WRITING WAR IN BRITAIN AND FRANCE, 1370–1854

Writing War in Britain and France, 1370–1854: A History of Emotions brings together leading scholars in medieval, early modern, eighteenth-century and Romantic studies. The assembled essays trace continuities and changes in the emotional register of war as it has been mediated by the written record over six centuries.

Through its wide selection of sites of utterance, genres of writing and contexts of publication and reception, *Writing War in Britain and France, 1370–1854* analyses the emotional history of war in relation to both the changing nature of conflicts and the changing creative modes in which they have been arrayed and experienced. Each chapter explores how different forms of writing define war – whether as political violence, civilian suffering or a theatre of heroism or barbarism – giving war shape and meaning, often retrospectively. The volume is especially interested in how the written production of war as emotional experience occurs within a wider historical range of cultural and social practices.

Writing War in Britain and France, 1370–1854: A History of Emotions will be of interest to students of the history of emotions, the history of pre-modern war and war literature.

Stephanie Downes is an honorary fellow at the University of Melbourne. She has published on late medieval literary and textual cultures and their modern reception, and on various social and cultural aspects of emotions history, including *Emotions and War: Medieval to Romantic Literature* (2015) with Andrew Lynch and Katrina O'Loughlin, and, with Sally Holloway and Sarah Randles, *Feeling Things: Emotions and Objects through History* (2018).

Andrew Lynch has recently retired as Professor in English and Cultural Studies at The University of Western Australia, and Director of the Australian Research Council Centre of Excellence for the History of Emotions. He has written extensively on medieval and modern medievalist literatures of war and peace. He is co-editor of the journal *Emotions: History, Culture, Society* and of *A Cultural History of Emotions* (2019)

Katrina O'Loughlin is Lecturer in English: Romantic and Nineteenth-Century Literature at Brunel Unversity, London. She has published on various aspects of Enlightenment and Romantic literature including *Women, Writing and Travel in the Eighteenth Century* (2018) and, with colleagues, two volumes on different aspects of the history of emotions.

Themes in Medieval and Early Modern History

This is a brand new series that straddles both medieval and early modern worlds, encouraging readers to examine historical change over time as well as promoting understanding of the historical continuity between events in the past, and to challenge perceptions of periodisation. It aims to meet the demand for conceptual or thematic topics that cross a relatively wide chronological span (any period between c. 500–1750), including a broad geographical scope.
Series Editor: Natasha Hodgson, Nottingham Trent University.

Available titles:

War in the Iberian Peninsula, 700–1600
Edited by Francisco García Fitz and João Gouveia Monteiro

Writing War in Britain and France, 1370–1854: A History of Emotions
Edited by Stephanie Downes, Andrew Lynch and Katrina O'Loughlin

WRITING WAR IN BRITAIN AND FRANCE, 1370–1854

A History of Emotions

Edited by Stephanie Downes, Andrew Lynch and Katrina O'Loughlin

LONDON AND NEW YORK

First published 2019
by Routledge
2 Park Square, Milton Park, Abingdon, Oxon OX14 4RN

and by Routledge
711 Third Avenue, New York, NY 10017

Routledge is an imprint of the Taylor & Francis Group, an informa business

© 2019 selection and editorial matter, Stephanie Downes, Andrew Lynch, Katrina O'Loughlin; individual chapters, the contributors

The right of Stephanie Downes, Andrew Lynch, Katrina O'Loughlin to be identified as the authors of the editorial material, and of the authors for their individual chapters, has been asserted in accordance with sections 77 and 78 of the Copyright, Designs and Patents Act 1988.

All rights reserved. No part of this book may be reprinted or reproduced or utilised in any form or by any electronic, mechanical, or other means, now known or hereafter invented, including photocopying and recording, or in any information storage or retrieval system, without permission in writing from the publishers.

Trademark notice: Product or corporate names may be trademarks or registered trademarks, and are used only for identification and explanation without intent to infringe.

British Library Cataloguing-in-Publication Data
A catalogue record for this book is available from the British Library

Library of Congress Cataloging-in-Publication Data
A catalog record has been requested for this book

ISBN: 9781138219168 (hbk)
ISBN: 9781138314139 (pbk)
ISBN: 9780429446245 (ebk)

Typeset in Bembo
by Florence Production Ltd, Stoodleigh, Devon, UK

Printed and bound in Great Britain by
TJ International Ltd, Padstow, Cornwall

CONTENTS

List of figures   vii
Notes on the contributors   ix
Acknowledgements   xiii

1. 'In form of war': war and emotional formation in European history   1
   Stephanie Downes and Andrew Lynch

2. Confessing the emotions of war in the Late Middle Ages: *Le livre des fais du bon messire Jehan le Maingre, dit Bouciquaut*   23
   Craig Taylor

3. Emotion and medieval 'violence': the Alliterative *Morte Arthure* and *The Siege of Jerusalem*   37
   Andrew Lynch

4. The Armagnac-Burgundian feud and the languages of anger   57
   Tracy Adams

5. Violent compassion in late medieval writing   73
   Catherine Nall

6. 'Thus of War, a Paradox I write': Thomas Dekker and a Londoner's view of continental war and peace   89
   Merridee L. Bailey

7 Corresponding romances: Henri II and the last campaigns of the Italian Wars 107
Susan Broomhall

8 Bellicose passions in Margaret Cavendish's *Playes* (1662) 127
Diana G. Barnes

9 'At Newburn foord, where brave Scots past the Tine': emotions, literature and the Battle of Newburn 145
Gordon D. Raeburn

10 'This humble monument of guiltless Blood': the emotional landscape of Covenanter monuments 163
Dolly MacKinnon

11 Paradoxes of form and chaos in the poetry of Waterloo 183
Robert White

12 War and emotion in the age of Biedermeier: the *United Service Journal* and the military tale 201
Neil Ramsay

13 'A possession for eternity': Thomas De Quincey's feeling for war 219
Michael Champion and Miranda Stanyon

Index 239

FIGURES

7.1 Autograph letter from Henri II to Diane de Poitiers [nd]. 111
Bibliothèque nationale de France, manuscrit français 3143, fol 2^r.
© Bibliothèque nationale de France
7.2 Autograph letter from Henri II and Diane de Poitiers to 117
Anne de Montmorency [1559] Bibliothèque nationale de France,
manuscrit français 3139, fol. 26^r. © Bibliothèque nationale
de France
10.1 Frontispiece, [Alexander Shields] *A Hind let loose, or An Historical* 164
Representation of the Testimonies, of the Church of Scotland, for the
Interest of Christ, with the true State thereof in all its Periods: Together
With A Vindication of the present Testimonie, against the Popish,
Prelatical, & Malignant Enemies of that Church . . . : Wherein Several
Controversies of Greatest Consequence are enquired into, and in some
measure cleared; concerning hearing of the Curats, owning of the present
Tyrannie, taking of ensnaring Oaths & Bonds, frequenting of field
meetings, Defensive Resistence of Tyrannical Violence . . . / By a Lover
of true Liberty. ([Edinburgh], 1687). The Burke Library at Union
Theological Seminary, Columbia University in the City of New
York. Image published with permission of ProQuest. Further
reproduction is prohibited without permission

CONTRIBUTORS

Tracy Adams received a Ph.D. in French from Johns Hopkins University, and is Associate Professor in French at the University of Auckland. She is the author of *Violent Passions: Managing Love in the Old French Verse Romance* (Palgrave Macmillan, 2005), *The Life and Afterlife of Isabeau of Bavaria* (The Johns Hopkins University Press, 2010), and *Christine de Pizan and the Fight for France* (Penn State University Press, 2014). With Christine Adams, she edited *Female Beauty Systems: Beauty as Social Capital in Western Europe and the US, Middle Ages to the Present* (Cambridge Scholars Publishing, 2015) and has co-authored *The Creation of the French Royal Mistress*, forthcoming with Penn State University Press.

Merridee L. Bailey is the S. Ernest Sprott Fellow for 2018, supported by The University of Melbourne, as well as an Associate Member of the Faculty of History at The University of Oxford. She is a social and cultural historian of late medieval and early modern England. Her first book, *Socialising the Child in Late Medieval England*, explored morality and courtesy in late medieval socialising discourses for young people. Additionally, she has written articles and chapters on the history of book culture, religious history, the history of emotions, and law and emotions. She is currently writing a book on the religious and social value of meekness from the Middle Ages to the present.

Diana G. Barnes is a Lecturer at the University of New England, who has been involved with the Australian Research Council Centre of Excellence for the History of Emotions from its inception, as a Research Associate and an Associate Investigator. Her book *Epistolary Community in Print, 1580–1664* was published in 2013. In the history of emotions she has published on Brilliana Harley and Puritan emotional ideals for marriage, Andrew Marvell's stoic response to civil war, and epistolary love in Shakespeare's *Merry Wives of Windsor*. She is currently researching the relationship between gender and early-modern neostoicism in literature.

x   Contributors

Susan Broomhall is Professor of History at The University of Western Australia, whose research explores gender, emotions, science and technologies, knowledge practices, material culture, cultural contact and the heritage of the early modern world. She currently holds an Australian Research Council Future Fellowship, researching the correspondence of Catherine de' Medici.

Michael Champion is Deputy Director of the Institute for Religion and Critical Inquiry at Australian Catholic University. He is the author of *Explaining the Cosmos: Creation and Cultural Interaction in Late Antiquity* (2014) and co-editor with Andrew Lynch of *Understanding Emotions in Early Europe* (2015) and with Juanita Ruys and Kirk Essary of *Before Emotion: The Language of Feeling, 400–1800* (2019).

Dolly MacKinnon, an Associate Professor in History at The University of Queensland, analyses the mental, physical and auditory landscapes of people in the past. Recent research includes '"[D]id ringe at oure parish churche . . . for joye that the Queene of Skotts was beheaded"', *Performing Emotions in Early Europe* 2018), and "Hearing madness and sounding cures"', *Journal Politiques de la communication* (automne 2017).

Catherine Nall is senior lecturer in medieval literature at Royal Holloway, University of London. She is author of *Reading and War in fifteenth-century England: from Lydgate to Malory*, a new biography of Henry IV for the Penguin Monarchs Series, and is currently working with Daniel Wakelin on a new edition of William Worcester's *Boke of Noblesse*.

Gordon D. Raeburn holds a PhD from the University of Durham, and from 2014–2017 was a postdoctoral research fellow in the Australian Research Council funded Centre of Excellence for the History of Emotions, based at the University of Melbourne. In 2018 he was the inaugural John Emmerson Research Fellow at the State Library of Victoria, Melbourne.

Dr Neil Ramsey is a Senior Lecturer in English Literature at the University of New South Wales, Canberra. He works on the literary and culture responses to warfare during the eighteenth century and Romantic eras, focusing on the representations of personal experience and the development of a modern culture of war. His first book, *The Military Memoir and Romantic Literary Culture*, 1780-1835, was published in 2011. His most recent, a collection co-edited with Gillian Russell, *Tracing War in British Enlightenment and Romantic Culture*, was published in 2015. He is currently completing a monograph on military writing of the Romantic era, the research for which was funded by an Australian Research Council Postdoctoral Fellowship that he held from 2010-2013.

Miranda Stanyon is a lecturer in Comparative Literature at King's College London, where her research focuses on Enlightenment and Romantic era writing in English and German, and on music and sound. Her work has appeared in edited collections on emotions history and on early modern musicology, as well as in *German Quarterly*, the *Journal of the Royal Musical Association*, *Studies in Romanticism*, and *Modern Philology*.

Craig Taylor is a Reader in Medieval History at the University of York. He is an intellectual and cultural historian who studies the politics and aristocracies of fourteenth- and fifteenth-century France and England. He has published on the Hundred Years War, chivalry, Joan of Arc, the Salic Law and propaganda, and is currently collaborating with Jane Taylor and Rosalind Brown-Grant in the translation of a series of fifteenth-century French chivalric biographies.

Robert White is Winthrop Professor in English and Cultural Studies at the University of Western Australia and a Chief Investigator in the Australian Research Council Centre of Excellence in the History of Emotions 1100–1800. He has held an Australian Research Council Professorial Fellowship. His publications are mainly in the field of early modern literature, especially Shakespeare, and also Romantic literature. They include *John Keats: A Literary Life* (2010, revised, paperback 2012); *Pacifism in English Literature: Minstrels of Peace* (2008); *Natural Rights and the Birth of Romanticism in the 1790s* (2005); and *Natural Law in English Renaissance Literature* (1996), as well as articles on peace and literature. Most recently he has published *Avant-Garde Hamlet* (2015), *Shakespeare's Cinema of Love* (2016), *The New Fortune Theatre: That Vast Open Stage* (co-ed. with Ciara Rawnsley) and *Ambivalent Macbeth* (2018).

ACKNOWLEDGEMENTS

Many of the essays in this collection take their origins from work conducted within the Australian Research Council Centre of Excellence for the History of Emotions (CHE) (CE110001011). We are deeply grateful to CHE for its strong support of various research projects and collaborations on emotions and war over the years. Bob White, Neil Ramsey and the late Philippa Maddern encouraged our efforts from the start. We thank the Centre's national staff – Tanya Tuffrey, Katrina Tap, Pam Bond and Erika Von Kaschke – along with Joanne McEwan, Stephanie Tarbin and Ciara Rawnsley, for their expert help in organising and promoting the academic events and visits through which we and the authors developed the volume. Thanks are also due to colleagues at the Universities of Melbourne and Western Australia, and in particular to Sue Broomhall, Jenny Gregory, Susan Takao, Audrey Barton, the Institute of Advanced Studies at The University of Western Australia, the UWA History Discipline, and the Perth Medieval and Renaissance Group.

Natasha Hodgson, Laura Pilsworth, Catherine Aitken, Morwenna Scott and Gabrielle Coakeley have kindly watched over the growth of *Writing War* at various stages. Violet Hamence-Davies gave great assistance with copy editing the submission. We also thank Alex Halliday at Florence Productions and Sara Barnes for their careful work in preparing the final product.

Above all, we thank our authors for their patience, hard work, inspiration and willingness to revise essays in response to comments from readers.

1

'IN FORM OF WAR'

War and emotional formation in European history

Stephanie Downes and Andrew Lynch

I. 'In form of war'

The phrase 'arrayed in form of war' is frequently found in late medieval English official and legal documents to introduce descriptions of the 'array' – the armour, weapons and organisation – of certain bands of male individuals (Paston 2004, p. 78). As a written formula, 'arrayed in form of war' is both technical and emotive, designed to place such men in maximum trouble with the law and to brand them as socially intolerable. The phrase encapsulates a central theme of this volume: that the emotions of war are 'arrayed' (that is, dressed and prepared) for use through complex negotiations between the two historical 'forms' of war and of writing. By reading form across both organised conflict and its textual representation, our goal is to broaden understandings of the social conditioning of human emotions in connection with war, throughout history. Feeling, too, takes forms – shared vocabularies, attitudes and gestures – which have a powerful impact on the way in which war in general, and individual wars in particular, garner meaning. The essays assembled here consider all writing(s) relating to war as 'genres' available for analysis and interpretation, from poetry and biography to tomb inscription. In placing the textual forms of war from various historical periods side by side our object is to identify both how the ways of writing war's emotions have shifted over time and how they have sometimes stubbornly refused change.

In covering a broad time-span, stretching from the fourteenth to the nineteenth centuries, we are not looking to write an overarching historical narrative in which uniform paradigm shifts in war's emotional experience will be evident. Rather, the chronological organisation of the volume highlights the varied expressive challenges and opportunities presented by new modes and technologies in both war and textual production. The volume asks: what are the variations, new ventures and recurrences in the 'emotional regimes' of war that result from these formal shifts? The essays it contains explore how different forms of writing define war – whether as political violence, civilian suffering, or a theatre of heroism or barbarism – giving war shape and meaning, often retrospectively.

War itself is a highly variable and historically contingent business. In insisting on war as a set of changing historical, cultural and literary forms, we wish to escape unitary and universalist notions of its emotional register – a sense of what war 'feels like', either in general, or in any given place or time – while still honouring the relation of its formal attributes to lived actualities of feeling. Such an approach understands cultural concepts of emotions and their location within human identity as deeply related to participation in textual culture. Monique Scheer has argued, for example, that the formation of an 'inner' emotional life in German bourgeois culture of the eighteenth and nineteenth centuries achieved its definition largely through the creation and consumption of written media: encyclopedias, diaries, 'intense epistolary exchanges', novels, and religious and philosophical discourse. Stuart Sherman makes a similar case for English culture in the early modern period (Sherman 1996). Scheer notes the decline of 'inside' and 'outside' in German definitions of emotion after 1840, but tracks a specific resurgence after the Second World War of 'interiority' as the place of the 'true self', allowing 'a refuge' and 'a return to 'inner values' as a reaction to the experience of dictatorship and war. She then goes on to chart the subsequent displacement of this view by behaviourist models of the emotions that redirected attention to the physical body as the site of 'real' emotional experience (Scheer 2014, pp. 35–39). For a while, historical trauma produced a resurgence of the idea and value of emotional interiority, and reframed the emotional life of a nation on an earlier model, which had developed in written and sociable form in an earlier period.

Scheer's study demonstrates that participation in written culture structures and informs the performance of emotional repertoires, but always within particular historical contexts. In this volume, and for this reason, we are especially attuned to war's emotions as historical experiences whose production is bound up in a wide range of bodily and cultural practices – including the forms of writing themselves. As Scheer elaborates in her discussion of how Bourdieu's *habitus* relates to the study of past emotions, bodily repertoires – including writing – are an intrinsic part of emotion's forms:

> [t]he formulation of thought is different when one is moving a pen across paper or typing on a keyboard as opposed to when one is speaking. Writing for oneself, as in a diary, while sitting alone has interiorizing effects, whereas speaking out loud while in view of a dialogic partner has exteriorizing ones. The social relationship of the two speakers affects the bodily dimension of the emotion in tone of voice, heart rate, and facial expression, which are all guided by the practical sense of the habitus, somewhere between deliberate control and unconscious habit.
>
> (Scheer 2012, p. 212)

Aspects of this idea of the formal repertoires of emotion, 'somewhere between deliberate control and unconscious habit', were adopted by Jan Plamper in his study of Bolshevik children's literature produced and consumed in times of war. Plamper suggests that, in certain conditions, reading can affect an 'emotional socialization' specifically related to war: 'less intentional, less signified, and less conscious aspects of the reading experience', 'get stored as practical knowledge that is also simultaneously cognitive and corporeal', and this 'can be recalled ... in different circumstances, including those of warfare' (Plamper 2014, p. 205). Catherine Nall identifies a similar process but in an earlier period, arguing that for the later medieval English ruling class, reading and the conduct of war were inseparable activities. In her view, there is a dynamic, 'circular' interaction between 'acts of textual production and reception, and the specific political and military circumstances in which they occurred' (Nall 2012, p. 2). Whether the process of emotional formation described by Plamper and Nall occurs through reading in general, or through reading about war in particular – whether it is understood as conscious or unconscious, and whatever the theoretical balance struck between the corporeal and cognitive elements of reading – both Plamper's and Nall's claims avowedly depend, in their different ways, on a thoroughly situated and historicised analysis of the texts and acts concerned.

Such historical analyses demand an awareness of the formal and aesthetic communicative potential that texts offer their contemporary readerships, as well as the evidence for readerly engagements with them. *Writing War* seeks to explore that awareness with greater historical depth. Through its wide selection of sites of utterance, written and theatrical genres, and contexts of publication and reception, the collection elaborates the emotional forms of wars past, both in relation to the nature of individual historical conflicts, and to the changing creative modes in which they have been 'arrayed' and experienced since.

II. War, history and writing

As Kate McLoughlin points out in her introduction to the *Cambridge Companion to War Writing*, war has been remembered in words so often throughout history that even certain literary forms have become synonymous with individual conflicts; the First World War's affinity with English lyric, for example, or the close connection of the 'war on terror' with the digital archive (McLoughlin 2009, p. 1). Some of these generic textual associations have great historical depth: for example, the Hundred Years' War, waged by the English and French crowns between 1337 and 1453, which is well remembered in its lyric forms and cross-Channel literary exchanges (Butterfield 2009; Strakhov 2014; Bellis 2016). The seventeenth-century civil wars in Britain take shape for us in a Georgic immersion in landscape. Understandings of frontier colonial violence from the early modern period are so often deflected through the literary-affective register of pastoralism. Observing that certain conflicts possess a characteristic 'poesis' usually requires a certain amount of distance – whether physical or temporal – from the conflict itself (McLoughlin 2009, p. 2). Of course, war and writing can unfold simultaneously, but the backward glance of history becomes crucial in evaluating how war, especially an individual war, will be culturally and socially remembered.

It is the trans-temporal potential of this poesis and its relationship to Western representations of emotional experience in and after wartime that this collection aims to explore in greater depth, with particular reference to England, France and Scotland from the Middle Ages through to the earlier nineteenth century. A 2015 publication, *Emotion, Politics and War*, edited by Linda Åhäll and Thomas Gregory, addresses its subject matter in a post-2001 setting, drawing on research by an international selection of social and political scientists and cultural theorists to emphasise the ways in which the study of emotion in warfare has been minimised or overlooked. 'Emotions,' Neta C. Crawford (2015, p. xviii) insists in her Preface, 'are constitutive of war and politics'. The volume pays close attention to the emotional resonances of war's past and present in the twenty-first century: it opens with a reflection on the emotional meanings demonstrated in the First World War commemorations of 2014 (Gregory & Åhäll 2015, p. 1); while an early chapter by Brian Massumi (2015, p. 17), reprinted from a 2013 multimedia project on 'Histories of Violence', looks back to 11 September 2001, to ask of the political, social and affective present, 'What remains of that day?'[1] Together, the volume's contributors consider the roles that various texts play in preserving the emotions of war, from letters and memoirs at the beginning of the previous century, to emails and online media, demonstrating the centrality of writing to war's emotions, even in the digital age. The collection's primary emphasis, however, remains on the emotional and literal politics of modern warfare and the various ways in which these are rendered intelligible in the twentieth and twenty-first centuries (Gregory & Åhäll 2015, p. 3).

Our volume seeks to understand and articulate this contingency of war, textual media and feeling over a much longer history. The following sections of the introduction focus on how works of literature from various historical periods are shaped by and in response to wars past, and how these literary-affective forms attempt to shape contemporary and future narratives of war. Our project is in no way constrained by this archive; here we seek to use the rich and varied example of literature in order to examine the role of writing and reading about war in war's long affective past. In the category of 'literature' we recognise the wide variety of poetic, narrative, theatrical and social forms which war has and might assume through writing which demonstrates some awareness or self-consciousness of its own formal vocabulary and structures, and through the associated range of emotions which it might be said to express or provoke. Such texts offer rich case studies for the expression and interpretation of war's emotions; but also case studies for war-writing in general. Is there an emotional or literary genre of war to be traced from the medieval period through the nineteenth century in the Western European tradition? What can we learn from literature about the history of the emotions of war?

III. War literature as emotional tradition

In medieval European literature, war was a central theme, closely linked with genres such as romance and epic. From Troy to Jerusalem, the locations of past wars and the emotions they produced and that had produced them were vividly imaged. Writers often adapted classical narrative traditions as commentary on current conditions of national and civil conflict, from the Crusades to the Hundred Years War and the Wars of the Roses. Medieval literature absorbed the culture of warfare, and metaphors drawn from the experience of war sustain some of the most famous and popular literary texts of the day, such as the siege of the captured and imprisoned 'Rose' in the thirteenth-century bestseller, the *Roman de la rose*. Perhaps more surprisingly, medieval literature also directly influenced the way wars were fought: during the fifteenth century, the revival of practical interest in Vegetius's late fourth-century treatise on the art and conduct of war, *De re militari*, meant that versions and adaptations were widely available in the vernacular and newly influential in these forms (Saunders 2009, pp. 84–85). Military manuals crossed temporal, geographical, linguistic and even political boundaries with ease. Christine de Pizan's *Livre des faits d'armes et de chevalerie* (1410), which drew directly on Vegetius's text, was extremely popular in England throughout the fifteenth and sixteenth centuries, while Catalan writer Raymond Lull's popular thirteenth-century text, *Libre qui es de l'ordre de cavalleria* (*The Book of the Order of Chivalry*), reached a wide readership in France throughout the later medieval period. Both works were translated into English and printed by William Caxton, England's 'first printer', in the late fifteenth century. Many of these vernacular manuals had an extraordinary longevity, influencing not only the reality of war, but the production of literature exploring its effects. Shakespeare, for example, is reported to have drawn from such works in his representation of just war in *Henry V* (Pugliatti 2010), while in the late fourteenth century, the poet John Gower called London 'newe Troye', reflecting the contemporary fascination with classical narratives of war, conflict and civic destruction.

In other famous literary texts from the medieval and early modern periods, war was thematised at the same time as it was curiously absent from the text, or consciously fictionalised into meta-narratives of war. In a famous scene from Chaucer's great love poem, *Troilus and Criseyde* (set during the Trojan war but with little reference to the conflict itself), Criseyde reads aloud from the story of the 'Siege of Thebes' with two of her ladies (Book 2, ll. 83–84).[2] Reading about war in times of war forms another kind of redaction of war into words: the words of one war are transposed onto the experience of another, shaping its experience and representation anew. Edmund Spenser's *The Faerie Queene* more subtly recalls classical models of warfare and warriors in its representation of Elizabethan political rule and expansion. The later books of Spenser's allegory (which includes moments of startlingly graphic violence throughout), offers readers a metaphorical reflection on Elizabeth's colonisation of Ireland (Fogarty 1989; Lim 1995). In Cervantes' roughly contemporaneous satirical novel, *Don Quixote,* the windmill-tilting protagonist draws on medieval chivalric rather than classical models in telling his own tales of war. Cervantes himself had first-hand experience of conflict as a soldier, having fought under Philip II in the Battle of Lepanto and various Spanish conflicts against the Turks. 'None in his poverty is as poor as he,' Don Quixote declares, 'for he depends on his miserable pay which comes late or never or on whatever he can steal with his own hands at great risk to life and conscience' (Cervantes 2005, p. 331). Don Quixote speaks here in the voice of a soldier, but his words recall the supplications of medieval poets to their patrons, suggesting the entanglement of literary form and soldiers' experience. Writing during the Dutch War of Independence (1568–1648), Cervantes glosses the use and abuse of earlier literatures in the representation of contemporary forms of violence.

Articulations of suffering in war literature have a distressingly marked longevity. In the introduction to his translation of *Beowulf*, the late Seamus Heaney recites a fragment from the poem of a scene of a Geat woman keening over the funeral pyre of her slain lord. This he describes as 'at once immemorial and oddly contemporary':

> A Geat woman too sang out in grief;
> with hair bound up, she unburdened herself
> of her worst fears, a wild litany
> of nightmare and lament: her nation invaded,
> enemies on the rampage, bodies in piles,
> slavery and abasement. Heaven swallowed the smoke.
>
> (ll. 3150–3155)

For Heaney (1999, p. xxiv), writing in 1999, the text's depiction of the woman's grief 'could come straight from a late twentieth-century news report, from Rwanda or Kosovo'. Her grief is expressed as a 'litany', in Old English a 'song sorg-cearig' (sorrowful song), terms which translate her cries of anguish into a form of oral poetry. Heaney captures a tautology typical of both modern and medieval efforts to articulate the experience and expression of trauma in words: poetry gives the subject space to 'unburden . . . herself', while simultaneously containing her cries and reducing them to a script and familiar textual performance.

IV. 'If poetry could truly tell it backwards'

If Heaney is right here that poetry asserts a continuity in the emotional experience of war across such different times, places and cultures, then a question arises: does poetry 'tell the truth' about wars, or does it shape later responses to them according to its own separate courses? 'The Last Post', written by Carol Ann Duffy to commemorate the centenary of the First World War in 2014, opens with the line: 'If poetry could tell it backwards, true, begin . . .' (Duffy 2014, p. 112). Duffy's conditional 'if' raises directly this issue of the reliability of the poetic war narrative. What, exactly, is poetry capable of expressing about war, or an experience of war?

Implicit in Duffy's provisional opening is the failure of form to represent war, or to capture an experience of war. The poem concludes: 'If poetry could truly tell it backwards, / then it would', underscoring its regenerative fiction and fragility. What the speaker of the poem implies in the lines in between is that even if it can't, it can still try, and that there is a value – even valour – in poetry's efforts to memorialise. The poem emphasises the importance of the act of writing about war by imagining the writer herself as a war hero, able to unearth the dead 'from History' by conjuring with words 'all those thousands dead / . . . shaking dried mud from their hair / and queuing up for home, freshly alive' (Duffy 2014, p. 113). In every attempt to narrate war, Duffy suggests, lies the potential for renewal after war: the chance to review, revise and reform the narrative of war's (or wars') past, for the better, in the present. Contemporary poetry about war, like Duffy's 'Last Post', very frequently turns on the speaker's discomfort with language's ability to represent the reality of war with an accuracy or intensity adequate to the experience. The process of translating war into words wields the worrying potential for distortion, manipulation and misrepresentation. War writing from Homer onwards acknowledges its inadequacy in this way, making good use of the 'inexpressibility topos' (Curtius 1952, pp. 159–162): – 'But how can I picture it all? It would take a god to tell the tale' (Homer *The Iliad*, Book 12, p. 225). Equally, the Chorus to *Henry V* asks 'can this cockpit hold / The vasty fields of France?' (*Henry V*, Prologue). In such ways, literature may be said not so much to compromise war's truth as to warn audiences that they can never read or hear it straight.

The question of how poetry and other textual accounts remember war, and how they consciously form and reform the past in the present, is central to this volume: in past centuries, as today, the ability and even the very value of using language to represent war was often called into question. Certain English 'clerkly' writers of the medieval period, including Chaucer, the *Gawain*-poet and Hoccleve, rather pointedly avoid the detailed description of war or fighting: they argue that their particular 'matere' is otherwise (*Troilus*, Book V, ll. 1765–1761); that they don't have time and it would be too much trouble, even boring (*Sir Gawain*, ll. 713–725); or that through their 'unkonnynge' they could not do justice to the subject (Hoccleve 'The Dialogue', ll. 582–588). Overall, this looks like a form of resistance to writing fight descriptions, that as poets they have better things for readers to invest their emotions in. When Chaucer provides a rare detailed fighting scene, as in the *Knight's Tale*, the outcome of the whole affair is eventually reduced to an 'aventure [accident]'; a further event, described as both 'miracle' and 'aventure', reverses the main outcome anyway (ll. 2569–2662). The language of bodily trauma – 'clothered blood'; 'venym and corrupcioun' – and its treatments – 'vomit upward' and 'downward laxatif' (ll. 2745–2756) – here intrudes viscerally on chivalric glamour. The overall effect inhibits any straightforward emotional engagement on the part of the reader with the story of victory or defeat in arms. In this respect, for all the abstract references to chivalry and the intense detail of its cultural practices, the *Knight's Tale* seems formed to make it difficult to 'know what to feel' about fighting, by complicating or even disabling some expected emotional attachments to the genres that mediate it in Chaucer's time.

The best part of four centuries later, *Tristram Shandy* instances another way in which literature problematises the emotions of war. Uncle Toby's 'Apologetical Oration' on war asks: 'If, when I was a school-boy, I could not hear a drum beat, but my heart beat with it – was it my fault? Did I plant the propensity there? – Did I sound the alarm within, or Nature?' (Sterne *Tristram Shandy*, p. 442).[3] Toby, a sympathetic and otherwise gentle character, claims that his 'propensity' to war is human nature. Yet his Apology reveals a childhood nurture saturated in the *Iliad* and in chapbook versions of medieval and Elizabethan military romances:

> When Guy, Earl of Warwick, and Parismus and Parismenus, and Valentine and Orson, and the Seven Champions of England, were handed around the school, – were they not all purchased with my own pocket-money?
> (Sterne *Tristram Shandy*, p. 442)

Toby acknowledges the influence, arguing that his schoolboy capacity to weep for Hector and feel for Priam's grief – 'you know, brother, I could not eat my dinner' – clears him of a mere selfish lust for war. He says nothing else of his extra-curricular childhood patronage of romances, but one must speculate that the extreme partiality of their outlook lies behind his assessment of war as only 'the getting together of quiet and harmless people, with their swords in their hands, to keep the ambitious and the turbulent within bounds' (Sterne *Tristram Shandy*, p. 444). Overall, reading seems to have given Toby (and possibly his school friends) the 'propensity' to see war as a matter of innate honour and morality, while containing the consciousness of its evils within a culture of educated literacy – Homeric *pathos*. Sterne may be comically deploying literature here to critique and control some of its potentially harmful social tendencies, for both high and low reading audiences.

A more complex situation, in which writing about war essentially distrusts itself, occurs when the emotions aroused by war are found to be too strong for words. Sarah Cole describes 'the inexpressibility of war experience' as 'a primary creed' of Great War writing, 'from rough diary notes to canonical poetry'. Might this be considered a form of war in and of itself? A shared belief in the 'extreme and ubiquitous failure of language' to speak feeling seems intrinsic to the deep affective relationships formed between male combatants. The peculiar intensity of feelings between serving soldiers has perhaps always created a further challenge to their expression in writing. As Cole suggests, in 'the case of personal relations, the problem of inadequate language is registered by a sense that it is impossible to translate into civilian terms the richness and precariousness of these new ties' (Cole 2003, p. 143). In a grimmer version of Uncle Toby's mysterious 'wound' that isolates him from normal civilian life, literature of the 'male friend' in war, Cole argues, shows him as eventually 'destroyed by a profound detachment from sustainable institutions, palpably lacking a cultural vocabulary that can be shared with the non-war world' (Cole 2003, p. 184). Septimus in Virginia Woolf's *Mrs Dalloway* is another such figure. Throughout the period covered by the essays in this volume, war literature suggests that the truth of war feelings cannot be told, but still requires us – as Woolf does – to be emotionally confronted by their human effects.

V. War writing and emotional subjectivities

Holly Crocker (2017, p. 88) has recently distinguished between approaches to the study of medieval emotions that 'treat . . . identity categories as already known' and those with a 'focus . . . not on specific feelings per se, but on what feelings – from emotions to affects – can do in the process of fashioning medieval subjectivities'. Crocker (2017, p. 94, n. 2) speaks of medieval 'affects' as 'the powers which are connected to the intellectual powers of reason and the will, and which are central to orienting subjects toward abstract categories that organise identity in ethical terms'. She notes, nevertheless, that while affects were supposed to rule the operations of the lower 'sensitive' soul, that process could be impaired or even reversed by strong emotions: 'Quite literally, the (e)motions of the sensitive soul *affected* the intellectual soul' (Crocker 2017, p. 84). In tracing these processes, Crocker (2017, pp. 91–92) goes on to argue, the study of 'literary representations' is 'crucial' because 'literary texts show what emotions did . . . Literatures demonstrate how identities might be changed; they fashion new affective affiliations, and they unmake old somatic alliances'. Crocker is speaking of medieval literature, but her statement applies more generally to literature (broadly interpreted) as a site for studying the history of emotions.

Crocker's appeal to medieval affect theory is perhaps especially relevant to the demonstrative capacities of war literature, where 'higher' motivations of reason, practicality and ethical alignment are mooted, but also all manner of passions are shown to be unleashed by and on the 'sensitive soul'. Her approach finds an echo in modern historical research, such as Joanna Bourke's study of fear in soldiers during the two world wars. Bourke (2001, p. 330) concludes that, for all the military's attempts to forge a 'man-machine',

> [the] murderous strength and rigidity of the machine was effortlessly subverted by the fluidity of the emotions: fear and anger, exhilaration and resignation – these were the stuff of the individual at war.

As Bourke shows, nothing could eradicate the cognitive and bodily effects of fear in humans. Not only were these manifested in very varied and unpredictable ways, but recognition of fear's continuing presence inspired a wide range of management strategies: it was variously proposed that soldiers should be punished for succumbing to fear, trained to deny it, told that it was normal and to 'live with it', or led to channel fear into 'positive' activities. The 'higher' desire of military commanders was for consistency and predictability in defining and containing combat emotions, but the written archive provides a set of narratives of differing behaviours, which makes the contingent and uncertain – 'fluid' – nature of the 'sensitive' emotion clear, both in the lived experience of the soldiers and in the baffled discursive responses of those observing them.

Writing about war is always, to some degree, a contest of this kind between form and formlessness, to which a host of ideological, generic and poetic strategies contribute their different emphases, and in which writers and readers easily find themselves emotionally confused. Patricia Di Marco (2000, pp. 29–30), commenting on the fourteenth-century poem *Les Voeux du Heron*, writes that in medieval chivalric narratives, 'deeds of arms lack any intrinsic ethical coding', while 'laments over the horror of war often coexist comfortably with strident defences of the necessity and righteousness of war'.[4] Towards the other end of the literary spectrum, in 'mirror for princes' literature, some modern readers understand a medieval clerk's anti-war advice to a ruler (Henry V) as a genuine moral intervention (Perkins 2001), while others see it as self-ingratiating window-dressing, designed to justify the king's ambitions while making him look properly reluctant to fight (Pearsall 1994, p. 389). There can be no simple readerly alignment of literary genre with war ideology, just as there was no simple response to war or the warrior in medieval society. Sir John Hawkwood, a famous mercenary adventurer in Italy, could be scorned as a pestilent 'robber', yet also given a noble tomb in the cathedral of Florence and later held up as a model of knighthood by William Caxton (Keen 1976, p. 32).

Similarly, in Shakespeare's *Henry V*, the spectator is exposed to every rhetorical strategy concerning war, from rousing nationalist enthusiasm – 'Once more unto the breach, dear friends' (Act 3, Scene 1) and 'St Crispin's Day!' (Act 4, Scene 3) – through the cynicism of Nym and Bardolph, and to ruminations on the king's moral responsibility for casualties. The king denies his hand in soldiers' *bad* deaths in the war he is waging, on the grounds that '[e]very subject's duty is the king's; but every subject's soul is his own'. Yet it is often pointed out that in answering this charge he dodges the broader question of whether the war itself is 'just' (Pugliatti 2010, pp. 217–218; Lake 2016, pp. 368–369). Blame for the war, in his version, falls solely on the French. But many think the play reveals from the outset 'Henry's underlying wish to conquer France for his own good' (Quabeck 2013, p. 158), and read 'his public justifications for the invasion . . . [as] Machiavellian fraud' (Mebane 2010, p. 258), or, rather more positively, as part of 'a series of political effects' worked by Henry's 'manipulation' of 'rhetoric' (Lake 2016, p. 363). That modern readers are able to see the play in these multiple lights is in part due to its polyvocality. Very unlike medieval chivalric texts, Shakespeare's play form allows representatives of common soldiers to speak for themselves as a means of bringing the official view into question. War's existence as an emotional entity is revealed to depend greatly on who is allowed to 'speak' of it, which is to say, who is given power over its language, and acknowledged as holding a legitimate interest in its practices and effects. This capacity to speak the cultural vocabulary of war is directly linked to the new possibilities made available in genre and poetic form.

One result of exposure to such a variety of war writing, and of responses to it, over the long course of time is a keen awareness of war as a hyper-mediated 'matter', which both arouses deeply emotional responses and renders them suspect. War's traditional status as a 'bottom line' proof of nobility, courage, masculinity and loyalty – of who 'does well', as romances and treatises on knighthood say – simultaneously sets up its liability as a cultural 'field' to exploitation by vested interests. Maurice Keen (1976, p. 34) notes, with reference to the late medieval period, that 'one reason for the failure of this age to keep the social problem of war within bounds lay, ironically, in the idealism of its attitude to war and the soldier, in what we may call the ethic of chivalry'. Those who could claim that their war was 'just' in their own eyes could represent it as a noble, even holy, activity. In this 'chivalric' view, warfare became an honourable, even a religious, undertaking because of the dangers and hardships that war itself created for combatants (Kaeuper 2009, pp. 94–115). At the same time 'because of . . . [chivalry's] underlying religious and idealistic justification, it made it difficult for men to look squarely at the parasitic activities of soldiers and to recognise them for what they were' (Keen 1976, pp. 34, 44–45).

VI. Sacred emotions of war

Religious reference is a common emotional and rhetorical vocabulary within modern war memorialisation, crossing and complicating a simultaneous view of war as human disaster, and providing another powerful example of the unstable semiotics of much war writing. Inscriptions on the Menin Gate Memorial in Ypres begin 'In Maiorem Dei Gloriam' ('To the Greater Glory of God'), and a scriptural text, chosen by Rudyard Kipling, is incorporated: 'Their name liveth for evermore' (Ecclesiasticus 44:14). The choice of text is misleading. The full verse is: 'Their bodies are buried in peace; but their name liveth for evermore', but the Gate commemorates 54,389 soldiers whose bodies could never be found for burial. War monuments from Britain to Burma to Australia carry the same words, adopting a sacralising vocabulary that both marks and obscures its own provenance. Confessional and ethnic communities have also used religious occasion and symbolism to claim a distinct place for their own war dead in honourable memory, and to assert their loyal contribution (Tierney 2017; Daley 2016). Through means like these, admiration for the courage of soldiers – and the wish to honour their sufferings – can be readily transferred to ideas of war itself as a moral, even a sacred, enterprise. Such slippage can confer a glorious 'name' on its fighters, while the names of non-combatant casualties and the bereaved remain unrecorded.

The process of sacralisation occurs more readily when literature and other cultural products maintain a focus on the 'deeds' of combatants and the defined 'field' of battle, especially in texts that ground their representation of warfare in traditional discourses of honour, loyal fellowship, courage, suffering and sacrifice. War experience has often been taken as both the classical and religious test of higher human qualities. Aristotle's long influence helped maintain the notion that facing death in war offered 'the finest conditions' for showing bravery because 'such deaths . . . occur in the greatest and finest danger' (Aristotle *Nichomachean Ethics*, Book 3, Chapter 6:8).[5] The Crusades buttressed this classical vocabulary with Christian piety and sacrifice. In modern times too, war has been treated as both a theatre of magnanimity and an unrivalled emotional education. These attitudes connect human experience across history, but also distinguish combatants in every epoch. For Oliver Wendell Holmes, speaking in 1884, the American Civil War:

> embodie[d] . . . in the most impressive form our belief that to act with enthusiasm and faith is the condition of acting greatly. . . . [T]he generation that carried on the war has been set apart by its experience. Through our great good fortune, in our youth our hearts were touched with fire. It was given to us to learn at the outset that life is a profound and passionate thing.
> (in Posner 1992)[6]

Holmes' words were used to preface the opening episode of Ken Burns' 1990 television documentary, *The Civil War*, which reached 40,000,000 viewers at its first showing and is widely used in US schools.[7] While the quotation does not speak for the mood of the entire series, or of Holmes' whole speech, its special prominence captures the lasting resilience of positive emotional attachments to war experience, even – or especially – in a recent 'liberal' American context.

> Feeling begets feeling, and great feeling begets great feeling. . . . the tattered flags of our regiments gathered in the Statehouses, are worth more to our young men by way of chastening and inspiration than the monuments of another hundred years of peaceful life could be.
> (in Posner 1992)[8]

Through such writing and its elevation of the tattered flag over a hundred years' life, war is granted a special emotional status – 'set apart' – that ranks it above peacetime in official cultural memories, and lends it moral authority.

It is no exaggeration to say that in its vocabulary of 'passion' and 'feeling' Holmes' speech presents the war as a fortunate and beneficial event. To treat the Civil War as he does depends on accepting a soldier's presence in it as primarily responsive to an emotional demand made primarily by 'life', although one clearly inflected by class and gender: 'as life is action and passion, it is required of a man that he should share the passion and action of his time at peril of being judged not to have lived' (in Posner 1992).[9] This approach to war through emotional attachment to a 'cause' lifts it to a level of abstraction, where each side legitimately holds its separate 'sacred convictions' yet is respectfully bonded in feeling with the enemy. Then, when battle is entered, individual agency is still further eclipsed, and '[t]he rest belongs to fate'. In effect, Holmes sets up in emotional terms the familiar conditions of a medieval chivalric literary 'field', where other motivations and effects are subordinated to the display of virtue and killing occurs without guilt: 'I slew him knightly' is a common self-exoneration in the world of *Le Morte Darthur*. As if in a medieval romance or chronicle, the combatants Holmes memorialises and addresses are clearly 'gentles' – 'gallant and distinguished officers', his 'friends', those with whom he mixes 'at the regimental dinner'. It is no surprise when he states that they displayed in war the 'high breeding' and 'romantic chivalry' of the '*ancien régime*'. One is reminded of the herald's casualty list in Shakespeare's *Henry V*, distinguishing those 'of name' from the 'rest' (Act 4, Scene 8). Of course, the practical, social and conceptual conditions of fighting the American Civil War differed hugely from those that operated in the much earlier wars described in this volume. It has become a cliché to say that the Civil War, with its industrial military technology – the Gatling Gun and the ironclad battleship – is 'the first modern war' (Phillips 2006). Yet for all those differences, Holmes' literary treatment largely erases that traditional periodisation in a long-familiar emotional register of war.

The point of such a comparison is in no way to suggest that all wars are the same, but to show that certain cultural forms of writing war are extraordinarily long-lived and resistant to other changes, or at least that they can operate long after most or all of the original circumstances in which they were first fashioned have disappeared. Holmes' outlook possibly harks back to Walter Scott's *Essay on Chivalry* (1834, p. 107), with its celebration of the 'constant and honourable opposition, unembittered by rancour or personal hatred' displayed in 'chivalry's 'most brilliant period ... during the wars between France and England'. One difference is, however, that Scott believed these great days had ended in the internecine conflicts of the fifteenth century, 'utterly inconsistent with the courtesy, fair play, and gentleness, proper to chivalry' (Scott 1834, p. 111) and he sharply distinguished between private modern instances of honourable conduct between enemies and the general carnage of war, especially civil war (Scott 1814, p. civ). For Holmes, chivalry, as an emotional opportunity in war, simply survives all other contingencies unscathed. If literary and cultural forms and symbols of war have a much longer life than its technologies, it seems that their longevity might be largely due to the continued provision of these forms and symbols as 'emotives' of war – that is, as performative means or 'inputs' to the self, by which particular emotional alignments towards war can be aroused and sustained (Reddy 2001, p. 322). The forms of emotional alignment constituted by literary vocabularies and cultural signs continue to make their presence felt even when they seem very distant from practical realities. To be in wartime, to remember it, or to read about it, means to some extent experiencing it through prevailing genres and vocabularies of representation, however that experience may jar with other emotional prompts.

VII. War genres, emotion and historical periodicity

Over the 600-year time-span covered by essays in this volume the precociousness, persistence and unpredictable re-emergence of emotional forms of war cast doubt on some modern versions of periodisation in Western emotions history. These include those that argue for an increasing restraint on emotional behaviours through a 'civilising process' as the West progressed into 'modernity', and those that relate an account of new developments in emotional life to changes in political, religious, familial and socio-economic arrangements. To these views, the careful examination of medieval and early-modern written evidence has come as a check, for example in considering the long history of grief in family bereavement, or conjugal affections. For all that empirical resistance to notions of emotional periodisation, it is still reasserted that '[t]he findings about modern change do tie together around a shared link to modernity; they are not random historical accidents' (Stearns 2014, p. 30). In this argument, when major historical changes are seen to establish 'modernity' as a unifying experiential paradigm, it can be easy to overlook the multiple and overlapping mediation of emotions through literary form, and the complex, temporally indeterminate, and often adversarial relationships that literature maintains with the societies and cultures within which it is produced and received. For 'modern' readers about war in the eighteenth and nineteenth centuries, for example, the age of capitalism, consumerism and Romanticism was simultaneously an age when Shakespeare and *The Pilgrim's Progress* found very wide audiences. There is never only one way of writing or reading – or even experiencing – war available to a given society. Therefore there can never be only one emotional response to be made to it, nor one fully consistent emotional temporality.

Rather than seeing war emotions as restricted to particular temporal periods on the grounds of widespread historical changes, we might instead see these emotions as potentiated by different and changing forms and genres of representation and apprehension. We can recognise these as operating more independently of time and place, while remaining conscious that genre and form are themselves subject to wider historical changes. As in Barbara Rosenwein's conception of 'emotional communities' as multi-centred and overlapping circles, we might appreciate war's potential for emotional subjectivity in any period as variously shared by and divided between literary and cultural forms and genres. And again, as in Rosenwein's (2009, p. 2) model, it becomes possible then to envisage individuals and groups as members of different formal and generic communities at the same time. In fact, given that there is nearly always some generic and formal choice to hand, it is perhaps harder to see how people might stay members of only one such community, rather than imagining and speaking within multiple registers at once.

It might then be argued that the abundance of continuing, vestigial, new and rapidly modifying genres in the last few centuries – set in contrast to the rather smaller array widely available, and perhaps more closely controlled, in earlier periods – may be a good part of what 'modernity' means in the context of war:

modernity *as* emotional polyphony in war writing. Yet prescriptive and linear periodisations of emotional subjectivity are, as Caroline Dinshaw suggests, always reductive, both of 'the times that are operant in the literature of the Middle Ages as well as the expansive *now* that can result from engagement with that literature' (Dinshaw 2012, p. xv). The varied generic and formal models of emotional being available to readers and audiences in any period work to reveal it as 'temporally heterogenous' (Dinshaw 2102, p. xiv), rather than as an 'age'. Chaucer's emotionally indeterminate image of war in the *Knight's Tale*, discussed above, is renewed in Stendhal's *La Chartreuse de Parme* (1839). Stendahl's radically oblique, decentred and emotively unstable account of Waterloo, part-farcical and part-anguished, was published shortly before the grand state funeral for Napoleon I, whose victories would subsequently be glorified in the imperial splendour of Les Invalides. Stendhal's own life-long conflicted response to Napoleon is well known (Richardson 1973, pp. 3–7). As viewed through the eyes of his naïve hero Fabrizio, the Waterloo scene refuses to respect any fixed emotional decorum, challenging the reader by not foreclosing on any of a multiplicity of impressions: pragmatism; horror; kindness; fear; absurdity; despair; and unlikely grandeur.

> "Give me four of your men," he said to the corporal in a faint voice, "I've got to be carried to the ambulance; my leg is shattered." "Go and f—— yourself!" replied the corporal, "you and all your generals. You've all of you betrayed the Emperor to-day."
>
> (Stendhal 1926, pp. 66–67)

New possibilities of emotional subjectivity are given scope, and former versions are troubled, when such a change in literary form takes the imaginary of war beyond former conceptual and expressive practices, even without leaving the literal war zone. Stendhal creates a war that is intensely visual, yet cannot be 'seen': a poetic medium in which the vast and creaking economy of the military and its hangers-on – the messy logistics of armies – signally fails to create a comprehensive 'field', but potentiates a collision of emotional styles and outcomes.

Like our earlier publication, *Emotions and War: Medieval to Romantic Literature* (2015), the present volume's concentration on the written forms of war is transhistorical, transnational (in the context of those historical periods in which the modern 'nation' can be said to exist), and cross-genre. The essays assembled here pay close attention to the ways in which writings in various genres or written forms of war – including poetry, chronicle, autobiography, romance, epic, theatre, treatise, letter, lyric, inscription and journal – have, in turn, helped form war as an emotional experience in Western literary tradition. Our contributors trace continuities and changes in the emotional register of violent conflict as it has been mediated and transmitted to modernity in the written record of the European past. The essays analyse the emotions of war from various viewpoints: representations of the experience of combatants, civilians and spectators; textual, literary and theatrical productions which adapt war themes for particular emotional effects;

studies of generic, historiographical and performance traditions of the emotions involved in war by reflecting on the historical, theoretical and thematic frameworks in which war writing is emotionally constructed. And they cover some of the most significant conflicts in Western European history, beginning with the Hundred Years War, and including the French Wars of Religion, the English Civil War and the Battle of Waterloo. Some contributors probe the fictionalisation of war's past as commentary on the experience of contemporary conflict; while others explore the dramatisation and textual formation of immediate solider and civilian experiences. The final essay considers a view from the mid-nineteenth century, looking back at the long history of European thought on the subject of war, shortly before the introduction of industrialised mass warfare radically changed apprehensions of its emotional and ethical texture.

As in this introduction, several of the contributors to this volume focus on how literary texts formalise the representation of war. Andrew Lynch explores the 'close relation of "violence" to emotion' in the medieval and early modern periods in a variety of fourteenth-century English fictions. Concentrating on two texts in particular – the Alliterative *Morte Arthure* and the *Siege of Jerusalem* – Lynch shows how form (verse) and style (alliteration) simultaneously contain and unleash a vast array of acts of 'violence' (which we might best understand in the modern sense of 'violation') in the context of warfare. Catherine Nall looks to a combination of literary and chronicle works in her discussion of what she identifies as the demonstration of 'violent compassion' in a variety of late medieval genres, including romance and mirrors for princes, as well as military treatises. The idea of compassion itself might be expressed and inflected in Middle English in a number of ways, from 'pite' to 'misericorde'. And yet, far from being used solely to curtail violence in these texts, compassion, as Nall shows, is often 'an emotion that acts as a precursor to vengeance'. Both the experience and expression of compassion, she demonstrates, form 'a crucial part of the affective foundation of the practice of violence' in an array of late medieval war narratives.

Concentrating on the political representation of war during the Anglo-French conflicts of the late fourteenth and fifteenth centuries, Craig Taylor and Tracy Adams treat a variety of genres, from the 'chivalric' biography to chronicle and lyric. These are all courtly forms of writing about war, and yet they form the emotions of war in very different ways. Taylor identifies a marked tendency among Francophone biographers to relegate the emotional experience of war to the backgrounds of their accounts. The exception to this rule is anger, which – in this medieval biographical register at least – consistently motivates the subject to righteous action, in a manner analogous to the role of pity in roughly contemporaneous English works discussed by Nall. In the conflicts of the Orléanist and Burgundian factions during the early fifteenth century, anger was similarly an essential ingredient in violent conflict. Adams examines the Burgundian 'Cour amoureuse' – a festival of love-poetry – as a 'theatre for defining relationships and enacting the emotional injuries that motivated its leaders to take up arms' [against the Orléanists]. Here, anger is a highly social emotion, and displays of anger that were formal (aristocratic) contrasted with those that were frenzied (popular). Although different types of anger were being mobilised with respect to the same situation of escalating political tension, as Adams shows, both were instrumental in bringing about armed conflict.

In the late sixteenth and seventeenth centuries, the English playwright Thomas Dekker drew on the currency of pamphlets treating news of war on the Continent in his work for both the popular media and the theatre. Merridee L. Bailey observes how Dekker's commercial interest in war narratives contributed actively to the making of 'a culture of war writing in the early modern period'. Dekker has long been of interest to scholars of both literature and history for the ways in which his works offer a window on the development of the theatre and the printing press in late Elizabethan and Jacobean civic life; in her chapter, Bailey reveals how the diversity of Dekker's references to war across his professional writings demonstrates particular attention to its emotional as well as economic effects. In whichever forum he was writing, Dekker deploys a range of linguistic devices and images to 'humanise' the impact of war on ordinary citizens, seeking to educate as well as entertain by 'giving voice to complex and contested views about war's value and cost'.

In the form of battle, war may look like a simple clash of angry opposites. In writing, we see better how it excites mixed emotional attachments and reactions. Gordon Raeburn explores how the battle of Newburn (1640) gave focus to complex expository strategies, in which the Scots victors stressed their reluctance to take up arms, and the defeated English tried to cast off shame by painting the invaders as both violently aggressive and fearful. Accusations of cowardice flew back and forth. Yet there was a broader view, more independent of partisan interests, in which the perceived actions of both sides – one wrongfully attacking, one too weakly defending – caused emotional pain to a much later commentator. Robert White, discussing poetry in the aftermath of Waterloo (1815), shows that British writers visiting the battlefield sometimes struggled to work the blank impact of mass slaughter into traditional forms of victory. In 1816 Wordsworth found the event laden with 'glory' and 'triumph', but when he and his sister visited the site in 1820, 'glory seemed betrayal' of the 'vast hoards of hidden carnage near'. Southey and Scott give similar witness to the emotional change made when the 'field' of victory 'reveals as much human degradation of nature as of human-kind'.

Dolly Mackinnon examines war's emotions over a much longer aftermath. Her essay reveals the 'continuing emotional community' built around memorials to Lowland Scots killed for upholding the national Covenant. Through renewed material practices, this community becomes both linked to and constitutive of 'emotional landscapes'. Encompassing monuments and graves, and examining both printed and oral accounts, Mackinnon shows that a wide network of witness across place and time empowers the Covenanter martyrdoms as 'tangible [and] permanent . . . markers', and makers, of Scottish history. In contrast, Neil Ramsey's account of British war memoirs of the earlier nineteenth century reveals how in a very different milieu, emotions around war were generated by newly adapting genres of writing. Faced with an audience emotionally educated by sentimental novels, writers of 'personal histories' succeeded 'because they wrote in such a way as to redefine the hardships and the horrors of war as a version of an ennobling pastoral experience in nature'. Increasingly, as the profession of war grew more scientific, Ramsay traces the ways in which the public 'were seen to have a connection with war that was now to be almost wholly constituted by feeling and emotion'. As in the medieval biographies examined by Taylor, the textual construction of emotions in these related genres of 'life writing' may hide as much as it reveals of their real place in war action and military culture.

Letters prove one of the most potent genres for combatants and non-combatants alike from the early modern period. Susan Broomhall's essay shows how French court correspondence during the Italian Wars of the mid-sixteenth century both 'forged a particular epistolary culture among ... four individuals' and 'created distinctive expressive capacity for feelings unique to their letters'. To Broomhall, 'war was ... a significant cultural force that provided the scaffolding of emotional expression in these letters, and more broadly, of the "chivalric" practice and display of feelings in the courtly environment'. Her analysis of the 'feeling rules' of letters written under the influence of chivalric romance suggests that they distributed opportunities and idioms for emotional expression unequally according to gender and the changing court situation. Diana Barnes' examination of plays written by Margaret Cavendish during the aftermath of the English Civil War and the Restoration also explores the emotional languages available to women in war, but in the medium of theatre, considering the roles that might have been adopted by elite women during the Early Modern period. Barnes shows how – in a post-war civil context that privileges masculinist forms of 'glory', virtue and self-government of the passions – Cavendish's plays question gender divisions by providing 'heroic' models of female strength in portraits of women's suffering, sympathy and honourable action. Cavendish's goal is 'to preserve exemplary feminine virtue in the national cultural memory' and to represent women's emotions as essential to the maintenance of social and political stability.

'History,' write Michael Champion and Miranda Stanyon, 'cannot escape from the realms of literature and personal memoir into science or philosophy, from emotional engagement and accident into detachment'. Their discussion of Thomas de Quincey's writings on war – and his writings *about* war – concludes this volume with a reflection on the generically hybrid, often highly intertextual nature of such work. De Quincey's attempts to avoid the war narrative becoming a Wordsworthian 'spontaneous overflow of powerful feelings' see him reaching back to classical models of historiography, especially the writings of Thucydides, in forming his own 'feeling' for the textual archive of war. The authors argue that attention to De Quincey's influences suggest 'that we should rethink both the dichotomy of form versus formlessness, and the equation of form with goodness'. There could be no truer statement for the goals of this collection in thinking about the historical relationship of war to emotion, which was understood etymologically in the early modern period as a specifically political form of violent or chaotic upheaval (Hochner 2016).

In writing about war writing and its forms – both in and across time – the essays collected here seek to understand the ways in which words have shaped both war's affects and effects, its meanings and its memory, with a multivocality that both constrains and liberates its subject. And yet war writing is not only a reflection, past or present, on war's losses. It may passionately celebrate war, or attempt to incite the passions of (and for) war. Whatever its agenda, writing about war often bears witness to an attempt to contain or control its violence; to direct its (human) impact, whether past, present or future; to give form, definition and meaning to its shapelessness. Order/disorder, control/chaos: the essays in *Writing War* attempt to read the ways in which writing about war in the West repeatedly sought to explain the emotional and practical mess of war with words.

Notes

1 See http://historiesofviolence.com.
2 For all references to Chaucer's works, see *The Riverside Chaucer* (1987).
3 *The Life and Opinions of Tristram Shandy, Gentleman*, Book 6, Chapter 32.
4 To Norris Lacy the same poem 'dramatizes the sinister process by which political manipulation . . . transforms a jovial court gathering into the prelude to a calamitous war' (Lacy 2000, p. 24).
5 *Nichomachean Ethics*, Book 3, Chapter 6:8.
6 www.people.virginia.edu/~mmd5f/memorial.htm
7 www.pbs.org/kenburns/civil-war/classroom/teaching-civil-war/
8 www.people.virginia.edu/~mmd5f/memorial.htm
9 www.people.virginia.edu/~mmd5f/memorial.htm

Reference list

Åhäll, L. & Gregory, T. (eds) 2015, *Emotions, Politics and War*, Routlege, London & New York.
Allmand, C. 1999, 'War and the Non-Combatant in the Middle Ages'. In M. Keen (ed.), *Medieval Warfare: A History*, Oxford University Press, Oxford, pp. 253–272.
Aristotle 1999, *Nichomachean Ethics*, trans. T Irwin, 2nd edn, Hackett, Indianapolis.
Bourke, J. 2001, 'The Emotions in War: Fear and the British and American Military, 1939–45', *Historical Research*, vol. 74, no. 185, pp. 314–330.
Butterfield, A. 2009, *The Familiar Enemy: Chaucer, Language and Nation in the Hundred Years War*, Oxford University Press, Oxford.
Cervantes, Miguel de 2005, *Don Quixote*, trans. E. Grossman, Vintage, London.
Chaucer, G. 1987, *The Riverside Chaucer*, ed. L. D. Benson, 3rd edn, Oxford University Press, Oxford.
Cole, S. 2003, *Modernism, Male Friendship, and the First World War*, Cambridge University Press, Cambridge.
Crocker, H. 2017, 'Medieval Affects Now', *Exemplaria*, vol. 29, no. 1, pp. 82–98.
Curtius, E. R. 1952, *European Literature and the Latin Middle Ages*, trans. W. R. Trask, Harper & Row, New York.
Daley, P. 2016, 'Divided Melbourne: When the Archbishop Turned St Patrick's Day into Propaganda', *The Guardian*, 22 April, viewed 19 October 2017, www.theguardian.com/

australia-news/postcolonial-blog/2016/apr/22/divided-melbourne-when-the-archbishop-turned-st-patricks-day-into-propaganda

Di Marco, P. 2000, 'Inscribing the Body with Meaning: Chivalric Culture and the Norms of Violence in *The Vows of the Heron*', in D. N. Baker (ed.), *Inscribing the Hundred Years' War in French and English Chronicles*, SUNY Press, New York, pp. 27–53.

Dinshaw, C. 2012, *How Soon is Now? Medieval Texts, Amateur Readers and the Queerness of Time*, Duke University Press, Durham, NC.

Downes, S., Lynch, A. & O'Loughlin, K. (eds) 2015, *Emotions and War: Medieval to Romantic Literature*, Palgrave Studies in the History of Emotions, Palgrave Macmillan, Basingstoke.

Duffy, C. A. (ed.) 2014, *1914: Poetry Remembers*, Faber & Faber, Suffolk.

Fogarty, A. 1989, 'The Colonization of Language: Narrative Strategies in A View of the Present State of Ireland and The Faerie Queene, Book IV', in P. Coughlan (ed.), *Spenser and Ireland: An Interdisciplinary Perspective*, Cork University Press, Cork, pp. 75–108.

Hoccleve, T. 2001, 'The Dialogue', in: R. Ellis (ed.),*'My Compleinte' and Other Poems*, University of Exeter Press, Exeter.

Hochner, N. 2016, 'Le corps social à l'origine de l'invention du mot "émotion"', *L'Atelier du Centre de recherches historiques*, vol. 16, 23 May, viewed 19 October 2017, https://acrh.revues.org/7357?lang=en.

Holmes, O. W. 1992, *The Essential Holmes: Selections From the Letters, Speeches, Judicial Opinions, and Other Writings of Oliver Wendell Holmes, Jr.*, ed. R. A. Posner, University of Chicago Press, Chicago, pp. 80–87, available at www.people.virginia.edu/~mmd5f/memorial.htm

Homer 1950, *The Iliad*, trans. E. V. Rieu, Penguin, London.

Kaeuper, R. W. 2009, *Holy Warriors: The Religious Ideology of Chivalry*, University of Pennsylvania Press, Philadelphia.

Keen, M. 1976, 'Chivalry, Nobility, and the Man-at-Arms', in C. T. Allmand (ed.), *War, Literature, and Politics in the Middle Ages*, Liverpool University Press, Liverpool, pp. 32–45.

Lacy, N. 2000, 'Warmongering in Verse: Les Voeux du Heron', in D. N. Baker (ed.), *Inscribing the Hundred Years' War in French and English Chronicles*, SUNY Press, New York, pp. 17–26.

Lake, P. 2016, *How Shakespeare Put Politics on the Stage: Power and Succession in the History Plays*, Yale University Press, New Haven.

Lim, W. S. H. 1995, 'Figuring Justice: Imperial Ideology and the Discourse of Colonialism in Book V of The Fairie Queen and A View of the Present State of Ireland', *Renaissance and Reformation / Renaissance and Réforme*, vol. 19, no. 1, pp. 45–70.

McLoughlin, K. 2009, *The Cambridge Companion to War Writing*, Cambridge University Press, Cambridge.

Mebane, J. 2007, '"Impious War": Religion and Ideology of Warfare in Henry V', *Studies in Philology*, vol. 104, no. 2, pp. 250–266.

Nall, C. 2012, *Reading and War in Fifteenth-Century England: From Lydgate to Malory*, D. S. Brewer, Cambridge.

Paston Letters and Papers of the Fifteenth Century, Part 1 2004, ed. N. Davis, Early English Text Society, Supplementary Series 20, Oxford University Press, Oxford.

Pearsall, D. 1994, 'Hoccleve's "Regement of Princes": The Poetics of Royal Self-Representation', *Speculum*, vol. 69, no. 2, pp. 386–410.

Perkins, N. 2001, *Hoccleve's 'Regiment of Princes': Counsel and Constraint*, D. S. Brewer, Cambridge.

Phillips, G. 2006, 'Was the American Civil War the First Modern War?', *History Today: History Review*, issue 56, December, viewed 9 October 2017, www.historytoday.com/gervase-phillips/was-american-civil-war-first-modern-war.

Plamper, J. 2013, 'L'histoire des émotions', in C. Granger (ed.), *À quoi pensent les historiens? Faire de l'histoire au xxie siècle*, Éditions Autremont, Paris, pp. 225–240.

Plamper, J. 2014, 'Ivan's Bravery', in U. Frevert *et al.* (eds), *Emotional Lexicons: Continuity and Change in the Vocabulary of Feeling 1700–2000*, Oxford University Press, Oxford, pp. 191–208.

Pugliatti, P. 2010, *Shakespeare and the Just War Tradition*, Ashgate, Farnham.

Quabeck, F. 2013, *Just and Unjust Wars in Shakespeare*, De Gruyter, Berlin.

Richardson, J. 1973, 'Stendahl and Napoleon', *History Today*, vol. 23, no. 1, pp. 3–7.

Saunders, C. 2009, 'Medieval Warfare', in K. McLoughlin (ed.), *The Cambridge Companion to War Writing*, Cambridge University Press, Cambridge.

Scheer, M. 2012, 'Are Emotions a Kind of Practice (and is That What Makes Them Have a History)? A Bourdieuian Approach to Understanding Emotion', *History and Theory*, vol. 51, no. 2, pp. 193–220.

Scheer, M. 2014, 'Topographies of Emotion', in U. Frevert *et al.* (eds), *Emotional Lexicons: Community and Change in the Vocabulary of Feeling 1700–2000*, Oxford University Press, Oxford.

Scott, W. 1834, *Essays on Chivalry, Romance and the Drama: The Miscellaneous Prose Works of Sir Walter Scott, Bart*, Robert Cadell, Edinburgh.

Scott, W. 1923, *Waverley* [1814], Archibald Constable, London.

Shakespeare, W. 2008, *Henry V*, ed. G Taylor, Oxford World's Classics, Oxford University Press, Oxford.

Sherman, S. 1997, *Telling Time: Clocks, Diaries, and English Diurnal Form, 1660–1785*, Chicago University Press, Chicago.

Sir Gawain and the Green Knight 1967, eds J. R. R. Tolkien & E. V. Gordon, 2nd edn, ed. N. Davis, Oxford University Press, Oxford.

Stendhal 1926, *The Charterhouse of Parma*, trans. C. K. Scott-Moncrieff, 2 vols, Chatto & Windus, London.

Stendhal 1961, *La Chartreuse de Parme* [1839], ed. H. Martineau, Garnier, Paris.

Sterne, L. 1986, *The Life and Opinions of Tristram Shandy, Gentleman* [1759–65], eds M. New & J. New, Penguin Classics, Harmondsworth.

Strakhov, Y. 2014, *Politics in Translation: Language, War and Lyric Form in Francophone Europe, 1337–1400*, unpublished doctoral thesis, University of Pennsylvania, Philadelphia.

Tierney, D. 2017, 'Catholics and Great War Memorialisation in Scotland', *Journal of Scottish Historical Studies*, vol. 37, no. 1, pp. 19–51.

2
CONFESSING THE EMOTIONS OF WAR IN THE LATE MIDDLE AGES

Le livre du bon messire Jehan le Maingre, dit Bouciquaut

Craig Taylor

Modern military historians have become increasingly interested in the combat experience of soldiers. Studying the actions and emotions of those directly engaged in the face of battle offers a crucial supplement to information gathered from the lofty and potentially distant perspective of those in command, and more importantly mitigates the risk of underestimating the brutal horror of war. Oral testimony, letters, diaries and memoirs can offer valuable insight into the personal experience of soldiers (Bourke 1999). Of course, such sources do need to be handled with care: the passage of time inevitably risks distorting the representation of combat, either because of lapses in memory or because of the influence of hindsight. Moreover, when such records are prepared away from the battlefield, different cultural and emotional pressures may also affect the evidence. In particular, military veterans may struggle to process and to articulate the horrors and realities of war, especially to those who have not shared their experiences (McLoughlin 2009; 2011; McLoughlin, Feigel & Martin 2017).

First-person accounts of war and the battlefield are very rare survivals from the Middle Ages. The personal correspondence and diaries that are a staple source for the modern military historian are almost completely absent. Few medieval soldiers committed their experiences to writing and therefore most surviving accounts of war were written by members of the clergy, who either mediated and filtered the accounts of military veterans or simply imagined the battlefield, independent of any first-hand knowledge. But, by the time of the Hundred Years War, a small handful of veterans were writing chronicles, led by Jean Le Bel, Enguerrand de Monstrelet and Jean de Wavrin, while others were the authors of military and chivalric manuals, including Geoffroi de Charny, Thomas Gray, Philippe de Mézières and Antoine de La Sale (Taylor 2013). All of these writers drew upon and discussed their own personal experiences of war, though their works are still a far cry from the military memoirs that began to appear in the early modern period, and which were first foreshadowed by the unusual autobiographical *Le Jouvencel* written by Jean de Bueil between 1461 and 1468 (Harari 2004; Ramsey 2011).[1]

The nearest medieval counterpart to the modern military memoir are the biographies of aristocratic commanders, usually written by a companion-in-arms. These narratives offered a very particular window into the military experiences and emotions of veterans during the late medieval period. Such works typically focused upon the lives of contemporary military leaders rather than the more anonymous members of their armies. Moreover, the biographies deliberately echoed chivalric romances that recounted the adventures of great heroes such as King Arthur or Alexander the Great, thereby presenting contemporary warriors as the counterparts of such legendary heroes and the embodiments of knightly values (Gaucher 1994; Tyson 1998). Prominent examples include: Jean de Joinville's biography of the French King Louis IX written between 1305 and 1309; Guillaume de Machaut's celebration of King Peter I of Cyprus in *La prise d'Alexandrie* written between 1372 and 1373; Cuvelier's biography of the leading French military commander Bertrand Du Guesclin completed by 1381; the Chandos Herald's life of the Black Prince written by 1385, but perhaps closer to the death of the Black Prince in 1376; *Le livre des fais* of Jean II Le Meingre, known as Boucicaut, completed in 1409; Jean Cabaret d'Orville's chronicle of the life of Louis II duke of Bourbon completed in 1429; and Guillaume Gruel's biography of Arthur de Richemont, written between 1458 and 1468 (Gaucher 1994; Tyson 1998).

In *Le livre des fais*, the biographer recounts the life of Jean II Le Meingre, marshal of France, from his birth in 1366 up until 6 March 1409. Unusually, the narrative was completed 12 years before the death of its subject (ed. Lalande 1985; Lalande 1988). The anonymous author takes great pains to deny that Boucicaut himself played any direct role in the creation of the biography, anxious to protect the marshal from any accusations of self-promotion. Instead the author explains that the book was commissioned

> by a number of renowned knights and gallant noblemen who themselves pursue noble and honourable deeds, and who knew the good and valiant marshal who is our subject, and knew of his ancestors – there are still many who are in that position.
> (ed. Lalande 1985, pp. 10–11)[2]

There is no doubt that the book did genuinely spring from this close circle of highly experienced military veterans. The biographer pays very close attention in the narrative to the companions who fought and served alongside Boucicaut, led by Jean d'Ony, Guillaume de Tholigny and his brother Hugues, Robert de Milly, Hugues Cholet, Gilibert de La Fayette, Guillaume de Meuillon, Amanieu de Montpezat, Jacques de Prades, Gilles de Preuilly, Macé de Richebaron and the Bastard of Varannes. Moreover, the author repeatedly draws upon eye-witness accounts of the military accomplishments of Boucicaut, particularly in the first book recounting the start of his career up until the Nicopolis expedition of 1396, and also in the fourth book that offered a more abstract discussion of Boucicaut's exemplary qualities (ed. Lalande 1985, pp. 10–11, 104, 417, 424–425, 427–428). This hearsay is supplemented by transcriptions of official documents, from the letter of the foundation of the knightly order that Boucicaut created on 11 April 1400 to the letter of defiance that the marshal sent to the Venetian doge and to their admiral Carlo Zeno on 6 June 1404, as well as accounts of two important diplomatic missions in 1407 and 1408 (ed. Lalande 1985, pp. 164–171, 277–291, 347–356, 371–372).

The author of the biography does not identify himself, but it is likely that he too was a member of this circle. Recent scholarship has debated whether *Le livre des fais* was written by Nicolas de Gonesse, a graduate of the University of Paris who served as Boucicaut's confessor from at least 16 December 1406 (Millet 1995; Lalande 1998). Gonesse was a celebrated writer, known above all for his completion in 1401 of a French translation of Valerius Maximus's *Facta et dicta memorabilia* that had been started by Simon de Hesdin in 1375 on the orders of King Charles V (Galderisi 2011, vol. 2, pp. 253–255). It seems likely that Gonesse did play some role in the creation of *Le livre des fais*, given the heavy use of this French translation of Valerius Maximus, which would not have been easy to access without his help so soon after it was completed (Croenen, Rouse & Rouse 2002, pp. 263–265). Yet upon closer examination, it is apparent that these citations are clustered in the fourth and final book of the biography, which abandons the narrative of Le Meingre's story in favour of a more abstract manual or mirror for princes that seeks to highlight his particular qualities as a leader. In contrast, the translation of Valerius Maximus is only used or cited in nine out of the ninety-two chapters of the previous three books of the biography, and then always to gloss and to underscore a particular point in that narrative, such as the claim that Boucicaut was a good man who had been undermined by jealous enemies and by perverse popular opinion (ed. Lalande 1985, pp. 99–101, 339–344, 438–447). Therefore, it seems most plausible that Gonesse was employed to embellish the biography by adding this fourth book that was finished on 9 April 1409 (ed. Lalande 1985, p. 456), and also by inserting comments and glosses into the life of Boucicaut that was completed on or soon after 6 March 1409 (ed. Lalande 1985, p. 378).

Logic would suggest that the author of the narrative portion of the biography was a more practical and experienced man than Gonesse. Jean d'Ony, for example, would have been well placed to write such a narrative account. The level of detail offered by the biographer significantly increases after 1400, when Ony had joined the entourage of Boucicaut. The biography also reports the confidential instructions that Boucicaut gave to Ony for his diplomatic missions, first to persuade the king of Cyprus to join Boucicaut's planned expedition to seize Alexandria in 1407, and then when Ony met with Paolo Orsini in Rome in April 1408. If Ony were the anonymous author of the main narrative, this might explain the lavish praise heaped upon him for his military and diplomatic exploits. For example, the biographer notes that Boucicaut selected Ony for the mission to Rome because this member of the marshal's entourage was known to be 'valiant, wise, virtuous and conscientious'. These qualities were on display during the subsequent negotiations with Orsini in Rome, because Ony quickly sniffed out the betrayal of Boucicaut by the Romans and rushed to pass the news to the marshal and his fleet so that they could set out from Porto Venere on 25 April 1408.

In short, *Le livre des fais* was the product of a highly experienced circle of military veterans and may have been written by one of those soldiers. But whether the anonymous author was Jean d'Ony or not, it is striking that the writer offers very few clues to his own identity and refrains from offering any personal reactions to the unfolding stories except where such comments embellish the key themes of the book. Moreover, the biographer largely refrains from putting words into the mouth of his subject, shunning the practice of contemporary writers of chivalric romances and also chroniclers who happily present dramatic speeches that reveal the thoughts and emotions of their subjects. In the biography of Boucicaut, the first-person speech of the marshal and his companions is rarely recorded. Instead, the author prefers to allow Jean II Le Meingre to speak for himself through official documents such as the letter of defiance that Boucicaut sent on 6 June 1404 to the doge of Venice, Michele Steno, expressing his outrage at the actions of the Venetian fleet under the command of Carlo Zeno (ed. Lalande 1985, pp. 277–291).

Indeed, if there is one emotion most commonly attributed to Boucicaut by his biographer, it is anger. This is most evident in his response to the reported treachery of the Venetians that undermined the marshal's expedition in 1403, culminating in their attack upon his fleet at Modone on 7 October (ed. Lalande 1985, pp. 262, 267–268, 276, 277–291). The narrator reports that the Frenchmen taken prisoner at Modone pleaded with Boucicaut to put aside his anger and desire for vengeance that undermined their chance of securing their freedom, but that although Le Meingre was moved to tears, he still could not abandon his plan to seek revenge on the Venetians (ed. Lalande 1985, pp. 272–274). This righteous anger on the part of Boucicaut in the face of injustice is a common theme that runs throughout the biography, closely linked to his overwhelming sense of pride. As a young man, he frequently takes up arms in personal combat out of anger, like a figure from a chivalric romance. For example, he responds to the insults of the Gascon Sicart de La Barde (ed. Lalande 1985, pp. 49–51) and wants to fight to avenge the Scottish knight William Douglas after he is murdered by some Englishmen at Königsberg in 1391 (ed. Lalande 1985, pp. 76–77). During the fateful Nicopolis expedition of 1396, Le Meingre and the other French leaders are annoyed when their allies fail to inform them quickly enough about the Turkish attack and are enraged at the loss of their comrades (ed. Lalande 1985, pp. 103, 108). Boucicaut is also angry that the count of Périgord has revolted against the king the following year (ed. Lalande 1985, pp. 130–131). Later in the narrative, the marshal is reportedly outraged by the treachery of the Pisans and their mistreatment of French prisoners in the summer of 1405 (ed. Lalande 1985, pp. 324–325, 320).

Early in the narrative, the biographer praises the young Boucicaut as a man who has been inspired by 'Love', invoking commonplace ideas found in contemporary romances and poetry; he also notes that Boucicaut was one of the authors of the *Livre des cent ballades*, a collection of verses recounting a dialogue between a young knight and a lady (ed. Lalande 1985, pp. 27–32, 52). Yet in practice, the biography provides very little detail regarding Boucicaut's love either for his wife or during his youth for the anonymous lady for whom he 'felt all those pangs of love that make loyal lovers so eager to see the object of their affections' (ed. Lalande 1985, p. 40). Far more common are discussions of male affection and friendship, though even here the narrator offers modest and superficial comments. Early in his career, Boucicaut enjoys the support of Louis II duke of Bourbon who is said to have been very fond of the young man (ed. Lalande 1985, pp. 43, 80). King Charles VI is also described as having a great affection for Boucicaut, which the biographer illustrates by citing a line from an anonymous *ballade:* 'If you are loved, you're not forgot, Because you're far away' (ed. Lalande 1985, p. 78). The marshal is also said to have enjoyed a close emotional bond with the men under his command. Describing Boucicaut's appointment to a command in the king's expedition to Brittany in 1392, the biographer notes that a thousand men-at-arms are delighted to serve under the marshal because of the affection that they feel and the respect that they have for him (ed. Lalande 1985, p. 84). The biographer emphasises Boucicaut's love for his men, as demonstrated by the pity that he feels for them after the battle of Modone in October 1403 when, 'he was sick at heart at the thought of his much-loved knights who had been taken prisoner' (ed. Lalande 1985, p. 268). When these men subsequently plead with him to make peace with the Venetians to secure their release, 'he could not for very nobleness of spirit prevent his tears, so greatly was he moved to pity and affection', though Boucicaut does not waver in his desire to continue fighting (ed. Lalande 1985, p. 273).

The confession by Boucicaut that he is moved to tears by the fate of these French prisoners of the Venetians is a rare discussion of sadness and grief on the part of the marshal. As a young man, he is said to have felt pain at leaving behind his unidentified lover, and later he is sad to be separated from his wife Antoinette de Turenne (ed. Lalande 1985, pp. 52–53, 205). But in general it is more common for civilians to be described as sad or grief-stricken, and in particular the lovers and wives of the knights. For example, the 'grief, tears and sobs' of the loved ones of the Frenchmen who leave on the Nicopolis expedition foreshadow the 'great mourning' that spread through France when news of the disaster arrives (ed. Lalande 1985, pp. 92, 118–119). Indeed, the narrator offers a highly emotive description of the fate of these Christians in the immediate aftermath of the battle, making it difficult to know whether he himself has witnessed this heart-rending scene, or is merely painting such a picture to affect his audience (ed. Lalande 1985, pp. 113–117).

The biographer frequently notes the joy experienced by Boucicaut and others in a perfunctory manner, without ever offering any real insight into the emotion of such moments. Boucicaut's men are often said to be happy after military victories, such as Châteaumorand's capture of a Saracen ship heading for Beirut in August 1403 (ed. Lalande 1985, p. 244). French prisoners captured at Nicopolis are also delighted to be released from captivity, and are greeted with great joy upon their return home (ed. Lalande 1985, pp. 122, 123, 126, 128). Immediately after the great jousts held at Saint-Inglevert in March 1390, the biographer underlines the accomplishments of Boucicaut and his companions by recording the joyful welcome that they receive in Paris from the king and the court (ed. Lalande 1985, p. 74). The narrative notes the same thing when Boucicaut returns from Prussia and meets with the king in late December 1391; Charles VI is 'naturally delighted' to see Boucicaut (ed. Lalande 1985, p. 79). According to the biographer, the citizens of Genoa also welcome Boucicaut with great joy and delight when he first arrives in October 1401 (ed. Lalande 1985, p. 191). They are similarly elated at the arrival of his wife Antoinette de Turenne in July 1402 and when the marshal returns to Genoa in October 1402 after the battle of Modone: 'no lord had ever been greeted with such warmth' (ed. Lalande 1985, pp. 205–206, 269). Finally, in late 1408, Boucicaut reaches the castle of Meyrargues after a difficult journey and there his wife 'was so overjoyed that she wept for love and sheer happiness' (ed. Lalande 1985, p. 382). Such accounts principally serve to underline the marshal's fame and the high esteem in which he is held. Indeed, the narrator suggests that Carlo Zeno and the Venetians make every effort to display joy and delight as they greet Boucicaut and his fleet in the summer of 1403, 'so that they all seemed fast friends', masking their treacherous plans to undermine the Genoese expedition (ed. Lalande 1985, p. 215).

On a few rare occasions within the narrative, Boucicaut's own joy is recorded upon rejoining his own loved ones. In the spring of 1391, Geoffroy Le Meingre travels to Prussia to join Boucicaut and the 'two brothers were delighted to see each other' (ed. Lalande 1985, p. 75). More common are descriptions of Boucicaut's joy either at the chance to take up arms or in celebration of victory. For example, he is described as being overjoyed at the news of the duke of Bourbon's plan to lead an expedition to Al-Mahdiya in 1390 and he is said to be delighted in July 1403 when a peace treaty between the king of Cyprus and Genoa gives him the opportunity to launch the expedition that later attacked Beirut (ed. Lalande 1985, pp. 74, 230).

In sum, the biography does consider Boucicaut's emotions before or after battle, but in a very limited fashion and there is almost no discussion of his immediate reactions to violence itself. The narrative concentrates on the actions of its hero and his companions – that is to say the deeds of arms identified in the title of the biography – rather than on their emotions. The biographer recounts an overwhelming list of expeditions, battles and encounters where Boucicaut and his circle display prowess and courage, rarely pausing to interrogate the specific emotions experienced by these Frenchmen. Early in the narrative, for example, the biography describes the deeds performed by the young Le Meingre during the battle of Roosebeke on 26 November 1382 (ed. Lalande 1985, p. 75). At one point, our

French hero faces a sturdy Fleming armed with a two-handed battleaxe who contemptuously dismisses the smaller Boucicaut, declaring that 'The French must be short of decent men if they have to enlist children'. Yet it is Le Meingre who emerges victorious in this encounter after stabbing his opponent with a dagger. The incident highlights Boucicaut's great prowess and courage in overcoming such a significantly more powerful opponent. But the biographer characteristically offers limited insight into the emotions of this highly charged moment, merely noting that the Fleming has initially been contemptuous of Boucicaut and that the Frenchman is anguished when he loses his own axe early in the struggle. Such details serve to underline the dramatic turn of events when Le Meingre turns the tables on his arrogant opponent, and then mocks the wounded man by asking him whether this is a game for Flemish children.

The narrator does not present Boucicaut's courage as a triumph over fear. Indeed, the biographer scrupulously avoids giving any hint that the marshal or his men are afraid in battle and there are very few occasions when the Frenchmen are explicitly described as feeling fear. One example appears early in the biography, when the author describes Le Meingre's disappointment at the king's refusal to allow him to join Louis de Bourbon's crusade to Al-Mahdiya in the summer of 1390. The author reports that Le Meingre felt fear ('paour') that King Charles VI would revoke the permission that he granted Boucicaut later in that year to travel to Prussia for the *Reise* (ed. Lalande 1985, pp. 74–75). This is the exact opposite of a cowardly fear of battle, and hence an honourable and worthy emotion.

Overall, *Le livre des fais* presents a very constrained representation of the emotional responses of its subject, Jean II Le Meingre, and his companions, to the face of battle. Very little attention is paid to their inner reactions to war, from the boredom, homesickness and even melancholia of campaign to the sheer terror of combat itself. This raises difficult questions regarding the ability of men like Boucicaut and his circle to articulate their true experiences of war. Does the narrative reveal the challenge that late medieval veterans faced in representing their personal experience of war, and of processing and expressing the emotions of war, particularly for a wider audience that had not experienced the battlefield? Or does *Le livre des fais* illustrate a martial culture that actively sought to mask weakness and fear? The fact that such heroic narratives concentrated upon the external demonstrations of bravery and courage, rather than the inner emotional experiences of warriors might suggest a deliberate conspiracy of silence regarding human weakness and insecurity in the face of such awful conditions (Taylor 1999). It has even been suggested that a textual culture that deliberately ignored the inner experiences, emotions or sensations of warriors such as Boucicaut may itself have been constitutive of the world of military combatants, encouraging them to worry more about their external behaviour and the audiences to their actions than about their inner feelings (Harari 2004; 2005; 2008).

Yet there are reasons to be cautious before advancing such bold claims, at least in relation to *Le livre des fais*. First and foremost, the biography of Boucicaut does not mask the horror and fear of the battlefield, but rather denies that either the marshal or his men are affected by this. A central theme of the narrative is the stereotyping of Saracens as cowardly and fearful, and hence the stark contrast between such enemies and the good Christians serving alongside Boucicaut. During the attack on Candelore in late June 1403, for example, the marshal conceives a cunning plan by which his men will pretend to be frightened and then stage a feigned retreat to draw the 'rats of Saracens' into an ambush. The fact that the French are pretending to be afraid serves to highlight the real terror of the Saracen army who does indeed turn tail in the face of this ambush (ed. Lalande 1985, pp. 227–228).

Le livre des fais repeatedly underlines the fearfulness of the enemies of the marshal. On 6 August 1403, Boucicaut's force of around 2,000 men engages with a Saracen army said to have numbered more than 15,000 at Tripoli. The fighting is fierce and the biographer acknowledges that the Saracens initially defend themselves with great ardour. But as the Christians renew their attack, their enemies become dismayed and ultimately flee from the battlefield, and the magnitude of this victory is emphasised by the narrator in citing the French translation and gloss on Valerius Maximus that argues that 'five hundred men of courage can often take on as many as ten thousand' (ed. Lalande 1985, pp. 236–240). When the marshal then staged a second attack against the Saracen positions, they again panicked and fled in the direction of some overgrown gardens (ed. Lalande 1985, pp. 241–243). Six days later, when the French attack Sidon, the Saracens are initially courageous but during the course of the battle become filled with fear in the face of the resolve of the marshal's army (ed. Lalande 1985, pp. 248–250). The contrast between the bravery of the Christians and the cowardice of their Saracen enemies is underlined much later in the narrative, when the marshal sends ambassadors in August 1407 to encourage Janus, king of Cyprus, to join an expedition to capture Alexandria. During the negotiations, the king declares that he has no fear of the sultan and his men because of his first-hand experience of their cowardice, and that he is therefore certain that a small number of good and well-trained men can overcome such an enemy (ed. Lalande 1985, pp. 259–360). The king subsequently decides not to join Boucicaut's proposed expedition but vigorously denies that this decision is motivated by cowardice (ed. Lalande 1985, p. 362).

It is not only Saracens who demonstrate fear and cowardice in the biography of Boucicaut. During the account of the battle of Nicopolis on 25 September 1396, the Ottoman Sultan Bayezid and his men are briefly alarmed by the valour shown by the Frenchmen and put to flight, at least until the Turks realise that they heavily outnumber their opponents (ed. Lalande 1985, p. 103). But the Hungarian allies of the French are the ones who panic on the battlefield, from the very first moment when the Turks first attack (ed. Lalande 1985, pp. 106–107). The biographer claims that most of the Hungarians are cowards and deserters who flee in the face of the Turkish archers, thereby justifying his contention that they are a people known to be reluctant to join battle. Indeed, the author even compares the Hungarians to the wicked and cowardly followers of Christ who abandon him when he is taken prisoner by his enemies (ed. Lalande 1985, p. 107).

This insistence upon the terror and cowardice shown by many of the Hungarians serves to underline the biographer's main contention that Boucicaut and the other French crusaders demonstrate extraordinary courage in the face of extreme circumstances. These men reveal themselves to be 'paragons of courage and defiance' in the face of the impending disaster (ed. Lalande 1985, p. 107). When Boucicaut finally realises that defeat is inevitable, he feels not terror but grief and dismay, and flings himself into the fray in order to ensure that his enemies will have to pay dearly to kill him (ed. Lalande 1985, p. 111). At that crucial moment in the text, the narrator calls upon the reader to recognise the tragedy at hand as Boucicaut is risking his life so bravely, and also to feel pity for the French company that has been deprived of support by their allies and has fallen victim to the cruelty of their enemies. This justifies the eternal shame that the narrator seeks to heap upon the Hungarians who have abandoned their allies and allowed the Turks to win the battle (ed. Lalande 1985, pp. 111–112). It also gives credence to the anonymous author's insistent denial of defamatory reports that many Frenchmen have actually fled in the face of the Turks, and that the ensuing chaos has played a crucial role in the defeat (ed. Lalande 1985, p. 104). This is a direct acknowledgement by the biographer that there were severe criticisms in France of the lack of discipline, organisation and courage shown by all the Christian warriors following the disaster at Nicopolis, most noticeably voiced by Michel Pintouin in his Latin chronicle of Saint-Denis (Gaucher 1996; eds Contamine & Paviot 2008).

Running through the narrative is an obsession with shame. The account of Nicopolis is framed by the subsequent battle to identify those who are to blame for the disaster and have therefore incurred eternal shame and opprobrium. The biographer of Boucicaut not only denounces the defamation of reports that blame all the Christians for the disaster, but also underlines his defence of the French contingent by reporting, for example, that just one single Hungarian, Count Nikola II Garai Miklós, stood firm alongside them in the battle, and that this man was 'filled with shame at the flagrant betrayal by the main body of Hungarians' (ed. Lalande 1985, pp. 107, 110). In contrast, Boucicaut not only refuses to retreat on the battlefield at Nicopolis, but also refuses to abandon the Frenchmen who were taken prisoner: 'If I left you here in so fearful a prison and fled to France, it would rightly be thought heinous and dishonourable' (ed. Lalande 1985, p. 123).

Fear of shame is consistently identified as a motivation for the actions of Boucicaut and his men. The biography argues that Boucicaut and his men prefer death to shame (ed. Lalande 1985, pp. 408–410). In the account of the siege of Oryahovo shortly before the battle of Nicopolis, the marshal is credited with a rare battle oration, warning his men that they will be shamed if others cross the bridge before them, and therefore urging them on to win honour and renown (ed. Lalande 1985, p. 96). Shame also frames the account of the fateful expedition of 1403 that culminates in the battle of Modone. The biographer presents

Boucicaut's own letter to the Venetians written on 6 June 1404, which describes the actions of Carlo Zeno and his men as 'a source of shame and humiliation to you and all your followers, showing as they do signal cowardice and disgrace' (ed. Lalande 1985, p. 288). Boucicaut declares himself willing to undertake a trial by combat to defend this charge, echoing the other occasions in the narrative when the marshal takes up arms out of righteous anger and to defend his own honour (ed. Lalande 1985, pp. 288–289). Shame also motivates Boucicaut's efforts to launch a crusading campaign in 1407, when he seeks not only 'to further the good of Christianity and bring honour to knighthood', but also to end 'the suffering and shame imposed on the Christians by their subjugation to the Saracens' living in the Holy Lands (ed. Lalande 1985, pp. 344–345). A similar motivation to protect others from shame underpins his earlier creation of the votive order of *La Dame Blanche à l'Écu Vert* on 11 April 1400: he and 12 other knights take oaths to take the field for any ladies of noble blood who lack a champion to defend their honour (ed. Lalande 1985, pp. 160–171).

The crucial point is that the biography itself was written as a defence of the honour of Jean II Le Meingre. *Le livre des fais* presents a carefully constructed defence of the actions of Boucicaut and his companions, not just during the Nicopolis expedition but throughout his subsequent governorship of Genoa following his appointment to that role by the French crown on 23 March 1401. Like other chivalric biographers, the author of *Le livre des fais* claims that he is writing to inspire the future generations of knights (ed. Lalande 1985, pp. 6–11, 447–451), but in fact such texts really served a more prosaic goal in defining the reputation of their subjects. This is particularly true of *Le livre des fais*, which was uniquely written while its subject was still alive, and hence less concerned with commemorating its subject than shoring up his reputation for eminently practical reasons. The book offers Boucicaut's version of events during a controversial period of 12 years, from the Nicopolis expedition in 1396 to his problematic involvement in further unsuccessful crusading ventures and the papal schism, all of which had inevitably called into question his abilities. Most important of all, Boucicaut was under severe threat from opponents in the city of Genoa and the region as a whole (Lalande 1988, pp. 98–165; Epstein 2001, pp. 257–260). On 16 November 1408, Gabriel Maria Visconti was arrested for his part in a Ghibellline plot to take control of Genoa. Immediately afterwards, Pileo de Marini, archbishop of Genoa, wrote to Paris, denouncing Le Meingre's rule as governor and his execution of Visconti for the plot (Puncuh 1978). Shortly after the biography was completed, Boucicaut's opponents took their chance to seize control of Genoa when the governor briefly left the city. His lieutenant, Hugues Cholet, was killed on the streets of the city on 3 September 1409 and three days later, Theodore II Paleologus, marquis of Montferrat, was appointed as the captain of the people.

It was against this backdrop that Boucicaut's friends prepared *Le livre des fais*, almost certainly for the audience at the French court. Following the Genoese uprising in September 1409, Boucicaut dispatched three envoys to Paris in March

1410 to appeal to the court for further financial support. They carried with them a dossier detailing his financial accounts and presumably also *Le livre des fais* that set out his version of events that had led Boucicaut to this perilous position. The biographer complained vigorously about the lies about the marshal that had been spread by the followers of the dukes of Orléans and Burgundy (Lalande 1988, pp. 337–338), and the narrative carefully defends the Boucicaut's judgement on the different occasions when these princes of the blood undermined him, for example in the aftermath of the disaster at Modone in 1403 and in the complex negotiations relating to Pisa in 1406 (Lalande 1988, pp. 272–291, 331–336).

The very practical purpose of *Le livre des fais* helps to explain the choices made by the author in constructing the narrative. The descriptions of emotion consistently served to underline the case being presented, from Boucicaut's righteous anger against his enemies, to the powerful contrast between the courageousness of his men and the fearfulness of their enemies. From a wider perspective, the biography echoed contemporary chivalric romances in celebrating the adventures of its protagonist and in the emphasis placed on his chivalric qualities. But where such romances typically used direct speech to give the audience access to the inner thoughts and emotions of a character, the biographer of Boucicaut carefully avoided putting words into the mouth of its subject. The biographer also rarely imposed his own voice as a narrator within the story, except as a commentator underlining the specific message to be drawn from specific anecdotes. These choices, together with the frequent resort to official documents, were intended to enhance the authority of the biographer and his narrative (Brown-Grant 2011).

In other words, the fact that the narrative offers limited insight into the emotions and inner experience of both Boucicaut and the biographer may have been a deliberate, tactical choice in service to the primary goal of the text – that is to say the presentation of the most convincing explanation for the marshal's actions, particularly as governor of Genoa. It would therefore be difficult to use a text such as *Le livre des fais* as evidence in support of the intriguing notion that soldiers in the late Middle Ages were emotionally constrained either because they lived in a martial culture that focused upon the external rather than the internal, or, more controversially, because they lacked the ability or interest to articulate their inner experiences. The biography of Boucicaut may have been the product of a circle of extremely experienced military veterans but, despite the claims of the author, it is implausible that this work, which survives in just one incomplete manuscript, was really intended to be an educational tool for young warriors or a simple mirror to the lives of military veterans. Rather, the biography was a carefully constructed defence of the actions of Boucicaut and his circle, artfully and manipulatively employing a range of techniques including the rhetoric of emotions to target a specific courtly audience. The goal of the text was to defend the public actions and behaviour of its subject, and therefore the narrator's interest in the emotions and inner experience of Boucicaut was always channelled towards that goal. It would therefore be wrong to read the limited discussion of the emotional experience of violence and the battlefield in *Le livre des fais* as evidence to support Harari's contention that veterans like those in service to Boucicaut had no interest in, or more importantly, no ability to express their reactions to such matters.[3]

Notes

1 Michelle Szkilnik is currently completing a new scholarly edition of *Le Jouvencel*.
2 All translations come from C. Taylor & J. H. N. Taylor (trans) 2016.
3 My monograph on Boucicaut and *Le livre des fais* will be published by York Medieval Press in 2019.

Reference list

Bourke, J. 1999, *An Intimate History of Killing: Face-to-Face Killing in Twentieth Century Warfare*, Granta, London.

Brown-Grant, R. 2011, 'Narrative Style in Burgundian Chronicles of the Later Middle Ages', *Viator*, vol. 42, no. 2, pp. 233–281.

Contamine, P. & Paviot, J. (eds) 2008, *Philippe de Mézières, Une epistre lamentable et consolatoire adressée en 1397 à Philippe le Hardi, duc de Bourgogne, sur la défaite de Nicopolis (1396)*, Société de l'Histoire de France, Paris.

Croenen, G., Rouse, M. & Rouse, R. 2002, 'Pierre de Liffol and the Manuscripts of Froissart's Chronicles', *Viator*, vol. 33, pp. 261–293.

Epstein, S. A. 2001, *Genoa and the Genoese, 958–1528*, University of North Carolina Press, Chapel Hill.

Galderisi, C. 2011, *Translations médiévales. Cinq siècles de traductions en français au Moyen Âge (XIe-XVe siècles). Étude et Répertoire*, vol. 1–2, Brepols, Turnhout.

Gaucher, E. 1993, 'Entre l'histoire et le roman: la biographie chevaleresque', *Revue des langues romanes*, vol. 97, no. 1, pp. 15–29.

Gaucher, E. 1994, *La biographie chevaleresque. Typologie d'un genre (XIIIe-XVe siècle)*, Honoré Champion. Paris.

Gaucher, E. 1996, 'Deux regards sur une défaite: Nicopolis (d'après la *Chronique du Religieux de Saint-Denis* et le *Livre des faits de Boucicaut*)', *Cahiers de Recherches Médiévales et Humanistes*, vol. 1, pp. 93–104.

Harari, Y. N. 2004, *Renaissance Military Memoirs. War, History, and Identity, 1450–1600*, The Boydell Press, Woodbridge.

Harari, Y. N. 2005, 'Martial Illusions: War and Disillusionment in Twentieth-Century and Renaissance Military Memoirs', *Journal of Military History*, vol. 69, no. 1, pp. 43–72.

Harari, Y. N. 2008, *The Ultimate Experience. Battlefield Revelations and the Making of Modern War Culture, 1450–2000*, Palgrave Macmillan, Basingstoke.

Lalande, D. (ed.) 1985, *Le livre des fais du bon messire Jehan Le Maingre, dit Bouciquaut, Mareschal de France et gouverneur de Jennes*, Librairie Droz, Geneva.

Lalande, D. 1988, *Jean II Le Meingre, dit Boucicaut (1366–1421): étude d'une biographie héroïque*, Librairie Droz, Geneva.

Lalande, D. 1998, 'Nicolas de Gonesse est-il l'auteur du *Livre des fais du Mareschal Bouciquaut*', in J. C. Faucon, A. Labbé & D. Quéruel (eds), *Miscellania Mediaevalia. Mélanges offerts à Philippe Ménard*, 2 vols, Honoré Champion, Paris, pp. 827–837.

McLoughlin, K. 2009, 'War and Words', in K. McLoughlin (ed.), *The Cambridge Companion to War Writing*, Cambridge University Press, Cambridge, pp. 15–24.

McLoughlin, K. 2011, *Authoring War. The Literary Representation of War from the Iliad to Iraq*, Cambridge University Press, Cambridge.

McLoughlin, K., Feigel, L. & Martin, N. 2017, *Writing War, Writing Lives*, Routledge, Abingdon.

Millet, H. 1995, 'Qui a écrit *Le livre des faits du bon messire Jehan Le Maingre dit Bouciquaut?*', in M. Ornato & N. Pons (eds), *Pratiques de la culture écrite en France au XVe siècle, Fédération internationale des instituts d'études médiévales*, Louvain-la-Neuve, pp. 135–150.

Puncuh, D. 1978, 'Il governo genovese del Boucicaut nella lettera di Pileo de Marini a Carlo VI di Francia 1409', *Mélanges de l'école française de Rome. Moyen Âge, Temps modernes*, vol. 90, no. 2, pp. 657–687.

Ramsey, N. 2011, *The Military Memoir and Romantic Literary Culture, 1780–1835*, VT: Ashgate, Burlington.

Taylor, A. 1999, 'Chivalric Conversation and the Denial of Male Fear', in: J. Murray (ed.), *Conflicted Identities and Multiple Masculinities: Men in the Medieval West*, Routledge, New York, pp. 169–188.

Taylor, C. 2013, *Chivalry and the Ideals of Knighthood in France During the Hundred Years War*, Cambridge University Press, Cambridge.

Taylor, C. & Taylor, J. H. N. (trans) 2016, *The Chivalric Biography of Boucicaut, Jean II Le Meingre*, The Boydell Press, Woodbridge.

Tyson, D. B. 1998, 'Authors, Patrons and Soldiers. Some Thoughts on Four Old French Soldiers' Lives', *Nottingham Medieval Studies*, vol. 42, pp. 105–120.

3

EMOTION AND MEDIEVAL 'VIOLENCE'

The Alliterative *Morte Arthure* and *The Siege of Jerusalem*

Andrew Lynch

The close relation of 'violence' to emotion in medieval and Early Modern Europe was a major topic for twentieth-century historians and continues to attract close attention (Broomhall & Finn 2015; Bellis & Slater 2016). As Susan Broomhall has recently remarked of the work of Johan Huizinga and Norbert Elias, '[b]oth appeared to understand the violence and the affective behaviours of medieval people as one and the same phenomen[on]' (Broomhall 2015, p. 4). Broomhall goes on to stress the key role of conceptual definitions in establishing the relation of emotion to violence, 'for these terms cannot be assumed to have shared meanings among disciplinary traditions, nor indeed among past and present populations' (Broomhall 2015, p. 5). In this essay, as an attempt to add clearer definition to the medieval concept of 'violence', or at least to avoid some confusion, I discuss the place of emotion in the construction and evaluation of 'violent' bodily actions in later medieval English war writings. Together with brief reference to early and late medieval poetic works, I pay special attention to two texts. One is the Alliterative *Morte Arthure*, a late fourteenth-century poem in the Arthurian tradition stemming from Geoffrey of Monmouth's 1130s *Historia regum Brittanie*. In this story, Roman ambassadors arrive in Britain and demand that Arthur pay tribute to the Emperor as overlord. In response, Arthur begins a new campaign against the Roman Empire, defeats the Emperor's forces, and is just about to win Rome itself when he hears that Mordred and Guinevere have rebelled and seized power in Britain. He returns and puts down the rebellion, but is killed in the last battle and is buried at Glastonbury. The other text is *The Siege of Jerusalem*, another anonymous alliterative poem, variously dated as between 1370 and 1400. It describes the total destruction of Jerusalem in CE 70 after a siege led by the Romans Vespasian and Titus. It is often, and very understandably, described as an unpleasantly violent work (Pearsall 1977, p. 169).

The word 'violence' had a different meaning in medieval times from that which it has today. In modern usage 'violence' primarily refers to '[t]he deliberate exercise of physical force against a person, property, etc'. Medieval usages of 'violence' refer, by contrast, to a former, now obsolete meaning: 'the abuse of power or authority to persecute or oppress' (*Oxford English Dictionary* 2017, violence, n. 1a). Anglo-Norman *violence* (the source of the English word) also supports the now obsolete meaning (*Anglo-Norman Dictionary* 1992, violence, s.). Medieval usages of 'violent' and 'violence', as they are applied to human actions, exclude many modern associations of the word because they always involve a judgement identifying some specially wrongful or dangerous use of force or superior power; these are misdirected, inappropriate, excessive, abusive, destructive or tyrannical acts and effects, rather than a description of physically aggressive actions and events in general.[1] They are instances of 'unreasonable violence', which was to be avoided because it 'discredited not only a particular enterprise but the entire "just war" theory as well' (Allmand 1999, p. 259). The general meaning of the medieval term is closer to modern 'violation'. Accordingly, it can be misleading to regard what modern Western culture calls 'violence' – fights and wars, for example – as instances of 'violence' in medieval understanding. If 'violence' involves the breaking of an explicit or implicit protocol, the term seems inappropriate for medieval fighters apparently represented as doing as they should, or to those battles in which normal rules are followed, however bloody the results. In much medieval literature if acts of physical force are shown as 'true to form', in line with generic convention, they are not presented as violent but as proper and socially beneficial. The judgement of right and wrong uses of force is always to some extent a response to aspects of form, including literary form and the emotive features of texts that direct readerly alignment towards character and action.

That is not, of course, to deny that medieval wars, like all wars, were very 'violent' in the modern sense (Hanley 2003, pp. 42–45), but to warn against the confusion of two different historical and evaluative frameworks in analysing medieval writings about war and combat. Without maintaining the distinction between these two meanings of 'violence', we may miss understanding the ways in which medieval literature both supports and critiques the motives and conduct of warfare. In particular, we may overlook the manner in which this literature relates judgement of physical force both to ethics and to emotion. In the discourse of medieval war poetry, descriptions of killing and maiming, including the Alliterative *Morte*'s 'obsession with the visual detail of damaged and dying bodies' (Baden-Daintree 2016, p. 57), are likely to be treated as ethically and emotionally positive, indeed honorific, matters, and presented to readers as honourable to behold. On the other hand, a condemnation of 'violence' may be sustained by a cool analysis of the circumstances in which an action is taken, with no graphic detail at all supplied.

The work of Chaucer provides instructive examples. The *Tale of Melibee* is an exercise in the tradition of prudential counsel. King Melibee is the victim of an unprovoked assault and angrily plans vengeance, but his adviser Dame Prudence refers to his proposed reaction of punitive war as a 'violence':

> And if ye seye that right axeth [asks] a man to defenden violence by violence and fightyng by fightyng, certes ye seye sooth, whan the defense is doon anon withouten intervalle or withouten tariyng or delay, for to deffenden hym and nat for to vengen hym [avenge himself]. And it bihoveth that a man putte swich attemperance in his deffense that men have no cause ne matiere to repreven hym that deffendeth hym of excesse and outrage, for ellis were it agayn resoun.
> (Chaucer *The Tale of Melibee*, in Benson 1990, p. 232)

Prudence's stipulation of the strict limits within which physical force may justifiably be used shows how such judgements of 'violence' belong to an ethical and relatively unemotional register of discourse. By contrast, in the *Knight's Tale*, Chaucer shows how differently a punitive war – waged by Thesesus against Creon out of pity for the Theban widows – looks within the discourse of chivalry:

> Thus rit [rides] this duc, thus rit this conquerour,
> And in his hoost of chivalrie the flour,
> Til that he cam to Thebes and alighte
> Faire in a feeld, ther as he thoughte to fighte.
> (Chaucer *The Knight's Tale*, in Benson 1990, ll. 981–984)

Prudence's critique of 'violence' finds no place here because in this kind of language the conqueror's motives and conduct appear unquestionably 'faire', a term that combines ethical and aesthetic approval. The *Knight's Tale* must employ other strategies to disrupt the smooth surface of chivalric war writing: a tour of the field strewn with bodies after the battle, and the miscellaneous semi-realist, semi-allegorical imagery of the Temple of Mars, where the grim and inglorious effects of war are shown.

Without some privileging of ethical judgement, or at least some suspension or disruption of chivalric language, charges of violence scarcely come into play in medieval texts. The word is rarely used in cases where modern writers would habitually use it, for example in relation to the fights and other aggressive behaviours described in Huizinga's famous opening chapter translated as '[t]he violent tenor of life', which became, in a later translation, '[t]he passionate intensity of life' (Huizinga 1924; 1996). 'Violence' is an identification inseparable from language which specifically encodes the cognitive, ethical and emotional grounds of 'violent' action. We cannot establish what it means 'in itself' as a known entity: it can only occur and be known historically, in its time, place and culturally situated utterance. Where one medieval writer rejoices in the noble scene of warfare, noting who 'does well', another writer, working from different ethical premises and in a different generic register, will represent the same deeds as pathological violence (Lynch 2016).

To give an idea of the vagueness that has surrounded the term 'violence' in its relation to medieval war: one essay collection on 'the impact of violence on society in medieval and early modern Europe' includes a study of the 'Peace of God' movement in thirteenth-century Aquitaine, which was designed to protect the church and the peasants from attack (Frassetto 1998). Another book on 'interpreting medieval violence' begins with an essay on Wiglaf's role in the dragon fight in *Beowulf* (Hill 2004). In one case, church authorities formally identify certain sections of society as illegitimate targets of military force, effectively casting aggression against them as a form of 'violence'. In the other, a young warrior achieves glory by helping to kill an enemy destroying his people, and, specifically, by aiding the kinsman and the lord to whom he owes allegiance. We are told that Wiglaf is doing what he should: 'swylc sceolde secg wesan, þegn æt ðearfe' – 'so should a warrior be, a thane in need' (*Beowulf*, ll. 2708–2709). It is clear that while both these examples are related to instances of 'violence' in the general modern sense, in one case only is the action or physical force concerned ideologically and institutionally established as 'violent'. Wiglaf's actions by contrast, are seen as praiseworthy and absolutely normative; *not* to act in that way violates an obligation. Violence is an ideological and institutional category, and an ethical interpretative category, not one simply established by identification of the use of force.

Nevertheless, something these two examples do have in common is emotion: strong feelings that conduce to action. Wiglaf does not only respond to Beowulf's plight with a cognitive sense of obligation; it is felt. The poet highlights Wiglaf's strong emotions: 'hiora in anum weoll / sefa wið sorgum sibb æfre ne mæg / wiht onwendan þam ðe wel þenceð' – 'The heart of one of them surged with sorrows; kinship can never change in one who thinks rightly' (*Beowulf*, ll. 2599–2601); 'his heart was sad in him' – 'him wæs sefa geomor' (*Beowulf*, l. 2632); he beholds Beowulf's dead body 'earfoðlice' – 'painfully' (*Beowulf*, l. 2822). Emotion drives his actions and models a correct emotional reaction for the audience. Similarly, the Peace of God could only be enforced when those who were militarily powerful were also afraid of spiritual penalties such as excommunication and denial of burial in consecrated ground. Churchmen decreed that killing peasants was wrong, but it was only the emotions that religious sanctions aroused in soldiers that could make the decrees effective (Frassetto 1998, pp. 18–20). Whether the result is to take or to limit actions involving physical force, and to approve them or deplore them, emotion figures in the judgement. As a corollary, the emotions elicited by witnessing extreme force will depend on cognitive alignments: the torments of Christ demand deep pity; those of a traitor are cause for laughter and satisfaction.[2] The emotions stirred or calmed by witnessing an event make it a 'violence' or not, in a way that shows the intersection of emotional, ideological and ethical judgements.

The kinds of questions asked in the Middle Ages about the use and abuse of physical force, and the ways they are answered, are always interactive with existing emotional regimes. They help to construct and modify these regimes, which are themselves always politically situated. The extension or refusal of emotional sympathy to particular actions, individuals and groups, and the narrative evocation of particular emotional repertoires concerning them, are institutionally and politically related matters (Reddy 2001; Colwell 2016). As Daniel Gross (2006, p. 4) puts it:

> the contours of our emotional world have been shaped by institutions . . . that simply afford some people greater emotional range than others, as they are shaped by a publicity that has nothing to do with the inherent value of each human life, and everything to do with technologies of social recognition and blindness.

Narrative genres and poetic strategies feature prominently among these technologies of recognition and repression. In complex poetic narratives, ideological and political evaluations are discovered or inferred from the emotional colour of each descriptive moment at its own place in the text. And, more specifically in the war poems I am considering, acts of force serve as focal points for emotional depictions and arousals that provide the narrative's most valued narrative currency and create the most intense impression of what the poetry is 'for': in these depictions emotion is at once a medium, an effect and a goal. Later medieval literary texts on war are quite rarely structured around philosophical or ethical propositions. In them, we are not often dealing with a clear 'concept' of 'war' or 'right', but with what Tomaž Mastnak – rejecting terms such as 'the concept of crusade, or 'the crusade idea' – calls instead 'something much vaguer, a magma of images, beliefs, fantasies, expectations, feelings, and sentiments' (Mastnak 2002, p. 56). To know how these texts establish and manage their inter-related ethical and emotional judgements about war is therefore necessarily a matter of literary analysis.

I. The Alliterative *Morte Arthure*

In later medieval English war literature, the merits of physically aggressive acts are not often discussed consistently according to a patent ethical system, and their descriptions usually omit explicit assessment of motivation. That effect is compounded in medieval alliterative verse narrative through its formal tendency to create a sequence of discrete narrative events – moral *topoi*, set speeches, summary catalogues, fights, rituals and descriptive loci – which establish their own separate significance and do not necessarily construct or appeal to an evident overall framework for interpretation. The Alliterative *Morte Arthure* is regularly seen as 'a fundamentally fragmented, fractured text' (Nievergelt 2010, p. 91).

We see this tendency in the very first lines of the poem, which invoke a long-term view of the narrative course, on a different scale and in a different evaluative mode from its detailed account of subsequent events. These lines may be read as anticipating the sad ending of the narrative – the final failure of Arthur's campaign – which is then obscured throughout nearly all of what follows:

> Now grete glorious God through grace of Himselven
> And the precious prayer of his pris Moder
> Sheld us fro shamesdeede and sinful workes
> And give us grace to guie and govern us here
> In this wretched world through virtuous living
>
> (*AMA* 1–5)[3]

The poem's summary view that this is a 'wretched world' can co-exist in different ways with its apparent enthusiasm for British prowess and conquest. It may be endorsing them as an example of 'virtuous living' in a world where wickedness is always present. The lines may also be read as exculpatory of Arthur's wars – he cannot be blamed for the failed outcome of his campaign against Rome, surely already known to readers and hearers, because the world is such an uncertain and wicked place. On the other hand, perhaps the opening provides a conceptual frame that limits the extent and the value of human agency, and leaves in question whether Arthur's actions in a 'wretched world' are 'sinful workes' or 'virtuous living'. Perhaps, in this large-scale view, emotional excitation towards an earthly goal would in itself be a part of human weakness, imperceptive of the need for divine grace, for all Arthur's many later claims to be a religious champion.

A further narrative check on the story's apparent enthusiasm for war is its scene-specific, disunifying treatment of character and motivation. While Mordred and Guinevere bear long-term ethical responsibility for the results of their treachery, their emotional credit at each stage of the story is rather detached from their involvement in future or past events. They act and react emotionally in more complex ways than their role as traitors in the plot would suggest. They seem not to possess essentially bad emotional motivations, but to accrue bad motivations circumstantially within the overall development of the action, so that blame for the bad outcome is not solely theirs. Even when a prior knowledge of the story can create a simple 'dramatic irony', unexpected emotional counter-effects of character ensue. For instance, Guinevere's grief at Arthur's departure to conquer Rome is genuine when it occurs, though we know she will later betray him with Mordred. Her comment, 'I may werye the wye thatt this war moved' – 'I may curse the man who urged this war' (*AMA* 699), shows an instinctive foresight that critiques Arthur himself, and underlines the mistaken confidence of his campaign: 'it shall to good turn!' (*AMA* 706). Mordred at this time seems not so much a villain in disguise as a man who fears, though he cannot know, his still-obscure future as traitor. The poem's grief-work for Gawain, its favourite son, is later movingly carried on in a speech by Mordred himself (*AMA* 3874–3885).

Despite the bellicose and simply antagonistic tone of much of the narrative, the potential it affords for ethical and emotional readings of the action is not fully controlled by sympathy and approval for Arthur's ambitions and condemnation of his enemies. We are allowed to think at times that the king's keenness for war creates the circumstances for his betrayal, and that it would have been better for him never to have broken the 12-year peace that reigned before the Roman ambassadors arrived.

Overall, evaluating the moral status of armed force in this story is a difficult business. The poem's beginning apparently offers an enthusiastic endorsement of warfare conducted by the right people:

> And I shall tell you a tale that trew is and noble
> Of the real renkes of the Round Table
> That chef were of chivalry and cheftains noble
> Both wary in their workes and wise men of armes,
> Doughty in their doings and dredde ay shame
>
> (*AMA* 16–20)

But, on a more careful reading, one realises that exactly what the poem is claiming here about Arthur and his men depends partly on the force one gives to the unalliterating final fourth stress in the verse lines. The grandiloquent sweep of the verse seems to celebrate Arthurian wisdom as well as prowess, but the less obtrusive ending to the line specifies only that they are wise in 'armes'. So one has to wonder if the prudent actions ('wary . . . workes') that we hear about refer only to short-term campaign and battle tactics, rather than deeper applications of foresight and wisdom. Does success in battle really count for other 'wise' and 'noble' virtues as well, or is the poem only setting up a seductive invitation for readers to think so, perhaps later to be corrected? When we are told that the 'tale' is 'true' and 'noble', do we associate those qualities particularly with the brave 'doings' of the 'noble' chieftains who figure in it, or with other instructive possibilities? The narrator, more in the manner of a preacher than a romance writer, hopes that his words will be '[p]lesand and profitable to the pople that them heres' (*AMA* 11; Werster 1994, p. 55), but does not indicate exactly where the pleasure or the profit will be found.

In direct speech – a major part of the narrative – a similar effect of splitting occurs. At first sight, emotional arousal seems to guide characters' declared evaluations of the action, or even to override them: action, emotional attachment and ethical approval appear to work together. Still, when King Aungers declares that Arthur is 'wisest and worthyest and wightest [strongest] of handes, / The knightlyest of counsel that ever crown bore' (*AMA* 290–291), or a Roman senator says 'He may be chosen cheftain, chef of all other / Both by chaunces of armes and chevalry noble, / For wisest and worthyest and wightest of handes' (*AMA* 530–532), how much should the qualification 'of handes' shape and limit the reader's notion of Arthur's wisdom, worthiness and strength? Does the praise extend to all these attributes or only his battle prowess? Or is he wisest and worthiest only so long as he is militarily strongest? And does 'knyghtlyest' counsel in a crowned king mean the highest kind of counsel, or the one most likely to please the tendencies of knights? More generally, how does success in the 'chaunces of armes', leading to supreme individual power, relate to wisdom and worthiness *per se*? Is it possible that the text looks forward here to the dream-scene of Fortune's wheel and the king's sudden fall (*AMA* 3370–3390)? There it seems that Arthur's previous success in war – his 'chaunces' – have lured him on towards Rome only to destroy him, with no sense that good or bad qualities and motivations have had any part to play. Fortune is concerned only with material gain and loss, making her reference to Christ seem deeply sardonic:

> 'King, thou carpes [complain] for nought, by Criste that me made!
> For thou sall lose this laik [game / pleasure] and thy life after;
> Thou has lived in delite and lordshippes ynow [enough]!'
> (*AMA* 3385–3387)

Even if readers do not make that long-range connection between scenes, the uncertain limits of the poem's praise for Arthur's virtue may still permit a response to the narrative that escapes emotional attachment to the means by which victory is won – strong leadership and strength in battle – and so resists implicitly treating them as endorsements of the king's moral aims and conduct. All the knightly participants, whether friends or enemies, show a great respect for chivalric prowess, but readers are also made aware that judgements of 'chivalry' or 'violence' are relative and perspectival. The Roman ambassadors praise Arthur's might in itself, but condemn him for his earlier conquest of Gaul and other places – 'thow has ridden and raimede [robbed] and ransound þe pople [held the people to ransom]' (*AMA* 100). They make, in effect, an accusation of 'violence' in medieval terms, but not out of any fundamental opposition to warfare as violent in itself. It is on the basis that he is 'rebel to Rome' (*AMA* 103) in withholding or intercepting revenues due to it, and therefore acting without a proper warrant. At the time it is made, the charge is angrily and patriotically denied. Arthur denies any allegiance to Rome, and claims his own right to its empire, but later events may allow readers to revisit this moment and judge differently.

Arthur's dream of himself and the rest of the Nine Worthies thrown from Fortune's wheel strongly contests the previous emotionally-charged endorsement of his campaign, amounting to suggestions of a Holy War, given the extensive reference to the non-Christian allies of the Romans and their exotic entourage (*AMA* 570–609, 2283–2288). Arthur goes to bed promising a Crusade '[t]o revenge the Renk [Man] that on the Rood died!' (*AMA* 3217) after he has taken Rome – a 'delirious messianic ambition' (Nievergelt 2010, p. 89). He awakes shivering with cold, as if he were about to die. Arthur's 'philosopher', purportedly an ethically independent voice in the poem, treats the dream as a sign that Fortune has deserted the king forever, and foretells that within 10 days he will hear of trouble at home (Mordred's rebellion). In addition, the philosopher uses the dream as an occasion to condemn Arthur retrospectively as an unjustified invader of foreign countries, an arrogant killer of the innocent:

> 'Thou has shed much blood and shalkes destroyed,
> Sakeles, in surquidrie, in sere kinges landes;
> Shrive thee of thy shame and shape for thine end.
> . . . .
> Found abbeyes in Fraunce, the fruites are thine owen,
> For Frolle and for Feraunt and for thir fers knightes
> That thou fremedly in Fraunce has fey beleved.'
>
> (*AMA* 3398–3405)

> 'You have shed much blood, and destroyed innocent men, through your arrogance, in many kingdoms. Confess your shameful deeds and prepare for your end. . . . Found abbeys in France – the benefits will be your own – for Frollo and Feraunt and for their keen knights whom you, as a foreign intruder, have left dead in France.'

References here to Arthur's arrogance and sinfulness, and to his campaigns as an alien intrusion into France and numerous other places, clearly represent his warfare as a sinful and shameful 'violence'. Yet one presumes that the speaker is one of the two 'sage philosophers', 'cunningest of clergy', who interpreted his earlier dream of the fight between the dragon and bear, *en route* to Normandy at the start of the campaign. In that reading, Arthur is told he has previously won all his kingdoms by 'right', that the dream enemy refers to violent, and therefore legitimate, targets – including 'tyrauntes that tormentes *thy pople*', taking his claim to imperial lordship for granted – and he is urged to continue his campaign and go on to victory 'through help of Our Lord' (*AMA* 806–831). The contrast is startling.

What is happening in this apparent radical reorientation of the clerical commentary? Is it merely that the new context of mutability and approaching death – all the Jewish and Pagan Worthies are already dead, and the Christian Worthies will also die – brings out a new generic emphasis on the need for repentance and minimising punishment in the next life? Possibly there is meant to be a more thorough ethical re-appraisal of the king's whole career, stretching back to his previous conquest of France, as well as the current campaign against Rome in which he has destroyed churches and hospitals (*AMA* 3038–3039; Kennedy 2015, pp. 111–112). Perhaps it is a simpler matter: that Arthur has always been an acquisitive hostage to Fortune, empowering her hold over him by his relentless ambition, and the changed assessment of his warfare merely reflects the harsh difference between winning and losing. When pursuing the 'chances of armes' turns out badly, attitudes to the value of maintaining the king's 'right' to conquest change too, along with the praise or blame that he gets for a campaign. Fourteenth-century English kings had wide experience of both outcomes (Given-Wilson 1997, pp. 116–123). In this light, perhaps the philosopher's moral comments are as responsive to Fortune as anything else in the poem.

Nevertheless, adding more uncertainty to judgement, the philosopher tones down his adverse finding by interspersing critique and calls to repentance with comments that link Arthur with Charlemagne and Godefroi of Bouillon as great warriors for Christ,[4] and by attributing the king's loss of rule to 'wicked men' (*AMA* 3447). He also promises Arthur both earthly and heavenly reward for his military prowess, in much the same terms.

> 'This [The Nine Worthies] shall in romaunce be redde with real [royal] knightes,
> Reckoned and renownd with riotous [bellicose] kinges,
> And deemed [judged] on Doomesday for deedes of armes,
> For the doughtiest that ever was dwelland [living] in erthe;
> So many clerkes and kinges shall carp [sing / recite] of your deedes
> And keep your conquestes in cronicle for ever'
> (*AMA* 3440–3445)

Christ in judgement, it seems, will personally praise Arthur for battle prowess. All of a sudden, the distance between military and moral understandings of conquest collapses, and no difference is made between the glory conferred by a 'romance', such as the one we are reading, and the reward of God in Heaven.

This is an extreme moment of Christian endorsement of Arthur, but not an isolated one. At many stages in the story, his mission is treated in the terms of later medieval piety, redolent of hagiography and miracle literature. He swoons on the dead Gawain's body, then treats it as a relic, and gathers up the blood in a helmet:

> 'It were worthy to be shrede [clothed] and shrined in gold,
> For it is sakless [guiltless] of sin, so help me our Lord!'
> (*AMA* 3991–3992)

Gawain too sees his role as religious, as a Crusader against Rome's Saracen allies:

> 'We shall end this day als excellent knightes,
> Ayer [Go] to endless joy with angeles unwemmed [immaculate];
> Though we have unwittyly [unwisely] wasted ourselven,
> We shall work all well in the worship of Crist!'
> (*AMA* 3800–3803)

In such scenes, the poem manages its evaluation of the use of force through a regulated excitation and direction of emotional energy: we are exhorted to feel for Gawain; we feel the extent of his loss by feeling how much Arthur (and even Mordred) feel for him. The intimate and unconditional emotional attachment that the poem demands for its heroes matches and motivates a pious hostility towards the Other. As readers participate in this emotional economy, they are encouraged to feel the sorrow, pity and anger elicited by the text as conferring both holy benefits and obligations. In the words of Catherine Nall, within late medieval war literature pity is 'the emotion that acts as a precursor to vengeance; as one that, far from limiting bloodshed, forms a crucial part of the affective foundation of the practice of violence' (Nall 2019, 74). Arthur's extreme display of sorrow at Gawain's death is only publicly tolerable if it feeds vengeance on his killer, Mordred; otherwise it will be scorned as womanish, 'bootless bale' – 'useless grief' (*AMA* 3976). Grief and vengeance are parts of the one impulse, heightened by blood-relationship as well as religious and chivalric fellowship. The veneration of Gawain's blood provides an intimate emotional bond between readers and the king, and the rightness of the feeling endorses the revenge as just.

The emotional intensity of such moments complicates reflection on their broader ethical context by invoking the feeling rules of a military caste; here a limited form of fellow feeling takes up the affective space. To a very large extent religion is made both a sanction and an intensifier in that process, not a curb on it. There *is* an ethical voice that asks empathy for the 'innocent' and 'foreign' victims of Arthur's invasion – and so briefly characterises his wars as a 'violence', the wrongful 'shed[ding]' of 'much blood' – but that too becomes largely subsumed into the commemoration of the king's greatness and the mourning for his end. The poem's strategic regulation and direction of emotional attachments, embedded as they are within descriptions of the action, largely protects its wars from critique. On the other hand, by taking the wider view that the poem intermittently establishes when considering the entire course of the king's career – whether in summary mode, as in the beginning, or through the dream symbolism of the Wheel of Fortune – a less emotional, more coolly critical assessment of Arthur's actions is permitted. Paradoxically, (and in contrast to the views of Huizinga and Elias), the increase of emotional heat and inclusion of graphic battle detail in the conduct of the narrative presents Arthur's actions as less, rather than more, 'violent' in medieval terms, because such a strategy of representation shows them as rightly motivated in feeling, and properly directed at notorious enemies. The outrage Arthur expresses vouches for these acts as justified, and not excessive or tyrannical. Yet we can also see that such emotions, though heartfelt, are not innocent of political purpose. They belong to a contemporary kingly repertoire of emotional display and control (Radulescu 2016, pp. 106–108). Anger, grief and love, expressed through discourses of chivalry, religion and family, and enacted in 'countenance', bodily movements and rituals, are shown as very effective means to bind the king's forces together and to both motivate and justify the courses of action he desires. To what extent the intense emotions expressed by the text's major figures, especially Arthur and Gawain, truly provide virtuous models of feeling and benign sources of emotional contagion for readers outside the text remains a question. How it is answered will decide whether or not Arthur's wars are 'violent'.

II. *The Siege of Jerusalem*

The late fourteenth-century English alliterative poem *The Siege of Jerusalem* is very commonly described today as an extremely violent work, and deservedly so. Yet such a judgement will be misleading if it draws attention from the work's self-presentation as an account of just vengeance.

The background to the poem is a conversion story that establishes an overriding emotional context for what follows. The Roman general Vespasian is miraculously cured of illness by hearing of the Vernicle, and becomes a fervent Christian, along with his son Titus. They take up Nero's quarrel with Judaea over non-payment of taxes, and transform it into a mission of vengeance on the Jews in Jerusalem for their treatment of Christ:

> 'Cytees vnder Syon, now is ȝour sorow uppe.
> Þe deþ of þe dereworþ crist der schal be ȝolden.
> Now is Bethleem þy bost ybroȝt to an ende,
> Jerusalem & Ierico forjuggyd wrecchys.
> Schal neuer kyng of ȝour kynde with croune be ynoyntid,
> Ne Jewe for Jesu sake iouke in ȝou more.
> (*SJ* 295–300)[5]

> 'Cities under Zion, now your sorrow begins. The death of the precious Christ shall be paid for dearly. Now, Bethlehem, your boasting is brought to an end; Jerusalem and Jericho are condemned wretches. Never shall a king from your race be annointed and crowned, and no more shall any Jew live within you, for Jesus's sake.'

The poem goes on to fulfill this warning in horrific detail, as the Jews are slaughtered in battle and reduced to famine by siege, their city utterly destroyed and their remnant sold into slavery.

Despite this framing story, it has been argued that the *Siege* contains an element of sympathy for the Jews. Christian readers of this poem, c. 1390, in an England from which Jews had been expelled a century before, were accustomed to understand religious and devotional references to 'Jerusalem' as applying typologically to the Christian community. Such readers might have identified with the sufferings of the Jews of the poem, and learned to fear a similar divine vengeance for sin, '[f]or in the Jews, medieval exegetes saw themselves' (Yeager 2004, p. 95). Given the medieval belief that the Crusaders' failure to keep control of Jerusalem was due to the immorality of Christians (Mandeville 1967, p. 101), together with the growing fear of attack from the non-Christian East, the poem's theme of divine vengeance has also been read as reflecting badly on contemporary European and

English societies. Suzanne M. Yeager writes that 'not only do the Jews of the poem represent Jewish groups who come before and after them, but they also represent medieval Christians', arguing that 'as the Jews of the siege are made to represent Christendom under threat, they are portrayed as a people with whom to sympathise and from whom to gain inspiration in the face of adversity' (Yeager 2004, p. 95). Elisa Narin Van Court suggests this ameliorative impulse can be found in the close narrative detail of the poem: '*The Siege of Jerusalem* offers many . . . discursive moments which invite audience and reader into active colloquy with the poem's complex representation of Jews' (Narin Van Court 2004, p. 153). Randy P. Schiff argues, in a related move, that Scottish, British and 'hyper-militaristic' English tendencies may be covert targets of the poem's anti-Jewish attack (Schiff 2008, p. 136).

I would find these readings of Christian and Western self-reflection in the poem's treatment of the Jews attractive, if I could agree with them, but I think they downplay the violently emotional framework and literal spirit in which Jewishness is conceived and maintained in the narrative, and, in Schiff's case, the 'theological' basis of the poem's action (Schiff 2008, p. 144). In its early stages, the *Siege* involves readers in detailed recollections of the life of Christ and the Passion as the emotional source – in pity, anger and contempt – of Vespasian's campaign:

> 'Byholdeþ þe heþyng [scorn] and þe harde woundes,
> Þe byndyng & þe betyng þat he on body hadde:
> Lat neuer þis lawles ledis [people] lauȝ at his harmys
> Þat bouȝt [redeemed] vs fram bale [evil] with blod of his herte.
>
> Y quyte-clayme [renounce] þe querels of alle quyk burnes [living men]
> And clayme of euereche kyng saue [except] of Crist one [alone],
> Þat [Whom] þis peple to pyne [torment] no pite ne hadde:
> As preueþ his passioun, whoso þe paas [passage] redeþ.'
>
> (*SJ* 497–504)

Vespasian's speech is founded in a particular distribution of emotion. Christians remember Christ's sufferings with pity. The Jews have proven themselves unworthy of pity because they denied it to Christ in his torment, and laugh at him still. The process of the Passion therefore still continues, and Christian compassion requires that Jewish laughter and mockery be repaid. The Jews are considered to have espoused, once and for all, and in the utmost degree, that wrongful use of force against a forbidden target which defines the very nature of violence. The force employed against them in the name of Christ is therefore not to be read as violence, but as justice, and its effects on the Jews should attract no sympathy. As Philippa C. Maddern has argued,

> 'when the world is viewed through a paradigm in which God has ordained certain expressions of violence as if they were forces of nature, types of

> violence performed by actors "in a right relationship with authority" are legitimized so much that they are "not simply just but justifying"'
>
> (Maddern 1992, pp. 84–87)

All the subsequent carnage of the poem's first battle and its aftermath, extreme even by the high standards of this genre, follows the impetus of this emotional programme. That includes the extensive judicial tortures – flayed alive, drawn with horses, hanged upside down – of the 'bishop' Caiaphas and the Jewish clerics, which are frankly offered as enjoyable to the Christian reader. In this context, the sorrow of the Jews watching from the city walls is deprived of effective emotional agency. Unable to produce a response from their Christian others, their feelings can only operate reflexively, on themselves:

> Þe Iewes walten [threw themselves] ouer þe walles for wo at þat tyme;
> Seuen hundred slow hemself for sorow of here clerkes [clergy].
> Somme hent hem [took themselves] by þe heere and fram þe hed pulled
> And somme doun for deil [grief] and daschen to grounde.
>
> (SJ 713–716)

Their sorrow intensifies the emotional atmosphere, but provides no grounds for Christian pity. Vespasian makes no immediate response to their grief. He first orders the bodies of Caiaphas and the Jewish clergy to be cut down and burned to ashes, and then lets the wind blow the dust towards the citizens watching from the walls:

> 'Þer is doust [powder] for ȝour drynke', adoun to hem crieþ
> And bidde hem bible [drink heartily] of þat broth for þe bischop soule.'
>
> (SJ 723–724)

Vespasian's delay in making this mocking reply, as much as its parodic content, models a correct lack of emotional availability to the unfolding situation, refusing in any way to allow the Jews' sufferings power to generate a dialogue with their others. Conversely, the refusal of the Jews, against massive odds, to surrender to Vespasian is represented as cursed stubbornness rather than courage. One reference to their brave defence is policed by the immediate comment that they were in the Devil's service (SJ 838). Even when surrendering the city at last, the Jews 'stubbornly' refuse to acknowledge that their defeat is a vengeance for killing Christ. They will, it seems, go on making the same blind error and so deserve the same treatment. Similarly, they refuse to parley with Vespasian and seek 'mercy'. This moves him to exemplary anger and another explicit denial of pity:

> Þan wroþ as a wode [mad] bore he wendeþ [turns] his bridul:
> 'Ȝif ȝe as dogges wol dey þe deuel haue þat recche [cares]!
> And or [before] I wende fro þis walle ȝe schul wordes schewe

> And efte spakloker speke or Y ȝour speche owene
> *[And answer more wisely before I acknowledge your speech]*.
>
> (*SJ* 781–784)

Jewish grief has been left unheeded by the Christian forces. Jewish silence is read as a further sign of emotional inversion, a refusal to participate in any dialogue, that frees Christians from caring about what happens to them. If the Jews are beyond mercy it is because, as in the Gospels, they have themselves chosen to be so. Since they will not 'more wisely' confess their defeat by Christ, the use of force is mandated, though it can only punish, never convert them. Christian emotions here are not understood as free agents responding to events as they please, but as both constitutive of and responsive to a regime, which properly directs when and where to feel and not to feel. It is made clear that readerly (Christian) sympathy for the justly punished Jews would, in itself, mean emotional infidelity to Christ. Under the conditions of this emotional regime the Christian-Jewish 'colloquy' that Narin Van Court (2004) speaks of is precisely what could not occur without fatally compromising the idea of 'Christian' and 'Jewish' that the poem constructs. An overriding emotional pattern is in place: when offered mercy Jews refuse it; their blood is on their own heads. Pity for their sufferings, or any positive emotional contact, is therefore pointless. If their fate can be read to provide a cognitive lesson for Christians, that interpretative move still represents no more than another despoliation of Jerusalem by Rome, allowing Jews sympathy only as proxy Christians, expressly excluding them from sympathy in their own right.

The poem stages later how young Titus learns this emotional lesson when he is mistakenly moved to pity for the besieged Jews after hearing of their appalling sufferings in the siege:

> Whan Titus told was þe tale, to trewe God he vouched
> Þat he propfred hem pes and grete pite hadde.
>
> Þo praied he Iosophus to preche þe peple to enforme [instruct]
> For to saue hemself and þe cite ȝelde [surrender].
> Bot Ion forsoke þe sawe so forto wyrche
> *[But John forsook the counsel to act in that way]*,
> With Symond þat oþer segge [man] þat þe cyte ladde.
>
> (*SJ* 1155–1160)

The Jews again reject pity. Those who do take up the offer to ask forgiveness for their sin against Christ are found to have cunningly swallowed their money to keep it from the Romans, and are disembowelled so it can be recovered, though without Titus's permission. The narrative works repeatedly to show young Titus's good emotional intentions thwarted by the tricks of the Jews themselves, in ways that exculpate his final response from being a violence. Finally learning the poem's emotional logic of the Christian-Jewish relationship, he concludes by resolving

'Neuer pyte ne pees profre hem more / Ne gome þat he gete may to no grace taken' – 'Never offer them pity or peace any more; nor let any man that is captured be given any mercy' (*SJ* 1179–1180). By the time the Jewish leaders do ask for peace and offer the keys to the gates of Jerusalem, Titus has already broken his own 'gate' ('road') through the wall. There is in effect no Jewish response to the siege that can either be effective of itself or draw a positive response from their Christian others. Mutuality of any kind, even in surrender, is consistently shown as impossible.

In these conditions, if medieval readers did observe a typological likeness in this poem between Jerusalem and Christendom, Jews and Christians, it was a cognitive effort in the context of a strategically coordinated series of emotional prompts and inhibitions that actively disabled any sympathetic potential in that likeness and made it thoroughly unilateral and aggressive. The poem is theologically framed by a crude Christian triumphalism, but its core is the literal destruction of an earthly Jerusalem. In this, I argue, the poem operates beyond David Nirenberg's persuasive analysis that Christian texts use the Jew as a cautionary figure in their struggle to maintain representative contact with transcendent truth, as 'a warning not to repeat their error of seeing only the letter of the law, the outer flesh rather than the inner spirit' (Nirenberg 2015, p. 13). The Jews of the *Siege* are stubborn literalists, but the poem delights in repaying them in kind, and has little or no interest in sustaining symbolic readings of events. Its retributive logic is deliberately imitative and complementary, not transcendent. One clear indication of this literalism is that the voice that cries 'woe' at the end of thåe siege does not address itself at large to 'the inhabitants of earth and the sea', as the angel does in Revelation 40. Instead the voice simply belongs to an unnamed 'wye [man] on þe wal', who laments specifically for 'Ierusalem þe Iewen toun' ['Jerusalem the Jews' town], crying 'Wo to þis worþly wone [wealthy city], and wo to myselue' (*SJ* 1229–1236). The relentless materiality of the poem's register extends to the detailed description of the looted treasures of the city, and the jeer that Jews who bought Christ for 30 pieces of silver are now sold at the rate of 30 to a penny.

It may seem absurd to argue that a poem full of the horrific detail of battle, torture, starvation and even cannibalism is not 'violent', but in its own medieval terms I think that is the case. These effects are not presented as the result of tyranny or the abuse of power, but of its opposite: a sanctioned military and religious enterprise which works according to a divine plan of just vengeance. And yet, there *is* a deep sense of 'violence' in this text, as an effect arising from its association of the harms suffered by the Jews with their *own* wrongdoing.

Speaking of later medieval devotion to the Virgin Mary. Miri Rubin writes of

> the potent dichotomy between this figure of utmost purity and nurture and the construction of utmost perversity and pollution in the late medieval Jew, the Jew of conspiracy and desecration, the Jew of treason and blasphemy.
> (Rubin 2009, p. 13)

We see that divisive process at work in *The Siege of Jerusalem*, but mainly centred around the figure of Christ rather than Mary. Since the Jews killed Christ, they are held to blame for their own sufferings, and the more they suffer the more they are to blame, because the more wrongful their suffering proves them to be. In this emotional-spiritual context of medieval piety, only the sufferings of Christ deserve pity, and since in later medieval religious tradition pity for Christ was largely inseparable from the imagination of his wounded body, it is fitting that the sufferings of the Jews should also be bodily, mandated by an alternate proper judicial process in place of the injustice done to Christ in his Passion. To the true Christian, pity for Christ should be endless and inexhaustible; its corollary, a lack of pity for the Jews, should be likewise. The specially perverse, arrogant and abusive quality of medieval 'violence' belongs to them, and is embodied in them, because they are to be understood as the originating and continuing violent agents: 'In a stunning historical inversion . . . [the] replayed scene of violence justifies the real and imagined persecution of medieval Jews' (Crocker 2017, p. 85; Bale 2010, p. 57). It is the poetic realisation of that logic, I think, that gives the description of the Jews' appalling sufferings, for all their horrors, an aura of blank detachment and distance that makes them peculiarly disturbing to a modern reader. As a shocking effect of the poetry's emotional unavailability to these sufferings, they falsely appear monumental, mysteriously naturalised as part of the condition of Jewishness rather than what they are, the work of Christians.

In conclusion, and thinking especially of the two main texts analysed here, I suggest that although medieval 'violence' is notionally a category established on ethical grounds, assessing permissible or wrongful uses of physical force, the first question to ask about an instance of extreme force in a medieval text is not whether it is justified or condemned on ethical grounds, as if one were discussing a case in abstraction, or even by 'by the way [it] derive[s] its meaning from larger systems of honor' (Di Marco 2000, pp. 29–30). What matters most is what kind and what degree of emotional engagement its written form is designed to display and to attract *in situ*. 'Violence' and its opposite, 'just force', are poetic achievements rather than consistent cognitive categories. 'Violent' actions include both physical and psychological motions; narration of them connects body and mind, endowing actions with motivations and ethical connections, while also indicating an appropriate emotional reaction to them, apparently tying together action and evaluation in a probative sequence. Yet the operations and outcomes of that process are elusive, because suggestions of 'violence' are neither governed by a single value system – they signify 'wrongful' or 'too much' or 'badly motivated' in a wide variety of ways – nor necessarily made explicit in abstract terms. The meaning and evaluation of extreme bodily force in later medieval English literature has less to do with the general nature of the force involved than with its poetic expression, with the links between aesthetics, ethics and action formed in texts, which are, as Sarah McNamer puts it, 'affective scripts in the history of emotion', that 'seek to generate emotional experience' (McNamer 2015, p. 1436). In this process, the literary generation of emotion in different generations of readers may qualify, or even oppose, responses to violence that might be reached by other criteria. In the long run, there are identifiable generic tendencies, but no consistent definition: what is 'violent' in medieval literature and what 'violence' means there will always remain a process of emotional affiliation for readers.

Notes

1 See *Middle English Dictionary*, violent, adj, 1. (a) 'Of an action, behavior, etc.: displaying physical force exercised injuriously, coercively, etc., brutally or violently performed'. http://quod.lib.umich.edu/cgi/m/mec/med-idx?type=id&id=MED51211
2 See, for example, the flaying alive of Godard in *Havelok the Dane*.
3 All references to the Alliterative *Morte Arthure* are to Benson, L. D. and Forster, E. E. (eds) 1994, *King Arthur's Death: The Middle English Stanzaic Morte Arthur and Alliterative Morte Arthure*, Medieval Institute Publications, Kalamazoo MI, designated as *AMA* with line numbers. Glosses and translations are the author's.
4 They win back the Crown of Thorns, sacred lance and the nails and the Holy Cross, respectively.
5 Hanna, R. & Lawton, D. (eds) 2003, *The Siege of Jerusalem*, EETS o.s. 320, Oxford University Press, Oxford, ll. 295–300. All subsequent quotation from the poem is from this edition, as *SJ* with line numbers. Translations and glosses are the author's.

Reference list

Allmand, C. 1999, 'War and the Non-Combatant in the Middle Ages', in M. Keen (ed.), *Medieval Warfare: A History*, Oxford University Press, Oxford, pp. 253–272.

Baden-Daintree, A. 2016, 'Visualising War: The Aesthetics of Violence in the Alliterative *Morte Arthure*', in J. Bellis & L. Slater (eds), *Representing War and Violence, 1250–1600*, Boydell and Brewer, Cambridge, pp. 56–75.

Bale, A. 2010, *Feeling Persecuted: Christians, Jews and Images of Violence in the Middle Ages*, Reaktion Books, London.

Bellis, J. & Slater, L. (eds) 2016, *Representing War and Violence, 1250–1600*, D. S. Brewer, Cambridge.

Benson, L. D. (ed.) 1990, *The Riverside Chaucer*, Houghton Mifflin, Boston.

Benson, L. D. and Forster, E. E. (eds) 1994, *King Arthur's Death: The Middle English Stanzaic Morte Arthur and Alliterative Morte Arthure*, Medieval Institute Publications, Kalamazoo MI.

Broomhall, S. & Finn, S. (eds) 2015, *Violence and Emotions in Early Modern Europe*, Routledge, London.

Colwell, T. M. 2016, 'Emotives and Emotional Regimes', in S. Broomhall (ed.), *Early Modern Emotions: An Introduction*, Routledge, London, pp. 7–10.

Crocker, H. 2017, 'Medieval Affects Now', *Exemplaria*, vol. 29, no. 1, pp. 82–98.

Di Marco, P. 2000, 'Inscribing the Body with Meaning: Chivalric Culture and the Norms of Violence in *The Vows of the Heron*', in D. N. Baker (ed.), *Inscribing the Hundred Years' War in French and English Chronicles*, SUNY Press, New York, pp. 27–53.

Frassetto, M. 1998, 'Violence, Knightly Piety and the Peace of God Movement in Aquitaine', in D. J. Kagay & L. J. Andrew Villalon (eds), *The Final Argument: The Impact of Violence on Society in Medieval and Early Modern Europe*, Boydell Press, Woodbridge, pp. 13–26.

Fulk, R. D., Bjork, R. E. & Niles, J. D. (eds) 2000, *Klaeber's Beowulf*, 4th edn, University of Toronto Press, Toronto.

Given-Wilson, C. 1997, 'Late Medieval England: 1215–1485', in N. Saul (ed.), *The Oxford Illustrated History of Medieval England*, Oxford University Press, Oxford.

Gross, D. M. 2006, *The Secret History of Emotion: From Aristotle's 'Rhetoric' to Modern Brain Science*, University of Chicago Press, Chicago.

Hanley, C. 2003, *War and Combat 1150–1270: The Evidence from Old French Literature*, D. S. Brewer, Cambridge.

Hanna, R. & Lawton, D. 2003, *The Siege of Jerusalem*, EETS o.s. 320, Oxford University Press, Oxford.

Hill, J. M. 2004, 'Violence and the Making of Wiglaf', in M. D. Myerson, D. Thiery & O. Falk (eds), *'A Great Effusion of Blood': Interpreting Medieval Violence*, University of Toronto Press, Toronto, pp. 19–33.

Huizinga, J. 1924, *The Waning of the Middle Ages*, trans. C. L. Kingsford, Arnold, London.

Huizinga, J. 1996, *The Autumn of the Midde Ages*, trans. R. J. Paynton & U. Mammitzch, University of Chicago Press, Chicago.

Kennedy, E. D. 2015, 'The Prose *Brut,* Hardyng's *Chronicle,* and the Alliterative *Morte Arthure*: The End of the Story', in J. Whitman (ed.), *Romance and History: Imagining Time from the Medieval to the Early Modern Period*, Cambridge University Press, Cambridge.

Lynch, A. 2016, '"With face pale": Melancholy Violence in John Lydgate's *Troy* and *Thebes*', in J. Bellis & L. Slater (eds.), *Representing War and Violence*, Boydell Press, Woodbridge, pp. 79–94.

McNamer, S. 2015, 'The Literariness of Literature and the History of Emotion', *PMLA*, vol. 130, no. 5, pp. 1433–1442.

Maddern, P. C. 1992, *Violence and Social Order*, University of Oxford Press, Oxford.

Mastnak, T. 2002, *Crusading Peace: Christendom, the Muslim World, and Western Political Order*, University of California Press, Berkeley.

Nall, C. 2018, 'Violent Compassion', in S. Downes, A. Lynch & K. O'Loughlin (eds), *Writing War in England and France, 1370–1854: A History of Emotions*, Routledge, London, pp. 73–88.

Narin Van Court, E. 2004, 'The Siege of Jerusalem and Recuperative Readings', in N. McDonald (ed.), *Pulp Fictions in Medieval England: Essays in Popular Romance*, Manchester University Press, Manchester, pp. 151–170.

Nievergelt, M. 2010, 'Conquest, Crusade and Pilgrimage: The Alliterative "Morte Arthure" in its Late Ricardian Crusading Context', *Arthuriana*, vol. 20, no. 2, pp. 89–116.

Nirenberg, D. 2015, *Aesthetic Theology and its Enemies: Judaism in Christian Painting, Poetry, and Politics*, Brandeis University Press, Lebanon NH.

Pearsall, D. 1977, *Old English and Middle English Poetry*, Routledge and Kegan Paul, London.

Radulescu, R. M. 2015, 'Tears and Lies: Malory's Arthurian World', in F. Brandsma, C. Larrington & C. Saunders (eds), *Emotions in Medieval Arthurian Literature: Mind, Body Voice*, D. S. Brewer, Cambridge, pp. 105–121.

Reddy, W. M. 2001, *The Navigation of Feeling: A Framework for the History of Emotions*, Cambridge University Press, Cambridge.

Rubin, M. 2009, *Emotion and Devotion: The Meaning of Mary in Medieval Religious Cultures*, Central European University Press, Budapest, p. 13.

Schiff, R. P. 2008, 'The Instructive Other Within: Secularized Jews in *The Siege of Jerusalem*', in J. Cohen (ed.), *Cultural Diversity in the British Middle Ages: Archipelago, Island, England*, Palgrave, Houndmills, pp. 135–152.

Seymour, M. C. (ed.) 1967, *Mandeville's Travels*, Clarendon Press, Oxford.

Werster, J. 1994, 'The Audience', in K. H. Göller (ed.), *The Alliterative Morte Arthure: A Reassessment of the Poem*, D. S. Brewer, Cambridge, pp. 44–56.

Yeager, S.; 2004, '*The Siege of Jerusalem* and Biblical Exegesis: Writing About Romans in Fourteenth-Century England', *Chaucer Review*, vol. 39, no. 1, pp. 70–102.

4

THE ARMAGNAC–BURGUNDIAN FEUD AND THE LANGUAGES OF ANGER

Tracy Adams

On 25 March 1410, a herald named Jacquemart David received payment from the *Hôtel de Ville* of Amiens, in the Burgundian territories, for delivering a message on behalf of the Prince d'Amour of Paris announcing a 'feste et assemblee' of the 'Cour amoureuse' to be held on 15 April, the feast of the Annunciation (Piaget 1902, p. 603). That the Amiénois would be informed of a love-poetry festival is not surprising: home of the Confraternity of the Puys of Our Lady of Amiens, founded in 1389, Amiens boasted many poets (Lavéant 2013). The planned date for the event, however, gives pause, for the Orleanist (or Armagnac)-Burgundian feud, smouldering for several years, was on the brink of reigniting into the civil war that would lead to the Treaty of Troyes and the occupation of France by the English.[1] Since December 1409, Jean Duke of Burgundy, who controlled Paris, and his cousin, the insane king, had been amassing troops near the city (Lehoux 1966–1968, vol. 3, p. 160, n. 6). In a *lit de justice* of 31 December 1409, Jean had taken over guardianship of the dauphin, and, as the chronicler Monstrelet notes, New Year's Day found him out working the crowds, that is, distributing large numbers of *étrennes* or presents in the form of jewelled images of his symbol, the *rabot* or carpenter's plane (Lehoux 1966–1968, vol. 2, pp. 57–58). Jean had recently excluded his uncles the Dukes of Berry and Bourbon from government. Furious, they had abruptly departed Paris sometime in February or March (Lehoux 1966–1968, vol. 3, p. 164, n. 1). In a letter dated 9 March 1410, an Italian merchant residing in Paris noted that war would have broken out already if not for the shortage of funds on both sides (Lehoux 1966–1968, vol. 3, p. 164, n. 2). On 15 April the Orleanists would form the League of Gien and begin to plan their march on Paris. Thus it seems an odd time for members of the Cour amoureuse – of which Jean was one of the 24 *conservateurs* – to have been thinking about love poetry.

Or perhaps not. In this chapter I examine how different chroniclers and court writers mediated the outrage that finally led the Orleanist and Burgundian factions to armed conflict, especially from the formation of the League of Gien to the 1419 assassination of Jean of Burgundy. In this context, I examine the Cour amoureuse as one Burgundian theatre for defining relationships and enacting the emotional injuries that motivated its leaders to take up arms (Bozzolo & Loyau 1982–1992; Bozzolo & Ornato 1986). In the first section I consider how the leaders of both factions competed for the moral high ground by performing what we might think of as aristocratic anger in a number of different settings. Contemporary writers offer vivid images of the faction leaders righteously proclaiming their duty to take up arms to save the king. The founding document of the Cour amoureuse, its charter, re-draws the royal hierarchy to favour the Burgundians, an insult to the Orleanists that could only arouse their anger, a legitimate, even obligatory, response to an insult. Anger was 'a deeply social passion', to use the words of Daniel M. Gross (2007, p. 2), 'an impulse, accompanied by pain, to a conspicuous revenge for a conspicuous slight directed without justification towards what concerns oneself or towards what concerns one's friends'. Indeed, enacting aristocratic anger in answer to injury was central to honour. To Queen Isabeau's request that he come to the negotiating table, Jean of Burgundy acknowledges that the king has assigned the queen the weighty task of appeasing the kingdom's divisions and assures her that he has always worked for the service and honour of her and the king, but refuses her because of the need to guard his own honour ('nécessité de garder [s]on honneur') (Juvénal des Ursins 1836, p. 466). Jean had just received a letter of challenge from the Orleans sons accusing him of treacherously murdering their father, and concern for his honour led him to continue cultivating anger rather than peace.

And yet, even though the war narrative of aristocratic anger clearly dominates in contemporary chronicles, it is frequently unsettled by traces of popular fury that challenge the feud leaders' righteousness, offering a contestatory, if disjointed, narrative running parallel to the chivalric one. In the second section of this chapter, I suggest that despite the chroniclers' apparent consensus that the 'people' were unreasoning, beast-like creatures, easily manipulated by cynical feud leaders into revolt, their anger was considered and complex. Slavoj Žižek's (2008, p. 1) distinction between subjective (agential, overt and spectacular) and objective violence (symbolic or systemic, and hidden from view), which has been widely drawn on in recent war scholarship, is a useful analytical tool for examining how popular anger related to the Orleanist-Burgundian feud.[2] Indeed, when we piece together the mentions of furious citizens that accompany accounts of the feud leaders' actions, we see that such outbursts of subjective violence respond to economic scarcity, itself to a large degree the result of the 'objectively violent' Valois ideology of kingship that, among other things, allowed an insane monarch to remain in power (Heckmann 2002; Autrand 1995, 1994, pp. 523–528, 661–668; Guenée 1988). Had the mad king simply left office and a permanent regent taken over until the dauphin came of age, much of the turbulence of the first decades of the fifteenth century would have been avoided. Using Žižek's terms, we can say that the subjective violence incited by the feud leaders as they fought for control of the king and dauphin deflected attention from the kingdom's ubiquitous systemic, or objective, violence, which worked by convincing subjects that the king ruled by the grace of God and therefore could not be removed. The relationship between popular anger and the feud, then, is complicated. The French people were good subjects ('of all the kingdoms and countries in the world, the people of France has the most natural and best love and obedience for their Prince,' as Christine de Pizan [1994, p. 93] wrote). But by remaining loyal to the king, they perpetuated their own misery.

Aristocratic Anger and the Orleanist-Burgundian Feud

The important events of the Orleanist-Burgundian conflict are well-known. Shortly after the first episode in 1392 of the intermittent mental illness that would permanently disable Charles VI, the king appointed his brother Louis (not yet the Duke of Orleans) to rule when he could not. The brother of the living king outranked everyone but the king's sons in the carefully ordered system of royal rank that had solidified during the course of the reign of Charles VI's father, Charles V (Guénee 1988). Although during Charles V's early reign his right to the throne had been challenged because of uncertainties in succession dating back to Philip VI or even Philip V, the system had worked during the middle and later years of the reign, supported by a politics of family love, manifested through royal ordinances, iconography and communications, oral and written, among members of the royal family. However, the system broke down with the onset of Charles VI's madness, because the king and Louis's uncle, Philip of Burgundy, tried to seize power for himself (Adams 2014, pp. 30–38). This power grab, in turn, triggered the factionalism that Jean of Burgundy so devastatingly intensified by having Louis of Orleans murdered in 1407 and that the dauphin, later Charles VII, futilely tried to end by ordering the slaying of Jean of Burgundy. Popular outrage against the terrible burden to the kingdom caused by the feud made little impression on the leaders, buoyed by their own performances of aristocratic anger in response to injuries from their rival throughout the decades of strife.

Early on, the warring members of the royal family managed their rivalry by means of symbolic displays of anger and insult. The Cour amoureuse, far from a pleasant diversion, had been founded by Philip of Burgundy and Queen Isabeau in January 1400 for the purpose – I suggest – of insulting Louis of Orleans, whose reputation for intelligent, generous speech would have been one more target for Philip's jealousy.[3] Poetry was central to courtly identity, reinforcing seigneurial authority. Great lords and knights, like Othon de Grandson, the Marshal Boucicaut and Louis of Orleans, were renowned not only for their martial skills but for their ability to compose verse, whether or not they in fact wrote the poetry attributed to them (Straub 1961; Kosta-Théfaine 2007; Piaget 1941; Jean le Sénéchal 1909, pp. liv–v, 119–120). In addition, recent studies emphasise the extent to which poets competed with each other for 'social capital' at court (Taylor 2007; Coldiron 2000; Armstrong 2000). Urban confraternities also hosted poetry competitions to augment the prestige of their cities. Amiens, as we have seen, along with Arras, Caen, Dieppe, Rouen, Valenciennes and Beauvais had long traditions of confraternities created to host literary *puys*, or lyric poetic competitions, often dedicated to the Virgin Mary (Reid 2006, pp. 152–153). Creating 'a form of spiritual kinship' and 'extending the trust that ideally existed between family members to a social group that was not blood related', confraternities helped to manage civil strife by uniting their members around various causes (Reid 2006, p. 151). In this they were like military orders: Louis of Bourbon's *Ordre de l'Escu d'or*, founded in 1368, Louis of Orleans's *Ordre du Porc-épic*, founded in 1394 and Boucicaut's *Ordre de la dame blanche à l'écu vert*, founded 1399. The associations also sought to defuse disruptive rivalries by re-directing them towards group goals (Boulton 1987, pp. 1–26).

As for the Cour amoureuse, through its charter Philip redrew the system of royal rank to which I have just referred to his own advantage, placing himself beside the king as the chief connoisseur of love poetry in the kingdom. The charter of the Cour amoureuse explains that the institution was to sponsor love poetry competitions and honour women. More importantly, however, I am proposing, it was also intended to injure Louis's honour. According to the charter, Philip of Burgundy was one of three *grands conservateurs* of the court, along with the king and the king's maternal uncle Louis of Bourbon (Bozzolo & Loyau 1982–1992, vol. 1, p. 37). Queen Isabeau's brother, Louis Duke of Bavaria and Philip's son, Jean (later Duke of Burgundy) are ranked before Louis in the list of 11 *conservateurs*. Furthermore, the charter specifies that on the chimney in his chamber the Duke of Burgundy's arms will hang next to those of the king's, with the Duke of Bourbon's to the left: the arms of the Duke of Orleans are not mentioned (Bozzolo & Loyau 1982–1992, vol. 1, p. 39).

If Louis read the charter, he apparently did not dignify the provocation with an answer. Regent not only by virtue of his proximity of relation to the king but also through the king's love and confidence, he did not concern himself with parrying insults or securing his popularity. Rather, he concentrated, as Françoise Autrand writes, on 'building an efficient and powerful state. . . .' (Autrand 2009, pp. 271–273). However, Christine de Pizan defends him against the aggression done him by the Cour amoureuse by re-asserting his loyalty and veneration of women in the *Dit de la rose*, which she presented to him in February 1402. This narrative poem dramatises the delivery of a message from the god of love by the goddess, Loyalty, to a group of 'noble folk', 'rich in honor, handsome, and well-bred', gathered at the hotel of 'that noble lord', the Duke of Orleans, for a poetry contest:

> Si fut voir qu'a Paris advint,
> Present nobles gens plus de vint,
> Joyeux et liez et senz esmois,

> L'an quatre cens et un, ou mois
> De janvier, plus de la moittié
> Ains la date de ce dittié,
> Du mois passé, quant ceste chose
> Advint en une maison close. . . .
>
> Notables sont et renommez,
> Des plus prisiez et miexul amez
> Du tres noble duc d'Orlïens,
> Qui Dieu gart de tous maulx lïens. . . .
>
> La n'ot parlé a ce mangier
> Fors de courtoisie et d'onnour,
> Senz diffamer grant ne menour,
> Et de beaulx livres et de dis,
> Et de balades plus de dix.
> Qui mieulx mieulx chascun devisoit,
> Ou d'amours qui s'en avisoit,
> Ou de demandes gracïeuses.
> (Fenster & Erler 1990, p. 92, ll. 25–32; p. 94, ll. 39–42, 68–75)

This contest and the feast in which the guests partake reflect the contests laid out in the charter of the Cour amoureuse. Loyalty offers the crowd the opportunity to pledge to treat ladies well: to keep each lady's reputation pure. The poem's narrator, presumably Christine, is later awakened from her sleep in that same hotel by a voice speaking from a brilliant cloud. The voice warns at length against the dangers of slanderers (both male and female), who are more evil ('plus male') and dangerous ('plus nuysant') than war-like people ('gent bataillereuse') (Fenster & Erler 1990, p. 115, ll. 447–449). The voice then orders Christine to leave the hotel, taking with her a letter, a bull, from the God of Love, to spread the news in 'every land/ Where noble people war against/ the ladies' (Fenster & Erler 1990, p. 117, ll. 521–522).

To put these virtual theatres for performing rivalry into their larger context, the ducal tension is mentioned explicitly for the first time by chroniclers during these same years. The monk of St. Denis, Michel Pintoin, official chronicler for the kings of France, describes the anger between Louis and his uncles, Philip and Jean of Berry, as the result of a lack of proper respect for rank. As I noted above, Louis, as the king's brother, preceded his uncles in rank. However, the uncles disputed this, pointing to their nephew's youth. According to the monk, the royal uncles were angry ('indignabantur') because Louis refused to support their call for the withdrawal of obedience from the Avignon pope Benedict XIII. But, more importantly, adds Pintoin, another hidden tension existed between them ('latebat et alius indignacionis fomes inter eos') (Pintoin 1994, vol. 3, p. 12). Louis, being closest to the king, monopolised power: he was 'impaciens consortis', that is, 'intolerant regarding shared heritage', in the eyes of the royal uncles, who felt their own honour diminished by his prominence (Pintoin 1994, vol. 3, p. 12).

Philip died in 1404, but the rivalry continued, with his son the new Duke of Burgundy, Jean, less easily satisfied than his father had been with 'staging' anger in response to what he understood as the unjustified preeminence of his cousin at his own expense. Jean turned to physical violence to answer as the perceived threat of armed conflict grew, and, finally, the assassination of Louis of Orleans at his order in 1407 set the stage for a cycle of subjective violence that would be unleashed as soon as Louis's sons reached an age to avenge their father's death. Too young at first to resist, the new duke, Charles, and his brothers were forced to participate in the Peace of Chartres of 9 March 1409, which was designed to appease their anger and reconcile them with the unrepentant Jean. The elaborately orchestrated peace ritual began with Charles and his brother, Philip Count of Vertus, entering the cathedral with the king, queen and the dauphin, while the other princes and took their places on a dais constructed for the occasion (Monstrelet 1857–1862, vol. 1, pp. 397–402). The Duke of Burgundy and his advocate entered through the front of the cathedral, where armed guards kept watch. As they approached the assembly at the front of the cathedral, all but the king, queen and dauphin rose. Kneeling before the king, the Duke of Burgundy's advocate proclaimed: 'Look, Sire, here is the Duke of Burgundy, your cousin and servant, who comes before you because you are angry ('indigné') about the act that he committed and had committed upon the person of Louis of Orleans, your brother, for the good of the kingdom, as he is ready to explain to you' (Monstrelet 1857–1862, vol. 1, p. 398). Jean then added, 'Sire, I pray you'. At this, the Duke of Berry rose and knelt before queen, speaking to her and the dauphin in a low voice, before kneeling before the king to ask that he favour this request (Monstrelet 1857–1862, vol. 1, p. 399). The king responded affirmatively. The Duke of Burgundy and his advocate then approached the Orleans sons, who were crying visibly (Monstrelet 1857–1862, vol. 1, p. 399).[4] The ritual was repeated, and the boys responded that they would remove rancour ('malevolence') from their hearts, because the king ordered them to do so.

The king then took control of the dukes' anger, so to speak, ordering them to be good friends henceforth and forbidding that they have or show hatred ('n'aiez à eulx, ne monstrez quelconque hayne') towards any person associated with the other, except for the Duke of Orleans' actual assassins, who were in any case banished forever (Monstrelet 1857–1862, vol. 1, p. 400). But the king's attempt to manage the new duke's outrage by prohibiting its display and deflecting it towards the men who had physically carried out the murder was destined to fail. According to Monstrelet, when the ceremony was over, the Duke of Burgundy, very happy about the peace thus restored ('très joieux de icelle paix ainsi faicte'), took his leave and rode off to dinner. But not everyone was so happy. Monstrelet notes that many of the lords left behind were greatly discontented, murmuring that from then on murder would be an option, because there was no longer any need to make reparation (Monstrelet 1857–1862, vol. 1, p. 400–401).

And young Charles' humiliation at being denied satisfaction for the injury to his family was extreme, and, in keeping with the aristocratic expectation of righteous fury as the proper response to such an insult, his anger was beyond measure. As Bernard Guenée has observed, the boy's wrath might have been appeased had Jean only repented of the assassination and made reparations rather than continuing to justify himself (Guenée 1992, 186). The process for reestablishing peace required an acknowledgement of fault. The perpetrator was then expected to leave the country, letting his relatives negotiate with the relatives of the victim to agree on a just compensation. Then the king would issue a pardon. Violence during the period was widespread, but hostility generally did not subsist, with wrongs most often settled through negotiation (Halsall 1998).

Although Jean's refusal to comport himself according to noble custom – a massive transgression – infuriated the Orleans sons, they had no means of asserting themselves until their uncles the Dukes of Berry and Bourbon fell out with Jean, as we have seen, and drew Charles and his brothers into the League of Gien. Solemnised on 15 April 1410, the League of Gien included, in addition to these allies, Bernard Count of Armagnac, the king's lieutenant-general for Languedoc, by whose name the party would then be known. On the day that the league was formed, Charles contracted to marry the Count of Armagnac's daughter, Bonne (Famiglietti 1986, pp. 88–89). On learning of the league, Jean went on the defensive, summoning his men-at-arms to Paris. The Duke of Berry and his allies sent justificatory letters to the king and the cities of the realm, articulating the cause of anger for their audiences. Their letter to the city of Amiens informs the citizens that they had recently written to the king and then repeats the contents of that letter. The allies express their anger as a measured and divinely-ordained response to Jean's illegitimate seizure of power. We will not rest, they inform the king (and the citizens of Amiens), until we see

> you restored and returned to honour and obedience of your royal majesty, and the authority and power of your dominion. And we are constrained, held, and obliged, greatly respected sovereign lord, to do this as much for the reasons cited as for fear, honor, and reverence of our Creator, from whom your birth and dominion proceed and also to satisfy justice and you, who are sovereign king on earth and our only lord, to whom for this reason and also because of our blood-ties we are entirely obligated. In truth, greatly respected sovereign lord, there is nothing in the world that we fear more than to offend and anger God, and, consequently, injure our honour, by letting these things take place, hidden from view.
> (Monstrelet 1857–1862, vol. 2, p. 85)

The letter, however, writes the chronicler Monstrelet, left the king and his council, as well as the Amienois, unmoved, for they all remained loyal to the Duke of Burgundy (Monstrelet, 1857–1862, vol. 2, p. 86). Therefore in August 1410 the Armagnacs defiantly marched on Paris to deliver the king and the dauphin from Jean. Summoned to mediate between the factions, Queen Isabeau met with the dukes at Marcoussis (Monstrelet 1857–1862, vol. 2, pp. 91–92). Hostilities were temporarily avoided when Jean agreed to negotiate, and on 2 November the peace of Bicêtre was signed. The faction leaders, including Jean, agreed to leave Paris and appoint a new set of counselors for the royal family.

However, peace did not last. The Duke of Berry was satisfied for the moment, having reasserted his authority. As Françoise Lehoux (1966–1968, vol. 3, pp. 205–206) explains, his interests were personal; he had no interest in avenging the death of his nephew. But the injury to the honour of Charles and his brothers remained. Monstrelet writes that

> at the beginning of the year, the Duke of Orleans, not happy that the king's guardians, that is, those in league with the Duke of Burgundy, had greater access to the king than anyone else, nor that every day the men who had been with his father [Louis of Orleans] and were now with him were further distanced from their office, sent ambassadors to remonstrate to the king about these problems and also to demand that the killers who had murdered his father be brought to justice....
> (Monstrelet 1857–1862, vol. 2, p. 115)

The Orleans sons issued a formal challenge to Jean in July 1411, carefully formulating the relationships that justified their anger:

> Charles, Duke of Orleans and Valois, count of Blois and Beaumont, seigneur of Coucy, Philip, count of Vertus, and Jean, Count of Angoulême, to you, Jean, who call yourself Duke of Burgundy. For the horrendous murder treasonously committed by you, the ambush set by the hired murderers upon the person of our greatly respected lord and father, Monseigneur Louis, Duke of Orleans, only brother of Monseigneur the king, our sovereign lord and yours ... and for the great betrayals, disloyalty, dishonour and evils that you perpetrated against our sovereign lord the king and against us in many ways, we inform you that from this hour on, we will injure you with all our power and with all means that we can muster; against you and your disloyalty and betrayal we call God and reason to our aid....
> (Monstrelet 1857–1862, vol. 2, pp. 152–153)

Jean replied on 13 August, justifying the murder of the Duke of Orleans by describing the late Duke of Orleans as so abusive of the mad king that Jean had acted rightly in having him killed:

> Charles, who call yourself Duke of Orleans and you Philip who call yourself Count of Vertus, and you, Jean, who call yourself Count of Angoulême, who have recently written us letters of challenge, you should know, and we

want everyone to know, that to foil the dreadful and evil betrayals and plotted ambushes treacherously carried out against Monseigneur the king, our greatly respected and sovereign lord and yours, and against his noble offspring, by the late Louis, your father, in several diverse ways, and to keep the false and disloyal traitor, your father, from achieving the detestable goal that he intended against your greatly respected and sovereign lord and his, and also against [the king's] offspring, so falsely and infamously that no decent man could let [Louis] live, we, who are cousin of my said lord . . . had assassinated, as we were obligated to do, this false and disloyal traitor. And in this way we please God. . . .

(Monstrelet 1857–1862, vol. 2, p. 153)

With these public declarations of enmity, the war had officially begun. Jean could not back down after such a challenge, even though the queen begged him to come to the table, as we have seen. The decade from 1410–1419, as described by contemporary observers, was marked by fulsome expressions of aristocratic anger as the feud continued, halted occasionally by a peace treaty, but always reigniting when one of the other of the parties violated the agreement. Charles of Orleans was taken prisoner by the English at the battle of Agincourt in 1415, bringing an end to his physical participation in the feud, which continued without him. Even the assassination of Jean of Burgundy at the hands of the dauphin's men on Montereau Bridge in September 1419, did not put an end to the feud, which continued without either of the two original leaders.

To return for the last time to the Cour amoureuse, in their two-volume study of the institution, Carla Bozzolo and Hélène Loyau gather information from the six manuscripts in which documents related to the institution are collected to offer a complete list of the approximately 950 participants from 1400 to 1440.[5] The members were preponderantly partisans of the Dukes of Burgundy, with a large influx of new members entering the ranks when Philip the Good succeeded his father, Jean, after his assassination by followers of the dauphin, Charles, later Charles VII (Bozzolo & Loyau 1982–1992, vol. 1, p. 18). It has never been clear to what extent the Cour amoureuse existed more on paper than in performance, although some evidence, including the document with which I began this chapter, suggests that it met at least occasionally. But whatever it was, the institution was carefully maintained by the Burgundians over a long period of time. In a sense, then, whether or not poetic competitions took place is irrelevant. The Burgundians obviously felt keeping up the Cour amoureuse to have been of symbolic importance in reinforcing group solidarity and creating and reiterating bonds that would motivate members to come to the aid of the Burgundian faction. Convening the Cour amoureuse just as the first hostilities between the Orleanists and Burgundians threatened to break out now makes perfect sense. The Burgundian institution served not only to unite the faction members around a common goal but also to assure them that its recourse to arms to express their anger was honourable.

Popular outrage

The stirring words of righteous anger and calls for vengeance are the stuff of chivalric adventure. In pronouncing their anger publicly, the dukes justified summoning their men to arms and amassing resources, often through taxing those least likely to profit from conflict to support their personal quarrel. That their men would respond to their calls for support was a given (or at least it is presented in such in contemporary writing with failures to do so condemned), and the feud is regarded through the lens of chivalry in most contemporary writing, until the 1420s. Such was the normal course of life among the aristocracy, which assumed armed conflict to be an ancient right, central to noble identity.

In contrast, the feud brought the people – referred to as 'gens', 'peuple', 'habitans', 'ignobili', 'cives', 'populi minori', 'oppidani', descriptions that did not adequately distinguish among very real differences among the non-nobles – only grief without the compensatory accrual of honour that was central to the aristocratic ethos. And yet, the rare contemporary descriptions of popular anger in the face of the hardship caused by war cast the emotion as unbridled, frenzied and destructive. But close attention to these descriptions suggests that although the chroniclers assume the entire kingdom to be divided between Armagnac and Burgundian, the people had their own agenda, one that corresponded to the objective of neither of the factions (which was, in each case, to control the king and government of the kingdom). In what follows, I trace the relationship between what contemporary writers describe as the frenzied wrath of the people and the very different type of anger between the dukes that underwrote the strife. I focus on two examples to make the point that descriptions of popular anger disrupt the narrative of chivalry throughout the chroniclers' narratives of the years between the formation of the League of Gien and the death of Jean of Burgundy.

But first, I offer some examples to suggest that the noble/non-noble divide was more profound than that between Armaganc and Burgundian, to set the stage for examining these two accounts of popular outrage. By the summer of 1412 the king had cast his lot with the Burgundians and set out with Jean of Burgundy and their combined armies to defeat the Armagnacs (Schnerb 1988, pp. 119–122; Famiglietti 1986, pp. 104–110). After crossing into Berry, they sent an order to the castle of Fontenay in the care of Captain Robert of Fontenay, whom the Monk of St. Denis describes as 'eminent arms bearer' ('insignis armiger', 'écuyer'), to surrender the castle to the king. Robert, man of the Duke of Berry, humbly but firmly declined to let the king enter as long as he and his government were under the control of Jean of Burgundy, in words so chivalrous that Pintoin records them (1994, vol. 4, p. 642). Indignant at hearing himself so slighted, Jean ordered a siege of the castle (Pintoin 1994, vol. 4, p. 642). But when the townspeople saw the army advancing they were terrified, and, excluded from their captain's chivalric world, they forced Robert of Fontenay to eat his brave words by sending him to the king with the keys to the castle. The second episode occurred in early August, in Orleans-held Dreux in the region of Beauce, which was torn between the

Armagnacs and Burgundians. The incident was too slight to retain chroniclers' attention, but the anonymous Bourgeois of Paris's description is suggestive, and a comparison between this account and Pintoin's is instructive (Pintoin 1994, vol. 4, pp. 672–676; Bourgeois de Paris 1990, pp. 53–54). Pintoin mentions Dreux in passing, just after proclaiming that he will now turn his attention from feats of arms ('militares conciones') to the pursuit of the enemy. The Count of Saint-Paul, constable of France, could not take Dreux, but quickly regrouped and ambushed the Armagnac army. In the subsequent disarray, the royal army took Dreux. The Bourgeois, however, complicates the picture, showing the commander of the royal town militias ('les communes') betraying the townspeople to the Armagnacs for money. The Armagnacs were stronger in the Beauce, writes the Bourgeois, but the people, heavily burdened by the armies, did not know whom to obey when the militias entered the region. When the militias arrived in Dreux, they found the townspeople rebellious (supporting the Armagnacs) and therefore killed many and laid siege. But just when the citizens of Dreux could no longer hold out, the leader of the militias accepted money from some of the besieged Armagnacs to abruptly desert the town. The Armagnacs would have slain the remaining militia members had they not departed immediately for Paris. Whom can one trust, the Bourgeois wonders indignantly. Exhausted by the summer heat and prodded by the dauphin, the factions re-established peace at Auxerre on 22 August (Famiglietti 1986, pp. 106–110).

Let us now consider two examples of chronicle entries in which the fury of the crowds overwhelms the chroniclers' ability to coherently order the mayhem within a chivalric narrative. Describing the state of the kingdom in spring, 1417, when the second dauphin had just died leaving only the youngest royal son, Charles, who was being raised in the Armagnac House of Anjou, Pintoin (1994, vol. 6, p. 62) writes that with 'the enemy of humankind, instigator of mortal discord, prodding...the French, noble and non-noble, motivated by an implacable hatred, fought among themselves . . . .'. The villages and towns were divided into Armagnac and Burgundian with the people referring to each other as the most terrible traitors ('proditores pessimos') (1994, vol. 6, p. 64). Pintoin (1994, vol. 6, p. 74) struggles to maintain the distinction between aristocratic and plebeian anger, but falters: knights and squires claiming to be in the service of one of the dukes were devastating the land; the king's men did not even try to stop the marauding bands. In the midst of 'stormy waves' ('undas procellosas') of the princes' dissension . . . the minds of the people 'swelled' ('fluctuarent') with 'varied motions' ('motibus variis') at the news of fresh hostilities. The dreadful situation, pronounces Pintoin (1994, vol. 6, p. 90), was the fault of the great lords who no longer drew their swords to chastise the iniquitous, but only to strike against each other. To make things worse, the English, having defeated the French at Agincourt in 1415, continued their advance into the kingdom.

And yet, in outraged response to an order from the constable of France, Bernard of Armagnac, to let the king's soldiers enter Rouen to defend the town against the impending English attack, the townspeople, writes Pintoin (1994, vol. 6, p. 92), the 'minoris populi', dashed through the streets as if in a 'crazed attack' ('vesano impetus'), shrieking not to obey the order. They did not want the alien robbers ('alienigenas predones') in their city. The townspeople then arrogated to themselves the guard of the town, taking the keys from the highly-placed burgers, and slew the king's bailli. The dauphin was dispatched to Rouen to calm the turbulence, but was refused entry unless he came unaccompanied by foreign troops (Pintoin 1994, vol. 6, p. 94). Peace was achieved only after the dauphin promised amnesty for all except those who had attacked the king's men (Pintoin 1994, vol. 6, p. 96).

Although Pintoin describes the behaviour of the Rouennais as frenzied and irrational, their reaction is understandable to anyone who has been reading the chronicle: having been harassed for several years by pillaging soldiers, they were unwilling to let yet more of the same into the town enclosure, especially the Gascon soldiers of Bernard of Armagnac who were especially feared for their rapaciousness, according to contemporary chroniclers. For the Rouennais, the men sent to protect them were at least as frightening as their 'enemies', Jean of Burgundy and the English, against whom they were to be protected.

Another example of chronicler dismay at the rioting crowds is the Bourgeois' attempt to depict the wild rush of the Burgundian Parisians to murder Armagnac Parisians when the Burgundians infiltrated Armagnac-held Paris in May 1418. The Burgundian Parisians massacred thousands, among them the Count of Armagnac, in a spree so furious that the Bourgeois's words failed him. He used the language of allegory to describe the horrors he observed. All social distinctions vanished, an effect he tries to capture in his description: 'Then arose the goddess of Discord, who was in the Tower of Ill-Counsel, and awakened Ire the insane ('ire la forcenée') and Covetousness and Rage ('enragerie') and Vengeance, and took arms in all manner and kicked out Raison, Justice, Memory, God, and Moderation' (Bourgeois de Paris 1990, p. 15).

Despite the impression of utter chaos conveyed by the Bourgeois, Michael Sizer has convincingly argued that the crowd's violence was not disordered but tactical. The Burgundians had suffered under Armagnac rule, and, in seeking their revenge, they aimed their fury at the persons and institutions that had caused them the most misery (Sizer 2007, pp. 766–768). As far as the chroniclers were concerned, however, the anger was completely unreasoned and violent, a sort of insanity that spread like an infection, unleashed by announcements made by the princes of the blood. Such a conception of anger evokes Augustine, for example, in the *City of God* 14.19, where he describes *ira* as moving the body: the initial movement is unavoidable, although, like lust, it can be regulated through the mind and reason ('mente atque ratione') (Knuuttila 2003, pp. 53–54). Humans share this type of emotions with animals; descriptions of the frenzied townspeople betray the chroniclers' perception that they were beasts. The anger of the townspeople, described as generalised fury, is a different emotion from the one that Aristotle describes and the one that Pintoin assumes to be behind the ducal enmity.

Conclusion

The social construction of anger as appropriate response to injury among the privileged classes and illegitimate fury among the less fortunate remains obvious today in media reports about urban unrest. As I write this chapter, rioting has broken out in Baltimore in the United States in response to yet one more police killing of a young black man. We read that:

> [r]ioters plunged part of Baltimore into chaos Monday, torching a pharmacy, setting police cars ablaze and throwing bricks at officers hours after thousands mourned the man who died from a severe spinal injury he suffered in police custody. . . . Earlier Monday, the smell of burned rubber wafted in the air in one neighborhood where youths were looting a liquor store. Police stood still nearby as people drank looted alcohol. Glass and trash littered the streets, and other small fires were scattered about. One person from a church tried to shout something from a megaphone as two cars burned.
>
> (Darcy 2015)

Numerous news outlets have compared such reports to descriptions that depict rioting by white students as justified in the wake of the firing of Joe Paterno, former coach of the Penn State Lions, who supported his assistant coach Jerry Sandusky as he sexually molested boys.

> After top Penn State officials announced that they had fired Joe Paterno on Wednesday night, thousands of students stormed the downtown area to display their anger and frustration, chanting the former coach's name, tearing down light poles and overturning a television news van parked along College Avenue . . . . The demonstrators congregated outside Penn State's administration building before stampeding into the tight grid of downtown streets. They turned their ire on a news van, a symbolic gesture that expressed a view held by many: that the news media had exaggerated Mr. Paterno's role in the scandal surrounding accusations that a former assistant coach, Jerry Sandusky, sexually assaulted young boys.
>
> (Schweber 2011)

Žižek's distinction between subjective and objective violence ties these late-medieval descriptions of popular outrage together, spotlighting what is a perdurable problem. The objective violence, that is, the appalling social situations that dominant ideologies naturalise into invisibility, gives rise to subject violence at certain flash points. But however justified, anger exercised outside of privileged circles tends to be treated as illegitimate and threatening. To return to the emotions of war, such constructions are clearer today than ever. Heads of state are called upon to respond 'presidentially', that is, with missiles, to aggression. Populations suffering the wars of their leaders, in contrast, are systematically killed for trying to defend themselves against occupying forces.

Notes

1. Stricken in 1392 by an intermittent mental illness that would disable him for the rest of his life, Charles VI of France appointed his brother Louis of Orleans by royal ordinance to carry out administration of the government when he, Charles, was incapacitated. However, the king's uncle, Philip of Burgundy, tried to seize power for himself. After Philip's death, his son Jean succeeded him as Duke of Burgundy and the conflict intensified until Jean had Louis assassinated in 1407. This episode was taken up in chronicles over the next several generations as the tragic source of all France's problems: the feud spanned generations, making possible Henry V's invasion and occupation of France and the brief but amazing appearance of Joan of Arc. It ended only with the Treaty of Arras of 1435, presided over by Charles VII and Philip of Burgundy.
2. 'At the forefront of our minds, the obvious signs of violence are acts of crime and terror, civil unrest, international conflict. But we should learn to step back, to disentangle ourselves from the fascinating lure of this directly visible 'subjective' violence, violence committed by a clearly identifiable agent. We need to preserve the contours of the background which generates such outbursts. A step back enables us to identify a violence that sustains our very efforts to fight violence and to promote tolerance' (Žižek 2008, p. 1). Some of the most recent examples of Žižek's categories in recent scholarship include Darling (2014), Vadén, (2014, pp. 127–154), and Wilson (2013, pp. 28–48).
3. Even Louis's contemporary detractors laud his intelligence and eloquence. Pintoin (1994, vol. 3, p. 36) reports that Philip of Burgundy admitted that his nephew was 'commendable for his affability and singular eloquence'. Louis was the most fluent man of his day, writes the monk, who goes on to relate that he had personally watched the duke orate against the best. A document recording the arguments of the Dukes of Bourbon, Orleans, Burgundy and Berry regarding the Schism supports Pintoin's evaluation (Douët-d'Arcq 1863, vol. 1, p. 143). Eloquent and self-effacing, the Duke of Orleans places the Schism in its larger context. He then works a *captatio benevolentiae*, explaining that he agrees with his opponents in principal, that the 'voie de cession', that is, the resignation of both popes so that a new one can be elected, is the only solution to the Schism but then enumerates why he believes that subtracting obedience from the Avignon pope will not result in the resignation of the two popes. Christine de Pizan (1936, vol. 1, p. 174) is warmly positive about the Duke's good nature and manners.
4. On the Orleans family's use of grief as propaganda see Hutchison (2016).
5. See Bozzolo, C. and Loyau, H. 1982–1992, *La Cour amoureuse, dite de Charles VI*, vol. 1, Léopard d'or, Paris, pp. 7–34.

Reference list

Adams, T. 2014, *Christine de Pizan and the Fight for France*, Pennsylvania State University Press, University Park, PA.

Armstrong, A. 2000, *Technique and Technology: Script, Print, and Poetics in France, 1470–1550*, Clarendon Press, Oxford.

Autrand, F. 1994, *Charles V*, Fayard, Paris.

Autrand, F. 1995, 'La succession à la couronne de France et les ordonnances de 1374', in J. Blanchard and P. Contamine (eds), *Représentation, pouvoir et royauté à la fin du moyen Âge*, Picard, Paris, pp. 25–32.

Autrand, F. 2009, *Christine de Pizan: une femme en politique*, Fayard, Paris.

Boulton, D. J. 1987, *The Knights of the Crown: The Monarchical Orders of Knighthood in Later Medieval Europe 1325–1520*, Boydell, Woodbridge.

Bozzolo, C. & Loyau, H. 1982–92, *La Cour amoureuse, dite de Charles VI*, 2 vols, Léopard d'or, Paris.

Bozzolo, C. & Ornato, M. 1986, 'Princes, prélats, barons et autres gens notables à propos de la cour amoureuse dite de Charles VI', in F. Autrand (ed.), *Prosopographie et genèse de l'état moderne*, École normale supérieure de jeunes filles, Paris, pp. 159–170.

Coldiron, A. 2000, *Canon, Period and the Poetry of Charles d'Orléans: Found in Translation*, University of Michigan Press, Ann Arbor.

Darcy, O. 2015, '"This Is One of Our Darkest Days": Baltimore Gripped By Violent Riots After Man's Death in Police Custody', *The Blaze*, www.theblaze.com/news/2015/04/28/baltimore-gripped-by-violent-riots-after-mans-death-in-police-custody/

Darling, J. 2014, 'Welcome to Sheffield: The Less Than Violent Geographies of Urban Asylum', in N. Megoran, F. McConnell & P. Williams (eds), *Geographies of Peace*, Palgrave Macmillan, New York, pp. 229–249.

de Monstrelet, E. 1857–62, *La chronique d'Enguerran de Monstrelet, 1400–1444*, ed. L. C. Douët-d'Arcq, 6 vols, Renouard, Paris.

de Pizan, C. 1936, *Le Livre des fais et bonnes meurs du sage roy Charles V*, trans. S. Solente, 2 vols, Champion, Paris.

de Pizan, C. 1990, *Poems of Cupid, God of Love: Christine de Pizan's* Epistre au Dieu d'amours *and* Dit de la Rose, *Thomas Hoccleve's* Letter of Cupid. *With George Sewell's The Proclamation of Cupid*, eds T. Fenster & M. C. Erler, Brill, Leiden.

de Pizan, C. 1994, *The Book of the Body Politic*, trans. K. L. Forhan, Cambridge University Press, Cambridge.

Douët-d'Arcq, L. C. 1863, *Choix de pièces inédites relatives au règne de Charles VI*, 2 vols, Renouard, Paris.

Famiglietti, R. C. 1986, *Royal Intrigue: Crisis at the Court of Charles VI, 1392–1420*, AMS Press, New York.

Gross, D. 2007, *The Secret History of Emotion: From Aristotle's Rhetoric to Modern Brain Science*, University of Chicago Press, Chicago.

Guenée, B. 1988, 'Le roi, ses parents et son royaume en France au XIVe siècle', *Bulletino dell'Istituto Storico Italiano per il Medio Evo et Archivio Muratoriano*, vol. 94, pp. 439–470.

Guenée, B. 1992, *Un Meurtre, une société: l'assassinat du duc d'Orléans, 23 novembre 1407*, Gallimard, Paris.

Halsall, G. 1998, 'Violence and Society: An Introductory Survey', in G. Halsall (ed.), *Violence and Society in the Early Medieval West*, Boydell Press, Woodbridge.

Heckmann, M. 2002, *Stellvertreter, Mit- und Ersatzherrscher. Regenten, Generalstatthalter, Kurfürsten und Reichsvikare in Regnum und Imperium vom 13. bis zum frühen 15. Jahrhundert*, 2 vols, Fahlbusch, Warendorf.

Hutchison, E. 2016, 'The Politics of Grief in the Outbreak of Civil War in France, 1407–1413', *Speculum*, vol. 91, pp. 422–452.

Journal d'un bourgeois de Paris 1990, ed. C. Beaune, Librairie Générale Française, Paris.

Juvénal des Ursins, J. 1836, 'Histoire de Charles VI, roy de France, et des choses mémorables advenues durant quarante-deux années de son règne. Depuis 1380 jusqu'à 1422', in J. F. Michaud & J. J. F. Poujoulat (eds), *Nouvelle collection des mémoires pour servir à l'histoire de France*, 1st edn, vol. 2, Editions du commentaire analytique du Code civil, Paris.

Knuuttila, S. 2002, 'Medieval Theories of the Passions of the Soul', in H. Lagerlund & M. Yrjönsuuri (eds), *Emotions and Choice from Boethius to Descartes*, Kluwer, Dordrecht, pp. 49–83.

Kosta-Théfaine, J. F. (ed.) 2007, *Othon de Grandson, chevalier et poète*, Éditions Paradigme, Orléans.

Lavéant, K. 2013, 'Personal Expression of a Playwright or Public Discourse of Confraternity? A Performance at the Puy de Notre-Dame in Amiens in 1473', in J. Bloemendal,

P. Eversmann, & E. Strietman (eds), *Drama, Performance and Debate: Theatre and Public Opinion in the Early Modern Period*, Brill, Leiden, pp. 19–34.

Lehoux, F. 1966–68, *Jean de France, Duc de Berri: sa vie. Son action politique (1340–1416)*, 4 vols, Picard, Paris.

le Sénéchal, J. 1905, *Les Cent ballades: poème du XIVe siècle*, ed. G. Raynaud, Firmin-Didot, Paris.

Piaget, A. 1902, *Oton de Grandson, sa vie et ses poesies*, Payot, Lausanne.

Piaget, A. 1902, 'Un manuscrit de la Cour amoureuse de Charles VI', *Romania*, vol. 31, pp. 597–603.

Pintoin, M. 1994, *Chronique du Religieux de Saint-Denys contenant le règne de Charles VI, de 1380–1422*, trans. L. Bellaguet, 6 vols., 2nd edn, Editions du Comité des travaux historiques et scientifiques, Paris.

Reid, D. 2006, 'Piety, Poetry and Politics: Rouen's Confraternity of the Immaculate Conception and the French Wars of Religion', in C. F. Black & P. Gravestock (eds), *Early Modern Confraternities in Europe and the Americas*, Ashgate, Aldershot & Burlington, pp. 151–170.

Schnerb, B. 1988, *Les Armagnacs et les Bourguignons. La maudite guerre*, Perrin, Paris.

Schweber, N. 2011, 'Penn State Students Clash With Police in Unrest After Announcement', The New York Times, www.nytimes.com/2011/11/11/sports/ncaafootball/penn-state-students-in-clashes-after-joe-paterno-is-ousted.html

Sizer, M. 2007, *Making Revolution Medieval: Revolt and Political Culture in Fifteenth-Century Paris*, doctoral thesis, University of Minnesota, Minnesota.

Straub, T. 1961, 'Die Grundung des Pariser Minnehofs von 1400', *Zeitschrift für romanische Philologie*, vol. 77, pp. 1–14.

Taylor, J. H. M. 2007, *The Making of Poetry: Late-medieval French Poetic Anthologies*, Brepols, Turnhout.

Vadén, T. 2014, *Heidegger, Žižek and Revolution*, Sense Publishers, Rotterdam.

Wilson, S. 2013, 'Violence and Love: In Which Yoko Ono Encourages Slavoj Žižek to Give Peace a Chance', in G. Matthews & S. Goodman (eds), *Violence and the Limits of Representation*, Palgrave Macmillan, New York, pp. 28–48.

Žižek, S. 2008, *Violence: Six Sideways Reflections*, Profile Books Ltd, London.

5

VIOLENT COMPASSION IN LATE MEDIEVAL WRITING

Catherine Nall

In Book Two of his *Troy Book* (1412–1420) the poet John Lydgate describes the attempted landing of the Greeks on Troy's shores. In the midst of the fighting that follows, as the Trojans attempt to prevent the landing, Protesilaus, a Greek, withdraws from the battle and stands on the shore. From this vantage point, he sees the massive slaughter inflicted on his men:

> Wher as him þou3t, his herte gan to ryue
> Of cruel Ire and also of pite,
> Þat he kau3t, only for to se
> His men lyn slayn endelong þe stronde,
> And some of hem comynge vp to londe,
> Dreint in þe se among þe flodis depe.
> For whiche þing he gan anoon to wepe
> Ful pitously, al wer it nat espied,
> Whos woful eyne my3te nat be dreyed
> For þe constreynt which sat so ny3e his hert.
> Til at þe last, among his peynys smert,
> So cruel Ire gan his hert enbrace,
> Þat sodeynly with a dispitous face,
> With-out abood, þou3te how þat he
> Vp-on her deth wolde avengid be.
> (Bergen 1906–1935, Book 2, ll. 8352–8366)

Lydgate here maps emotional and somatic change in a way that his source does not.[1] In Lydgate's version, Protesilaus begins by feeling both 'cruel Ire' (anger) and pity – the effect of which is to make him feel that his heart will split apart or tear ('ryue'). Looking at his men dead and dying, he weeps '[f]ul pitously' –

his weeping is both full of pity and produces pity in those who witness it, although, as Lydgate tells us, in this case there is no witness ('al wer it nat espied'). But then, 'at last', anger begins to 'enbrace' – affect or influence – his heart, so much so that with 'dispitous face' he enters the fighting 'where he saw þat þer was grettest pres' (l. 8372), and kills every Trojan he encounters. In order to avenge the deaths of his men, pity has to give way to anger. The face that was full of pity, the weeping, 'woful' eyes, becomes 'dispitous' – cruel, pitiless – a carefully chosen word which emphasises the connection between cruelty and lack of pity, and, in particular, the renunciation of pity required for Protesilaus to go and kill other men.

Pity has a conspicuous presence in late medieval war writing. As one of the key attributes of good kingship, occupying a central place as a virtue to be practised both by rulers and by those who prosecute war, pity is primarily associated in a range of genres – from romance to *speculum principis* to military treatise – with the restraint of violence. In such idealising genres, pity comes into effect to spare the life of an opponent, to see the ransoming rather than the execution of prisoners, to prevent the captured town from being razed to the ground, to stay the hand of the victor. Yet, as the above example illustrates, pity also has a different realisation in late medieval war writing as the emotion that acts as a precursor to vengeance; as one that, far from limiting bloodshed, forms a crucial part of the affective foundation of the practice of violence.

The terms pity, 'routhe', mercy, 'misericorde', and compassion are frequently collocated in late medieval writing, and are often used to explicate each another.[2] Two Middle English works derived in whole or in part from Giles of Rome's *De Regimine Principum* (c. 1280) gesture towards the relatedness of these terms. In his translation of *De Regimine Principum* (c. 1400), John Trevisa glosses 'misericordia' as mercy and as 'rewþe' (pity, compassion). His definition, based on Aristotle's definition of pity, explains that if a man

> is sory for anoþeris harme and troweth namlich þat he hath wrongfullich þat harme, þat is misericordia, rewþe; for, ii Rethoricorum, it is iseid þat misericordia is not elles but a certein sorwe of harme þat is iseie and iknowe and corrumpeth [corrupts] a man and maketh hym sory þat hath þat harm with wrong.[3]

While he who has 'reuthe of no thing' is cruel, to have 'rewthe of al þyng' is 'mollis (nesche)', that is tender, soft or weak, and 'wommanliche'. The merciful man is the one who has compassion or 'rewþe' in the right quantity and in the right circumstance, following Aristotle's doctrine of the mean: 'And he þat hath rewþe of hem þat hauen harme wrongfulliche is mene and is to preisyng and is icleped mysericors, merciable' (*Governance*, p. 136).

In his *Regiment of Princes* (c. 1411), also based in part on *De Regimine Principum*, Thomas Hoccleve explains, following St Augustine, that 'Mercy . . . Of herte is a verray conpassioun / Of othir mennes harm', while pity works to make men 'fonde / To help him þat men sen in meschif smert'.[4] He explains the relationship between the two by stating that mercy 'springs' and 'grows' out of pity: 'Out of pitee growith mercy and spryngith'. A man without pity cannot perform acts of mercy: 'For pitelees man can do no mercy' (*Regiment*, ll. 3305–3306). Deeds of mercy, then, are not empty of emotion, but are generated by and depend upon the presence of the feeling of pity.

This affective dimension to the virtues of pity and mercy is present across many different definitions. St Augustine, citing Cicero, argues that ' "Among your virtues none is more admirable and agreeable than your compassion". And what is compassion but a fellow-feeling for another's misery, which prompts us to help him if we can?' (Augustine 1950, p. 285). Chaucer's Parson describes 'misericorde' as 'a vertu by which the corage of a man is stired by the mysese of hym that is mysesed. / Upon which misericorde folweth pitee in parfournynge of charitable werkes of misericorde'.[5] Brunetto Latini's definition of 'Misericorde' in *Li Livres dou Tresor* (c. 1260–1266) explains that it 'est une vertus par qui li corages est esmeus sour les mesaisiés et sor la poverté des tormentés' ('is a virtue through which the heart is moved by those who suffer and by the poverty of the tormented') (Carmody 1948, p. 292; Barrette & Baldwin 1993, p. 257) . The twelfth-century *Moralium dogma philosophorum* explains that 'Misericorde est une vertuz qui fait le cuer tendre et pitex vers celx qui sont apressé de mesaise' ('Mercy is a virtue that makes the heart tender and piteous towards those who are oppressed by suffering') (Holmberg 1929, p. 30, my translation) . These definitions also emphasise the connection between (felt) emotion and (resultant) action. Those who feel pity, compassion or mercy are moved to act; they are prompted to relieve those for whom they feel pity.

Theseus and the Theban widows

In Chaucer's 'Knight's Tale' pity works both to limit and to perpetuate violence. It is the display of the weeping pity of the women who beg for the lives of Arcite and Palamon that produces compassion in Theseus and prevents him from administrating strict justice: 'And eek his herte had compassioun / Of wommen, for they wepen evere in oon' (ll. 1770–1771). But it is this emotion, too, that leads to the devastating violence inflicted on Thebes, as Theseus kills Creon, puts the people to flight, 'And by assaut he wan the citee after, / And rente adoun bothe wall and sparre and rafter' (ll. 989–990).[6]

As Theseus returns to Athens following his conquest of the Amazons, he is interrupted by a group of grieving widows, who make 'swich a cry and swich a wo . . . / That in this world nys creature lyvynge/ That herde swich another waymentynge' (ll. 900–902). They tell Theseus that their husbands died fighting against Thebes but that the tyrant Creon – the ruler of Thebes – has denied the bodies proper burial: he ' "wol nat suffren hem, by noon assent, / Neither to been yburied nor ybrent, / But maketh houndes ete hem in despit" ' (ll. 945–947).[7] On two occasions in this long speech, the widows implore Theseus to feel the pity so notably absent in Creon. On the first occasion, the widow of Cappaneus begs Theseus to:

> "Have mercy on oure wo and oure distresse!
> Som drope of pitee thurgh thy gentillesse,
> Upon us wrecched wommen lat thou falle"
>
> (ll. 919–921)

The widow links Theseus's nobility – his 'gentillesse' – with his ability to feel pity (the drop of pity can fall *because of* his nobility). On the second occasion, having fallen on the ground ('They fillen gruf and criden pitously', l. 949) – a traditional posture of supplication – the widows collectively reiterate their plea:

> "Have on us wrecched wommen som mercy,
> And lat oure sorwe synken in thyn herte"
>
> (ll. 950–951)

The repetition of 'lat' ('allow') in both of these supplications is interesting. Theseus must allow a drop of pity to fall; he must allow 'their sorrow [to] sink in his heart'. To have mercy requires opening oneself up to a kind of transference of another's suffering – allowing *their* sorrow to sink in *his* heart. But it is also something that is controlled and that is subject to reason – one can decide whether or not to allow oneself to feel pity.

These are injunctions to feel pity. In linking Theseus's status with the demonstration of pity, the women emphasise what is at stake in this moment – a failure to feel pity would be an indictment of Theseus's nobility. If anything, Chaucer lessens the coercive element of his source: in Boccaccio's *Il Teseida*, the women say that 'If high nobility, as we believe, dwells within you, take pity upon us now' (Havely 1980, p. 109). But Chaucer also makes it clear that Theseus does feel this emotion.[8] He carefully delineates the emotional process taking place in Theseus:

> This gentil duc doun from his courser sterte
> With herte pitous, whan he herde hem speke.
> Hym thoughte that his herte wolde breke,
> Whan he saugh hem so pitous and so maat,
> That whilom weren of so greet estaat
>
> (ll. 952–956)[9]

Witnessing the women's suffering – through hearing them speak and seeing them 'pitous' and 'maat' (helpless) – makes the 'herte pitous', and the compassionate heart is vulnerable – Theseus thinks that his heart will break.[10] Chaucer also emphasises the cognitive aspects of pity – that feeling of pity is partly produced by a knowledge that the women were once of such high status. It is not presented as an irrational emotion in this sense, but one that is produced through Theseus's judgement and evaluation of the women's condition. At the same time, that their status is relevant at all points to the discriminatory nature of compassion, as it differentiates between those who deserve to be pitied, and those who do not.

Chaucer provides an explanation for why Theseus can be moved in such a way. As he puts it on four occasions, and in one instance specifically in relation to Theseus, 'Pitee renneth soone in gentil herte'.[11] This seems to be both figurative and literal: pity has a liquid quality; it can 'run'. Medieval texts regularly figure pity in this way, as something that moistens the heart: the *Ayenbite of Inwit* explains how pity 'bedeaweþ þe herte', and writes of the 'wetnesse of pite' (Gradon 1965, p. 116, l. 24; p. 242, l. 16); a late fifteenth-century sermon refers to the 'moystnes of pite' (cited in Langum 2015, p. 269).[12] Stephen Scrope's mid-fifteenth century translation of Christine de Pizan's *Epitre d'Othea* explains that 'Ingratitude ... drieth þe welle of pite, þe dewe of grace and þe ryuer of merci' (1970, p. 67, ll. 17–18). Such phrases are usually understood in their figurative sense alone, but they surely also relate to wider understandings of the physiology of emotion, of the movement of vital spirits to and from the heart. The 'moistness' of pity explains why it was understood that as the body dries in later life there was a corresponding decline of pity and compassion; why the phlegmatic was thought to be piteous; and why women, naturally more moist, were supposedly more compassionate (Langum 2015, pp. 269–270).[13] It also explains why weeping – a purging of excess moisture – is so closely identified as an outward sign of sorrow and pity, and why, in the example discussed above, Lydgate's Protesilaus's 'woful eyne myȝte nat be dreyed / For þe constreynt which sat so nyȝe his hert'.[14] Similarly, the common image of a drop of pity plays on this quality of pity, seeming to mean not only a small amount, but also a liquid drop. Asserting that pity runs quickly in a noble heart posits an essential difference between the heart of a noble and that of a non-noble. Indeed, for some writers, what is at issue is not only that noblemen naturally feel pity, but that a churl is incapable of feeling it.[15] The ability to feel pity, then, reinforces class difference and supports hierarchy; the ability not only to feel it but crucially to *act* on the piteous impulse makes manifest and maintains privilege, specifically masculine, aristocratic privilege.

Arthur and the giant

For the author of the Alliterative *Morte Arthure* (c. 1400) the generation of pity in both his protagonist and in his audience is crucial. In his description of Arthur's encounter with the giant, the poet foregrounds pity, and in so doing departs from previous accounts of their meeting, including those of his sources. When Arthur arrives in France in the initial stages of his campaign against Rome, he hears news of a giant who has been terrorising the local inhabitants and has abducted the duchess of Brittany. This moment in the account of Arthur's reign appears across the Arthurian chronicle tradition. It originates in Geoffrey of Monmouth's *History of the Kings of Britain* in the late 1130s and then reappears in subsequent versions

– in the Anglo-Norman of Wace, the early Middle English of Layamon's *Brut*, the Alliterative *Morte Arthure* and Malory's *Morte Darthur*.

Geoffrey of Monmouth simply reports that 'news reached Arthur that a huge giant had come from Spain' (Reeve 2007, p. 224). Geoffrey does not give the details of Arthur's response to this news. Rather, he states that '[s]o mighty a warrior as Arthur was unwilling to lead his army against such a monster, as he could destroy it single-handed and wanted to encourage his troops by doing so' (Reeve 2007, p. 224).

Wace's account is similarly indirect, but more graphic in terms of what the giant has done. The point of this description, though, seems to be to emphasise that nobody has dared challenge the giant until this point: 'There was no man in the land so bold, no young man, whether noble or peasant, however proud or brave, who dared to fight the giant or venture into his neighbourhood' (Wace 1999, p. 285). In both Geoffrey's and Wace's versions, the encounter serves to highlight Arthur's courage and his ability to inspire courage in his men.

Layamon's account differs more substantially. Rather than the news being reported second-hand, a 'hende cniht' ('noble knight') comes to Arthur to tell him what the giant has been doing. It is a long speech, comprising 20 lines, which goes further in outlining the injuries inflicted on the people. However, we are not shown Arthur's emotional reaction to what he has heard (Layamon 2001, ll. 12802–12829).

The author of the Alliterative *Morte Arthure* realises the dramatic potential of this moment. A Templar knight makes the following speech to Arthur:[16]

> "Here is a tyraunt beside   that tormentes thy pople,
> A grete giaunt of Gene,   engendered of fendes;
> He has freten of folk   mo than five hundreth,
> And als fele fauntekins   of free-born childer.
> This has been his sustenaunce   all this seven winteres,
> And yet is that sot not sad,   so well him it likes!
> In the countree of Constantine   no kind has he leved
> Withouten kidd casteles,   enclosed with walles,
> That he ne has clenly distroyed   all the knave childer,
> And them carried to the crag   and clenly devoured".[17]

He goes on to tell Arthur that the giant has taken the duchess, '"the flowr of all Fraunce   or of five rewmes, / And one of the fairest   that formed was ever"' (ll. 861–862), intending to '"lie by that lady   ay whiles her life lasts"' (l. 856). In case this speech has not produced the appropriate emotional response of pity, the Templar ends his speech to the king with the following, original, injunction:

> "As thou art rightwise king,   rew on thy pople
> And fonde for to venge them   that thus are rebuked!".

(ll. 867–868)

The words of the Templar map out the connection between Arthur's claim to be a 'rightwise king', feeling pity, and the victims' status as Arthur's people, as his subjects: 'rew on thy pople'. As with the Theseus example, emotion is tied to a claim to status and identity – in this instance that of being a righteous king. Again, as with Theseus, Arthur does then feel the emotion he has been told to feel – and this is one of this author's remarkable innovations:

> Then romes the rich king   for rewth of the pople,
> Raikes right to a tent and   restes no lenger;
> He welteres, he wresteles,   he wringes his handes;
> There was no wye of this world   that wiste what he mened.
>
> (ll. 889–892)

This is a heightened representation of emotional state and emotional process. Arthur's pity causes him to bellow, to writhe and contort, and to wring his hands. Pity produces an array of outward signs here: the wringing of hands is often associated with the feeling of pity for both genders – men and women alike wring their hands as expressions of sorrow in the Alliterative *Morte Arthure*, and in medieval literature more generally.[18] Arthur does not, however, respond in the way most often associated with the feeling of pity in various generic and textual contexts: he does not weep. Rather, the writhing and contortion of the body are this author's way of expressing the presence of extreme mental and emotional anguish.[19]

When Malory used the Alliterative *Morte Arthure* as the basis for the second tale of his *Morte Darthur*, he altered his source in a way that strengthened the connection between defence of subjects, the claims and obligations of conquest, pity, and violence. The Templar here becomes the 'husbandeman' – a farmer – a member of that group in society that suffers most through war. The 'husbandeman' outlines the activities of the giant; the speech is truncated but is essentially the same as that given by the Templar in the source.[20] The husbandman then makes explicit the effect that this description ought to have Arthur: '"Now, as thou arte oure ryghtwos kynge, rewe on this lady and on thy lyege peple, and revenge us as a noble conquerroure sholde"' (p. 154, ll. 24–26). Malory doubles the coercive part of this – maintaining the 'ryghtwos kynge' of his source but adding that a 'noble conquerroure' should exact vengeance. He thus emphasises the connection between pity, vengeance and claims to other identifiers – those of being a righteous king and a 'noble conquerroure'. Defence of subjects, taking action on their behalf, and the emotional dimensions of political rule are connected here, and made part of two overlapping responsibilities – those pertaining to kingship and those pertaining to conquest.

Malory chooses not to include the description of Arthur's extreme outward display of pity given in the Alliterative *Morte Arthure*. Initially the effect that the husbandman's words have had on Arthur is only registered by the king's statement that '"Thy soth sawys have greved sore my herte"' (p. 155, ll. 4–5). Arthur returns to his tent and 'carpys but lytyll' (p. 155, l. 6). The affective response is deferred until Arthur actually sees what the giant is doing. He sees the giant 'gnawyng on a lymme of a large man', and three ladies turning 'three brochis'; on those skewers are 'twelve chyldir but late borne, and they were broched in maner lyke birdis. Whan the kyng behylde that syghte his herte was nyghe bledyng for sorow. Than he haylesed hym with angirfull wordys' (p. 156, ll. 28–34). There is an easier movement from sorrow to anger, here, than in the example from Lydgate. While Lydgate, Chaucer and the author of the Alliterative *Morte Arthure* dwell on emotional processes, Malory acknowledges the presence of emotion, but does not focus on the movement from one state to another.[21]

Elsewhere in the *Morte Darthur*, not to avenge one's people or defend them is about individual shame – but shame as something anticipated conditionally rather than directly experienced. At the beginning of 'Balyn le Sauvage', Arthur is told that King Royns of North Wales has entered Arthur's land and 'brente and slew the kyngis trew lyege people'. Arthur responds by stating that '"Iff thys be trew . . . hit were grete shame unto myne astate but that he were myghtyly withstonde"' (p. 47, ll. 9–12).[22] Later on in the opening tale, Arthur is informed that five kings have entered his lands 'and brent and slewe and distroyed clene byfore hem bothe the citeis and castels, that hit was pité to here' (p. 100, ll. 33–35). Arthur responds by exclaiming '"Alas!' . . . yet had I never reste one monethe syne I was kyng crowned of this londe. Now shall I never reste tylle I mete with tho kyngis in a fayre felde, that I make myne avow; for my trwe lyege peple shall nat be destroyed in my defaughte"' (p. 101, ll. 1–4). In these instances, the responsibility of kingship is recognised, but there is no explicit emotional reaction, but rather a pre-empting of an emotional state: the potential to feel shame, and to be shamed, in consequence.

It is tempting to see this emotional shift over the course of the *Morte Darthur* as evidence of Arthur's maturation. The giant episode is commonly seen as a kind of rite of passage for Arthur (and for heroes more generally), in the sense that it demonstrates Arthur's ability to rule and his mastery of sinful impulses such as lechery and gluttony (Cohen 1999). The capacity to feel pity, not just anticipate shame, becomes part of the crucial formula of Arthur's kingship. In this sense, pity's relationship to power is once more important. As Felicity Riddy puts it, '[p]ity as a social virtue sanctifies hierarchy, since it is predicated on the difference between higher and lower, or between weaker and stronger: it is a mode of relationship with one's inferiors' (Riddy 1994, p. 57). Arthur's pity makes manifest and legitimises the political power he already has over his conquered subjects – hence why the husbandmen in his speech emphasises Arthur's status as conqueror as well as king, both by elaborating on the duties attendant on conquest and by addressing Arthur as 'Sir Conquerrour' (p. 154, l. 33).[23]

Pity is not realised by these writers simply as a virtue to be performed. Those whose actions make the virtue of pity manifest are also depicted as having been moved to act. Theseus and Arthur are exemplary producers of emotion, using emotion in the correct way. Killing a giant is clearly not the same kind of violence, in either scale or consequence, as razing a city to the ground, but both instances depend on an understanding that violence might be the outcome of compassionate pity. In his 1487 translation and edition of Jacques le Grand's *Book of Good Manners*, William Caxton urges his readers to 'take the waye of pyte & to leue vengeance' (book 3, ch. 1, STC 15394, sig. Eijr). In these examples, to 'take the waye of pyte' is not to reject vengeance, but to enact it.

The politics of pity

The cultivation of pity in one context is clearly inappropriate for the actual practice of violence, which depends on the suppression of pity. Perhaps more than any other state, war requires the active management of compassion; the ability to feel and not feel as circumstances dictate. In the instances of Arthur and Theseus, compassion for one group of people does not translate into compassion for another group. Perhaps no ethical question is raised by Arthur: the authors work hard to demonstrate the giant's monstrosity, as compassionate king is juxtaposed with inhuman, baby-eating giant. In the case of Theseus though, such discriminatory compassion is more problematic. Compassion for the widows leads to the dispossession of the Theban people, the destruction of the city, and the production of a 'taas of bodyes dede' (l. 1005). Significantly, Chaucer omits the detail given in Boccaccio's *Il Teseida* that Theseus had those bodies buried (McCoy 1974). The outcome of Theseus's compassionate violence is not so unlike the situation that gave rise to his compassion in the first place: one pile of unburied bodies replaces another.

These examples rely to varying degrees on images of suffering in order to generate pity: the dead men lining the shore or drowning in the sea; the grieving, swooning widows; the devoured children; the abducted, raped and murdered duchess. Indeed, images of suffering can be used to support violence as much as to contest it. Writing on what she terms 'shock-pictures' – photographs of atrocity – Susan Sontag questions the presumption that such images could 'only stimulate the repudiation of war', asking whether it is not also the case that they can 'foster greater militancy' (Sontag 2004, pp. 7–8). She calls attention to the different, indeed antithetical, responses (for peace, for revenge) such images may evoke (Sontag 2004, pp. 11–12). Images of suffering in the examples I have considered support the notion that suffering is best met with violence, with yet more suffering.

The ethical complexities of compassion, the division of people into those who do or do not deserve to suffer, those who do or do not deserve compassion, are perhaps nowhere so evident as in the rhetoric of crusading, particularly as it emerged in the late fourteenth and early fifteenth centuries. Written against the backdrop of arguments for Anglo-French peace, calls to crusade in this period attempt to inculcate compassion for one group of people only to then urge violence against another.[24] When in c. 1411 Thomas Hoccleve argues for peace between England and France, compassion is key. He urges his addressees of 'Cristen Princes' to 'haven conpassioun' of 'Cristen blood'; he refers to the death and destruction wrought by war, of lives, buildings, crops and the rape of women; and exhorts his readers to 'Lat your pitee now awake / That longe hath slept, and pees betwixt yow make' (*Regiment*, ll. 5534–5340). But, once peace has been made, he urges that those whose pity has been awakened should 'on the foos of Cryst, your redemptour,/ Werreieth' (*Regiment*, ll. 5430–5432).

The *Letter to King Richard II*, probably written in 1395, by Philippe de Mézières (b. 1327–d. 1405), a monk, and former chancellor of Cyprus and member of Charles V's council, uses compassion in a similar way. This text has multiple agendas – a marriage between Richard and Isabella, daughter of Charles VI, peace between France and England, an end of the papal schism, and, crucially in this context, a new crusade in the East. Philippe, referring to himself as 'this Old Solitary', constructs the very writing of the text as an act produced by compassion: 'he feels compassion now for those who have died by reason of it [the wound of war] and still more concern and compassion for his Christian brethren who are now alive . . .' (Coopland 1975, pp. 7–8, 80).[25]

In this text, pity works more explicitly both in the service of arguments to limit and to commit violence. In the opening 'lamentation' Philippe refers to the destruction of nobles and churches, and to the creation of widows and orphans as a result of the ongoing Anglo-French conflict (Coopland 1975, pp. 7, 79). Later, as part of his argument to promote peace between England and France, he urges Richard to 'have true compassion and bitter grief for the blood of Christian men' (Coopland 1975, pp. 43, 116). He constructs the killing of other Christians as a re-enactment of the crucifixion: 'by shedding the blood of our fellow creatures, English and French alike, once more we have killed sweet Jesus Christ'. Instead, 'a new compassion' ('fresche compassion') should be shown 'for the death of our gentle Redeemer . . . and heart-felt horror at the effusion of the blood of our Christian brothers' (Coopland 1975, pp. 44, 117).

Sarah McNamer uses these examples to demonstrate the existence of a 'significant current of protest against violence in late medieval England'. She argues that '[p]ity for Christ [. . .] becomes the foundation of an ethics of nonviolence toward other Christians' (McNamer 2010, p. 154). While I agree that Philippe and Hoccleve do indeed move from a focus on compassion for Christ to a call for compassion for Christians, to read these texts as protesting violence is problematic. Both authors also actively promote violence: it is just that the target of violence is shifted from the Christian to the non-Christian. The compassion that in one context is designed to limit Christian bloodshed, in another supports the shedding of the blood of non-Christians. Pity serves to legitimise and encourage violence towards non-Christians. According to Philippe, a new campaign in the East requires compassion. He refers to how the king's subjects who live in Jerusalem 'are held in serfdom by King Vigilant' (earlier identified as the sultan of Babylon). He refers to how these subjects are 'beaten and ill-treated, and how they pay great tributes and aids, to the shame and dishonour of all Christian kings', and to Richard and Charles in particular. The 'Catholic Faith . . . is trodden under foot, dishonoured, destroyed, deserted and abandoned'; the holy places 'lie profaned, ruined, and emptied'. 'What man is there', asks Philippe:

> baptised in the name of the blessed Jesus, whose heart is so steeled that he can hear tell of these great wrongs and not be moved to compassion, and so to offer in devotion to God his body, his goods and all that lies in his power, to remedy the very great evils and dishonour of Christendom, here briefly recited? There is a great danger that those Christians who do not have compassion will be deprived of a share in Jerusalem triumphant . . .
> (Coopland 1975, pp. 29, 102)

As with the earlier injunctions to feel pity, Philippe performs a number of manoeuvres that link the performance of that feeling to wider identity claims. First, Philippe links compassion to kingly authority – those who suffer are not simply Christian brothers in the East, but the king's subjects: they thus have a particular claim on Richard. Philippe then makes compassion part of a specifically Christian identity: 'What man is there, baptised in the name of the blessed Jesus, whose heart is so steeled that he can hear tell of these wrongs and not be moved to compassion?' The rhetorical question connects a hard heart – in this case a heart of steel ('cuer d'acier') – with the inability to feel compassion, which is a commonplace in Middle English texts too.[26] The appropriate response to hearing about what is inflicted on these subjects is one of compassion, and feeling that compassion manifests itself in the commitment of body and goods to a new crusade. To not feel compassion in response to hearing of the injuries and insults endured is not without risk. Philippe spells out the consequences of such an affective deficiency: the failure to feel compassion becomes a dereliction of Christian duty, with very exact consequences for the reader in the afterlife. These injunctions, then, construct compassion as a crucial part of noble, kingly and, indeed, Christian identity.

These images of pitying-conquering kingship evoke the model of divine pity and punishment, of God 'of pitee the auctour' (*Regiment*, l. 3025). This movement from the suffering of the people, to pity for them, and then to (new) violence, is one modelled on biblical precedent. In particular, it relates to Exodus, chapter 22, verse 27: 'si clamaverit ad me, exaudiam eum, quia misericors sum' ('if he cry to me, I will hear him, because I am compassionate' [*Biblia Sacra Latina Ex Biblia Sacra Vulgatae Editionis* 1970, p. 53.]). This precedent was well known to readers and writers of the fifteenth century. A fifteenth-century Middle English translation of Alain Chartier's *Quadrilogue Invectif* (1422), for example, warns that

> it is oftentymes founde in the olde writyngis that for the myserye of the powr people [and] the wepyngis and sorowis of them . . . the diuine iugementis hath yevyn full egre and sharpe punycion. Wherfor I counseile euery man that fyndith hymself gilti in this trespas that he bewar, for it is not to thynke that the turmentis of so many coragis and the pituous and

lamentable voice which addressyn their cryes, wepyngis and compleintis vp to the high hevyn move nat with pite the mekenes of the right mercifull and all-puyssaunt Creatour, that His iustice procedith nat to the confusion of theim that cause the iniquityf wikednes.

(Blayney 1980, vol. 1, p. 172)

The presence of particular types of emotion in accounts of war-making does important work for audiences, and part of that work is to communicate the justness or legality of war. In particular, the presence of pity in the examples considered here helps to mark the war as just, the violence as legitimate. According to just war theory, defence of the rights of subjects is a legitimate reason to make war. William Worcester, for example, in his *Boke of Noblesse* presented to Edward IV in 1475 states that 'the second [just cause for war] is to withestande all soche mysdoers the whiche wolde defoule grief and oppresse the peple of the contre that the kyng or Prince is gouernoure of' (British Library, ms Royal 18.B.XXII, fol. 4ʳ). Nicholas Upton, in his military and heraldic text *De Studio militari* finished in 1446, argues that a war is just if it is waged in order '[t]o Avenge the wronges off poore people; to poorge & rydde the cowntry off wykkyd lyuers' (Walker 1998, vol. 1, p. 22). The coercive element of this responsibility to defend subjects is made clear in Caxton's translation of Christine de Pizan's *Livre des faits d'armes*, published in 1489: war is just if it is for the defence of subjects and this, with other just reasons, means that it: 'is not onely leefful [lawful] to a prynce to moeue warre or to mayntene it / but it is to hym pure dette to make it by oblygacion of tytle of seignourie & iuredicion / yf he wyll vse it after rightfull duete' (Caxton 1937, p. 12). Defence of subjects is a responsibility, an obligation of kingship and rule, a 'pure dette' as Caxton has it.

There is, however, an affective gap in this theorisation. The emotional dimension of how one goes from hearing about injustices committed to one's subjects to violence – the emotional process it might involve – is not articulated in these theorisations of the just war. This gap can either be left blank or filled with other emotions – shame, for instance, as in the examples cited earlier from the *Morte Darthur*, or righteous indignation. The authors of the examples considered here chose to fill that affective gap with pity itself. That pity has been felt legitimises the violence that follows, and becomes the necessary emotion for any further violence. A connection that is implied in just war theory – between pity and violence – is made explicit by these authors: it is not an implied affective underpinning, but an explicit emotional process, in which the experience of feeling pity leads to acts of violence.

Pity has particular value in accounts of war-making. As such an essential part of the ideology of kingship, to depict a ruler feeling pity constructs other kingly and noble characteristics at the same time: to feel pity in one context implies one's ability to feel it appropriately in another. While the presence of shame, for example, might suggest a consciousness of failing in some duty or expectation, to pity brings with it an assertion of power – the power that comes with pitying another.[27] It acts, then, to communicate political subjection. Indeed, in some narratives, a people's subjection to a would-be ruler's pity is but the first phase in a process which will culminate in their subjection to other kinds of forces – legal, political, or military – as a ruler's pity brings about the willing subjection of a city under siege.[28]

Notes

1 This interest in, and emphasis on, emotion, is characteristic of Lydgate's handling of his source in general. For the equivalent passage in Guido delle Colonne's *Historia destructionis Troiae*, see *The History of the Destruction of Troy* (1974), trans. M. E. Meek, Indiana University Press, Bloomington, p. 120.
2 For an extremely useful discussion of these terms, and their relationship to one another, see Burnley, J. D. 1979, *Chaucer's Language and the Philosophers' Tradition*, D. S. Brewer, Cambridge.
3 Fowler, D. C., Briggs, C. F. & Remley, P. G. (eds) 1997, *The Governance of Kings and Princes: John Trevisa's Middle English Translation of the De Regimine Principum of Aegidius Romanus*, Routledge, New York, p. 135. Hereafter referred to as *Governance*. The definition is based on Aristotle, *The Art of Rhetoric*, 2.8.
4 Hoccleve, T. 1999, *The Regiment of Princes*, ed. C. R. Blyth, Medieval Institute Publications, Kalamazoo, Michigan, ll. 3312–4, 2999–3000. Hereafter referred to as *Regiment*.
5 'The Parson's Tale', in *The Riverside Chaucer* (1987), ed. L. D. Benson, 3rd edn, Oxford University Press, Oxford, ll. 806–807. Subsequent references to the *Canterbury Tales* are taken from this edition.
6 These two episodes have generated a great deal of discussion. See, in particular, Blamires, A. 2006, *Chaucer, Ethics, and Gender*, Oxford University Press, Oxford, pp. 27–29; Crane, S. 1994, *Gender and Romance in Chaucer's Canterbury Tales*, Princeton University Press, Princeton, pp. 20–23; Harding, W. 1997, 'The Function of Pity in Three Canterbury Tales', *The Chaucer Review*, vol. 32, no. 2, pp. 163–166; Mann, J. 1991, *Geoffrey Chaucer*, Harvester Wheatsheaf, Hemel Hempstead, pp. 171–175; Nolan, B. 1992, *Chaucer and the Tradition of the 'Roman Antique'*, Cambridge University Press, Cambridge, pp. 263–267.
7 Lack of burial itself suggests an absence of pity. In a Christian context, burial of the dead was of course one of the works of mercy. For the author of the *Book of Virtues and Vices*, an English translation of the *Somme le Roi* made in c. 1375, burial of the dead also depends on the presence of 'rewthe and pitee'. The author argues that 'ȝif kynde and pitee moueth thes sarazenes and Iues and mysbilueyng folke to birie the deede, moche more scholde moeue vs rewthe and pitee and cristene bileue' (Francis 1942, p. 211).
8 That Theseus feels something is important. Barbara Nolan reads Theseus's behaviour in this scene as according with Seneca's recommendation that the 'practitioner of true Stoic *clementia* will "come to the aid of those who weep, but without weeping with them"' (Nolan 1992, p. 266). Although I agree that a distinction is made here (and indeed in the case of King Arthur, considered below) between the weeping women and what Alcuin Blamires (2006, p. 155, n. 14) terms the 'active compassion' of Theseus, Seneca's point more broadly is that the wise man will not feel pity at all: ameliorative acts will be performed 'with unruffled mind, and a countenance under control. The wise man, therefore, will not pity, but will succour' (Seneca cited in Basore 1928, II.6.3, p. 441). Tears are one manifestation of the feeling of pity, a heart that seems like it might break, as does Theseus's, is another.

9 For Jill Mann (1991, pp. 172, 173), pity has 'a levelling, unifying nature' with the 'power to overturn and obliterate the relationship between conqueror and suppliant', and she suggests that having Theseus dismount works to 'illustrate dramatically the levelling of conqueror with victims'. My understanding of pity in relation to power is different, as I suggest below, and I would further add that it is significant that the first thing Theseus does, having dismounted, is to raise the widows up from their still prostrate position on the ground ('he hem alle up hente', l. 957), as it is an act that dramatises their relative, differentiated, positions of power.
10 Hence the almost parodic response of Harry Bailly after hearing the 'Physician's Tale' where he says that grief almost caused him to have a heart attack ('I almost have caught a cardynacle') and that his 'herte is lost for pitee of this mayde' ('The Introduction to the Pardoner's Tale', ll. 313, 317).
11 The line appears in the 'Knight's Tale', l. 1761, 'Squire's Tale', l. 479, 'Merchant's Tale', l. 1986, and *Legend of Good Women*, F Prologue, l. 503. See also the 'Man of Law's Tale', l. 660: 'As gentil herte is fulfild of pitee'.
12 See Langum 2015, pp. 269–270 for discussion of the moistness of pity.
13 For the phlegmatic as piteous, see Yonge, J. 1898, *Gouernaunce of Prynces* in *Three Prose Versions of the Secreta Secretorum*, ed. R. Steele, EETS e.s. 74, Kegan Paul, Trench, Trübner & Co., London, p. 220, l. 11.
14 For a discussion of weeping across different categories of text, see Lynch, A. 1991, '"Now, fye on youre wepynge!": Tears in Medieval English Romance', *Parergon*, vol. 9, no. 1, pp. 43–62.
15 See, for example, Lydgate, J. 1924–1927, *Fall of Princes*, ed. H. Bergen, EETS e.s. 121, 122, 123, 124, 4 vols, Oxford University Press, London, 4.2961.
16 Helen Nicholson (2001, p. 98) suggests that given the association between the Templars and defence of the Holy Land, 'the appearance of the Templar was a signal to the audience that what followed was a holy war, depicting Arthur as a champion of Christianity'.
17 Benson, L. D. (ed.) and Foster, E. E. (rev.) 1994, *King Arthur's Death: The Middle English Stanzaic Morte Arthur and Alliterative Morte Arthure*, Medieval Institute Publications, Kalamazoo, ll. 843–852. Subsequent references are to this edition.
18 For other instances in the Alliterative *Morte Arthure*, see ll. 951, 2679, 3155, 3920, 4286 and of course the moment where the 'bold men' reprimand Arthur for his response to Gawain's death, saying 'This is bootless bale, for better bes it never! / It is no worship, iwis, to wring thine hands / To weep als a woman', ll. 3975–3977.
19 When Arthur learns that Gawain has landed, and fears he is dead, 'He al to-writhes for wo, and wringand his handes', l. 3920.
20 Malory, T. 2013, *Le Morte Darthur*, ed. P. J. C. Field, D. S. Brewer, Cambridge, vol. I, p. 154, ll. 11–24. Subsequent references are to this edition.
21 This is characteristic of Malory's style. As Andrew Lynch writes, 'the emotional cast of Malory's work can be hard to articulate, partly because the text seems sparing in interpretative commentary on the subject': *Malory's Book of Arms: The Narrative of Combat in Le Morte Darthur,* (D. S. Brewer 1997, Cambridge), p. 134.
22 Malory adds the detail that those killed were Arthur's 'trew lyege people'.
23 Similarly, Theseus's status as conqueror is emphasised in the widows' supplication.
24 For similar arguments following the fall of Constantinople in 1453, see Harris, J. 2017, 'Byzantine refugees as crusade propagandists: the Travels of Nicholas Agallon', in N. Housley (ed.), *The Crusade in the Fifteenth Century: Converging and Competing Cultures*, Routledge, London and New York, pp. 34–46.
25 I have slightly modified the translation. Alain Chartier also presents himself as 'moved by compassion' to write his *Quadrilogue Invectif* (Chartier 2011, p. 8, l. 4).
26 For example, a fifteenth-century sermon collection states that 'prowde men arn [. . .] harde in herte wyth-oute compassioun' (*Jacob's Well* 1900, ed. A. Brandeis, EETS o.s. 115, Kegan Paul, Trench, Trübner & Co, London, reprint 1973, p. 236, l. 29.

27 For discussion of treatments of shame in Middle English texts, see Trigg, S. 2012, *Shame and Honor: A Vulgar History of the Order of the Garter*, University of Pennsylvania Press, Philadelphia, pp. 130–132; Flannery, M. C. 2012, 'The Concept of Shame in Late-Medieval English Literature', *Literature Compass*, vol. 9, no. 2, pp. 166–182.

28 I am thinking here of accounts of Henry V's siege of Rouen (1418–1419). See, for example, the account of the siege written by John Page (Bellis, J. (ed.) 2015, *John Page's The Siege of Rouen*, Middle English Texts 51, Universitätsverlag Winter, Heidelberg).

Reference list

Augustine 1950, *City of God*, trans. Marcus Dods, Random House, New York.

Benson, L. D. Benson, L. D. (ed.) and Foster, E. E. (rev.) 1994, *King Arthur's Death: The Middle English Stanzaic Morte Arthur and Alliterative Morte Arthure*, Medieval Institute Publications, Kalamazoo.

Bergen, H. (ed.) 1906–35, *Lydgate's Troy Book*, EETS e.s. 97, 103, 106, 126, 4 vols, Kegan Paul, Trench, Trübner & Co., Oxford University Press, London.

Biblia Sacra Latina Ex Biblia Sacra Vulgatae Editionis, 1970, Samuel Bagster & Sons, London.

Blamires, A. 2006, *Chaucer, Ethics, and Gender*, Oxford University Press, Oxford.

Blayney, M. S. (ed.) 1974, 1980, *Fifteenth-Century English Translations of Alain Chartier's Le Traité de l'Esperance and Le Quadrilogue Invectif*, 2 vols, EETS o.s. 270, 281, Oxford University Press, Oxford.

Boccaccio, G. 1974, *The Book of Theseus*, trans. B. M. McCoy, Medieval Text Association, New York.

British Library, London ms Royal 18.B.XXII

Caxton, W. (trans.) 1937, *The Book of Fayttes of Armes and of Chyualrye*, ed. A. T. P. Byles, EETS o.s. 189, Oxford University Press, Oxford.

Chartier, A. 2011, *Le Quadrilogue Invectif*, ed. F. Bouchet, Honoré Champion, Paris.

Chaucer, G. 1987, *The Riverside Chaucer*, ed. L. D. Benson, 3rd edn, Oxford University Press, Oxford.

Cohen, J. J. 1999, *Of Giants: Sex, Monsters, and the Middle Ages*, University of Minnesota Press, Minneapolis.

Dan Michel's Ayenbite of Inwyt; or Remorse of Conscience 1965, ed. P. Gradon, EETS, o.s. 23, Oxford University Press, London.

Das Moralium Dogma Philosophorum des Guillaume de Conches, 1929, ed. J. Holmberg, Almquist & Wiksells, Uppsala.

de Mézières, P. 1975, *Letter to King Richard II*, trans. GW Coopland, Liverpool University Press, Liverpool.

Fowler, D. C., Briggs, C. F. & Remley, P. G. (eds) 1997, *The Governance of Kings and Princes: John Trevisa's Middle English Translation of the De Regimine Principum of Aegidius Romanus*, Routledge, New York.

Geoffrey of Monmouth 2007, *The History of the Kings of Britain: an edition and translation of De gestis Britonum [Historia Regum Britanniae]*, ed. M. Reeve & trans. N. Wright, Boydell Press, Woodbridge.

Havely, N. R. (ed. & trans.) 1980, *Chaucer's Boccaccio: Sources of Troilus and the Knight's and Franklin's Tales*, D. S. Brewer, Cambridge.

Langum, V. 2015, '"The Wounded Surgeon": Devotion, Compassion and Metaphor', in L. Tracy & K. DeVries (eds), *Wounds and Wound Repair in Medieval Culture*, Brill, Leiden.

Latini, B. 1948, *Li Livres dou Tresor*, ed. F. J. Carmody, University of California Press, Berkeley and Los Angeles.

Latini, B. 1993, *The Book of the Treasure (Li Livres dou Tresor)*, trans. P. Barrette & S. Baldwin, Garland, New York & London.

Layamon 2001, *Layamon's Arthur: The Arthurian Section of Layamon's Brut*, revised edn, ed. & trans. W. R. J. Barron & S. C. Weinberg, University of Exeter Press, Exeter.

McNamer, S. 2010, *Affective Meditation and the Invention of Medieval Compassion*, University of Pennsylvania Press, Philadelphia.

Malory, T. 2013, *Le Morte Darthur*, ed. P. J. C. Field. D. S. Brewer, Cambridge.

Mann, J. 1991, *Geoffrey Chaucer*, Harvester Wheatsheaf, Hemel Hempstead.

Nicholson, H. 2001, *Love, War and the Grail: Templars, Hospitallers and Teutonic Knights in Medieval Epic and Romance, 1150–1500*, Brill, Leiden.

Nolan, B. 1992, *Chaucer and the Tradition of the 'Roman Antique'*, Cambridge University Press, Cambridge.

Riddy, F. 1994, 'Engendering Pity in the Franklin's Tale', in R. Evans & L. Johnson (eds), *Feminist Readings in Middle English Literature: The Wife of Bath and All Her Sect*, Routledge, London.

Scrope, S. 1970, *The Epistle of Othea*, ed. C. F. Bühler, EETS o.s. 264, Oxford University Press, London.

Seneca, L. A. 1928, *Moral Essays*, vol. 1, trans. J. W. Basore, Heinemann, London & New York.

Sontag, S. 2004, *Regarding the Pain of Others*, Penguin, London.

The Book of Vices and Virtues: A Fourteenth Century English Translation of the 'Somme le Roi' of Lorens D'Orléans, 1942, ed. W. N. Francis, EETS o.s. 217, Oxford University Press, London.

Wace 1999, *Roman de Brut: A History of the British*, ed. & trans. by J. Weiss, Exeter University Press, Exeter.

Walker, C. G. 1998, An Edition with Introduction and Commentary of John Blount's English Translation of Nicholas Upton's *De Studio Militari*, 2 vols, unpublished doctoral thesis, University of Oxford, Oxford.

6

'THUS OF WAR, A PARADOX I WRITE'

Thomas Dekker and a Londoner's view of continental war and peace

Merridee L. Bailey

In the late sixteenth and early seventeenth centuries men and women in England could be forgiven for thinking war was all around them: the English war with Ireland, begun in 1594, had ended in ignoble fashion in 1603; the Spanish-Dutch war had started in 1566 as a revolt of the Seventeen Provinces against the Spanish Empire; England and Spain were in the grip of their own uneasy relationship, punctuated from 1585 by intermittent bursts of violence; and closer to home on English soil, apprehension about a possible state of civil war loomed. The succession of James I to the English throne in 1603 would turn out to be a smooth and unproblematic affair but an ageing Elizabeth I's refusal to name James publicly as her heir had encouraged a mood of insecurity. The circulation of information, rumours and reports about war in cheap pamphlets, as well as the public discussion about the scope of England's engagement in war in political treatises, contributed to the steady stream of late sixteenth- and early seventeenth-century literature alerting English audiences to military conflict. These contemporary writings about real and anticipated warfare reflected, intensified and gave voice to the varied and dissenting voices that could be heard speaking about war.

In these guises, war became a fashionable topic for the English presses. Reports on wars in Ireland, France and in the Netherlands made popular reading for English men and women, attested to in the growing proliferation of news pamphlets (Raymond 2006; Pettegree 2014). The appetite for news about war on the Continent was unsurprising given the close geographical and commercial ties between the English and the Dutch, as well as the ramifications conflict between Spain and the Dutch Republic had on English commercial and dynastic interests. With some speed, Thomas Dekker, who made a living writing professionally for London's theatres and the printing presses, turned the threat of war and the close commercial and political interests between England and the Continent into scenes in his plays and pamphlets. Performed on stage and read by London audiences, Dekker's writings became part of a culture of war writing in the early modern period.

This chapter explores Dekker's contribution to the contemporary literature on war. From Dekker's known works I identify 17 texts that refer to war, which I have included among his war writings. These are: *The Shoemaker's Holiday* (1600), *The Wonderfull Yeare* (1603), *The Meeting of Gallants* (possibly with Thomas Middleton, 1604), *Nevves from Graves-End Sent to Nobody* (again with Middleton, 1604), *The Seven Deadly Sinnes of London* (1606), *The Double PP* (1606), *A Worke for Armourers* (1609), *The Ravens Almanacke* (1609), *Foure Birdes of Noah's Arke* (1609), *The Roaring Girl* (with Middleton, 1611), *If it be not good, the Diuel is in it* (1612), *O per se O* (1616), *The Owles Almanacke* (attributed to Dekker, 1618), *A Rod for Run-Awayes* (1625), *Warres, Warres, Warres* (1628), *Looke vp and see Vvonders* (attributed to Dekker, 1628) and *The Honest Whore, Part II* (1630).[1] I focus on one of Dekker's central war themes from the first decade of the 1600s concerning overseas wars and London's commercial interests.[2] The texts, *A Shoemaker's Holiday*, *The Seven Deadly Sinnes of London*, and the related *A Worke for Armourers*, *The Meeting of Gallants* and *Warres, Warres, Warres*, form the core of this chapter, but other works are discussed when relevant.

Richard Strier has convincingly demonstrated that emotion was celebrated in sixteenth and seventeenth century drama. Early modern writers displayed 'emotional animation' and worldly enjoyment. Moreover, passion and pride 'unrepentantly' pervaded the period's plays (Strier 2011). Bridget Escolme (2013, p. xvi) also hypothesised that early modern theatre audiences 'went to watch extremes of emotion and to consider when those extremes became excesses'. To reflect on the emotional affect Dekker's war writings might have had on his audience I first make a close examination of how Dekker portrayed the negative effects of military conflict on two characters in *The Shoemaker's Holiday*.[3] Dekker gave teeth to war's emotional effect by focusing on its impact on ordinary citizens. Humanising the effects of war heightened the drama of the subject matter and served as a reflection of the ways in which war shook ordinary people in their day-to-day lives. However, I also agree with Strier and Escolme that while early modern people went to playhouses (and read books) to test the boundaries of social, political and emotional norms, we may be overlooking the more obvious point that people also wanted to be entertained. While this chapter focuses on the moral consequences of war and explores Dekker's skill in giving voice to complex and contested views about war's value and cost, that he was also trying to rouse emotions of enjoyment to retain his audience even about topics like war, death and grief, is quite likely.

The chapter first provides a portrait of Dekker and why his social commentary on war is worth exploring for the insights it gives into the intersections between early modern drama, reactions to war and early modern mentalities. I then examine the timing and content of particular works in relation to events occurring on the Continent. I discuss how the Anglo-Dutch relationship was viewed, particularly in terms of how the Dutch were represented in early modern drama, and why paying close attention to this clarifies how audiences interpreted the cultural and physical proximity between England and the Low Countries and made sense of war narratives. Throughout the chapter, the social, political and dramatic function that emotional language served in war writing is examined. Dekker drew on the playwright's craft of heightened emotional tone, rhetorical devices and allegorical imagery to influence his audiences' reactions to war.

Thomas Dekker: 'a professionally articulate man'

Literary scholars and historians who have written about Dekker have tended to justify their focus on him in one of two ways. Laura Caroline Stevenson (1984, p. 50) sees Dekker as representative of those 'professionally articulate men' who made their living in late Elizabethan and Jacobean London as writers for both the stage and the printing presses. Dekker's biography can indeed be mined for nuggets which locate him within his wider circle of peers who were writing citizen comedies for London's theatre-going crowds on topics that we assume entertained London's middle orders. In the first decade or so of his career Dekker wrote prolifically for the Henslowe Companies. After Elizabeth's death in 1603, Dekker, like Thomas Heywood, wrote for the Queen's Men. Again, like Heywood, Dekker penned numerous pamphlets about London city life and like many other popular writers incorporated the issues and concerns of day-to-day Londoners into his texts. As Stevenson remarks about Dekker and the popular playwrights of the day, including Heywood and William Haughton (1984, p. 50): 'The popularity of their works suggests that their attempts to reach a great number of people were successful'. Dekker's career milestones can be seen as typical for those in his chosen profession. Even Dekker's struggles with debt and poverty – he was imprisoned for debt in 1598 and 1599 and then again from *c.* 1612 until 1619 – were common hazards for professional writers, given the precariousness of writing for the playhouses in periods when plague threatened their closure.

Dekker also appeals to historians who can mine his writings for insight into the social history of non-elite London. Dekker's sensitivity to the particularities of London merchant livelihoods has been widely seen as a consistent feature of his writing and one of his strengths as an early modern voice of, and perhaps for, the non-elite. Dekker is increasingly viewed as an astute commentator on early modern life. Julia Gasper (1990) has attempted to see Dekker as driven by strong militant Protestantism, Normand Berlin (1966) and John Twyning (1998) have focused on the darker, angry, themes in Dekker's texts, while Matthew Kendrick (2011) explores the 'artisanal consciousness' of Dekker's plays. Common themes in early modern drama at this time included commercial life, overseas wars, material success, positive mercantile identity and a social order that was in flux. Dekker's concerns with commercial stability and prosperity, topics consistently incorporated into his war writings as they were in his other texts, were subjects that were valued by the majority of London's citizens who were engaged in trade and who were the audiences for much of the literature and drama that appeared in print and in the playhouses at this time.

Anna Bayman (2014) makes the crucial point that Dekker's most significant contribution to understanding early modern literature and its intersections with contemporary forms of thinking, including warfare, lies not just in exposing what was popular but in exposing the multiple contradictory voices and viewpoints about political decisions and social structures heard across London. Dekker penned sections in his texts that explicitly highlighted paradoxical reasoning, for example writing 'A paradox in praise of going to Law', 'A paradox in praise of a Pen' and 'A paradox in praise of Vacations' in *The dead tearme* (1608) and 'a Paradox in praise of Serieants' in *Jests to make you merie* (1607). The paradox of war with which I began this chapter also played out in Dekker's works, in which he represented the destructive and constructive aspects of both war and peace. War brought horror and death on a dramatic scale ('tread, Knee deep in blood, and trample on the Dead', 1628, B1v);[4] but it also curbed the excessive abundance and consumerism created by peace ('To cleanse the rancke-world, for to thee is giuen, The skill of Minerals, [lead, iron and steele]', 1628, B2v). Dekker's, *Warres, Warres, Warres*, (1628) shows him at his most explicit in voicing war's complexity, but this type of paradoxical thinking was typical for him, and his concern with the economic and social consequences of war and peace in particular accounts forms many of the paradoxes that can be found in his writings (Stevenson 1984; Seaver 2003; Bevington 2003).

The wider contemporary acknowledgement of contradictory and dissenting views about warfare has not gone unnoticed. Bayman (2014, p. 147) notes that 'even in 1623–5' there were dissenting voices in England about the direction of engagement in war, despite historians like Thomas Cogswell and Richard Cust arguing that there was an 'unusual degree' of public pressure driving attitudes. As well as providing a way for us to read Dekker's war writings, historians rightly point out that Elizabethan and Jacobean life was more generally awash with contradictory views and tensions about warfare, mercantile identity, social order, consumerism, trustworthiness and a host of other concerns (Seaver 2003; Bevington 2003; Mortenson 1976). As Bayman (2014, p. 147) argues, if anything helped the presses to thrive it was not 'uniformity and consensus' but multiple viewpoints, contradictory ideas and dissenting voices. Dekker's literary works were part of a wide tolerance during the early modern period for ambiguous and differing beliefs. Dekker's paradoxical writings on war are most revealingly read in this light.

The connection between contemporary wars and Dekker's works needs to be treated with some care since it is usually in a writer's best interests to promote the contemporary relevance of their work to increase their audience (Bayman 2014, p. 79). However, there are undeniable moments of intersection between Dekker's choice of topics and contemporary conflicts. The cultural proximity between this literature and attitudes towards the Dutch and to trade is an important point of connection in Dekker's war writings. But more than this, as Bayman (2014) suggests, to fail to note the broader intersections between Dekker's writings and current events means we fail to see how Dekker contributed to his period's wider cultural understanding of war and conflict. Plays and pamphlets which featured London soldiers, such as in *A Shoemaker's Holiday* (1600), war in an allegorical city much like London, described in *A Worke for Armourers* (1609), and the connections between war and London's outbreaks of plague, for example in *The Meeting of Gallants* (1604), made war relevant to London audiences, just as Dekker himself benefited from their timeliness.

The impact of war on mercantile London: overseas wars and trade

Real-world conflict in the Low Countries provided Dekker with opportunities to write – and importantly to sell – commercially relevant works. Much of Dekker's audience was centered upon the capital, given the higher literacy rates in towns in this period, the likely overlap between London's theatre-going audiences and those who were reading pamphlets, and the explicit London specificity that saturated Dekker's descriptions of space and day-to-day activities (Bayman 2014, pp. 29–36). In London, trade dominated the activities of the vast majority of the city's middle ranking population. These were the men and women who were involved with or touched by commercial interests in the everyday course of their lives. This was either through direct involvement in processing raw materials, making items for sale, or buying and selling commercial quantities of textiles, metalwork and foodstuffs, as well as those who worked in what would now be labeled the hospitality trade, which included anyone working in London's pubs, theatres and on the waterways. In addition, there was the informal illegal work of prostitutes and hucksters and the informal legal work of wives, daughters and sisters in household workshops. With most Londoners immersed to some degree in commerce, we should not under-estimate the city's preoccupation with events that impacted on supply, costs and overseas markets. Continental wars effected trade and commercial activities and became part of the everyday gossip that circulated within the city and grist for Dekker and his contemporaries' writings on war. For this reason, Dekker's war writings extend beyond technical or emotive descriptions of warfare to scrutinise ideas about honest labour, livelihoods and economic damage, all of which mattered in people's daily lives.

Since Elizabeth's reign, the economic implications of the Dutch-Spanish war had been among the most serious of these matters. Formal military assistance to the Dutch had been provided in the 1585 'treaty of assistance' in which the English provided 4,000 foot soldiers and 400 mounted soldiers.[5] Elizabeth's intention had been to protect the port of Antwerp, an economically significant goal given England's loss of its European port at Calais in 1558 (Poot 2013, p. 15). As Anton Poot (2013, p. 15) notes, this treaty was not a conventional diplomatic one but negotiated in terms of contractual exchange in which England supplied goods and services (soldiers) in exchange for cash payments and with further collateral for repayment set in the form of England's right to station troops in key overseas towns. Over the next few decades the English state would seek repayment for the agreed costs of this military help, a tangled state of affairs which mirrored the difficulties ordinary merchants so often faced when seeking repayment of loans; a theme often used in the plots of mercantile dramas and city-comedies from this same period (Poot 2013, p. 21). England's own commercial interests were complicated further by their conflict with Spain and the partially vested interests they had in an ongoing Spanish-Dutch war. While England provided support to the Dutch Republic in its war against Spain, following the Anglo-Spanish peace and commercial treaty in 1604 English commercial interests had benefitted from the Spanish embargoes preventing the Dutch from similar free trade with Iberia, which in turn left English merchants free to trade in the Peninsula. With the start of the 12-year truce between the Dutch and Spanish in 1609 these embargoes were lifted, meaning the Dutch and the English found themselves in direct trading competition.

Dekker's *The Seven Deadly Sinnes of London* (1606) and its spin-off, *A Worke for Armourers* (1609), were timed to take advantage of these events.[6] *The Seven Deadly Sinnes* was published in 1606 when the Dutch-Spanish war was at a stalemate, largely because neither side was able to fund the armies needed to mount a decisive victory. Instead, in 1606 reluctant peace negotiations between Spain and the Netherlands began. The conflict between the Spanish and the Dutch was cited in the second part of *The Seven Deadly Sinnes*, entitled 'Warres': 'No, nor all those late acts of warre and death, commenced by Hispaniolized Netherlanders' (Dekker 1606, B4r). This was only one of several wars Dekker referred to in the passage but a margin note: 'Low country warres' draws attention to this conflict and uses readers' current knowledge about neighbouring countries to introduce the allegorical tale in which Money and Poverty fight a war for dominion over the earth.

Other references to war appeared in the opening to *The Seven Deadly Sinnes* (1606) proper, in which Continental conflicts were again a focus of attention:

> Antwerp (the eldest daughter of Brabant) hath falne in her pride, the Citties of rich Burgundy in theyr greatnes. Those seuenteene Dutch Virgins of Belgia, (that had Kingdomes to theyr dowries, and were worthy to be courted by Nations) are now no more Virgins: the Souldier hath deflowred them, and robd them of theyr Mayden honor.
> (Dekker 1606, A1v–A2r)

Dekker's language is rhetorically forceful and plays upon the notion of war and the stain of rape, but also of war as polluting and contaminating: 'the Warre hath still vse of their noble bodyes, and discouereth theyr nakednes like prostituted Strumpets' (1606, A2r). There is an emotional shift between the imagery of maidens' honour and prostituted strumpets, but in both cases the language is intended to arouse an emotional reaction to the destruction and pollution of war.

Dekker extends the themes of pollution and destruction by stating that London faced even more devastation than its neighbouring war-torn countries because of the plague's arrival in the city. War, plague and famine were recurring and often connected themes for Dekker. The emotions and language attributed to plague in particular often closely mirror those associated with war, and vice versa.[7] In *The Meeting of Gallants* (1604) the personifications of War, Famine and Pestilence try to outdo each other in descriptions of their destructive power. Pestilence uses the language and imagery of war to evoke terror at its power:

> As for lame persons, and maimed Souldiers
> There I outstrip thée too; how many Swarmes
> Of bruised and crackt people did I leaue
> Their Groines sore pier'st with pestilentiall Shot:
> Their Arme-pits digd with Blaines, and vicerous Sores,
> Lurking like poysoned Bullets in their flesh?
> (Middleton & Dekker 1604, A3r)

While war was a theme that allowed Dekker to explore the uncertainties of living in the early modern period, the plague's impact on the London population was highly acute for Dekker and his contemporaries. The astronomical death rates, loss of livelihoods and a state of pervasive fear were all felt close to home. Dekker's many plague-writings reveal the heavy cost recurrent plague outbreaks caused in London. However, by drawing attention to the likenesses between plague and war in his works, including the application of military expressions and war machinery to descriptions of plague ('pier'st with pestilentiall *Shot*', 'poysoned *Bullets*'), Dekker coupled the experiences of both, heightening the emotional content of each and reinforcing their analogous destructive power.

The timing for the publication of *The Seven Deadly Sinnes* (1606) and the republication of the section 'Warres' a few years later is significant. The peace negotiations between Spain and the Netherlands, which had begun when *The Seven Deadly Sinnes* was published were successfully concluded with the signing of a 12-year truce in 1609 for which England and France acted as guarantees (Poot 2013, p. 19). With some speed Dekker and his publisher, Nathaniel Butter, took advantage of the newsworthiness of the 1609 treaty and reissued 'Warres' as a discrete work complete with a new title, *A Worke for Armourers* (1609). A newly written dedication and opening referred to the now ended wars between Spain and the Netherlands: 'The Hollander and the Spaniard haue bene (and I thinke still are) your best Lords and Maisters' and again: 'Yet euen those Dutch warres, haue bene vnto you that seru'd in them, but as wares in these dead times are to Merchants and Tradsemen' (Dekker 1609, A1r, A1v). Apart from the new opening the rest of the tale was left intact since the allegorical story which explored socio-economic conflict, the gap between the rich and the poor, and the ethics of consumption had ongoing relevance (as well as requiring much less revision) making the turn-around even faster for Dekker and Butter. The point Dekker was making *in A Worke for Armourers* was that all of these real wars were as nothing compared to the bloodshed and violence about to unfold in his allegorical tale when the rich and the poor would do battle. While Dekker thus wrote about real wars he also explored war in fictional registers, often using one of his favoured literary styles of allegory or writing dialogues between different personifications, for example, War, Famine and Pestilence in *The Meeting of Gallants* (1604) or the cities, London and Westminster, in *The dead tearme* (1608). These highly fictionalised works provided Dekker with a separate register through which to present his audience with abstract cautionary tales about war's consequences.[8]

The Dutch in England: comic figures and darker military subplots

To understand why Dekker's war writings from the 1600s were so observant of conflicts happening in the lowlands, just as they were of the threat of civil war and turbulent socio-economic conditions, we need not only to understand the impact that war between the Dutch and Spanish had on London's commercial stability, but also to appreciate the sheer number of foreigners of Dutch origins living in London at that time. From the mid-sixteenth to the early seventeenth centuries the Dutch were the largest alien population in the city (Rubright 2014, pp. 2, 12). Many of these migrants were seeking an escape from the conflict with Spain. The close commercial ties between London merchants and the Dutch meant that exchanges between groups and individuals were both personal and professional. Marjorie Rubright (2014) identifies the complex ways in which the Dutch were represented in literary texts at this time, sometimes as friends and allies, sometimes as deceitful or as figures of fun.

In one of Dekker's most successful plays, *The Shoemaker's Holiday* (1600), the connection between war and (pseudo-) Dutch characters is key to the play's plot. One of the central characters, the aristocrat Roland Lacy, deserts from the English army having hypocritically conscripted another central character, the journeyman Rafe. Lacy spends the majority of the play impersonating a Dutch shoemaker to comic affect – ironically in Rafe's own former workshop. Lacy speaks with a deliberately dreadful Dutch accent – 'Yaw yaw...voour mack shoes groot and cleane' (Dekker 1600, C3v) – a trope Rubright (2014, p. 44) identifies as 'inauthentic stage Dutch'. Lacy's speech patterns were intended for comic effect but we should remember that Londoners heard authentic Dutch spoken throughout the city's streets (Rubright 2014, p. 92).[9] Lacy's Dutch persona is a comic one and he is by no means a sinister figure – perhaps because the war in this play takes place between the English and the French – but his characterisation no doubt played upon Londoners' ambiguous attitudes towards skilled Dutch craftsmen by reinforcing stereotyped differences between the native English and Dutch peoples.

Dekker's other well-known play, *The Roaring Girl* (1611), co-written with Middleton, reworked similar themes. In this play the villainous English-speaking Tearcat assumes a Dutch accent to cheat money from Moll, Sir Beauteous and

Jack Dapper. But Tearcat also claimed to have been wounded in wars overseas in order to gain sympathy. He identifies himself as: 'A man beaten from the wars sir', while another character, Trapdoor, remarks: 'Your Worship will not abuse a souldier' (Middleton & Dekker 1611, K3v, K3r). Because of the emotional connotations war carries in the plays, it is an inducement to sympathy and concern. But it also begets falsity and provides easy opportunities for deception. These themes are more fully developed in *A Shoemaker's Holiday* (1600). Sitting alongside the comic-romantic plot in which Lacy's Dutch persona is a figure of fun is a much darker military theme which gives voice to the social and emotional implications of war. Major themes include the turmoil caused by conscription; the anguish of losing loved ones to war either through their absence or death; the emotional costs paid by returning wounded soldiers; and the disruption war brings to honest household workshops.

While much of *The Shoemaker's Holiday* (1600) is a reworking of Delaney's *The Gentle Craft* (published 1597), Dekker overlaid the original story with a new focus on military service, returning soldiers, conscription and desertion (Womack 2008, pp. 157–161). While Dekker's play was published in 1600 it is set in an unspecified past around the time of England's fifteenth century wars in France, but the play's theme of conscription was highly topical for London at the start of the seventeenth century. 12,000 men had recently been mustered to fight in Ireland with a further 4,000 needed almost immediately after, with London supplying 1,000 men (Seaver 2003, pp. 87–89). Dekker created the character Rafe who is conscripted to fight in France and who is central to the war arc and through whom we see many of war's social, economic and emotional consequences. This included war's effects on different characters' emotional constancy. Throughout the play Dekker associates war with injustice of different types, although he does so subtly without explicitly referring to unfairness in any of the speeches. However, it is there for the London audience to spot. The honest merchant Rafe's war injuries were unjust because the aristocratic deserter Lacy had conscripted him. Lacy unjustly suffers no loss of aristocratic status through his own desertion. Rafe's young wife, Jane, is lied to and deceived over her husband's supposed death and tricked by the villainous (albeit strangely sincere) Hammond into near marriage. These injustices are given colour and narrative impact because they are related to crises in personal relationships. This gives Dekker room to write about the emotional costs of warfare for ordinary citizens.

Much of this emotional work is done through various characters' reports on the emotions and physical demeanours of others, not all of which is sympathetic. Before she even speaks, the references to Jane focus on her tears at Rafe's departure: 'Leaue whining, leaue whining, away with this whimpring, this pewling, these blubbring teares, and these wet eies' (Dekker 1600, B3r). She is also introduced as: 'and this is blubbered Iane' and then again: 'She cannot speake for weeping' (Dekker 1600, B3r, B4r). It is possible the other characters see her tears as insincere. In her first lines, Jane herself describes her dread at Rafe's departure: 'O let him stay, else I shal be vndone' (Dekker 1600, B3r). The 'vndone' hints at her –

ultimately correct – realisation that her husband's conscription into the army means her security as the newly married wife of an honest guildsman is about to change. Her fears continue to be associated with her financial security: 'what shal I do when he is gone?' The character Firk answers 'be not idle', that is, work and earn an honest living. The character Eyre is even more direct, hinting that Jane has been unused to manual work: 'Let me see thy hand Iane, this fine hand, this white hand, these prettie fingers must spin, must card, must worke, worke you bembast cotten-candle-queane, worke for your liuing with a pox to you' (Dekker 1600, B4v). Jane's emotions, and the physical display of them in the form of her tears, are obliquely styled as being not the 'right' kind and her peers dismiss them and her. Jane's love is not self-less and her tears and fearful exclamations may have been intended to disturb audiences. This was not because her reactions were excessive but because they were nakedly self-focused. We know negative responses were not a knee-jerk reaction to tears. When Rafe later cries in the play the characters respond quite differently. We know the actor would have simulated crying on the stage because other characters draw attention to his tears, asking: 'Rafe, why dost thou weepe?' and again 'hees ouercome with sorrowe, he does but as I doe, weepe for the losse of any good thing' (Dekker 1600, E4v). Rafe's tears are sympathetically viewed and his tears are not dismissed as Jane's had been. Dekker uses explicit dialogue between the other characters to show their reactions to tears and emotions in order to influence the audience into forming a particular view of individual personalities, trustworthiness and likeability.

Dekker, however, manipulates several emotional registers in the Rafe-Jane relationship and it is not ultimately clear that Jane's fearful state is focused on the financial cost of war. Rafe himself emphasises her emotional, romantic, commitment to him – 'Now gentle wife, my louing louely Iane' – giving her a gift of a pair of shoes. The shoes represent his craftsman's skill and his hours of labour, but Rafe's description also presses home how intimate his gift is: 'And euerie morning when thou pull'st them on, Remember me, and pray for my returne, Make much of them, for I have made them so, That I can know them from a thousand mo' (Dekker 1600, B4v).[10] Jane herself later grieves for his presumed death overseas and repeatedly reiterates her love for Rafe: 'I haue but one heart, and that hearts his due'; 'Thogh he be dead, my loue to him shal not be buried' (Dekker 1600, F4v, G1r). Jane's emotional experiences unfold in more complex ways over the course of the play with the audience shown how her grief moulds her actions and decisions. Her tears in the later scenes are commented on more sympathetically by her would-be suitor, Hammond: 'Come, weepe not: mourning though it rise from loue, Helpes not the mourned, yet hurtes them that mourne' (Dekker 1600, G1r). By drawing attention to theirs as a marriage of on-going affection as well as one of financial security, Dekker heightens the emotional impact of Jane's loss. For her, the wars are bitter because of her personal suffering at many levels: 'Prest was he to these bitter warres in France, Bitter they are to me by wanting him' (Dekker 1600, F4v).

One consequence of war is that soldiers return to their homes after the fighting is over. Returning soldiers were frequently identified as a threat to Elizabethan and Jacobean London because they were thought to be unruly, threated good order and were often unemployed (Ruff 2001, pp. 64–66). Dekker comments on this problem in *Warres, Warres, Warres* (1628, D3r) when he writes about the bleakness of the returning soldier's plight:

> Thus, Home at last, the Souldier comes,
> As vselesse as the Hung-vp Drums:
> And (but by Noble hands being Fed,
> May beg hard; hardly yet get Bread.

Dekker was sympathetic to the difficulties soldiers faced. In *Newes from Graves-End* (1604, D2r) he draws attention to the unfairness of the physical toll they were forced to pay for England's peace: 'The Souldiers staruing at the doore, Ragd, leane, and pale through want of blood, Sold cheape by him for Countries good'.[11] Many soldiers returned to their homes maimed and physically altered by their experiences and injured soldiers would have been a fairly common sight in London. When Rafe returns to London missing one of his legs he fears what has become of Jane in his absence and how he will now support her. His concerns over how his injuries will affect his livelihood, however, are dealt with summarily:

> Rafe.
> ...Where liues my poore heart? sheel be poore indeed
> Now I want limbs to get whereon to feed.
> Roger.
> Limbs? hast thou not hands man? thou shalt neuer see a shoomaker want bread, though he haue but three fingers on a hand.
> Rafe.
> Yet all this while I heare not of my Iane.
>
> (Dekker 1600, E4r)

In this play, the cost of Rafe's war injuries is not his productivity (he can still work to make shoes with his hands) or even his emotional sense of wholeness as a man, but his relationship with Jane. In this tale, wartime injuries are significant, not because they threaten social harmony and public order, but because they play on an intimate and primal fear about surviving war, but being left unrecognisable to the people left behind.

Quickly sidestepping the real economic harm of injuries sustained in war frees Dekker to concentrate on the emotional toll it exacts from those who fought. Far more pressing than whether Rafe can work again is that his wounds have made him unrecognisable to Jane and when he finally finds her she does not know him: 'I lookte vpon her, and she vpon me . . . my lame leg, and my trauel beyond sea made me vnknown' (Dekker 1600, H4v). The play fudges the question of why

Jane cannot recognise him, given that he has, after all, lost his leg and not suffered injuries to his face. The full nature of Rafe's war wounds is never made entirely clear. One stage direction notes: 'Enter Rafe being lame' and shortly after one of the characters exclaims: 'Lord how the warres haue made him Sunburnt: the left leg is not wel it was a faire gift of God the infirmitie tooke not hold a litle higher' (Dekker 1600, E4r).

War also created opportunities for people to take advantage of others and act duplicitously or falsely. Rafe learns that the villainous, and wealthier, Hammond has told Jane that Rafe has died overseas, leaving her free to remarry, despite her ongoing commitment to remain a widow. However, Hammond's lies are exposed and Rafe is finally revealed to her by the intervention of Rafe's co-worker Hodge, who still has to point out to Jane that the unrecognisable man 'lamed by war' is her husband:

> Hodge
> > Ile shew you: Iane, dost thou know this man? tis Rafe I can tell thee: nay, tis he in faith, though he be lamde by the warres, yet looke not strange, but run to him, fold him about the necke and kisse him.
> Iane
> > Liues then my husband? oh God let me go,
> > Let me embrace my Rafe.
>
> > > > > > > > > > > > > > (Dekker 1600, L1r)

The emotional outbursts from Rafe and Jane, again often depicted through descriptions of their weeping, allows Dekker to focus his audience's attention on war's cost for human subjects. Jane and Rafe weep at different moments in the play to physically express their feelings. The other characters draw attention to their tears, sometimes sympathetically and sometimes less so, but each time, their explicit dialogue about the character's emotional presentation highlights the emotional salience of war to the audience. By separating his young couple through Rafe's conscription, by making them verbally express their suffering and by showing them weeping, Dekker made war and the plight of ordinary soldiers and families highly personal and intimate.

At the very end of the play Dekker extends war's impact beyond the personal and individual. The play ends on a jarring note at the final celebratory banquet when all of the romantic entanglements have been satisfactorily untangled and everyone should exit the stage happy and satisfied. Instead, the King announces that war with France will begin anew with another round of conscription: 'We wil incorporate a new supply: Before one summer more passe ore my head, France shal repent England was iniured' (Dekker 1600, K3v). The final lines of the play are given to the call for war: 'When all our sports, and banquetings are done, Warres must right wrongs which frenchmen haue begun' (Dekker 1600, K4v). But this final scene is ambiguous. The lines lack a celebratory ring and the overall effect is one of being jolted out of the successful conclusion of the romantic and comic plot and back into the real world where war looms on London's horizon (Mortenson 1976, pp. 251–252).

Afterword: War in the 1620s

War did, in fact, loom. While *A Shoemaker's Holiday* (1600) was ostensibly set in the past and referred to older wars in France, audiences could easily have related the tale to current events. The relations between the Dutch and the English had become increasingly strained during the 1610s, so that by 1621 when the 12-year truce had ended, competition over fishing rights, whaling and the cloth trade meant that relations between English and Dutch merchants were particularly poor (Poot 2013, p. 24). The 1623 Amboyna incident, when the Dutch East India Company (VOC) summarily executed 10 Englishmen from the competing English East India Company (EIC) on dubious treason charges, led to worsening trade relations between the Dutch and the English. Because of what would now be described as heavy media reporting in England, public reaction and sentiment to the Dutch worsened.[12] At the same time, it was politically useful for James I to agree to the Anglo-Dutch mutual defence treaty in June 1624, not least as England was enmeshed in an even messier situation with Spain over the possible marriage of James's son, Charles, to Phillip III's daughter, dubbed the 'Spanish Match' (Poot 2013, pp. 25–26). There was significant debate in Parliament and among the general population about whether peace or war with Spain was the desirable course of action. In 1625, Dekker wrote about the array of conflicts in Europe and Spain's role in (literally) fuelling war by flinging about its 'fire-brands':

> Looke vpon Denmarke, Sweden, and those Easterne Countries: How often hath the voice of the Drumme called them vp? Euen now, at this houre, the Marches are there beating. How hath the Sword mowed downe the goodly Fields of Italy? What Massacres hath in our memory beene in France? Oh Germany! what foundations of bloud haue thy Cities beene drowned in? what horrors, what terrors, what hellish inventions haue not warre found out to destroy thy buildings, demollish thy Free States, and vtterly to confound thy 17. Prouinces? . . . In all these thy miseries, the Spaniard hath had his triumphs; his Fire-brands haue been flung about to kindle and feede all thy burnings; his furies haue for almost foure score yeeres stood, and still stand beating at the Anuils, and forging Thunder-bolts to batter thee, and all thy neighbouring Kingdomes in pieces.
>
> (1625, A3v)

By this time James's early interest in diplomacy with Spain had changed dramatically and England declared war in 1625, a policy about-face that Cogswell (2005, p. 1) sums up as part of the 'murkier aspects' of the period's foreign and domestic policy. A few years later, in 1628, Dekker reflected on England's position in relation to war: 'Thy Land-Souldiers (O England) shall not stand in feare of any Italian Spin[. . .]|laes; nor thy Nauy Royall of any Spanish Armadoes: For, thine enemies that rise agaynst thee, shall fall before thy face' (1628, B2r).

Public debates about England's involvement in war in the 1610s and 1620s ranged from supportive to dissenting across a range of genres, including plays, pamphlets, sermons, openly spoken resistance in public places like alehouses, and royal proclamations (Cogswell 2005, p. 312). Understanding how the public debated war and peace has occupied historians for some time, however, as Bayman (2014) suggests, there was a greater diversity of opinion about war's merits and costs than has perhaps been recognised. Dekker's "paradoxical" writings about war were not an attempt to work through competing claims to achieve a resolution to the 'problem' of war, but rather indicate a deeper acceptance of conflicting impulses about the nature of war in the early modern period. Bayman (2014, p. 143) argues that: 'commercial prosperity and the social order – rather than confessional struggle, international harmony, and the balance of European power relations through dynastic unions – were the principle considerations' of Dekker's war writings. That is, to Dekker it was the ordinary implications of war, rather than war's international, political ramifications, that preoccupied him. To this I would add that Dekker not only represented war's effects on ordinary citizens to give these multiple perspectives a voice, but that part of how he did so was by acknowledging the emotional cost of warfare on ordinary people and the toll war took on the emotional quality of people's lives.

Conclusion

For Dekker, war tropes, along with other catastrophic events such as the plague, served as means to explore subject matters perennially preoccupying him. Perfectly fitting the turbulence of his times, war was one of Dekker's themes – although not his only choice of themes – to scrutinise certain social and emotional features of the early modern world. That war became a way to comment on social practices and uncertainty with life in early modern London is not surprising given how easy it is for war to act as a lightning rod for social, cultural and emotional anxieties. Within these texts several themes are repeated. The emotional cost of warfare, the fate of returning injured soldiers, and the deceit and falsity that war encouraged in men and women are all identified and reflected upon through different story arcs. Plays such as *The Shoemaker's Holiday* (1600) emphasised the consequences of warfare on honest merchants, the damage war caused to personal (romantic) and domestic relationships and the injustices of war. The plight of soldiers was also noticed in *Warres, Warres, Warres* (1628), a text that finds Dekker at his most explicit in talking about the paradox of war. *The Seven Deadly Sinnes* (1606) and *A Worke for Armourers* (1609) display a keen attention to current events on the Continent. War writings such as *A Meeting of Gallants* (1604) focused on war and plague in a fictional register through a dialogue between War, Famine and Pestilence. Allegory was also used in *A Worke for Armourers* to draw parallels between an allegorical city under siege and London. In the midst of such turbulence Dekker takes care to underscore the costs of war but also its ambiguities. In the context of almost endemic warfare in Europe, fears over civil war, and debates about England's involvement in conflicts, Dekker's texts draw attention to the multifaceted nature of war and the breadth of its impact on Londoners.

Notes

1. Not all of these texts exclusively concern war. Instead, each text describes war or refers to war or soldiers in a way that is helpful in understanding the theme of war across Dekker's corpus. This is not an exhaustive list: war is also tangentially referred to in many other plays and pamphlets not mentioned here. *The Wonderfull Yeare*, *The Ravens Almanacke* and *Foure Birdes of Noah's Arke* allude to fears with war on English soil.
2. War has been analysed as a key plot device or backdrop in Dekker's stories. Morrow (2014) highlights how Dekker uses war to explore national and occupational identity; Bayman (2014) gives consideration to the threat of civil war; Cañadas (2002) explores war through the lens of interclass conflict; Lee (2015) makes connections between war and money's role in mercantile social cohesion.
3. Getting at the emotional reactions Dekker's audiences may have had when reading or hearing his work, or when going to his plays, can only be speculative, a point Escolme (2013) raises and which Hobgood's (2014) more extensive study of the theatre as a place of 'emotional practice' still only nods towards.
4. The quotation in this chapter's title is found on D3v.
5. This was extended with further foot and mounted soldiers after the fall of Antwerp in the 'treaty of increased assistance' (Poot 2013, p. 15)
6. The text is also described as: an example of prison writing (Shaw 1947); a pamphlet on London's sins with an appended section on war (Bayman 2014, p. 133); a plague pamphlet (Munro 2000); and a discussion on contemporary sins (Harris 2008).
7. Famine is a third recurring topic. See *The Ravens Almanacke* (1609), with Middleton in *A Meeting of Gallants* (1604), *The Colde Year* (1614), *A Rod for Run-Awayes* (1625) and Dekker and Middleton in *Newes from Graves-End* (1604).
8. I have elsewhere written about the economic meaning of *A Worke for Armourers* (Bailey 2018).
9. On whether such effects marginalised foreigners see Burke (2004); Dillon (2006) and Kermode (2009).
10. The significance of Rafe's gift of shoes has been explored by Kendrick (2011, pp. 268–269).
11. In *O per se O* Dekker also calls for people to give alms to maimed soldiers.
12. On how attitudes to the Dutch changed in the period's drama after the 'Amboyna massacre' see Rubright (2014, pp. 212–234).

Reference list

Bailey, M. L. 2018, 'The Importance of Equilibrium in Thomas Dekker's *A Worke For Armourers (1609)*', *English Studies*, vol 99.2, pp. 1–17.

Bayman, A. 2014, *Thomas Dekker and the Culture of Pamphleteering in Early Modern London*, Ashgate, Farnham.

Berlin, N. 1966, 'Thomas Dekker: A Partial Reappraisal', *Studies in English Literature*, vol. 6, no. 2, pp. 263–277.

Bevington, D. 2003, 'Theatre as Holiday', in D. L. Smith, R. Strier & D. Bevington (eds), *The Theatrical City: Culture, Theatre and Politics in London, 1576–1649*, Cambridge University Press, Cambridge, pp. 101–116.

Burke, P. 2004, *Languages and Communities in Early Modern Europe*, Cambridge University Press, Cambridge.

Cañadas, I. 2002, 'Class, Gender and Community in Thomas Dekker's *The Shoemaker's Holiday* and Lope de Vega's *Fuente Ovejuna*', *Parergon*, vol. 19, pp. 119–150.

Cogswell, T. 2005, *The Blessed Revolution: English Politics and the Coming of War, 1621–1624*, Cambridge University Press, Cambridge.

Dekker, T. 1600, *The shomakers holiday. Or The gentle craft VVith the humorous life of Simon Eyre, shoomaker, and Lord Maior of London . . .*, Valentine Sims, London.

Dekker, T. 1604, *Newes from Graves-End Sent to Nobody*, T[homas] C[reede] for Thomas Archer, London.

Dekker, T. 1606, *The seuen deadly sinnes of London drawne in seuen seuerall coaches, through the seuen seuerall gates of the citie bringing the plague with them. Opus septem dierum*, E[dward] A[llde and S. Stafford] for Nathaniel Butter, London.

Dekker, T. 1609, *Worke for armorours: or, The peace is broken Open warres likely to happin this yeare 1609*, Printed [by Nicholas Okes] for Nathaniel Butter, London.

Dekker, T. 1625, *A rod for run-awayes Gods tokens, of his feareful iudgements, sundry wayes pronounced vpon this city, and on seuerall persons, both flying from it, and staying in it. Expressed in many dreadfull examples of sudden death*, [By G. Purslowe] for Iohn Trundle, London.

Dekker, T. 1628, *Looke vp and see vvonders A miraculous apparition in the ayre, lately seene in Barke-shire at Bawlkin Greene neere Hatford. April. 9th. 1628* [By N. Okes] for Roger Michell, London.

Dekker, T. 1628, *Warres, warre[s,] warres*, [By Nicholas Okes] for I. G[rismand?], London.

Dillon, J. 2006, *Language and Stage in Medieval and Renaissance England*, Cambridge University Press, Cambridge.

Escolme, B. 2013, *Emotional Excess on the Shakespearean Stage*, Bloomsbury Arden Shakespeare, London.

Gasper, J. 1990, *The Dragon and the Dove: The Plays of Thomas Dekker*, Oxford University Press, Oxford.

Harris, J. G. 2008, 'Ludgate Time: Simon Eyre's Oath and the Temporal Economies of *The Shoemaker's Holiday*', *Huntington Library Quarterly*, vol. 71, pp. 11–32.

Hobgood, A. P. 2014, *Passionate Playgoing in Early Modern England*, Cambridge University Press, Cambridge.

Kendrick, M. 2011, '"A Shoemaker Sell Flesh and Blood – O Indignity!": The Labouring Body and Community in The Shoemaker's Holiday', *English Studies*, vol. 92, pp. 259–273.

Kermode, L. E. 2009, *Aliens and Englishness in Elizabethan Drama*, Cambridge University Press, Cambridge.

Lee, H. L. 2015, 'The Social Meaning of Money in Dekker's *The Shoemaker's Holiday* and Shakespeare's *The Merchant of Venice*', *Comparative Drama*, vol. 49, pp. 335–366.

Middleton, T. & Dekker, T. 1604, *The meeting of gallants at an ordinarie: or The walkes in Powles*, T. C[reede], London.

Middleton, T. & Dekkar, T. 1611, *The roaring girle. Or Moll Cut-Purse As it hath lately beene acted on the Fortune-stage by the Prince his Players*, [By Nicholas Okes] for Thomas Archer, London.

Morrow, C. L. 2014, 'Corporate Nationalism in Thomas Dekker's The Shoemaker's Holiday', *Studies in English Literature*, vol. 54, pp. 423–454.

Mortenson, P. 1976, 'The Economics of Joy in the Shoemaker's Holiday', *Studies in English Literature*, vol. 16, pp. 241–252.

Munro, I. 2000, 'The City and its Double: Plague Time in Early Modern London', *English Literary Renaissance*, vol. 30, pp. 241–261.

Pettegree, A. 2014, *The Invention of News: How the World Came to Know About Itself*, Yale University Press, New Haven & London.

Poot, A. 2013, *Crucial Years in Anglo-Dutch Relations (1625–1642): The Political and Diplomatic Contacts*, Verloren, Hilversum.

Raymond, J. 2006, *Pamphlets and Pamphleteering in Early Modern Britain*, Cambridge University Press, Cambridge.

Rubright, M. 2014, *Doppelgänger Dilemmas: Anglo-Dutch Relations in Early Modern English Literature and Culture*, University of Pennsylvania Press, Philadelphia.

Ruff, J. R. 2001, *Violence in Early Modern Europe 1500–1800*, Cambridge University Press, Cambridge.

Seaver, P. S. 2003, 'The Artisanal World', in D. L. Smith, R. Strier & D. Bevington (eds), *The Theatrical City: Culture, Theatre and Politics in London, 1576–1649*, Cambridge University Press, Cambridge, pp. 87–100.

Shaw, P. 1947, 'The Position of Thomas Dekker in Jacobean Prison Literature', *MLA*, vol. 62, pp. 366–391.

Stevenson, L. C. 1984, *Praise and Paradox: Merchants and Craftsmen in Elizabethan Popular Literature*, Cambridge University Press, Cambridge.

Strier, R. 2011, *The Unrepentant Renaissance: From Petrarch to Shakespeare to Milton*, University of Chicago Press, Chicago.

Twyning, J. 1998, *London Dispossessed: Literature and Social Space in the Early Modern City*, St Martin's Press, New York.

Womack, P. 2008, *English Renaissance Drama*, Blackwell, Malden.

7

CORRESPONDING ROMANCES

Henri II and the last campaigns of the Italian Wars

Susan Broomhall

In the last days of the Italian Wars, a conflict that had divided European states for more than 50 years, four key political protagonists in France exchanged letters. French campaigns against Habsburg forces in the north had separated the king, Henri II, from his queen Catherine de' Medici, his mistress Diane de Poitiers, the Duchess of Valentinois, and his chief military advisor, the constable Anne de Montmorency. During this time, four individuals whose political fates were tightly interwoven took to letters to express their hopes, desires and fears at war. Courtly correspondence always operated within particular rhetorical and material conventions, and with symbolic and practical purposes. War, as this chapter argues, not only forged a particular epistolary culture among these four individuals, but created distinctive expressive capacity for feelings unique to their letters.

Henri's letters were composed both as he led military campaigns away from the court, and as campaigns separated him from his leading political advisors. The constable Montmorency, for example, was captured at the French defeat of the Battle of Saint-Quentin and securing his release appears a key motivation for Henri's negotiations of the Peace of Cateau-Cambrésis in August 1559, which definitively ended the Italian Wars. As Henri's designated regent while on campaign, Catherine maintained, with his council, the everyday business of government and negotiated war's exceptional demands for military provisions and financial support. She conducted complementary operations in the advancement of Valois political objectives during the wars, often at a distance from her husband (Broomhall 2018a). While these letters talk about the details of war, including troop movements, supplies, specific actions within particular campaigns and liaisons between military leaders, in this chapter I focus on war's emotionally expressive dimensions within this epistolary culture. War created opportunities for articulation of sentiments by all four protagonists in letters. These sentiments differed not only from each other but from the feelings expressed in other political contexts in which each of the four also wrote letters. War was not simply the context in which these letters were produced. As this chapter argues, war was also a significant cultural force that provided the scaffolding of feeling expression in these letters, and more broadly, the practice and display of feelings in the courtly environment.

In particular, this chapter examines the epistolary production of feeling by the man who was at the court's centre, Henri II. The rhetorical expertise of early modern elite women in the genre of letter writing is now receiving important scholarly attention (Daybell 2001, 2006; Caine 2015; Daybell & Gordon 2016). This includes analysis of the distinctive communicative strategies of Catherine de' Medici and Diane de Poitiers (Crawford 2001, 2004; McCartney 2005; Crouzet 2008; Gellard 2015; Broomhall 2018b). By contrast, the extensive correspondence of, and between, Henri II and Anne de Montmorency has primarily served as key evidence in analyses of their military and political achievements (Decrue 1885; Baumgartner 1988; Rentet 2011). Only recently have scholars begun to consider the wealth of correspondence produced in the course of these responsibilities for its textual and epistolary insights (Pardanaud 2006). Feelings were also perceptible in the material qualities of the letters' exchanges among these protagonists – autograph components, and postscript additions among them – in ways that both reflected and actively shaped relationships. Although we may never know whether or how Henri and his correspondents experienced the feelings that they expressed, we can fruitfully consider how the articulation of certain feelings in precise ways to particular individuals within the letter form was designed to achieve political effect in a time of war. These were political statements, but that did not mean they were not lived experiences. Furthermore, these epistolary emotional behaviours of individuals at war require us to investigate further the expression of sentiments between ruling men and their subordinates, and as they were declared to male and female recipients in an intimate circle.

Catherine, 'my friend'

From the beginning of his reign, Henri II pursued an aggressive military policy designed to regain some of the territory and much of the French pride lost under the ill-fated campaigns of his father, François I. Moreover, Henri keenly desired to participate personally at the battlefront. On the occasions where he toured newly acquired territories in Piedmont in July 1548, or led French campaigns on the Rhine and the northern France in the summers of 1552, 1553, 1554 and 1557, Henri delegated his wife, Catherine de' Medici, to head his council and manage his affairs.

This generated an exchange of letters between husband, wife and Henri's senior councillor at the front, Montmorency. Catherine had long sought to cultivate Montmorency as an ally soon after her arrival at the French court. Although he had been disgraced under François I in 1541, Catherine evidently perceived the senior stateman's powerful influence over her young and impressionable husband. She encouraged Montmorency to form a close-knit relationship with her and to 'no longer write to me in ceremony for you know well that you need not do that for me', and assuring him that he 'had no better friend, male or female' (La Ferrière-Percy 1880, pp. 3 n3; 6).[1] In return, she regularly expressed anxiety for Henri's health and wellbeing, a sign of her wifely devotion. While on campaign with Montmorency in Avignon in August 1536, Henri had fallen from his horse, and Catherine anxiously asked Montmorency for more information (La Ferrière-Percy 1880, p. 3). After the French defeat at Thérouanne and Hesdin in July 1553, in which a significant number of France's noblemen had been taken prisoner (including Montmorency's eldest son François), Catherine more than once expressed fears to Montmorency about Henri's personal safety, 'as a wife and as a person who will have nothing' should Henri be killed or kidnapped (La Ferrière-Percy 1880, p. 78).[2]

In these letters to Montmorency at the frontline, Catherine's devotion was not only to her husband's wellbeing. She also repeatedly insisted upon her dedication to performing reliably as Henri's regent and her dependency on their approval of her actions: 'I will not be easy until I know that King and you are content' (La Ferrière-Percy 1880, p. 56).[3] She wrote explicitly of her growing political education:

> My *compère*, you will see by the letter that I wrote to the King that I lost no time in learning the state and charge of a *munitionnaire*; so that if each does his duty to hold and observe what he promised, I assure you that I am going to be a past mistress of this; for from one hour to the next I study nothing but this.
>
> (La Ferrière-Percy 1880, p. 56)[4]

In return, Montmorency regularly assured Catherine that her letters were a 'thing from which I am sure he [Henri] will receive great contentment, as also I know that he has with all that you have done until now in the charge that he has left to you' (Ribier 1666, p. 414).[5] But Montmorency evidently also saw Catherine's successful political interventions as a potential threat to his own power as an advisor to the king. He warned Catherine not to over-reach her power in the last days of her regency before the king's return.

> Madame, because I know that the thing in the world that you desire the most is to satisfy only the King, I did not want to be remiss, for the old and devoted service and obedience that I hold for you, in warning you that it seems to me, as the King is so close to you, that you must not enter into any expense nor make any ordonnances without first letting him know about it and knowing his pleasure.
>
> (Ribier 1666, p. 414)[6]

Significantly, the senior counsellor made the couple's feelings for each other the basis for offering his warning for Catherine to restrain any personal ambitions of power.

Montmorency's fears about Catherine's insertion into an intimate political circle around the king had some foundation. In addition to her exchange of lettters with the constable, the king was also directly communicating with Catherine, whom he addressed as 'the Queen my wife', 'My Friend' (Ribier 1666, p. 415).[7] Henri's direct correspondence with Catherine was far less frequent than that she received from Montmorency or that Henri wrote to the constable. These were by and large practical missives seeking to secure his immediate needs for supplies or tactical support at the front. However, Henri carefully framed his requests for Catherine's assistance with consideration of her feelings, strategically sensible since she was his voice before the council. In his phrasing, Henri conveyed respect for and acknowledgement of Catherine's skills to operate on his behalf. When he required further supplies at camp, he asked Catherine to intervene with his council: 'I beg you, My Friend, to . . . make known my intention' and assured her that he was grateful for her support of his requests, 'it being impossible, as I knew, that you could have done more about it than you have' (Ribier 1666, p. 415).[8] He delegated diplomatic responsibilities to her, sending away foreign envoys from the frontline to address Catherine on his behalf at the court (La Ferrière-Percy, p. 60). Henri wrote supportively of Catherine's abilities, assuming positive benefits from her interventions and increasingly he explicitly delegated diplomatic interviews to her decision. Of one audience with Ferdinand de Saint Severino, prince of Salerno (1507–1568), Henri concluded his advice by assuring Catherine 'you know well how to add other good remonstrances . . . tell me straightaway what you can draw from him' (Ribier 1666, p. 416).[9] Henri's letter to his wife evoked a partnership founded on respect for Catherine's intellectual capacity and his support for her political development. That this was understood by political colleagues is reflected in Montmorency's warnings for Catherine not to overstep her delegated and temporary authority. These letters between Catherine, her husband and his leading statesman, Montmorency, made the queen's ostensibly fragile emotional state central to their discourse, in which Catherine's feelings were fashioned as responsive to Henri's personal safety in the military conflict and to his happiness with her actions.

Honest love and chivalric romance: Diane

The correspondence that Catherine exchanged with Henri and Montmorency at the battlefront shared characteristics of coupling demands for assistance regarding her husband's political goals with explicit rhetorical attention to Catherine's emotional state. By contrast, distinct vocabularies of feeling shaped by a courtly culture steeped in contemporary literary conventions of chivalric prose romance permeated the exchange of missives between Henri, Montmorency and the king's longstanding partner, Diane de Poitiers, Duchess of Valentinois. Here, expression of sentiments was primarily the privilege of Henri, but the experience of strong feelings was acknowledged and implicitly underpinned epistolary discussions.

As he did with Catherine, Henri addressed Diane as 'my friend'; his concerns for her health creating an informal, quasi-domestic context for their discussions. However, his autograph letters of absence from Diane were filled with explicit expressions of longing, service and duty to his lady. 'I beg you to send me news of your health, for the pain that I'm in to have heard of your illness', Henri wrote. 'For if you continue to be ill, I would not hesitate to go to you to be able to be

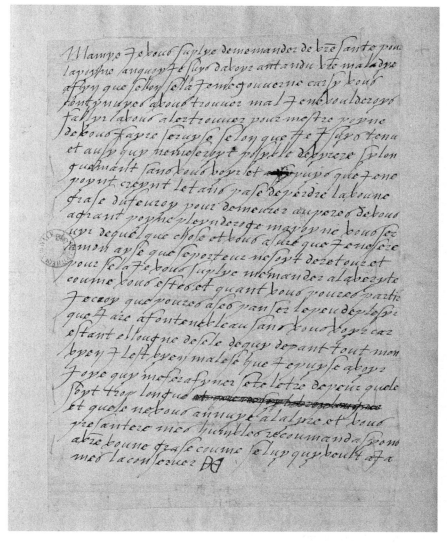

FIGURE 7.1 Autograph letter from Henri II to Diane de Poitiers [nd]. Bibliothèque nationale de France, manuscrit français 3143, fol 2ʳ.

© Bibliothèque nationale de France

of service to you, as I am bound to, and because it is not possible to live so long without seeing you' (BNF ms fr 3143, fol. 2ʳ).¹⁰ From the first years of his reign, Henri's epistolary expression fashioned an identity as an attentive and subordinate partner, eager to please – a position that a man of power could willingly adopt and express by choice. 'Being distant from she from whom depends all my wellbeing, it is impossible for me to be happy' (BNF ms fr 3143, fol. 2ʳ, Fig 1.).¹¹ Upon hearing of her improved health, Henri wrote gratefully for her response: ' I cannot live without you, if you only know the little leisure that I have here, you would have pity on me' (BNF ms fr 3143, fol. 5ʳ).¹² In such letters, as with those of Catherine, discussion of emotional states was central. Here, however, the king coupled discussion of his duties to kingdom and government with explicit attestations of his passion.

The combination of explicit expression of the king's feelings, and in particular his longing and concerns to be remembered by his loved one, likewise occupied Henri's letters at war. In May 1552, Henri was encamped at Wallerfangen as part of an alliance of convenience, the Treaty of Chambord, with German Protestants against Emperor Charles V. From there he penned a short missive to 'Madame my friend'. He begged Diane 'to imagine how beautiful and well disciplined my army is' and hoped that she would have in her thoughts 'he who has never known but one God and one friend'. Suffering the exile of war, Henri went further, assuring Diane that 'I have no shame in giving myself the name of servant, [a role] that I beg you will keep me in as always' (BNF ms fr 2991, fol. 9ʳ).¹³ Some years later, in August 1558, from the French camp at Pierrepont, the tenor of Henri's war correspondence to Diane was unchanged. He acknowledged her expected interest in the conflict, indicating that the courier would provide her with all the details of their most recent developments. The letter itself was thus devoted to the ways in which Diane's love made his war service possible. She had sent her royal lover a simple gift. Henri expressed his 'hope to be worthy of being able to wear the scarf that you sent me' (BNF ms fr 3143, fol. 3ʳ).¹⁴ In exchange, Henri enclosed a ring: 'I beg you always to remember he who has never loved nor will ever love any but you. I beg you, my friend, to willingly wear this ring for love of me' (BNF ms fr 3143, fol. 3ʳ).¹⁵ These may have been simply keepsakes of a loving couple separated by war and the possibility of death, but Henri had rendered them central to his military offensive for France.

Moreover, Henri signed each of these letters to Diane with a particular device (Figure 7.1), an uppercase H that embedded two back-to-back uppercase Ds. This was a symbol that he used widely from the time he became *dauphin* in 1536. The interlaced letters could be read as an H and C for Henri and his wife Catherine. However, most contemporaries understood the device to represent the partnership of Henri and Diane, as did an eyewitness attending the introduction of Venetian ambassador Giovanni Capello to the king at the Louvre, who observed that the king's apparel was embroidered,

> with two gold crescents fashioned in a manner to seem to be two Ds. In this interweaving of Ds, one can see first an H, the initial of the name of

His Majesty, then also an E, the second letter of the same name, Henri. One can also see two Ds, which are the double initials of the Duchess of Valentinois, also called madame la Sénéchale. Her real name is Diane and the allusion is clear in these two crescents so united and joined by the embrace of the two Ds. Thus are, in effect, the souls of the two lovers united and reunited in a close bond.

(Baschet 1862, p. 443)[16]

Certainly, it was a device that Henri used only in his letters to Diane but never for those to his wife, Catherine.

Nonetheless, Catherine supported the convenient fiction that the symbol represented her own partnership with the king. She was depicted wearing the symbol while *dauphine* and queen (Quentin-Bauchart 1891, pp. 185–188). Likewise, she tolerated Diane's position as a senior figure in her immediate entourage. This position enabled Diane to write openly of her proximity to power, providing news of the movements of the royal couple to a range of interlocutors. Ostensibly for her particular services to the queen, Henri even rewarded Diane with a gift of 5500 *livres* (Guiffrey 1866, pp. 78–79). Diane's assistance to the queen, like the queen's share in the HD/HC symbol, was widely understood to be a fiction; nevertheless, these were narratives considered vital to the stability and morality of the court as a whole.

These outward presentations of the nature of the relationship between Henri, Diane and Catherine were made possible by a courtly culture energetically enacting a practice derived from contemporary prose romance. The popularity of translated chivalric literature from Spain and Italy, most notably the long-running blockbuster *Amadís de Gaule*, was at its height during the reign of François I and his son Henri. Such texts promoted concepts of chaste love and devotion to a single lady for whom a servant knight or prince could overcome all manner of obstacles, interspersed with masculine comraderie developed through acts of bravery and courage in military service. Significantly for its pertinence to Henri's emotional relationships, the protagonist, Amadís, consummates his relationship with his lover outside the conventions of formalised marriage. Translated editions of successive volumes were immensely popular both at court and among a wider reading populace during the 1540s and 1550s (Baret 1853; Bourciez 1886; Rothstein 1994; Cazauran 2000; Bideaux 2005). Ambitious translators and publishers saw a ready connection to the king's twinned interests of love and war, dedicating volumes to his senior military advisor Anne de Montmorency and to his companion Diane de Poitiers.

Indeed, translators argued strongly to the reading public the value of these books in teaching moral and military codes of feeling. In a prefatory poem to Book 8 of *Amadís*, translated by Nicolas de Herberay, sieur des Essarts, and dedicated to Montmorency, Michel Sevin suggests that the work 'praises those who, with right courage, love the love that leads to marriage' (de Herberay 1548, sig. Aiii^r).[17] The epic, Sevin emphasised, could provide courtly readers with instruction in love and war: 'It also treats love and feat of arms, representing knights and men of arms, who love with an honest love, and yet are strong and chivalrous, for this novel brings together Mars and Venus' (de Herberay 1548, sigs. Aiiii^v–v^r).[18] Jacques Gohory's translation of Book 11 and Guillaume Aubert's of Book 12, both dedicated to Diane de Poitiers, continued the story of the hero Agesilan de Colchos, 'in the long pursuit of the love of Diane, the most beautiful princess in the world', with hinted correspondences between the fictive palace of Diane and Diane de Poitiers's château of Anet (Gohory 1554; Gorris 2000).[19] In his address to readers, Aubert argued that the power of the work resided in the purety and simplicity of its language, and its enjoyment of what 'the extremes of love could do to people'. Readers could 'see the experience of military art, be spurred to arms through the praise of prowess and by the rebuke of cowardice, contemplate . . . diverse changes in fortune, the inconstance of human things and the luck of war' (Aubert 1556, sig. Aiiii^r).[20] In the eyes of their translators, these works could reflect lived and desirable emotional experiences at court – honest love, courage and bravery.

Moreover, these publications also fostered nationalistic sentiment for the current French campaigns of the Italian Wars. Herberay's translations of *Amadís* were lauded for adapting 'primitive' Spanish into the 'gentle, ornate, orderly and rich' language of France (de Herberay 1540, sig. Aii^v).[21] The translations of Spanish and Italian epics were justified as cultural appropriations that reflected and aided the French war effort (Cooper 1990, p. 197). A poetic dedication to François I in 1543, repurposed as equally appropriate to the hawkish Henri in the 1555 edition of Book 4, promised that 'you will see here, Sire, how with great happiness your Amadís knew so well how to pursue his enemies, that he defeated the Emperor' (de Herberay 1543; 1555, sig. Aii^r).[22] In his contribution, Gohory likened Henri to Julius Caesar who had also, with his 'warring legions and the French forces with their great military discipline, reduced the Empire to his obedience' (Gohory 1554, sig. Aii^v).[23] Translation itself thus became a form of conquering act. 'It is certain', wrote Michel le Clerc, for de Herberay's Book 1 translation in 1540, 'that Spain knows well that in this matter, France has the advantage in speaking beautifully, as much as in good conduct' (de Herberay 1540, sig. Aii^r).[24] That contemporaries mocked as unreal the outdated forms of war that were represented in these texts does not mean that they held less meaning as practised, or simply ideal, models of feeling codes for the court, and in particular its king (Cooper 1990, p. 191). Indeed, Aubert drew a line between the protagonist Princess Diane and her dedicatee Diane de Poitiers that paralleled contemporary Franco-Spanish military rivalries, arguing that 'the heavenly destinies . . . wanted the history of your perfections to be known by the Spanish before your birth' but 'discovered by the French in your lifetime' (Aubert 1556, sig. Aii^r).[25] These sixteenth-century chivalric interpretations of both love and war were, I argue, enacted in Henri's letters to Diane from the battlefront that voiced the devotion of a warrior-king-servant for his distant, beloved lady.

Henri's missives even drew upon the works of contemporary French poets who had been inspired by popular prose romances. In one letter to Diane that the king likely composed from the war front in 1552, he copied out a sonnet by Joachim du Bellay, first published in his collection imbued with Neoplatonic themes, *L'Olive*, in 1549. Du Bellay's poem was inspired by Ludovico Ariosto's *Orlando Furioso*, a work that itself underwent some 11 French editions during the period (Hope 1982; Cooper 1990, p. 234). This sonnet was coupled with three other verses, perhaps of Henri's own invention, adopting Petrarchan motifs, lamenting his departure and submitting his heart to her protection (BNF ms fr 3143, fols. 6–9ʳ). War and the romance of his honest love for Diane went hand in hand for Henri. In fact, war was part of the chivalric romance that Henri was constructing as his emotional experience in these letters.

The king's 'honest love' for Diane, his lady, both mirrored and constructed through its relationship to contemporary chivalric romance, was itself stimulated by the context of Henri's campaigns within the Italian Wars. That the king's love was of a particular, honest and discreet kind was vital for the moral functioning of the court. *Histoire de Primaleon de Grece* likened its hero's 'chivalry and courtesy' to that of Henri himself (Vernassal 1550, sig. Aivᵛ).[26] A hallmark of the *Amadís* series, as Gohory opined in his introduction to Book 10, was that it served as an ideal introduction to youth at court as 'an example and model of chivalry, courtesy and discretion, which lifts their hearts to virtue, teaching them the acts which they must follow or avoid' (Gohory 1552, sig. Aiiiʳ).[27] Chivalry of the kind these romances advanced demanded discretion.

Chivalry also demanded the co-operation of Henri's acknowledged female partners, Catherine and Diane. Within this framework of chivalric discretion, Henri's further dalliances, even those that led to illegitimate children, as with Italian Filippa Duci, Nicole de Savigny and Jane Stewart, could be managed within the courtly culture. But indiscretion could not be tolerated. The widowed Scotswoman Stewart, Lady Fleming, governess to the young Mary Queen of Scots and *dauphine* of France, for example, boasted too broadly of her relationship with the monarch, which resulted in the birth of a son, Henri, in 1551, and was soon sent back to Scotland. Many years later, Catherine de' Medici reflected on uxorial and courtly discretion in Henri's day, emphasising the importance of courtly protocols and appropriate emotional demeanours.

> I had the honour to have married the King my lord . . . but the thing that annoyed him the most was when he knew that I knew of such things; and when Madame de Fleming was pregnant, he found it very good when she was sent away
>
> (Baguenault de Puchesse 1901, p. 36)[28]

Indeed, she called upon the example of the more subtle behaviour of Diane de Poitiers, in order to make her point. 'With Madame de Valentinois, it was, as with Madame d'Estampes [Anne de Pisseleu, mistress of François I], most honourable, but those who were so silly as to disrupt things he [Henri] would have been very annoyed if I had retained them close to me' (Baguenault de Puchesse 1901, p. 36).[29] Catherine stressed the importance of repressing visible affective display about affairs of the heart, and their consequences, for the political and social stability of the court.

Discretion was one half of the courtly chivalric romance fiction that Henri imposed; emotional discipline was the other. Many years after the deaths of both Henri and Diane, Catherine reflected upon her emotional experiences at the court of her husband. 'If I made good cheer for Madame de Valentinois, it was the King who I was really entertaining . . . for never did a woman who loved her husband succeed in loving his whore. For one cannot call her otherwise, although the word is a horrid one to us' (Baguenault de Puchesse 1901, p. 181).[30] Henri's version of chivalric romantic culture at court, which was practised in his correspondence at war, demanded considerable emotional discipline and discretion from others.

No letters of Diane to Henri have yet been uncovered to reveal her views. Perhaps the chivalry of the king extended to destroying missives that could potentially compromise his partner. However, those that Diane composed for other men within his military forces make clear, explicitly so, her intimate knowledge of the course of the war and the king's movements. War offered Diane the opportunity to use her correspondence with far-flung servants to the king to offer herself as a mediator between them and Henri. She assured those on campaign that she could employ her physical and emotional proximity to the monarch to remind the king of their important contribution (Broomhall, 2018b). Letters to Henri's trusted advisor and her political rival Montmorency, however, required particular care. In August 1547, Diane had wed her younger daughter, Louise de Brézé, into the dynasty that was Montmorency's rival, the Guise family. While the Guise favoured a continuation of aggressive campaigns during the late 1550s, the defeat of the French troops and Montmorency's capture at Saint-Quentin had convinced Henri of the value of peace negotiations with Philip II. Diane thus astutely expanded her allegiances at court. Her letters to the imprisoned constable now reflected her 'hope' that Montmorency's negotiations would see the stateman return to influence at court (Guiffrey 1866, p. 155). She began to seek a marriage of her grand-daughter, Antoinette de la Marck, to Montmorency's second son, Henri I, Duke of Damville, in June 1558.

However, in March 1559, Montmorency was to receive a significant letter that revealed as much through its material qualities as its content (Figure 7.2). Diane commenced the short missive to the captive statesmen with thanks for his most recent news. Then the quill was taken over by Henri, who continued by thanking him for writing in his own hand at such a busy time during the peace talks. He then concluded that 'the secretary who has completed half of my letter and me recommend ourselves to your good grace', with Diane completing the main letter text by wishing God's blessing upon their recipient. Henri scrawled the complimentary close, 'Your longstanding & best friends', before each author penned their own name (BNF ms fr 3139, fol. 26ʳ).[31] (Figure 7.2) This remarkable letter interspersing the voice and penmanship of the king and his partner clearly signalled the intimate nature of their relationship and the power of Diane's access and reach into the king's affairs. There could be no minsunderstanding by Montmorency of Diane's power.

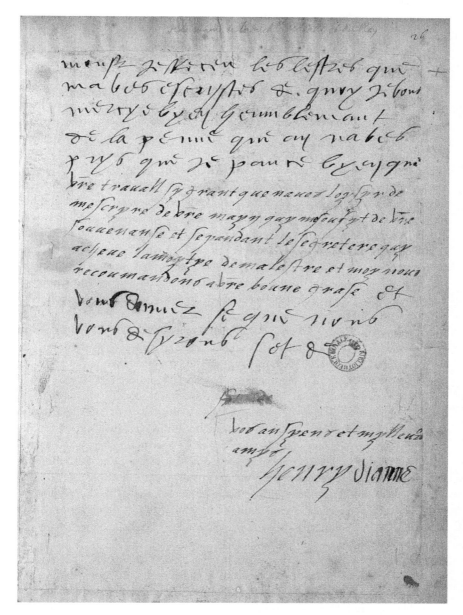

FIGURE 7.2 Autograph letter from Henri II and Diane de Poitiers to Anne de Montmorency [1559] Bibliothèque nationale de France, manuscrit français 3139, fol. 26ʳ.

© Bibliothèque nationale de France

Brotherly love: Anne de Montmorency

But why had Diane been driven to such a course of action, whether the double letter was her idea or an idea of Henri's that she had accepted? Henri's war correspondence with Montmorency had revealed some startling information, principally in terms of how Henri addressed the elder courtly figure. The emotional rhetoric of Henri's letters during the campaigns, coupled with his political response to Montmorency's capture, suggested a powerful bond of feeling between themen, one that appeared to threaten the affective supremacy of his longstanding partner, if not his wife.

Montmorency had risen under François I to the supreme position of the French army as constable, and had a demonstrated record of military achievement, particularly in crushing imperial forces in Provence. However, he had found himself at odds with another royal mistress, Anne de Pisseleu, soon after and had been exiled from court. With Henri's accession to the throne, and a renewed emphasis on pursuing conflict against the Emperor, Montmorency had been recalled to the court and his former position. He campaigned with Henri, and as demonstrated above, regularly corresponded for the king with senior court members, including the queen. Catherine had identified the strong influence of Montmorency early on in her marriage and had attempted to forge a close connection with a figure who could potentially provide an alliance against Diane de Poitiers. When they were apart, Henri's letters intermingled directions about the campaign with his concerns for Montmorency's safety and his desire to share the experience of war with his friend (BNF ms fr 3129, fol. 8ʳ).[32] In the spring and summer of 1554, for example, Henri concluded one letter by begging Montmorency: 'keep yourself well that you do not fall ill, for you would make me die' (BNF ms fr 3129, fol. 4ʳ).[33] Another repeated the phrasing, 'praying that you look after yourself, so that you do not fall ill, and remember the person in this world who loves you the most and who will forever remain, if you please, your good *compère* and friend' (BNF ms fr 3129, fol. 12ʳ).[34] Henri requested in a post-script that Montmorency should destroy these letters so that no one could see them (BNF ms fr 3129, fol. 12ʳ). Montmorency, like Diane, did not. Henri's use of the word '*conpere*' (*compère*) was a sign of their spiritual kinship, for Henri was the godfather of Anne's son, Henri, who would later marry Diane de Poitiers's grand-daughter (Brantôme 1864, p. 331).

In August 1557, after the collapse of the truce of Vaucelles that had been signed between Henri and Philip II in February 1556, Montmorency took the head of the army at Saint-Quentin. Here, the French were resoundingly defeated and the constable captured. Henri's undated letters from this period continued to express longing for the older man: 'telling you that my greatest desire in all the world is to see you happy again' (BNF ms fr 3139, fol. 14ʳ).[35] Henri's words of comfort as a 'good and loyal friend' were no mere complimentary close; the negotiations that concluded the Italian Wars were shaped by the king's feelings for Montmorency.[36] Lamenting their distance, Henri assured his friend and councilor: 'as to my health,

I have no ease or contentment since it pleases God that I am away from you. I beg you to believe nothing else in this world could ever divert me from the friendship that I hold for you' (BNF ms fr 3139, fol. 1ʳ).[37] This was the language of a chivalric, quasi-romantic attachment between brothers at arms. It mirrored the language and tone of the set pieces of rhetoric within the *Amadís* series. These texts were so popular that the key speeches of the first 12 books of *Amadís* were gathered together in a treasury in 1559 (Benhaïm 2000). Their compiler assured readers that they could be of particular value as tools of epistolary expression, 'as much for familiar as all sorts of missives' (*Thresor* 1560, sig. A1ᵛ).

As part of the process for Montmorency's ransom and the ongoing negotiations for a peace between the warring monarchs, Montmorency was released on parole to communicate with the king. Henri begged him to 'hurry as soon as you can so that I can enjoy seeing you again, not being able to live without you' (BNF ms fr 3139, fol. 3ʳ).[38] Contemporaries observed in Henri's actions what they could not have read in his intimate letters – a strong emotional bond and familiarity between the men. When in October 1558, Montmorency was released to visit the king at Beauvais, Henri came to meet him hat in hand and held the constable in an embrace lasting minutes, in full view of witnesses including the Ferrarese ambassador Julio Alvarotti who understood from the gesture the full extent of Montmorency's influence. The men then retired, the king sharing his bed for the next two nights with Montmorency (Romier 1913, p. 301). The constable was back just two weeks later in early November, attending the king, queen and Diane at court and the wedding of eleven-year-old Claude de Valois, the king's daughter, to Charles III, Duke of Lorraine, in early January 1559. The Venetian ambassador Giovanni Michieli reported that Henri had Montmorency sit at his table, next to his master, and had arranged a bed for the older man 'in the wardrobe next to his chamber, continuing more than ever to bestow favours on him in public and in private' (Romier 1913, p. 310).[39] By mid-February Montmorency was again with Henri, at Villers-Cotterêts, before returning again in early March. With each visit enabling the advancement of the peace treaty negotiations, the two men were never long out of each other's company.

But loss and longing at a time of war were relative. Between these encounters, Henri and Montmorency exchanged letters. Some contained practical points of negotiation, but details were more commonly left to his envoys, making Henri's epistolary space one for expression of particular feelings. Upon one occasion of Montmorency's return to Habsburg captivity, Henri wrote at length:

> My friend, this letter will serve that which I could not do when I said goodbye to you, for my heart was so broken that it was impossible to say anything to you. I beg you to believe that you are the person in the world that I love the most, and for all that, I know nothing to offer you, for, since my heart is yours, I think that you know well that I would spare nothing I own or nothing in my power to have the happiness to see you again.
>
> (BNF ms fr 3139, fol. 16ʳ)[40]

The king's haste to see Montmorency return was repeatedly expressed across multiple letters: 'My friend, I don't know how to speak of the regret that I have to be separated from you without doing anything . . . I beg you to excuse me if I importune you too much about your ransom, but my desire to see you makes me do it.' (BNF ms fr 3139, fol. 20ʳ).[41] Henri's feelings also gave power to the Habsburg negotiators, particularly in driving up the price of Montmorency's freedom. For, as Henri wrote: 'nothing but death could separate me from you, I would think myself happy and would die content when I see a good peace and the man whom I love and esteem most in the world, and so do not be afraid to set the ransom at any price, for I will spare nothing that is in my power to see you again' (BNF ms fr 3139, fol. 5ʳ).[42]

Henri's letters to Montmorency were embedded in a specific courtly rhetoric of chivalric warfare that prioritised brotherhood forged in shared combat and which allowed for intense emotional expression. An enormous sum was the final price of this friendship and Montmorency's permanent release, in addition to the signing of the Peace of Cateau-Cambrésis that ended the Italian Wars permanently, a deeply unpopular resolution to the conflict among many in France. However, as a dedicatory poem in Book 8 of *Amadís* had suggested to Montmorency in 1548, if the prose romances taught the captain sent to war how to willingly acquire honour and glory, it also instructed 'the Prince how to govern himself so well as to long reign in peace' (de Herberay 1548, sig. Aiiiᵛ).[43] And, as Jacques Gohory had suggested to Henri's sister, Marguerite, in his dedication of Book 10 to her in 1552, after war come 'the good alliances and marriages of Princes and Princesses', just so was Marguerite married in June 1559 to Emanuel Philibert of Savoy (1528–1580), the Emperor's ally who had routed Montmorency at Saint-Quentin in 1557 (Gohory 1552, sig. aiiiʳ).[44]

Conclusions

Letters exchanged between Henri, Catherine, Diane and Montmorency, written in the context of the last campaigns of the Italian Wars, demonstrate how that military context offered new political opportunities and alliances that were expressed in a specific, gendered language of care, concern, friendship and love within the epistolary genre. These letters also articulated crucial understandings about the nature of war; specifically, about the feeling rules of war itself. The context of war – or rather, a particular view of chivalric military engagement practised by the mid-sixteenth-century French court – enabled Henri to articulate strong sentiments of passion in his letters. His emotional expression functioned within a specific courtly culture in which the knight errant/king could earn the favour of his treasured lady and signify a bond of brotherhood with fellow men through acts of bravery in military conflict.

The key protagonists of this epistolary exchange may have been exchanging missives about feelings in war, but it did not mean that the emotional expression made available to them in this 'romance' or their articulation of particular affective experiences was 'corresponding'. The rules of war's emotions in this cultural milieu were dependent on both gender and status in the hierarchy of the court. By right of his status, Henri held the power to articulate feeling about and through war in his letters – love, loss, longing, a sense of exile from his most cherished supporters. Others too spoke of their sentiments, such as his consort Catherine, but the expressive capability and range of female-authored letters to men at the battlefront was far more limited. The rules of chivalric romance did not voice female passion for male partners, and accordingly neither Catherine nor Diane openly articulated passionate love for a male partner in times of war. Rather, Catherine's epistolary expression of fears, primarily concerns for the emotional and physical wellbeing of a loved one in danger, implied her uxorial emotional duties. Nor did the feeling rules of courtly romance legitimise the objects of male affection, in this case both Diane and Montmorency, to voice a response or reciprocation to his sentiments in the epistolary form, either because they could not be expressed in that format, or because they could not be left for the eyes of others.

Notes

1 [nd] 'ne m'esecripvié pleus en syrimonye, car vous savés byen que se net pas à moy à quy l'an fo fère', La Ferrière 1880, 3, n.3; [June 1543], 'vous n'avés pount de mylleures amys ne amye', La Ferrière 1880, 6. 'et qui set quindé afoler', La Ferrière 1880, 3.
2 [15–20] August 1553, 'en femme et an personne qui n'ayra rien'.
3 20 May [1552], 'j'espère que le tout bien acheminé et estably, comme il est, vous en serez satisfait . . . n'y perdray point ma peine jusques à ce que je sçache comme le Roy et vous en serez contens'.
4 'Mon compère, vous verrez par la lecture que j'escris au Roy que ie n'a pas perdu temps à apprendre l'estat et charge de munitionnaire; en quoy si chacun fait son devoir de tenir et observer ce qu'il a promis, je vous asseure que je m'en vais maistresse passé; car d'heure à autre je n'estudie que cela'.
5 30 May 1552, 'chose dont ie suis seur qu'il receura grand contentement, comme aussi connois-je qu'il a de tout ce que vous auez fait jusques – icy en la charge qu'il vous auoit laissée'.
6 30 May 1552, 'Madame, pource que ie sçay que la chose du monde que vous desirez le plus, est de satisfaire seulement au Roy, ie n'ay voulu manquer, pour l'ancienne & devote servitude & obeissance que ie vous porte, vous advertir qu'il me semble, estant ledit Seigneur si prochain de vous, qu'il sera doresnavant, que vous ne devez entrer en aucune despense, ny plus faire ordonnance d'aucuns deniers, sans premierement le luy faire sçauoit & entendre son bon plaisir'.
7 8 June 1552, 'à la Reyne ma Femme', 'ma mie'.
8 'ie vous prie, Ma Mie, ordonner aux gens de mon Conseil, auquel vous ferez à tous entendre mon intention, qu'ils ayent à ne vaquer à autre chose', 'estant impossible, comme j'ay sçeu, que vous y'eussiez plus fait que vous auez'.
9 '& autres bonnes remonstrances que vous y sçaurez bien adjouster, . . . & de ce que vous pourez tirer de luy, vou s m'aduertirez incontinent'.
10 [1547] 'Mamye Je vous suplye de me mander de vre santé, pour la poyne anquoy je suys davoyr antandu vre maladye afyn que sellon sella je me gouuerne car sy vous contynuyes a vous trouuer mal je ne vouldreroys fallyr la vous aler trouver pour mestre poyne de vous fayre servyse selon que je i suys tenu et ausy quy ne me feroyt posyble de vyvere sy longuemant sans vous voyr'.

11 'vous asure que je ne sere a mon ayse que se porteur ne soyt de retour . . . le peu de plesyr que jare a fontenebleau sans vous voyr car estant ellongne de sele de quy depant tout mon byen il est bien malese que je puysse avoyr joye'.

12 [1547] 'je ne puys vyvere sans vous et sy vous sauyes le peu de pasetans que je isy vous aryes pytyé de moy'.

13 [May 1552] 'Madame mamye . . . je vous suplye de panser que mon armee est belle et an boune voulante . . . je vous suplye avoyr souvenanse de seluy qui na james conu que ung dyu et une amye et vous asurer que nares point de honte de mavoyr doune le non de servyteur lequel je vous suplye me conserver pour james'.

14 'estre dyne de pouuoyr porter lescharpe que maves anvoye'.

15 'je vous suplye avoyr toujours souuenanse de seluy quy na james ayme ny nemera james que vous . . . je vous suplye mamie vouloyr porter set bague pour lamour de moy'.

16 'de deux croissants d'or accommodés de manière à sembler être entre deux D. Dans cet enlacement des D, on voit d'abord un H, intiiale du nom de Sa Majesté: on voit aussi un E, seconde lettre du même nom de Henri; on y peut voir aussi deux D; lesquesl sont la double initiales de la duchesse de Valentinois, appelée aussi madame la Sénéchale. Son vrai nom est Diane, et l'allusion est bien manifeste dans ces deux croissants si unis et si joints par l'embrassement des deux D; ainso soit, en effet, les deux âmes des deux amants, unies et réunies dans un étroit attachement'.

17 'Il louë aussi ceux quie de bon courage/ Ayment d'amour tendants a mariage'.

18 'Il traite aussi les amours & faitz d'armes/ Representant Chevaliers & gens d'armes/ Qui de l'honneste amour sont amoureux:/ Et toutesfois forts, & chevalereux/ Car ce Romant assemble /Mars, & Venus'.

19 'au long pourchas de l'amour de Diane, la plus belle Princesse du monde'.

20 'en considerant que peut l'extremité de l'amour sur les humains, voir l'experience de l'art militaire, s'encourager aux armes par la louange de la prouesse, & par la vituperation de la couardie, contempler . . . les diuers changemens de la fortune, l'inconstance des choses humaines, les hazards de la guerre'.

21 'doulx, aorné, proper, & riche'.

22 'Vous y verrez (Sire) que par grand heur/ Vostre Amadis sceut si tresbien poursuyvre/ Ses ennemys, qu'il deffit l'Empereur'.

23 'ses legions aguerries, & forces Françoises auec sa bonne discipline militaire, reduit l'Empire à son obeissance'.

24 'Et soit certain qu'Espagne en cest affaire/ Cognoistra bien que France a l'aduantage/ Au bien parler autant comme au bien faire'.

25 'celestes destinées, qui ont voulu que l'histoire de voz perfections fust entenduë par les Espagnolz deuant votre naissance, & descouuerte aux Françoys en vostre viuant'.

26 'les chevaleries et courtoisie'.

27 'un exemple & patron de chevalerie, courtoisie, & discretion, qui leur eleuast le cueur à la vertu, enseignant les actes qu'ilz doivent ensuyure ou euiter'.

28 12 June 1582. 'J'ay eu cet honneur d'avoyr espousé le Roy mon seigneur . . . mais la chouse du monde de quoy yl estoit plus mary, c'estoit quand yl savoit que je seuse de ces nouveles là; et, quand Madame de Flamin fut grose, yl trouva très bon quant on l'an envoya'.

29 'De Madame de Valentinois, c'estèt, comme Madame d'Estampes, en tout honneur; mais celes qui estoient si foles que d'en fayre voler les esclats, yl eust esté bien marry que je les eusse retenues auprès de moy'.

30 25 April 1584. 'cet je fèse bonne chère à madame de Valantynnois, c'estoyt le Roy, et encore je luy fèsèt tousjours conestre que s'étoyt à mon très grent regret: car jeamès fame qui aymèt son mary n'éma sa puteyn; car on ne le peust apeler aultrement, encore que le mot souyt vylayn à dyre à bous aultres'.

31 'la segretère quy achève la moytye de ma lestre et moy nous recoumandons a vre boune grase' 'vos ansyens et mylleurs amys, henry, dianne'.

32 'couneses byen la grande anvie que je d'estre au canp'.

33 'je vous prye, garde vous byen que ne soyes malade car vous me feries mourir'.
34 'vous pryer vous byen garder afyn que ne soyes malade et avoyr souvenanse de la persoune de se monde quy vous ayme le plus et quy veult a james demourer sy vous plait vre bon conpere et amy'.
35 'la plus grande anuye que je aye an se monde est de vous reuoyr contant'.
36 'bon et leal amy'.
37 'quant a ma sante mes aveque peu dayse nyde contantement puys quy playt adyeu que je soys absant et elougne de vous et vous prie de croye que nule chose de se monde ne me saroyt detourner de lamitie que je vous porte'.
38 'vous depecher le plustost que poures afin que je se byen de vous voyr ne pouant vyuere sans vous'.
39 5 November 1558. 'preparare un letto nella guardarobba contingua alla sua camera, continuando più che mai i favori verso di lui in pubblico et in privato'.
40 'Mon amy sete lestre fera lofyse que je ne peu fayre quant je vous e dyst adyeu pour avoyr le ceur sy sere quy mestoyt inposyble de vous ryens dyre Je vous prye de croyre que vous estes la persoune de se monde que jeme le plus et pour sela je ne vous saroys ryens oferyr car puys que mon ceur est a vous je croy que vous panses byen que je nepergnere mes byens ny se quy sera an ma puysanse pour avoyr set heur que de vous ravoyr'.
41 'Mon amy je ne saroys vous dyre le regueret que je de vous voyr separer sans ryens fayre ... Je vous prye mescuser sy je vous prye mescuser sy je [sic] vous importune tant de vre ranson mes l'anuye que je de vous voyr me le fayt fayre'.
42 'autre ocasyon que sele de la mort ne me saroyt separer daueque vous la quele jestimeroys heureuse et mouroys contant quant je veroys une bonne pays et loume du monde que jayme et estime le plus et pour sela necregnes de vous mestre à ranson à quelque pris que se soyt car ie nepargnere chose quy soyt an ma puysanse pour vous ravoyr'.
43 'Au Prince enseigne à bien se gouverner/ Si longuement il veult en pais regner'.
44 'bons accordz & mariages des Princes & Princesses'.

Reference list

Aubert, G. 1556, *Le douziesme livre d'Amadis de Gaule*, Vincent Sertenas, Paris.

Baguenault de Puchesse, G. 1901, *Lettres de Catherine de Médicis*, vol. 8, Imprimerie nationale, Paris.

Baret, E. 1853, *De l'Amadis de Gaule et de son influence sur les moeurs et la littterature au XVIe siècle et au XVIIe siècle*, Auguste Durand, Paris.

Baschet, A. 1862, *La diplomatie vénitienne: Les princes de l'Europe au XVIe siècle*, H. Plon, Paris.

Baumgartner, F. J. 1988, *Henry II: King of France 1547–1559*, Duke University Press, Durham.

Benhaïm, V. 2000, 'Les Thresors d'Amadis', in N. Cazauran & M. Bideaux (eds), *Les Amadis en France au XVIe siècle*, Presses de l'Ecole Normale Supérieure, Paris.

Bibliothèque nationale de France (BNF)
  ms fr 3129. Recueil de lettres. XVIe siècle.
  ms fr 3139. Recueil de lettres. XVIe siècle.
  ms fr 3143. Recueil de lettres. XVIe siècle.

Bideaux, M. 2005, 'Les romans de chevalerie: romans à lire, romans à vivre', in M. Clément & P. Mounier (eds), *Le Roman français au XVIe siècle ou le renouveau d'un genre dans le contexte européen*, Presses universitaires de Strasbourg, Strasbourg, pp. 173–187.

Bourciez, E. 1886, *Les Moeurs polies et la littérature de cour sous Henri II*, Hachette, Paris.

Brantôme, P. 1864, *Oeuvres complètes de Pierre de Bourdeille*, vol. 1, Vve Jules Renouard, Paris.

Broomhall, S. 2018a, 'Counsel as performative practice of power in Catherine de Medici's early regencies', in H. Graham-Matheson & J. Paul (eds), *Queenship and Counsel in the Early Modern World*, Palgrave, Basingstoke.

Broomhall, S. 2018b, '"The King and I": Rhetorics of power in the letters of Diane de Poitiers', in S. Broomhall (ed.), *Women and Power at the French Court, 1483–1563*, Amsterdam University Press, Amsterdam.

Caine, B. (ed.) 2015, 'Special Issue: "Letters between Mothers and Daughters"', *Women's History Review*, vol. 24, no. 4.

Cazauran, N. 2000, 'Amadis de Gaule en 1540', in N. Cazauran & M. Bideaux (eds), *Les Amadis en France au XVIe siècle*, Presses de l'Ecole Normale Supérieure, Paris.

Cooper, R. 1990, '"Nostre histoire renouvelée": The Reception of the Romances of Chivalry in Renaissance France (with bibliography)', in S. Anglo (ed.), *Chivalry in the Renaissance*, Boydell Press, Woodbridge, pp. 175–238.

Crawford, K. 2000, 'Catherine de Médicis and the Performance of Political Motherhood', *Sixteenth Century Journal*, vol. 31, no. 3, pp. 643–673.

Crawford, K. 2004, 'Catherine de Médicis: Staging the Political Woman', in K. Crawford, *Perilous Performances: Gender and Regency in Early Modern France*, Harvard University Press, Cambridge, pp. 24–58.

Crouzet, D. 2008, '"A strong desire to be a mother to all your subjects": A Rhetorical Experiment by Catherine de Medici', *Journal of Medieval and Early Modern Studies*, vol. 38, no. 1, pp. 104–118.

Daybell, J. 2001, *Early Modern Women's Letter Writing, 1450–1700*, Palgrave, Basingstoke.

Daybell, J. 2006, *Women Letter-Writers in Tudor England*, Oxford University Press, Oxford.

Daybell, J. & Gordon, A. (eds) 2016, *Women and Epistolary Agency in Early Modern Culture, 1450–1690*, Routledge, London.

Decrue, F. 1885, *Anne de Montmorency*, Plon, Paris.

de Herberay des Essarts, N. 1540, *Le premier livre d'Amadis de Gaule*, Denis Janot, Paris.

de Herberay des Essarts, N. 1543, *Le quatriesme livre d'Amadis de Gaule*, Denis Janot, Paris.

de Herberay des Essarts, N. 1548, *Le huitiesme livre d'Amadis de Gaule*, Ian Longis, Paris.

Gellard, M. 2015, *Une reine épistolaire. Lettres et pouvoir au temps de Catherine de Médicis*, Classiques Garnier, Paris.

Gohory, J. 1552, *Le dixiesme livre d'Amadis de Gaule*, Etienne Groulleau, Paris.

Gohory, J. 1554, *L'onziesme livre d'Amadis de Gaule*, Jean Longis, Paris.

Gorris, R. 2000, 'Pour une lecture stéganographique des Amadis de Jacques Gohory' in N. Cazauran & M. Bideaux (eds), *Les Amadis en France au XVIe siècle*, Presses de l'Ecole Normale Supérieure, Paris.

Guiffrey, G. 1866, *Lettres inédites de Dianne de Poytiers*, Vve Jules Renouard, Paris.

Hope, G. R. 1982, 'The Verses of Henri II: A Note on Attribution', *Bibliothèque d'Humanisme et Renaissance*, vol. 44, no. 1, pp. 127–131.

La Ferrière-Percy, H. de 1880, *Lettres de Catherine de Médicis*, vol. 1, Imprimerie nationale, Paris.

Le Thresor des douze livres d'Amadis, 1560, Vincent Sertenas, Paris.

McCartney, E. 2005, 'In the Queen's words: Perceptions of Regency Government Gleaned from the Correspondence of Catherine de Médicis' in J. Couchman & A. Crabb (eds), *Women's Letters Across Europe, 1400–1700: Form And Persuasion*, Ashgate, Aldershot, pp. 207–222.

Pardanaud, C. 2006, 'James mestre n'ema tant servyteur que je vous ayme»: quelques lettres autographes inédites du roi Henri II au connétable Anne de Montmorency, relatives à la bataille de Saint-Quentin et à la captivité du connétable (été 1557–hiver 1558)', *Réforme, Humanisme, Renaissance*, vol. 63, pp. 111–131.

Quentin-Bauchart, E. 1891, *La Bibliothèque de Fontainebleau et les livres des derniers Valois à la Bibliothèque nationale (1515–1589)*, E. M. Paul, L. Huard et Guillemin, Paris.

Rentet, T. 2011, *Anne de Montmorency. Grand maître de François Ier*, Pressses universitaires de Rennes, Rennes.

Ribier, G. 1666, *Lettres et mémoires d'estat*, vol. 2, François Clozier et la veuve Aubouyn, Paris.

Romier, L. 1913, *Les origines politiques des guerres de religion*, vol. 2, Perrin, Paris.

Rothstein, M. 1994, 'Clandestine Marriage and *Amadis de Gaule*: The Text, the World, and the Reader', *Sixteenth Century Journal*, vol. 25, no. 4, pp. 873–886.

Vernassal, F. de 1550, *Histoire de Primaleon de Grece*, P. Le Pellier pour E. Groulleau, Paris.

8
BELLICOSE PASSIONS IN MARGARET CAVENDISH'S *PLAYES* (1662)

Diana G. Barnes

When Margaret Cavendish, Duchess of Newcastle, employed emotional terms to justify her decision to publish, rather than stage, her *Playes* (1662), she positioned her contribution within a pressing political and philosophical debate. In 'The Epistle Dedicatory' to her husband William Cavendish, Duke of Newcastle, she identifies the risks of performance: 'If *Envy* did make a faction against them, they would have had a publick Condemnation; and though I am not such a *Coward*, as to be *afraid* of the hissing Serpents, or stinged Tongues of *Envy*, yet it would have made me a little *Melancholy* to have my harmless and innocent Playes go *weeping* from the Stage' (my italics). Here Cavendish distinguishes her volume from the kind of public discourse that incites the emotions that fuel faction, and breed civil war. As Stephen Zwicker (1993, p. 1) reminds us, in the years immediately following the restoration of monarchy in 1660, 'the memory of that lamented translation from language to arms remained vivid and potent'. The whole historical period should be seen in these terms: David Armitage (2017, p. 11) stresses that 'slaughter on such a scale scythes through families, shatters communities, shapes nations. It can scar also imaginations for centuries to come'. All literary genres carried the collective emotional scars of war but, as Cavendish and her contemporaries recognised, this was particularly true of drama. The public theatres were closed by Parliament after the outbreak of civil war in 1642, and reopened after the restoration of monarchy in 1660. By 1662 when Cavendish's *Playes* were published, drama was a literary genre, and the theatre a cultural institution, deeply implicated in the recent experience of civil war. In choosing to print rather than stage her dramatic works, Cavendish does not shy away from politico-literary polemic. In post-civil-war Britain tears, print drama and the fear, envy, shame and melancholy Cavendish associates with them had a collective political significance as the terms of what Alexandra Bennett (2009) calls the 'theatre of war'. Cavendish's *Playes* is an ideal focal point for considering the relationship between war and emotion. She theorises the relationship between civil war, emotion and theatre in the prefatory materials, while *Bell in Campo*, parts 1 & 2, and *Loves Adventure*, parts 1 & 2, directly concern war, specifically women's emotional roles within it.

When Cavendish writes of plays that 'go weeping from the Stage', tears are not associated with a specific emotion. She cites cowardice, envy and melancholy, but implies shame, pride and courage. As Thomas Dixon (2015, p. 7) argues, 'A tear [. . .] is a universal sign because, depending on the mental, social, and narrative context, it can mean almost anything'. That is not to say that tears do mean anything, but rather they have had a range of specific meanings at different points in time. Nevertheless, as recent scholarship on the cultural history of emotions shows, the broad connotative implications of tears are relevant here. First, tears register emotion that exceeds other modes of expression, such as language and gesture, as Tom Lutz (cited in Rambuss 2013, pp. 258–259) points out: 'We recognize in crying [. . .] a surplus of feeling over thinking, and an overwhelming of our powers of articulation'. Second, tears have meaning within a community. As Dixon (2015, p. 8) puts it: they 'are not best thought of as expressions of individual emotion, but rather as a kind of liquid social bond'. Third, as a social activity, crying is gendered. Bernard Capp (2014, p. 75ff) argues that in seventeenth-century England the 'elite and essentially male code' of civility that had largely displaced medieval courtesy constructed tears as feminine, Roman Catholic, bestial and plebeian, that is, as the antithesis of masculine decorum, decency and control. Dixon's history of Englishness and tears also documents the emergence and ascendency of a masculine emotional regime. Literature is important to Dixon's account: he cites Shakespearean drama as evidence for a mounting national crisis that culminated in the English civil war and then produced lachrymose poetry such as Richard Crashaw's 'The Weeper' (1646). Crashaw's poem is a good example of courtly Roman Catholic discourse adapted to address war (Rambuss 2013, pp. 61–63), but we need to look further than this to understand the significance of Cavendish's invocation of weeping plays and a public divided by factionalism.

A different emotional history emerges, however, if we foreground the complaint and the history play, popular native English literary genres that deal in emotional excess, and deploy it in political and gendered terms. Both draw plotlines from chronicle history and cast them into emotion-rich and tearful, literary forms. Jean Howard's work on the gendering of theatrical passions, and relatedly on theatrical tears, in history plays of the 1590s written by Thomas Heywood and William Shakespeare is important here. In Shakespeare, while tears are often a sign of effeminacy or weakness in a man, especially a king (Richard II), they can connote authentic feeling (Richard Duke of York), or ruthless feigning (Shakespeare's Richard III). Early modern stage tears are ideologically contested, and as such they presage a new emotional code of representation (Howard 2016). Heywood defended the theatre in *An Apology for Actors* (1612), on emotional grounds, specifically its 'power to new mold the harts of the spectators and fashion them to the shape of any noble and notable attempt'. As Howard (1999, p. 136) points out, 'the history play was privileged as a didactic and patriotic genre' and one primarily focused on male heroes and male spectators, but it drew on emotional techniques of impersonation, that is, embodiment of passion in a character, and then transference of that passion from actor to spectator (in Heywood's words 'as if the Personator were the man Personated') derived from the complaint. The *locus classicus*, Ovid's *Heroides*, associated feminine emotional excess of the kind that manifests in tears with a heroic capacity for eloquent and just defiance of oppressive powers. This literary tradition did not depict female tears pejoratively (Helgerson 1999; Clarke 2000). Ovid's tragic and emotional heroines had a special place in the grammar school curriculum 'as affecting *subjects* worth studying and imitating' by men (Enterline 2012, pp. 124–139). The form and its affective techniques were popularised in the male and female complaints of characters from English chronicle history in *The Mirror for Magistrates* (1559). These poems and later male and female historical complaints by Michael Drayton and Samuel Daniel provided playwrights with a powerful model for emotional characterisation (Kerrigan 1991; Manley 1995; Fox 2009; Thorne 2010; Kaegi 2015). Cavendish's *Playes* draws upon these traditions.

In 1662 Cavendish had ample personal justification for tears of grief and for tears of fear that civil war could re-erupt. Born around 1623 to a staunchly royalist family, her formative years were dominated by the mounting civil unrest of the 1630s, the outbreak of civil war in 1640s, and the interregnum of the 1650s (Whitaker 2002, pp. 42–60; Murphy 2012, pp. 272–273, 276). In 'A True Relation of my Birth, Breeding and Life' (Cavendish *Natures Pictures*), she subscribes to a causal mechanistic understanding of emotions, and presents herself as born with a familial emotional disposition, or humour, that was honed by circumstance. She describes her father, Thomas Lucas, as a nobleman and not a peer. As a noble, that is, loyal, constant and upright, to his core, he 'did not esteem titles unless they were gained by heroic actions; and [under Elizabeth I and James I] the kingdome being in a happy peace with all other nations, and in itself [. . .] there was no employments for heroic spirits' (Cavendish *Natures Pictures*, p. 187). This portrait opens a bifurcated account of lives radically reshaped by war. Before the war her parents took a simple approach to raising their family: lavish children with 'superfluity' and they shall never be 'sharking', 'mean' or base'; dress them 'to the height of their estate' and they will recognise their own social superiority; protect them from 'vulgar' influences and 'unseemly actions' and they will not suffer 'infection by ill examples'; and 'please', 'delight' and 'reason' rather than scold, threaten or beat and they will willingly curb base impulses and embrace reason (Cavendish *Natures Pictures*, pp. 188–190). This emotional grooming produced a close-knit family of 'like agreeable natures and affectionable dispositions' (Cavendish *Natures Pictures*, p. 192). Their life, routinely divided between county obligations and fashionable London pastimes, was interrupted by 'an unnatural war [that] like a whirlwind [. . .] felled down their houses' and 'crusht [some] to death' (Cavendish *Natures Pictures*, p. 192). Although Cavendish (*Natures Pictures*, p. 198) would 'lament' these losses for the rest of her life, she recognised that civil war afforded unique opportunities for noble action, heroism and just reward.

In Cavendish's account a powerful and disorienting emotional experience, such as grief and its expression in tears, represents a liminal emotional state between two extremes: passionate loss of control and reasoned heroic action. The emotional devastation (grief, fear, anger etc.) wreaked by war necessitated an important exercise of individual liberty: namely to choose how to respond. One of her brothers, Sir Charles Lucas, was 'shot to death for his loyal service' and faced it with 'a superfluity of courage' (Cavendish *Natures Pictures*, p. 198; Whitaker 2002, pp. 105–106). Wartime heroism was not restricted to men; Cavendish (*Natures Pictures*, p. 196) recalls that her mother shed ample tears over her husband and sons, yet 'in such misfortunes [she] was of an heroic spirit, in suffering patiently where there is no remedie, [and being] industrious where she thought she could help'. War also impelled Cavendish into action. Hearing that the Queen's entourage was diminished, she petitioned successfully to be a maid of honour (*Natures Pictures*, p. 193). Cavendish (*Natures Pictures*, p. 198) celebrates her family's capacity to embrace wartime opportunities for constancy, loyalty and service, but she acknowledged the extremity of bereavement, reporting without judgement that her eldest sister died of grief following her daughter's death.

When Cavendish served as a maid of honour to the Queen, first at Oxford and then Paris, she was part of an emotional regime bound by loyalism and the longing and nostalgia of political exile. At the French court she met her future husband, William Cavendish, Duke of Newcastle, Commander of the Royalist Northern Army, who had fled England after a devastating loss at the Battle of Marston Moor. As a privy councillor and one-time tutor to the future Charles II he was a leading figure in the expatriate royalist community. Although she was dowerless and well below Newcastle's class, he admired her bashful reticence, that is, her humoral or emotional disposition, and fell in love with her. She 'had not the power to refuse him, by reason [her] affections were fixed on him,' but she stresses, this 'love was honest and honorable', and not 'infected' with 'amorous love', which she viewed as 'a disease, or a passion' (*Natures Pictures*, pp. 194–195; Fitzmaurice 2004). Whatever the underlying balance of reason and emotion, marriage to Newcastle positioned Cavendish within a political community of entitled and self-sacrificing royalists anticipating just rewards after the wars, *and* actively debating the relationship between emotions and war in intellectual, literary and political terms.

Newcastle and his brother, Sir Charles Cavendish, were at the centre of an intellectual circle devoted to discussing new philosophical ideas, in particular the passions, and the causes of civil war (Jacob & Raylor 1991, pp. 215–227). They hosted a salon in Paris, patronised intellectuals and *literati*, and maintained a wide intellectual correspondence network (Jacquot 1952; Malcolm 1996; Whitaker 2002, pp. 91–94).[1] Two participants, Thomas Hobbes and René Descartes, wrote extensively about the passions. Their understanding of the passions was far more capacious than ours is of the emotions. They not only classified states that we recognise as emotions, such as love, envy, hate, fear and melancholy, as passions, but also character traits (good nature, bashfulness and greed), passive states (wonder), drives, (appetite, desire or aversion), and ephemeral states (sudden glory) (Schmitter 2014; 2016). The passions were gaining definition but there was no consensus. Whereas Descartes defined them as receptive passive states, a kind of thinking involving rudimentary judgement and somatic memory, that could be shaped via education, Hobbes saw them as the first stirrings of action or movement (James 1999, pp. 87–108, 124–136). The new philosophy theorised physical motion, and psychological emotion, in order to establish a grand system of how the world worked. Newcastle valued such schemes as aids to understanding how civil war could erupt (Sarasohn 1999).[2] Such theoretical endeavour was intimately connected to his well-developed views of how statesmen should serve crown and country, and the public utility of cultural practice (Cavendish 1984).

Prior to the war Newcastle had written plays for the London stage, and had been patron to a number of dramatists, including Ben Jonson, Richard Brome, William Davenant and James Shirley. On the surface humoral comedy and social farce of the kind modelled by Jonson, and adapted by Shirley, Brome, Newcastle and others, was not overtly political. Defining characters primarily by a dominant trait, such as anger, pride or vanity, however, provided a forum to explore how different emotions colour the character of a community. The readiness of dramatists associated with Newcastle to enlist in military service (Shirley and Davenant, for example, and Jonson before them) suggests the easy transition they perceived between theatrical practice and war (Pathsupati 2012; Donaldson 2011, pp. 93–98). Davenant made an important position statement in his Preface to *Gondibert* (1650), laying forth a post-war literary tradition determined to serve political ends by giving readers an emotional education. It was published with Hobbes' endorsement of its philosophical underpinnings. Davenant argued that civil war occurred when 'the State and People are divided, as wee may say a man is divided within him selfe, when reason and passion (and Passion is folly) dispute about consequent actions' (*Gondibert*, p. 36). In cases of 'intestine warre' he continued 'we must side with Reason' and thereby honour 'natures Law [which] hath taken deep impression in the Heart of Man' (*Gondibert*, p. 36). To this end he proposed instilling virtue via heroic verse in dramatic five-act form that employed characters representing 'the distempers of Love, or Ambition', plots drawn from myth, and gentle persuasion rather than force (*Gondibert*, pp. 10–13, 38; Chua 2014; Shershaw 1999). By 1653 Davenant had left *Gondibert* half-written and was actively promoting dramatic performance of martial scenes drawn from recent history to the commonwealth government in London (Jacob & Raylor 1991, p. 213) and conceptualising his operatic drama *The Siege of Rhodes* (1656) (Chua 2014, pp. 51–55).

In the early restoration when Cavendish's *Playes* were published, the English public theatre was being redefined under pressure of recent and endemic war. The royalist spin opposed Puritan emotional constraint to royalist liberty of feeling and celebrated the formal reopening of the theatres as the return of a royalist institution.

As Paulina Kewes (2004, p. 133) argues: 'The myth of the abiding royalism of pre-civil War drama' provided a 'convenient' means for 'aspiring playwrights' to 'cast the intervening years as an aberration'. In fact, as David Scott Kastan (1999, pp. 201–220) explains, the closure of theatres by Parliamentary ordinance in 1642 was motivated less by Puritanism, and more by the imperative to restrict freedoms of association and assembly. Parliament recognised the theatre's capacity to 'make publics', that is, groups of people who judge and take action (Yachnin & Eberhart 2014; Wilson & Yachnin 2010). Theatrical practice did not cease completely between 1642 and 1660 (Potter 1989, pp. 72–112; Straznicky 2004), but adapted and gained political force, particularly in print (Kastan 1999, p. 217). The stage became a key term employed by all parties, in political and religious discussion of the war particularly in print (Wiseman 1998, pp. 2–6; Barnes 2013, pp. 116, 124).

The dedications, letters and introductory dialogues appended to published plays, already an established forum for polemic on the 'affective technologies' of drama, and the civilities of audience response (Mullaney 2007), were readily adapted to royalist ends. In the copious paratexts appended to one of the most significant royalist dramatic publications of the period, Humphrey Moseley's 1647 folio edition of Francis Beaumont and John Fletcher's *Comedies and Tragedies*, for example, metatheatrical discussion of passion nurtures wistful affection for traditions and values interrupted by war. In a letter 'To the Reader', Shirley acclaims drama '*the most absolute*' art owing to its emotional versatility: it can represent 'not only the Phlegm and folly of thick-skinn'd men, but [. . .] the Vertues and passions of every noble condition'. Nostalgically he recalls that 'the very Pleasure [of watching a play] did edify' but, he tells readers, '*in this* Tragicall Age *where the Theatre hath been so much out acted, congratulate thy owne happiness, that in this silence of the Stage, thou hast a liberty to reade these inimitable Playes*' (Beaumont & Fletcher 1647, n.p.). Print plays sustain liberty and effect the reproduction of 'happiness' and other politically contingent passions. Far more effective than 'the sowrer ways of education', in drama 'passions [are] raised to that excellent pitch and by such insinuating degrees that you shall not chuse but consent, & go along with them, finding yourself at last grown insensibly the very same person you read, and then stand admiring the subtile trackes of your engagement' (Beaumont & Fletcher 1647, n.p.).

Moseley's Beaumont and Fletcher folio entrenched in royalist discourse the argument that print drama stimulates audience identification and emulation and thus nourishes a threatened emotional regime. In the preface to *Loves Dominion* (1654) Richard Flecknoe, another associate of the Cavendishes (Whitaker 2004, pp. 120–121), also presents drama's pedagogical advantage over sullen sermons in his programme for 'the Reformed Stage', a text that instills virtue via delightful persuasion; 'let who's list take the *black melancholy spirit* [he asserts, but], give me the *light cheerful one*' (Flecknoe 1654, n.p.). War permeates discussions of royalist affect, for example, William Chamberlayne described *Loves Victory* (1658) as 'begot while Clamourous War's cry was hot' and 'the mourning Stage was silent' (quoted in Rollins 1921, p. 59). In the preface to the 1658 reprint of Thomas Heywood's defence of theatre, Thomas Cartwright presents drama as a cultural defence, explaining that he overcame his wariness of print because it 'was better to wear rusty Armour, than go naked' (Heywood 1658). Playing on the political resonance of these terms in the early restoration, Flecknoe insisted that he would rather an audience encounter *Erminia* (1661) in print than badly staged (Keenan 2014, pp. 42–45). When royalist polemicists presented drama as an 'academy' for emotional civilities that ensure peace (Flecknoe 1654), they articulated a mechanistic view of the passions as pre-rational feelings or judgements triggered by external stimuli, which the average spectator cannot, or will not, self-regulate.

Cavendish uses the paratexts to her *Playes* to position her work within royalist theatrical discourse about the passions – and to preempt her critics. These aims overlap to a degree. By 1662 Cavendish had published five titles amid some controversy: the fact that she had published at all; whether her works were her own; the quality of her writing and philosophical reasoning; and the question of her sanity. The paratexts to *Playes* appear in following sequence: a poem, 'The Dedication'; 'The Epistle Dedicatory' to Newcastle; 10 letters to the reader; a poem, 'To the Lady Marquess of Newcastle', by her husband; a poem, 'A General Prologue to all my Playes'; and a dialogue entitled, 'An Introduction'. Cavendish's agenda is most clearly spelled out in her dedication to her husband. The letters to the reader cover a range of topics: the first advertises the forthcoming biography of her husband (n.p.); the second justifies publishing plays written while the theatres were closed (n.p.); the third presents natural variety as a more effective means of teaching about the passions than classical dramatic unities of time, place and action (sig. Aiv^r); the fourth is a pitch for noble rather than paid actors in public theatres; the fifth concerns her rejection of conventional 'Rules, Forms and Terms' (n.p.); the sixth debunks the assumption that authors speak as they write; the seventh insists that her plays 'join edifying Profit and Delight together' (n.p.); the eighth asserts that no-one helped 'sow' the scenes together (n.p.); the ninth acknowledges songs and scenes contributed by Newcastle (sig. Avi^r); and the tenth recommends that 'Playes must be read to the nature of those several humours, or passions [. . .] as if they were spoke or Acted' (sig. Avi^v). Inconsistency of pagination, print formatting and devices suggests that letters 1, 2, 4, 5, 7 and 8 were interpolated after printing, evidently as a defensive measure.[3]

Playes opens with 'A Dedication', a poem describing the author's 'pleasure and delight' in rehearsing the plays in her mind. The lines, 'For all the time my Playes a making were,/ My brain the Stage, my thoughts were acting there' (sig. Aii^r; see Gallagher 1988; Tomlinson 1992; Barnes 2013 p. 163 ff.), rich with royalist connotation, contextualise the volume within the interregnum. When the theatres' doors were shut, in her mind's eye Cavendish was free to imagine performances irrespective of adverse external conditions. Delight, generated imaginatively, represents royalist hope, nourished by her husband. In the dedicatory letter to Newcastle, she credits him with having 'Create[d] a desire in [her] Mind to write Playes' (sig. Aiii^r). She counterpoises the 'natural life, and [. . .] quick spirit' of his plays with her own 'dull dead statues' (sig. Aiii^r). Whereas his were written for and performed in the Caroline theatre, hers were written while the theatres were closed. Print offers Cavendish certain advantages: it protects her on the one hand from 'the fear of having them hissed off from the Stage' if the audience does not favour them; and on the other, if the plays deserve applause, envy, faction and condemnation (*Playes*, sig. Aiii^r). Cavendish swears she is no 'Coward', but here admits it 'would have made [her] a little Melancholy to have [her] harmless and innocent Playes go weeping from the Stage, and whipt by malicious and hardhearted censurers' (*Playes*, sig. Aiii^v). Asserting the liberty afforded her to embrace and creatively bolster royalism by marriage, she concludes: 'but the truth is, I am careless, for so I have your applause I desire no more' (*Playes*, sig. Aiii^v). In a dedicatory poem to the author Newcastle affirms her role as a print playwright in ensuring the reproduction of royalist affect: 'When we read your each Passion in each Play [. . .] at your pleasure all our passions ly' (n.p). When Cavendish describes the extremes of delight and melancholy, she identifies emotional disequilibrium as the underlying cause of the recent wars, and sympathy as its cure. Marriage to Newcastle stimulates her imagination, bridles melancholy, allays fear, instills hope and insulates her from judgement driven by passions that fuel faction and war.

Dramatic form allows Cavendish to enter a politicised debate about emotions through character. When Cavendish warns readers in 'A General Prologue' to expect 'Cottages of Prose and Rhime' wrought from her own imagination rather than Jonsonian masterpieces (*Playes*, sigs Avii–Avii^v), she acknowledges a precedent that her plays emulate and exceed (Williams 2000, p. 205; Dodds 2013, pp. 159–182). Most of her characters are named for emotional states: Lady Bashful, Lady Passionate, Lord Peaceable Studious, and so on. In the tradition of humoral comedy, this device signals embedded moral argument and social commentary. But whereas England was at peace when Jonson wrote, the aftermath of civil war dominated Cavendish's writing life. Her overriding concern is peace and women's contribution to achieving and maintaining it. As Lady Speaker of *The Female Academy* explains, drama is the ideal host for such discussion because: 'A Theatre is a publick place for publick Actions, Orations, Disputations, Presentations, whereunto is a publick resort; but there are only two Theatres, which are the chief, and the most frequented; the one is of War, the other of Peace; the Theatre of Warr is the Field, and the Battles they fight are the Plays they act' (*The Female Academy*, IV: 22, p. 669). Civil war reverberates throughout the emotional fabric of *Playes*, but *Loves Adventure*, parts 1 and 2, and *Bell in Campo*, parts 1 and 2, directly concern war.

In *Loves Adventure*,[4] parts 1 and 2, Lady Orphant, cross-dressed as the page Affectionata, navigates war with emotional competency. The plot concerns her courtship with Lord Singularity, the General, named for his stated aversion to marriage. The time and place are not specified but, as in England, the characters hail from a country recovering from recent war, and they meet in a distant land where Lord Singularity is fighting another war. At their first meeting, they discuss the correlation between emotion and war:

SINGULARITY: Pray how is my Country, and Countrey-men, live they still in happy peace, and flourishing with plenty?
AFFECTIONATA: There is no noise of war, or fear of famine.
SINGULARITY: Pray Jove continue it.
AFFECTIONATA: It is likely so to continue, unless their pride and luxurie begets a factious childe, that is born with war, and fed with ruine.
SINGULARITY: Do you know what faction is?
AFFECTIONATA: There is no man that lives, and feels it not, the very thoughts are factious in the mind, and in Rebellious passions arises warring against the soul.
SINGULARITY: Thou cannot speak thus by experience boy, thou art too young, not yet at mans Estate.
AFFECTIONATA: But children have thoughts, and said to have a rational soul, as much as those that are grown up to men; but if souls grow as bodies doth, and thoughts increases with their years, then may the wars within the mind be like to School-boys quarrels, that falls out for a toy, and for a toy are friends.

(LA 1. III: 16, p. 48)

According to Affectionata, all people, even children, have the potential for war within; their thoughts tend naturally to the creation of factions, and their passions battle within their minds. Cavendish identifies two emotional regimes: a chaotic and combative one in which individuals are drawn to faction and perpetual war; and a well-governed orderly one in which individuals govern their passions and live sociably with others. This sounds very like Hobbes. In *De Cive* (Hobbes 1642, p. 116), a work dedicated to Newcastle, he describes the state of nature as 'a Dominion of Passions, war, fear, poverty, slovinlinesse, solitude, barbarisme, ignorance, cruelty', and the commonwealth or society as 'the Dominion of reason, peace, security, riches, decency, society, elegancy, sciences, and benevolence'. In the state of nature man is led willy-nilly by his passions and senses, but in society contract bridles and directs men's passions for the common good. In the *Leviathan* (1651 XVII, p. 359), Hobbes identifies 'The passions that incline men to peace [as]: fear of death; and desire of such things as are necessary to commodious living'. These passions move men to restrain those negative passions that foster what Hobbes (1651 XIII, p. 351) describes as a 'disposition' to war. Like Hobbes, Cavendish is concerned to distinguish between 'what drives conflict and what allows cooperative endeavor' (Schmitter 2014). In the scene cited above Cavendish identifies pride, greed and fear as passions, or appetites, that fuel conflict. In contradistinction to Hobbes, in her dedication to Newcastle she presents sympathy and unguarded approval of the kind fostered by marriage, rather than fear and self-interest, as passions that mitigate the warring potential of envy and melancholy. For Cavendish, then, marriage is ideally a bridge between different and potentially opposed parties.[5]

Cavendish's plays connect commentary on marriage to political theory. Affectionata defines war as an emotional conflict between positive and negative passions, or the virtues and graces, on the one hand, and vices and follies, on the other:

> AFFECTIONATA: [. . .] the souls of all mankind, they are like Commonwealths, where the several vertues, and the good graces are the Citizens therein, and the natural subjects thereof; but vices and follies, as thievish Borderers, and Neighbour-enemies, which makes inrodes, factions, mutinies, intrudes and usurps Authority, and if the follies be more than the good graces, and the vices too strong for the vertues, the Monarchy of a good life falls to ruine, also it is endangered by Civil-wars amongst the passions.
>
> (LA 1. IV, p. 56)

Sympathetic marriage is an emotional contract that secures the natural sociability essential to peace by quelling 'anger, malice, and despair', the emotions in each person's mind that Affectionata identifies as the most significant threats to what is pointedly described as 'the Monarchy of a good life' (LA 1. IV, p. 56). As Affectionata states, 'no man ought to be a Master of a Family, but those that can govern orderly and peaceably' (LA 2. IV: 28, p. 95). This idea is developed in another plotline in which Lady Ignorant, frustrated by the quiet life and her husband Lord Peaceable Studious's absorption in books, persuades him to go with her into society. Peaceable Studious embraces the experience. He flirts with other women openly, making Ignorant very uneasy. After she has learned her lesson they resume their old routines. Peaceable Studious observes that when husbands 'take it as a great pleasure to make wives jealouse', they 'separate their affections, and [. . .] make a disorder in their Families' which, like war, is characterised by 'plot and design' (LA 2. II: 14, p. 82). But, he explains: 'when a man lives to himself within his own Family [. . .] he governs orderly, eats peaceably, sleeps quietly, lives contentedly, and most commonly, plentifully and pleasantly, ruling and governing his little Family to his own humour, wherein he commands with love, and is obeyed with duty' (LA 2. II: 14, p. 82). '[W]ho,' he asks rhetorically, 'that is wise, and is not mad, would quit this heavenly life to live in hellish Societies', responding, those who shun this 'stand upon a Quagmire, or rotten Foundation, that will never hold or indure, that is, they are neither grounded on honesty, nor supported with honour' (LA 2. II: 14, p. 82). Ideally, marriage is a mini-commonwealth grounded on a sympathetic contract, fostering humours that support a peaceful emotional regime within the body politic.

When Affectionata is faced with the challenge of gaining the sympathy of a man opposed to marriage, that is, a man whose affective philosophy carries the seeds of war, she shuns eloquence in favour of heroic action. Affectionata's heroism comprises both valiant bravery enabled by 'acting a masculine part upon the Worlds great Stage' (LA 2. V: 34, p. 100), and the more conventionally understood feminine activity of crying. She sheds tears to persuade Singularity to allow her to accompany him to battle, again to persuade him to refuse the Duke of Venice's offer to adopt her, and finally to express 'love, shame, grief and fear' when conflicted by her seemingly impossible love for Singularity and the consequences of her disguise for her elderly guardians, Foster Trusty and Nurse Fondly (LA 2. V: 34, p. 100). Each occasion sparks discussion of the passions. When Singularity observes: 'But thy tears seems as if they were produced from some passion', Affectionata relays the following emotional theory: 'Indeed they are produced from passions and appetites, for passions are the rayes of the mind, and appetites the vapour of the sense, and the rayes of the mind hath drawn up the vapour of my sense into thick moist clouds, which falls in showering tears' (LA 2. V: 34, p. 100). Although, by this account, tears reflect passionate disequilibrium, over and again they effect a sympathetic response in Singularity who endeavours to subdue her melancholy.

Tears mingled with blood gush through civil-war royalist elegy, lament and complaint, giving poetic and political expression to a grief that exceeds words and comprehension. Whereas early civil war royalist elegy celebrated 'the soldier's sacrificial bargain to suffer his own maiming or extinction in order to keep an ideological body intact' (Gray 2013, p. 172), late civil-war elegy, including poetic tributes to Cavendish's brother, Sir Charles Lucas, expressed a more ambivalent attitude toward bloodshed and military virtue. In *Fons Lachrymarum, or Fountain of Tears* (1648), a collection dedicated to Lucas's memory, Francis Quarles has England beg: 'Convert my *tydes of blood* to *streams of tears,* / [. . .] let me / Dissolve to tears (dear God) and weep to thee:/ [. . .] To send these *showres* to *wash away that blood* / VVhich I have lost' ('England's Petition to Heaven', in Quarles 1648, pp. 27–28). The blood flowing through the verse is men's, but the tears are shed by poets, muses, England, God, wives, mothers and men.

Although women were involved in all aspects of the civil war, royalist elegy celebrates military heroism as a masculine virtue, and presents women as widows and mothers, that is, as the embodiment of grief and constancy. Quarles (1648, p. 2) describes being so 'distracted' with grief that all his muses had dispersed, except the tragic muse '*Melpomene,* who now appears / Like *Nioby,* a monument of tears'. Here Quarles cites Niobe, the bereaved mother and widow, as a classical personification of despair conventional to debates about emotional authenticity (Oakley-Brown 2006, p. 69; Enterline 2012, pp. 138–139; Steggle 2007) that gained force during the civil wars. In the *Metamorphoses,* Ovid recounts Niobe's proud defiance of the God Latona, the murder of her seven sons and seven daughters and the suicide of her husband, her metamorphosis into stone, and the tears that continue to flow. Niobe also adorns the frontispiece of *Lachrymae Musarum, Tears of the Muses* (1649), the elegies commemorating the death of royalist Colonel-General, Sir Henry Hastings collated by playwright Richard Brome. She is depicted as a weeping statue surrounded by the muses, signalling the resonance of her intensely felt, but silent, memorialisation of bereavement to civil war elegy.[6] As Ovid (1567, V ll. 396–397) tells it, the story of Niobe taught 'men and women' to '[fear]' the 'open ire' of the Gods, and to worship 'with far greater sumptuousness and earnester desire'. Zealousness motivated by fear was not the lesson royalist poets drew from Niobe; rather in the much admired Ovidian style popularised by the historical female complaints, they admired her fearlessness, dignity, pride of family, position and lineage, and her refusal to capitulate to oppressive religious strictures. Niobe paid the ultimate emotional price for her heroic stand, but she does not buckle: tears flow over her stony form and she continues to emote. In his contribution to *Lachrymae Musarum*, Francis Standish praises Hastings's mother for her 'Stoick' 'Philosophie' and 'patient suffering of affliction' distinguishing her from Niobe's 'still weeping Marble-monument' ('Upon the right Honourable, LUCIE Countess of Huntingdon's Heroick and most Christian bearing of that grand Affliction, the death of her onely Son, The young Lord HASTINGS') (Brome 1649, p. 25). In a compendium of ancient and modern sources bearing 'relation to the late warr', Robert Grove identifies Niobe as a reference point for a philosophical debate about the fitting expression of extreme emotions, citing Seneca '*Cur*[a]*es loquuntur, ingentes stupent*' (Light sorrows speak but the deepest sorrows stupefy) (1651, p. 62).[7]

Cavendish does not mention Niobe in her civil war plays, but the moral debate about managing overpowering emotion associated with Niobe, and the heroic female complaint and its popular adaptation to English history in verse and drama, inform her treatment of wartime grief in *Bell in Campo*.[8] The play presents an argument about emotion, gender and war through its characters Madam Passionate, Lady Victoria, Madam Jantil, and a chorus of angry, then grieving, women. True to her name, Passionate is a slave to her emotions: she slumps into melancholy when her husband, Monsieur La Hardy, goes to war; 'her Spirits are drown'd in sorrow' when he dies (BC 1. IV: 19, p. 130); she is seduced by the flattery of a young suitor and remarries, unhappily thereafter. When Jantil's husband, Seigneur Valeroso, leaves for war, she says jealously: 'I cannot chuse but take it unkindly that you will go without me, do you mistrust my affection?' (BC 1. II: 7, p. 115). She dreams presciently of his death, and in the terms of royalist elegy envisages, 'His wounds fresh bleeding blood like rubies bright' (BC 1. III: 3, p. 127). When his death is confirmed, Jantil 'seems not disturb'd' although her maid, Nell Careless, weeps profusely (BC 1. III: 14, p. 129). Jantil advises Careless that 'Life's a curse [but] since you cannot weep out life, bear it with patience' (BC 1. IV: 21, p. 131). To this end Jantil commissions her husband's biography and designs a magnificent tomb celebrating his valour. Within she places 'the Statues of the four Cardinal Virtues [. . .] sitting as in weeping posture', and without a grove of 'Trees [in which] the Birds may sit and sing his Elegy' (BC 1. IV: 21, p. 132). Jantil explains: 'Although my sorrow appears not outwardly, yet my heart is dead within me' and embracing her grief she lives out her remaining days within her husband's tomb (BC 1. V: 25, p. 137). Only Victoria succeeds in persuading her husband, The Lord General, to allow her to accompany him to war. Victoria is the *femme forte*; she argues that custom alone has made women 'weak and fearful', unfit for public office, and suited only for breeding (BC 1. II: 9, p. 119). When the Amazonian army is stricken with tearful grief over brothers, fathers, husbands, sons and friends lost in war, she declares that while 'tis both natural and human to grieve for the Death of our friends [. . .] tears nor lamentations cannot bring them out of the grave'. Therefore she urges in terms resonant of early-civil-war royalist elegy, 'let your justice give them Death for Death [. . .] instead of weeping eyes, let us make them weep through their Veins' (BC 1. IV: 17, p. 128). Victoria redirects the women's inchoate grief into virtuous heroic action through education comprised of speeches and a fortifying training programme involving military drills, strict discipline, asceticism and marching songs celebrating 'the heroic actions done in former times by heroical women' (BC 1. III: 11, p. 124).

In *Bell in Campo*, then, Passionate stands at one end of the emotional spectrum oscillating uncontrollably from love to melancholic pining, inconsolable grief and tears, desire and infatuation and, ultimately, unhappiness and regret. By contrast Victoria and Jantil govern their feelings stoically, but to different ends.[9] Jantil, 'the tragic elegist', channels her sorrow towards honouring her husband's life and, like Niobe, casts her feelings in stone and thereby memorialises the national trauma of war (Nelson & Alker 2008, p. 29). Victoria channels women's anger and grief into victorious heroic military action and for this gains fame and public honour. Her likeness is 'cast in Brass, and then set in the midst of the City' (BC 2. V: 20, pp. 167–168), memorialising female heroism born of the emotional devastation of war.[10] Thus in *Bell in Campo* Cavendish presents the emotional biographies of wartime wives within an ongoing neostoic moral and political debate about emotional governance in public life intensified by the recent civil wars.

In her fifth letter to the reader Cavendish challenges the 'scholastic' convention of gendering the emotions declaring that her plays:

> [D]o not keep strictly to the Masculine and Feminine Genders [. . .] as for example, a Lock and a Key, the one is the Masculine Gender, the other the Feminine Gender, so Love is the Masculine Gender, Hate the Feminine Gender, and the Furies are shees, and the Graces are shees, the Virtues are shees, and the seven deadly Sins are shees, which [she writes] I am sorry for; but I know no reason but that I may as well make them Hees for my use, as others did Shees, or Shees as others did Hees.
>
> (*Playes*, sig. Aiv)

Recognising that rejecting convention involves the risk of being misunderstood, she objects 'we may as well understand the meaning or sense of a Speaker or Writer by the names of Love or Hate, as by the names of he or she, and better; for the division of Masculine and Feminine Genders doth confound a Scholar more' (*Playes*, n.p.). Amy Schmitter (2014) argues that seventeenth-century philosophers neither wrote of emotions as gendered nor attributed particular emotional expertise to women. Cavendish's renunciation of 'the nicities of Rules, Forms, and Terms' of gender and emotion is pitched at the philosophy of emotions foundational to Davenant's theatrical reform.

In 'A Proposition for Advancement of Moralitie' (1653) Davenant asserts the correlation between civility, masculinity and preparedness for war, stating that: 'the civilizing of a Nation makes [people] not effeminate, or too soft for such discipline of war as enables them to affront their Enemies, but takes off that rudeness by which they grow injurious to one another and impudent towards authority' (Jacob & Raylor 1991, p. 242). Davenant distinguishes here between foreign and civil war and, in well-established terms, advocates emotional education as an antidote to the latter. He writes 'People will ever be unquiet while they are ignorant of themselves, and unacquainted with those Engins that scrue them up, which are their passions' (Jacob & Raylor 1991, p. 244). He outlines how dramatic spectacle stimulates delight and wonder, and thereby enhances an audience's tractability to the state. But he urges theatrical reform, stressing the importance of wholesome, heroic subject matter drawn from recent history particularly 'those famous Battels at Land and Sea by which this Nation is renown'd [. . .] which will not, like the softer arguments of Playes, make people effeminate, but warme and incite them to Heroicall Attempts' (Jacob & Raylor 1991, p. 246). Relatedly he specifies that men should not act women's parts. Davenant proposes staging passions that were both devoid of that worrying feminine tendency of pre-civil war drama and derived from men's experience of war. Such public performances would literally engender obedience to the governing regime and a readiness to fight in its defence.

Cavendish rejects this gendered emotional economy. She embraces cross-dressing as a plot device capable of ensuring a happy resolution, as in *Loves Adventures*, when Affectionata's true sex is revealed, and Singularity accepts it and unflinchingly takes her as his wife. Cavendish also regenders emotions themselves, for example, by attributing heroic virtue to women. Affectionata and Victoria, for instance, are eloquent and rational in the tradition of the female complaint, and valiant on the battlefield. Furthermore their military courage is based on sound emotional principles. Affectionata becomes a thrashing machine and kills countless opponents when her true love is threatened, and Victoria commands her army in a just war to save the masculine army – and the nation. As Victoria asserts, this 'prove[s] the courage of our Sex, to get liberty and freedome from the Female Slavery, and makes [women] equal with men' (BC 2. I: 3, p. 143). The liberty Cavendish's Amazonian 'Heroickesses' embraces, then, is the freedom to exercise courage, the passion conventional to battle, and thus claim a species of 'glory' once reserved for men. The early moderns categorised glory as an inherently social passion, conferred on a person by others. They viewed it as crucial to a well-run society because people heed and emulate a glorious person. In Cavendish's plays the characters who achieve glory not only model lives in which the passions are well-governed and directed to positive action, but embed that affect into aesthetic monuments (stone, brass or words) that preserve exemplary feminine virtue in the national cultural memory. As Cavendish signals in her paratexts such works are important because glory can stimulate envy and faction; if it is not well managed, it will undermine the sociable contract.

In her *Playes* Cavendish sought to depict a new emotional landscape born out of England's recent history of war and to articulate a heroic civil code that would fit the newly restored state and enfranchise women in the emergent royalist emotional regime. Cavendish challenged the royalist theatrical and philosophical discourses that were gaining solid form as an emotional regime. She recognised the importance of emotional discourse as a conduit for political values and as a stabilising foundation crucial for a political regime after civil war; but she contested the gendering of the discourse that was gaining authority.

Notes

1. Participants included René Descartes, Marin Mersenne, Thomas Hobbes, John Bramhall, Anna van Schurman and Christina of Sweden.
2. Hobbes had a long association with the Cavendish family and dedicated a number of works to William Cavendish, Duke of Newcastle. See Sarasohn 1999.
3. I thank Gweno Williams and Alan Stewart for discussing this with me.
4. All subsequent references to *Loves Adventure* are cited in-text as 'LA', and followed by Act, Scene, and line numbers. All page numbers are from the Shaver (1999) edition.
5. For Cavendish's treatment of marriage in *Sociable Letters* (1664) see Barnes 2013, p. 144 ff.
6. Interestingly, the short Latin verse on the frontispiece compares tears to a seeping pustule. Hastings died of smallpox rather than battle wounds. I am grateful to Michael Bennett for the following translation 'How the muse Niobe would lie weeping at a revered hero's urn so at your corpse and, O Argus, at yours. Just as the spiteful pain of disease flowed and the pustule swelled up so [will] a tear well up in a thousand eyes. Weep goddesses this flower of the Britons has been laid under the earth. Unprompted, amongst the tears, the Castalian spring spouts'.
7. Robert Grove, *Gleanings, or a Collection of Some memorable Passages, Both Ancient and Modern, Many in relation to the late warre* (1651).
8. All subsequent reference to *Bell in Campo* will be cited in-text as 'BC', followed by Act, Scene and line numbers. All page numbers are from the Shaver (1999) edition.
9. On stoicism in *The Unnatural Tragedy* (Cavendish 1662), see Bennett (2011).
10. On Lady Victoria, see Stanton (2007) and Raber (2000).

Reference list

Barnes, G. 2013, *Epistolary Community in Print, 1580–1664*, Ashgate, Farnham.
Barnes, G. 2015, 'Remembering Civil War in Andrew Marvell's "Upon Appleton House"', in S. Downes, A. Lynch & K. O'Laughlin (eds), *Emotions and War: Medieval to Romantic Literature*, Palgrave Macmillan, Basingstoke, pp. 185–202.
Beaumont, F. & Fletcher, J. 1647, *Comedies and Tragedies*, London.
Bennett, A. 2009, 'Margaret Cavendish and the Theatre of War', in S. H. Mendelson (ed.), *Ashgate Critical Essays on Women Writers in England, 1550–1700*, Ashgate, Farnham, pp. 103–113.
Bennett, A. 2011, '"Yes, and": Margaret Cavendish, the Passions and Hermaphrodite Agency', in P. Salzman & J. Walwork (eds), *Early Modern Englishwomen Testing Ideas*, Ashgate, Farnham, pp. 75–87.
Brome, R. 1649, *Lachrymae Musarum, Tears of the Muses*, London.
Capp, B. 2014, '"Jesus Wept" but did the Englishman? Masculinity and Emotion in Early Modern England', *Past & Present*, vol. 224, no. 1, pp. 75–108.

Cavendish, M. 1662, *Playes*, London.
Cavendish, M. 1915, 'A True Relation of My Birth and Breeding', in *Natures Pictures* 1656, reprinted as 'Memoirs' in E. Rhys (ed.), *Margaret, Duchess of Newcastle: Life of the Duke, Memoirs of her own Life and Certain Sociable Letters*, Dent, London, pp. 187–213.
Cavendish, M. 1999, *The Convent of Pleasure and Other Plays*, ed. A. Shaver, Johns Hopkins University Press, Baltimore.
Cavendish, W. 1984, *Ideology and Politics on the Eve of Restoration: Newcastle's Advice to Charles II*, ed. Thomas P. Slaughter, American Philosophical Society, Pennsylvania.
Chua, B. 2014, 'The Purposes of Playing on the Post Civil War Stage: The Politics of Affection in William Davenant's Dramatic Theory', *Exemplaria*, vol. 26, no. 1, pp. 39–57.
Clarke, D. 2000, '"Formed into words by your divided lips": Women, Rhetoric and the Ovidian Tradition', in D. Clarke & E. Clarke (eds), *'This Double Voice': Gendered Writing in Early Modern England*, Palgrave Macmillan, Basingstoke, pp. 61–87.
Davenant, W. 1971, *Sir William Davenant's, Gondibert*, ed. D. F. Gladish, Oxford University Press, Oxford.
Dixon, T. 2015, *Weeping Britannia: Portrait of a Nation in Tears*, Oxford University Press, Oxford.
Dodds, L. A. 2013, *The Literary Invention of Margaret Cavendish*, Duquesne University Press, Pennsylvania.
Donaldson, I. 2011, *Ben Jonson: A Life*, Oxford University Press, Oxford.
Enterline, L. 2012, *Shakespeare's Schoolroom: Rhetoric, Discipline, Emotion*, University of Pennsylvania Press, Pennsylvania.
Fitzmaurice, J. 2004, 'The Intellectual and Literary Courtship of Margaret Cavendish', *Early Modern Literary Studies*, Special Issue 14, viewed 6 October 2017, http://purl.oclc.org/emls/si-14/fitzinte.html
Flecknoe, R. 1654, *Love's Dominion, A Dramatique Piece, Full of Excellent Moralitie; Written as a Pattern for the REFORMED STAGE*, London.
Flecknoe, R. 1661, *Erminia*, London.
Fox, C. 2009, *Ovid and the Politics of Emotion in Elizabethan England*, Macmillan, New York.
Gallagher, C. 1988, 'Embracing the Absolute: The Politics of the Female Subject in Seventeenth-Century England', *Genders*, no. 1, pp. 24–39.
Gray, C. 2013, 'Wild Civility: Men at War in Royalist Elegy', in J. Feather & C. E. Thomas (eds), *Violent Masculinities: Male Aggression in Early Modern Texts and Culture*, Palgrave Macmillan, Basingstoke, pp. 169–189.
Grove, R. 1651, *Gleanings, or a Collection of Some memorable Passages, Both Ancient and Modern*, London.
Helgerson, R. 1999, 'Weeping for Jane Shaw', *South Atlantic Quarterly*, vol. 98, no. 3, pp. 451–476.
Heywood, T. 1658, *The Actors Vindication containing, three brief treatises, viz. I. Their antiquity, II. Their antient dignity, III. The true use of their quality*, London.
Hobbes, T. 1651, *Leviathan or the Matter, Forme and Power of a Common-Wealth Ecclesiastical and Civil*, London.
Hobbes, T. 1998, *On the Citizen*, eds R. Tuck & M. Silverthorne, *Cambridge Texts in the History of Political Thought*, Cambridge University Press, Cambridge.
Howard, J. E. 1999, 'Other Englands: the View from the Non-Shakespearean History Play', in H. Ostovich, M. V. Silcox & G. Roebuck (eds), *Other Voices, Other Views: Expanding the Canon in English Renaissance Studies*, University of Delaware Press, Delaware, pp. 135–153.

Howard, J. E. 2012, 'Thomas Heywood: Dramatist of London and Playwright of the Passions', in T. Hoenselaars (ed.), *Cambridge Companion to Shakespeare and Contemporary Dramatists*, Cambridge University Press, Cambridge, pp. 120–133.

Howard, J. E. 2016, 'Monarchs Who Cry: The Gendered Politics of Weeping in the English History Play', in D. Callaghan (ed.), *A Feminist Companion to Shakespeare*, Wiley Blackwell, New Jersey, pp. 457–466.

Howard, J. E. & Rackin, P. 1997, *Engendering a Nation: A Feminist Account of English Histories*, Routledge, Oxford.

Jacob, J. R. & Raylor, T. 1991, 'Opera and Obedience: Thomas Hobbes and A Proposition for Advancement of Moralitie by Sir William Davenant', *The Seventeenth Century*, vol. 6, no. 2, pp. 205–250.

Jacquot, J. 1952, 'Sir Charles Cavendish and his Learned Friends', *Annals of Science*, vol. 8, no. 1, pp. 13–27, 175–191.

James, S. 1999, *Philosophy and Action: The Emotions in Seventeenth-Century Philosophy*, Oxford University Press, Oxford.

Kaegi, A. 2015, '(S)wept from Power: Two Versions of Tyrannicide in Richard III', in R. Meek & E. Sullivan (eds), *The Renaissance of Emotion: Understanding Affect in Shakespeare and his Contemporaries*, Manchester University Press, Manchester, pp. 200–220.

Kastan, D. S. 1999, *Shakespeare After Theory*, Routledge, Oxford.

Keenan, T. 2014, *Restoration Staging 1660–74*, Routledge, Oxford.

Kerrigan, J. 1991, *Motives of Woe: Shakespeare and Female Complaint*, Clarendon, Oxford.

Kewes, P. 2004, 'Dryden's Theatre and the Passions of Politics' in S. N. Zwicker (ed.), *The Cambridge Companion to John Dryden*, Cambridge University Press, Cambridge, pp. 131–155.

Lawrence, M. 1995, 'London and the Languages of Tudor Complaint', in M. Lawrence (ed.). *Literature and Culture in Early Modern England*, Cambridge University Press, Cambridge, pp. 62–122.

Malcolm, N. 1996, 'A Summary Biography of Hobbes', in T. Sorrell (ed.), *The Cambridge Companion to Hobbes*, Cambridge University Press, Cambridge, pp. 13–44.

Mullaney, S. 2007, 'Affective Technologies: Toward an Emotional Logic of the Elizabethan Stage', in M. Floyd-Wilson & G. A. Sullivan Jr. (eds), *Environment and Embodiment in Early Modern England*, Palgrave, Hampshire, pp. 71–89.

Murphy, E. 2012, 'Wartimes Seventeenth-Century Women's Writing and Its Afterlives', in A. B. Coiro & T. Fulton (eds), *Rethinking Historicism From Shakespeare to Milton*, Cambridge University Press, Cambridge, pp. 257–281.

Nelson, H. F. & Alker, S. 2008, 'Memory, Monuments, and Melancholic Genius in Margaret Cavendish's *Bell in Campo*', *Eighteenth Century Fiction*, vol. 21, no. 1, pp. 13–35.

Oakley-Brown, L. 2006, *Ovid and the Cultural Politics of Translation in Early Modern England*, Ashgate, Farnham.

Ovid 1567, *The XV Books of P. Ovidius Naso, entitled Metamorphosis, translated oute of Latin into English by Arthur Golding*, London.

Pasupathi, V. C. 2012, 'Arms and the Book: "Workes," "Playes," and "Warlike Accoutrements" in William Cavendish's *The Country Captain*', *Philological Quarterly*, vol. 91, no. 2, pp. 277–303.

Potter, L. 1989, *Secret Rites and Secret Writing: Royalist Literature 1641–1660*, Cambridge University Press, Cambridge.

Quarles, F. 1648, *Fons Lachrymarum, or Fountain of Tears*, London.

Raber, K. 2000, 'Warrior Women in the Plays of Cavendish and Killigrew', *Studies in English Literature, 1500–1900*, vol. 40, no. 3, pp. 413–430.

Rambuss, R. 2013, 'Crashaw and the Metaphysical Shudder; Or, How to Do Things with Tears', in S. McClary (ed.), *Structures of Feeling in Seventeenth-Century Cultural Expression*, University of Toronto Press, Toronto, pp. 253–271.

Rollins, H. E. 1921, *A Contribution to the History of the English Commonwealth Drama*, Chapel Hill.

Sarasohn, L. 1999, 'Thomas Hobbes and the Duke of Newcastle: Study in the Mutuality of Patronage before the Establishment of the Royal Society', *Isis*, vol. 90, no. 4, pp. 715–737.

Schmitter, A. M. 2014, '17th and 18th Century Theories of Emotions', *The Stanford Encyclopedia of Philosophy*, ed. EN Zalta, viewed 15 June 2015, http://plato.stanford.edu/archives/spr2014/entries/emotions-17th18th/ and 2016 edn. viewed 25 September 2017, https://plato.stanford/win2016/entries/emotions-17th18th [links broken].

Shershaw, S. C. 1999, 'Windings and Turnings: The Metaphoric Labyrinth of Restoration Dramatic Theory', *Comparative Drama*, vol. 26, no. 1, pp. 1–18.

Stanton, K. S. 2007, '"An Amazonian Heroickess": The Military Leadership of Queen Henrietta Maria in Margaret Cavendish's Bell in Campo (1662)', *Early Theatre*, vol. 10, no. 2, pp. 71–86.

Steggle, M. 2007, *Laughing and Weeping in Early Modern Theatres*, Ashgate, Farnham.

Straznicky, M. 2004, *Privacy, Playreading, and Women's Closet Drama, 1550–1700*, Cambridge University Press, Cambridge.

Thorne, A. 2010 '"O Lawful let it be/ That I have room . . . to curse a while": Voicing the Nation's Conscience in Female Complaint in *Richard III*, *King John*, and *Henry VIII*', in W. Maley & M. Tudeau-Clayton (eds), *This England, That Shakespeare: New Angles on Englishness and the Bard*, Ashgate, Burlington, pp. 105–126.

Tomlinson, S. 1992, '"My Brain the Stage": Margaret Cavendish and the Fantasy of Female Performance', in C. Brant & D. Purkiss (eds) *Women, Texts and Histories 1575–1760*, Routledge, London, pp. 143–163.

Whitaker, K. 2002, *Mad Madge: The Extraordinary Life of Margaret Cavendish, Duchess of Newcastle, the First Woman to Live by her Pen*, Basic, New York.

Williams, G. 2000, '"No Silent Woman": The Plays of Margaret Cavendish, Duchess of Newcastle', in A. Findlay & S. Hodgson-Wright (eds), *Women and Dramatic Production 1550–1700*, Routledge, London, pp. 95–122.

Wilson, B. & Yachnin, P. (eds) 2010, *Making Publics in Early Modern Europe: People, Things, Forms of Knowledge*, Routledge, London.

Wiseman, S. 2004, *Drama and Politics in the English Civil War*, Cambridge University Press, Cambridge.

Yachnin, P. & Eberhart, M. (eds) 2014, *Forms of Association: Making Publics in Early Modern Europe*, University of Massachusetts Press, Massachusetts.

9

'AT NEWBURN FOORD, WHERE BRAVE SCOTS PAST THE TINE'

Emotions, literature, and the Battle of Newburn[1]

Gordon D. Raeburn

On 20 August 1640 a Scottish Covenanter army, led by General Alexander Leslie, crossed the River Tweed at Coldstream, thereby entering England. Eight days later they met and defeated an English royalist force at Newburn Ford, on the River Tyne, six miles outside of Newcastle. The resulting Scottish occupation of a large part of Northern England, including Newcastle and Durham, forced Charles I to a truce, and an agreement to pay the expenses of the Scottish army.[2]

The Battle of Newburn was the only battle of the Second Bishops' War, a conflict that had arisen from ongoing attempts to impose ecclesiastical uniformity with England upon Scotland. The subsequent signing of the National Covenant in Edinburgh in 1638, and the First Bishops' War in 1639, had ended, as far as the Scots were concerned, with an agreement as to the preservation of Scottish laws and religion. It would seem, however, that Charles I had no intention of abandoning his attempts to impose episcopacy in Scotland, and by 1640 conflict was once again on the horizon.[3]

In addition to the concessions made by Charles I following the Battle of Newburn, the invasion of England by Leslie's forces in 1640 unsurprisingly resulted in much correspondence, propaganda and printed works on both sides of the conflict, both before and after the crossings of the Tweed and Tyne. In many instances these works, either private letters or works for public consumption, were possessed of and displayed true emotion, but in certain cases they were also clear attempts to shape the emotional responses of the audience to the battle and its aftermath.

Before the Battle

In the run up to the Battle of Newburn several pamphlets and broadsides, anonymously authored, but on behalf of the 'Scottish people', were printed within

Scotland that addressed an English audience, explaining the Scottish position and intentions. These were all relatively short works which all contained distinct emotional elements. The first of these printed works, *Information from the Estaits of the kingdome of Scotland, to the kingdome of England*, began:

> The troubles which these years bygone afflicted this nation, and storms which threatned both kingdomes, being apparently concluded by capitulation at the borders; The subjects of this kingdome re-turned from thence, not only very confident to have enjoyed peace among themselves, by the Parliament & Assembly promised for settling all disorders arisen for the want of these, but also to have gained the English in a further degree of friendship, having cleared the calumnies laid to our charge, both by our carriage and by discovering the fountaines, whence the mischief then escaped, had flowed.
> (Information from the Estaits of the kingdome of Scotland 1640, p. 3)

This is a very clear attempt to establish quickly a friendship between Scotland and England in the minds of the common English man and woman who may have read this work, and to highlight this international friendship as an outcome of the events of the previous year. It is also quite important to note that the author or authors were very quick to suggest that the Scottish army and the Scottish people had been lied about by the English authorities, an extension of which is that the English authorities were lying to the English people. This in turn could have been an attempt to suggest to the English audience that there was a degree of separation between them and the English authorities, and perhaps more common ground with the Scots could be found. Indeed, as was subsequently emphasised:

> for as we hold that no obligation bindeth so fast, as that of Religion, so do those who are contrary to our Religion hold the same; and as that *maxime* doth make them hold fast together, should not likewise all good Christians and Patriots in this isle, labour to mantaine love and friendship among our selves, and with the rest of the Protestants about us? Should we not be stirred up by the valour and successe of lesse powerfull nations, to joyn with united armes against the whore of *Babel* and her supports; should we not open our ears to the lamentations of the princely children of our Kings only sister, who in severall parts of the world (but all banished from their own inheritance) are crying for pitie and relief, rather than break the bonds, whereby we are so often tyed, and make sport to the Pope and his children, the Bishops, by killing one another, to mantaine their pride and usurpation?
> (Information from the Estaits of the kingdome of Scotland 1640, pp. 8–9)

This section again highlights the shared bond of friendship between England and Scotland, but this time emphasises that this friendship was also due to the commonality of religion. As befits two nations who shared the same religion should they not join together against those who would oppose them, namely Charles I, as he would have attempted to impose changes to their religion? In addition to friendship and shared religion, however, this piece also appeals to a sense of shared emotional response to the suffering of others. Such a sympathetic response to the lamentations of those banished from their inheritance, in conjunction with the bonds of common religion, should, for the authors of this piece, draw the Scots and English together, an outcome that would have proven unhappy for their enemies. Any conflict between Scotland and England would serve only to please Charles I and the Pope, enemies, in the minds of the Covenanters, to true religion. By using such affective terminology in an appeal to their international friends the authors were clearly attempting to elicit an emotional response from their audience, hopefully leading to an increased sense of solidarity for the Scots among the English people. Of course, friendship and a common religion did not mean that there was no separation between Scotland and England:

> For as we meddle not with the laws of England, nor their Parliaments, when there is difference betwixt the King and them, so ought not the English to meddle with us: For the kingdomes are independent of each other, and their government distinct, and will not therein be ordered the one by the others example, even in things needfull.
> (Information from the Estaits of the kingdome of Scotland 1640, pp. 9–10)

Despite the friendship between Scotland and the English people, it was clear that Scotland would not willingly have changes to their religion imposed upon them. Surely the English people could understand that?

The second piece to be printed in Scotland was a broadside entitled *Information from the Scottish Nation, to all the true English, concerning the present Expedition*, the first paragraph of which ended:

> To maintain an Army on the borders is above our strength, & cannot be a safety unto us by Sea: To retire homeward, were to call on our Enemies to follow us, & to make our selves & our Countrey, a prey by land, as our Ships & goods are made at Sea. We are therefore constrained at this time to come into *England*, not to make warre, but for seeking our relief and preservation.
> (Information from the Scottish Nation 1640)

Having established a friendship between England and Scotland in the previous work it was clearly important to the author that the English people understood that the army, which was about to cross the border, was not there with violence in mind. Indeed, as was subsequently stated, '*Duetie* obligeth us to love *England* as our selves: Your grievances are ours, The preservation or ruine of Religion & Liberties, is common to both Nations: We must now stand or fall together' (*Information from the Scottish Nation* 1640). The Scots were clearly attempting to emphasise that they were not there to take from or hurt the friends they had in the English. The honourable intentions of the Scottish army were further reinforced by stating, 'And where it may be conceived, that an Army cannot come into *England* but they will waste & spoile, We declare, that no Souldiours shall be allowed to commit any out-rage, or do the smallest wrong, but shalbe punished with severity' (*Information from the Scottish Nation* 1640). The author of this piece was clearly trying to instil in the English people that the Scottish army would encounter upon crossing the border a sense of trust and common feeling rather than the understandable fear of an invading army. As with the previous example this work also utilised affective language and terminology in order, perhaps, to increase the depth of feeling for their cause among the English audience, by appealing once more to sympathetic feelings south of the border. The author stresses that the Scottish people love the English, and hopefully the same can be said of the English for the Scots. Once more, this affection for one another should allow for a sympathetic response from those in England.

A similar attempt was made in the subsequent printed work, *The Intentions of the Army of the Kingdome of Scotland, Declared to their Brethren of England*, in which was stated:

> Wee now before GOD and the world, make offer in generall, and will make offer to so many of them as will require it in particular, of the strongest and most inviolable bond of our solemne Oath and religious attestation of the great Name of GOD, who is our feare & our dread, & from whom we hope for a blessing upon our Expedition, that we intend no enimitie or rapine, and shall take no mans goods, nor ingage our selves in blood by fighting, unlesse we be forced unto it.
>
> (The Intentions of the Army of the Kingdome of Scotland 1640, p. 6)

This statement of intent is slightly different in that it contains the qualifying statement that the Scottish army would fight if they were forced to, which could be read as an appeal for solidarity as well as a warning not to oppose them. Indeed, this work is the first in which the probability of conflict is alluded to, although the Scots must have known all along that this was inevitable:

> All the designe of both Kingdomes is, for the trueth of Religion, and for the just Liberty of the Subject; and all the devices and doings of the enemy are for oppressing of both, that our Religion may bee turned into Superstition and Atheisme, and our Libertie into base servitude and bondage: To bring this to passe, they have certainly conceived, that the blocking up

of this Kingdome by Sea and Land, would proove a powerfull and infallible meane: for either within a very short time shall wee through want of trade, and spoyling of our goods, bee brought to such extreamity, poverty, and confusion, that we shall miserably desire the conditions which wee now despise and declyne, and bee forced to embrace their will for a Law, both in Kirk and Policie, which will bee a precedent for the like misery in *England*, taught by our example to be more wise. Or upon the other part, we shall by this invasion bee constrayned furiously, and without order, to breake into *England*, which we beleeve is their more earnest desire, because a more speedy execution of their designe: For we doubt not but upon our comming, clamours will bee raysed, posts sent, and Proclamations made through the Kingdome, to slander our pious and just intentions, as if this had been our meaning from the beginning, To stirre up all the English against us, that once being entred in blood, they may with their owne swords, extirpat their own Religion, lay a present foundation with their own hands for building of *Rome*, in the midst of them, and be made the authors both of their own and our slavery, to continue for ever.
(The Intentions of the Army of the Kingdome of Scotland 1640, pp. 7–8)

The authors were clearly making the case that their hand was being forced; they had no choice but to enter England. If they did not enter England they would be besieged by English forces on land and sea, intent on forcibly altering their religion. They did this, however, not just for themselves, but also to save their potential English allies from their own inevitable religious suppression. The Scots were aware they would be painted as an invading horde, but continued to stress that nothing could be further from the truth; their intentions were pious and just.

It is possible that at the same time as the Scots were printing material aimed at quieting the fears of the English people they were also engaged in a more clandestine manipulation of the English authorities. In a letter dated 3 August 1640, to the Secretary of State Francis Windebank, Edward Viscount Conway, the commander of the English forces in the north, wrote:

You yesterday received another letter from Sir John Conyers wherein he says the same person did write that Carr had returned with a bond wherein 63 noblemen and gentlemen had bound themselves to join with the Scots. I am absolutely of opinion that both these letters were counterfeit, sent only to deceive us, and to make us suspect ourselves. Neither do I believe the Scots will come into England; this that they do is only to brag; but, however, I will look to myself as well as a man may that has no money in his purse. I would send for more of the foot from Selby but I fear unpaid soldiers more than I do the Scots, and the Devil to boot – God keep you from all three.
(Hamilton 1880, pp. 548–549)

If Conway's suspicions concerning the authenticity of these letters were true then it is probable that the Scots were attempting to spread doubt and fear among the English command. Indeed, if true, this shows a fascinating divergence in approach to the manipulation of the emotions of the English public and armed forces. The authors of the publicly available printed works seen above were engaged in clear attempts to elicit sympathy from the English, and to highlight the commonalities between the English and Scots, while at the same time emphasising their differences. These differences, however, merely allowed for a greater bond between the two nations, based on love and respect. In private, however, the approach was rather different, and the authors of those letters attempted to manipulate the fears of the English forces so as to reduce their willingness to fight a clearly prepared force. Such an attempt is less likely to have reached the common man and woman, and if it had it would have come from the English authorities themselves, and could be responded to from Scotland with the aforementioned public expression of love and friendship. If the letters described above were in fact attempts to spread fear and doubt then this shows a clearly thought out strategy towards the subtle manipulation of English emotions at all levels of society.

Interestingly, Conway's belief that the Scots would not enter England was not shared by all. On 11 August 1640 Sir Jacob Astley wrote to Conway:

> I think the Scots had better advance a good way into Northumberland without resistance than we send this army to encounter them without pay; for then, without all question, they will prove more ravenous upon the country than the Scots, who, for their own ends and to gain a party here, I believe will give the country all the fair quarter that may be, which our men neither can nor will do.
>
> (Gardiner 1884, pp. 185–186)

Astley, at least, seemed to believe that the Scots truly did intend to prevent their soldiers committing any atrocities, and that this level of self-control may well endear them to the common English man and woman.

A further example of the more subtle manipulation of English fears can be seen from a letter dated 15 August 1640 from Sir John Clavering to Conway:

> My son like a young man more forward than wise, without any advice from me or assurance from them, ventured into their camp at Chouseley Wood, and by means of some acquaintance had a sight of their general and other nobles who were then going to a council of war at Dunse Castle on Wednesday afternoon last. He went to their camp where he had a particular view of each regiment, 196 in number, and eight more expected, which, they tell him, shall no sooner come than they are to march for England, still declaring how little harm they intend in their passage; and to make it more prob[able they told] him they have provided 10,000 sheep and 500 beasts, with a fortnights provision for all their army, and that they will bring with

them a canvas tent for every six soldiers, a free gift of their dear sisters of Edinburgh, that they should not spoil the hedges and groves of any in England.

(Hamilton 1880, p. 587)

While it is possible that the acquaintances of Clavering's son truly believed in what they told him, it could also be the case that this was a further attempt at the manipulation of the English forces, and it certainly filtered through to Conway's command in the form of Clavering's letter.[4]

The English, however, produced their own materials aimed at the manipulation of people's fear. On 20 August 1640, the day the Scots entered England, a piece entitled 'Leslie's speech to his soldiers after they were passed the Tweed' appeared:

Fellow soldiers and countrymen, give me leave to bid you heartily welcome thus far. We are now with Caesar past the Rubicon, and this night you are to lie on English ground. This is the land of promise, which as yet ye see but afar off. Do but follow me, I will be your Joshua. Your turf cottages you shall ere long exchange for stately houses, and let not the thought of your wives and bearns and such like lumber which you leave behind trouble you, for having done your business you shall have choice of English lasses, whereon you may beget a new and better world. Was not their great William the Conqueror a bastard? And in some things we are not inferior to him, and will never despair of as great a fortune; nay, in many things we have far greater advantages than that Norman duke, and shall we be such dastards not to pursue them? At his first entrance he had no party to trust to, but we have already many a fair town; yea, London itself is as sure to us as the good town of Edinburgh. Their purses which have been shut to their King, doubt not but you shall find open to you. The brethren, who have in their hearts long since sworn the Covenant, are already providing change of raiment for you and the sisters clean linen, and do but long for your coming to fetch it. You have fast friends both in court and city, fathers, brothers, and kindred that will employ their utmost ability to solicit your cause, and if occasion be, their swords I trust shall be as ready to make way for you, as your own. Our informations, our declarations, and especially our late intentions are generally well liked of and approved by all. What remains but that like true Scots we lay hold of this blessed opportunity. I shall quickly bring you to the sight of gay coats, caps and feathers, goodly horses, bonny lasses, fair houses. What shall I say? Win them and wear them. When we are once in possession they shall know more of our minds. Return to Scotland they that list for Leslie!

(Hamilton 1880, p. 612)

This is a fascinating piece, hence its reproduction in full. The piece is clearly aimed at instilling fear in the English populace in opposition to the earlier Scottish attempts to the contrary. The Scottish army, and indeed the Scottish nation as a whole, were painted as contemporary Border Reivers, entering England to steal clothes, money and English women. They had abandoned their wives and children, indeed, they had abandoned their entire country. Why would they have returned to Scotland once they had taken charge of England? Interestingly, the piece does suggest a religious motive behind the invasion, in that Leslie was reported as telling his army the hearts of many of the English had already signed the Covenant. Perhaps in this instance to deny a religious motive would have been a step too far for the intended audience, and would have led to the realisation that this was propaganda? It is unfortunately unclear how widely this piece was disseminated.

Following their entry into England the Scots printed one last piece, *The Lawfulnesse of ovr Expedition into England Manifested*, in which was reiterated:

> It was not premeditate nor affected by us (God knows,) but our enemies haue necessitat & redacted us unto it, & that of purpose to sowe the seed of Nationall quarrels; yet as God hitherto hath turned all their plots against themselves, and to effects quite contrary to those that they intended: so are we hopefull, that our going into *England*, so much wished and desired by our adversaries for producing a Nationall quarrel, shall so farre disappoint them of their aymes, that it shall link the two Nations together in straiter & stronger bonds both of civill and Christian love, then ever before.
> (The Lawfulnesse of ovr Expedition into England Manifested 1640, sig. A3^r)

Once again the author of this piece was emphasising the Scottish friendship with the English, even though the Scottish army had by this stage crossed the border. However, they stressed to the English people that this was still done with pious intent, and the side effect would be a strengthening of the bond between the two nations and the victory of Protestantism over the plotting of their Catholic adversaries.

After the battle

As was the case in the days and weeks leading up to the battle, following the Scottish victory at Newburn there were several works printed, as well as correspondence, relating to the events of late August 1640.

Very shortly after the battle, on 4 September 1640, a petition was sent to the King from the Scottish commissioners of the disbanded parliament, in which was stated:

> That whereas through many sufferings, in this time past, *Extream* necessity hath constrained us, for our reliefs, and obtaining our humble and just desires, to come unto *England*; where according to our Intentions formerly delivered, we have in all our Convoy, lived upon our own Means, Victuals

and Goods brought along with us; and nither troubling the Peace of the Kingdom of *England*, nor hurting any of your Majesties Subjects of whatsoever quality in their Persons or Goods, having carried ourselves in a most peaceable manner, till we were pressed by strength of Arms to put such forces out of the way, as did without our deservings, and (as some of them at their point of death have confessed) against their own Consciences opposed our peacable passage at *Newburne* upon *Tine*; and have brought their own blood upon their own heads against our purposes and desires, expressed by Letters sent to them at *Newcastle*.

(Rushworth 1659, p. 1255)

In a similar vein to those publications aimed at an English audience prior to the battle, in this petition the Scottish commissioners highlighted the army's good carriage after entering England. True to their word they lived off their own supplies, and only fought when prevented from crossing the Tyne. The petition also stated, however, that those English that were captured or killed at Newburn admitted to their own reluctance to fight the Scots, suggesting that their deaths were the fault of the English, not the Scots. The Scots were clearly attempting to absolve themselves of blame and guilt, while at the same time possibly attempting to stir up feelings of guilt and remorse among the English. The petition went on to state that, in order to prevent further violence and death, the Scots desired access to the King, so that they could profess their loyalty, but also press him to address their concerns regarding episcopacy, their true reason for entering England in the first place. Charles, perhaps unsurprisingly, did not particularly believe these claims (Rushworth 1659, pp. 1255–1256). However, in a letter of 2 September 1640 from the Scottish forces in England to the Earl of Lanrick, the Secretary of Scottish affairs, the Scots stated:

Wee are debarred from sending or carring our suplications in ane ordinarey way, wich makes ws to haue adresse to your Lordschips, earnistly intreatting your (Lo:) in our names to present this our petition heirin inclosed to his Matie, and in humility to bege ane anssuer therwnto, to be sent with the bearir to ws, quho shall endeuor to approue ourselues his Maiesties loyall subiectes, and most unwilling to shed aney christian blood, far lesse the Englishe, quherof wee haue giuen werey good prouffe, by our bygane carriadge, to euery one quho with violence hath opposed ws; zea euen to thosse that entred in blood with us, and wer takin prissoners, quhom wee haue lettin goe with meat and money. Notwithstanding that all thesse of oures, quho did debord from ther quarters, are miserablie massacared by these we can tearme no otherwayes then cutthrottes. Our behauior to thesse that are in Neucastle can vittnes our intentions, wich is to liue at peace with all, and rather suffer than offend.

(Balfour 1824, pp. 392–393)

Again, the Scots stressed their peaceable intentions and their desire for friendship with the English, and suggested that this, along with an acknowledgement of their grievances, was all that they were seeking. Of course, this letter was written to a supporter of the King, and in support of a petition to Charles I, but it does seem that the Scots genuinely went out of their way to make sure their actions in England would endear them to the English.

It is interesting to note, and a possible result of Scottish attempts to endear themselves to the common English people, as well as their occupation of parts of Northern England, that following the defeat at Newburn the commanders of the English forces continued to attempt to spread anti-Scottish propaganda. In a letter of 10 September 1640 Captain Thomas Dymoke wrote to Windebank that early on the day after the battle, 29 August 1640, 'Newcastle was deserted by us and possessed by the enemy, but Leslie and his guards did not enter till Sunday, where he heard a sermon, and dining with the Mayor for requital turned him out of doors and seized his house and goods to his own use' (Hamilton 1882, p. 39). Dymoke here was clearly attempting to suggest to Windebank that the Scots, and in particular Leslie, behaved poorly following the occupation of Newcastle. Leslie's reported actions, however, seem unlikely, as the mayor of Newcastle, Robert Bewick, was a puritan, and as such was likely to have sympathised with the Scottish position (Terry 1899, p. 127, n. 1). Of course, this does not mean that Leslie did not evict Bewick, and it is the sort of behaviour one might expect during an occupation, but there are no other sources supporting this, so it is likely that Dymock was attempting to reinforce the notion that the Scots were lying about their intended treatment of the English, and had entered England as nothing more than rebels.

Another interesting aspect of this conflict is that there was support for the Scottish cause among the English population, and as such not everyone south of the border was overly concerned by the Scottish presence. John Fenwick, an English Presbyterian and supporter of the Covenant, wrote that when the Scottish army approached Newburn:

> there was flying indeed to purpose, the swiftest flight was the greatest honour to the *Newcastilian* new dubd knights, a good Boat, a paire of Oares, a good Horse, (especially that would carrie two men) was more worth then the valour or honour of a new knighthood. Surely Vicar *Alvey* too would have given his Vicaridge for a horse when he for haste leapt on horseback behinde a countrie-man without a cushion, his faith and qualifications failing him, he might well feare to fall from grace by the *Scots* coming.
>
> (Fenwicke 1643, p. 4)

Fenwick painted a vivid picture of cowardice among the English forces and clergy in Newcastle who fled before the Scots. This, however, was another work of propaganda in that, while the English army and clergy did abandon Newcastle and its citizens to the encroaching Scottish forces, it is probably not the case that they did so two to a horse, offering their knighthoods in exchange for safe passage. Indeed, Fenwick, although native to Newcastle, is unlikely to have seen these scenes himself, as he had accompanied the Scottish army into England, having fled to Scotland the previous year.

Perhaps the most interesting response to the Battle of Newburn came from the Presbyterian minister Zachary Boyd. In 1643 Boyd produced *The Battel of Nevvbvrne: Where the Scots Armie obtained a notable victorie against the English Papists, Prelats and Arminians*, a work of poetry which a few lines in stated 'At *Newburn* foord, where brave Scots past the *Tine* / Under CHRISTS colours with courage divine' (Boyd 1643, p. 4). Boyd is not known for being a particularly skilful poet but this piece is fascinating in another respect. Boyd seemed in some ways to be exulting not only in the victory of the Scots over the English, but also in the injuries and deaths that the English forces suffered:

> Yea, legs and armes which in the air did flee
> Were then cut of (like gibblets) fearfully:
> The Scottish Bals so dash'd them with disdain;
> That *hips ov'rhead*, their skul did spew their brain
> Both legs and armes and heads, like dust, did flee
> Into the air, with fearfull mutinie.
>
> (Boyd 1643, p. 6)

It could, of course, merely be the case that Boyd was attempting to describe the horrors of war in a particularly vivid fashion, and it was not his intention to glory in the deaths of the English. However, considering that Boyd was a Covenanting minister, the similarity of the imagery present in this work with that of the Last Judgment is unlikely to be coincidental. Indeed, the main aim of this work was describing the Scottish victory as that of God's victory over those who would corrupt true Christianity. This can be seen in the divine courage of the Scots described previously, and throughout the piece as a whole, but it may also justify the rather gruesome passage above. Perhaps, through their rejection of Presbyterianism and the Covenant, the enemies of the Scots, indeed, the enemies of Christ, were somehow de-humanised, and as such less deserving of pity. This is reinforced by the line 'All was made Hodge-Podge, some began to croole, / Who fights for prelats is a beastly foole' (Boyd 1643, p. 7). Other examples of God's intervention in the battle, and the nature of the battle itself, can be seen in lines such as 'Terrours from heaven made all the footmen flee / By an backside with blushing infamie:' (Boyd 1643, p. 8). and 'Yea, Reek and Fire a great battell did fight, The one for Darknesse, th'other for the Light' (Boyd 1643, p. 10). It is also interesting to note that Boyd, possibly to further emphasise the intervention of God, or from a desire to heighten the drama of the battle, seemed to imply that at one point the English had had the upper hand:

> Thus stood the case, but God of heaven at last,
> Fought for the *Scots*, so that their foes agast
> Did flee with fear like *Hindes* before the *Hounds*,
> Their *back* not *face* receiv'd most shamefull wounds.
>
> (Boyd 1643, p. 12)

Throughout this work it is clear that Boyd firmly believed that God had given the Scots a victory over the English as it was the Scots who were supporters of Presbyterianism and the Covenant, and Boyd did not want the Scots to forget this. In a section of the work addressed to Leslie, Boyd wrote; 'To this great work th'*Almighty* did thee raise, / He honour'd thee, but see that thou him praise' (Boyd 1643, p. 16). Boyd was clearly telling Leslie, and indeed Scotland as a whole, that he and they had only achieved victory over the English with the help of God. This was an emotionally-driven plea from Boyd to the Scottish nation that they should continue to thank God for that victory. Boyd feared that Leslie, the Scottish army, and perhaps the Scottish nation as a whole would forget that their victory came only through God, and he feared the result of not acknowledging God's role in the battle. As he subsequently noted, 'We were not sav'd be Canons, Spears, nor Swords, Or strength of men, the Battell was the LORDS' (Boyd 1643, p. 23). Should God not properly be praised, Boyd believed that the punishment would be the defeat of the Scots, and the crushing of the Covenant, and as such he stressed as much in this work.

Later representations of the battle

Another noteworthy aspect of the emotional responses to the Battle of Newburn was the fact that such responses continued to be produced for so long after the battle itself. Zachary Boyd wrote about the battle three years after the fact, for instance, and others wrote later still, such as David Buchanan who wrote on the issues surrounding the Second Bishops' War in 1645. Others, however, continued to produce emotionally-charged accounts of the Battle of Newburn years and even decades after the events of 1640.

Patrick Gordon, writing at some point between 1647 and 1660, stated:

> the king hoppt weill of his armie, throw the confidence he had in his leaders; as also, that the bodie of the people of which this armie was made vp was not yet infected, nether ware they capable of those deipe misteries and high plots which, as strong and euer rolleing wheilles, careid along this ingeine of the Couenant. But the malitius influence of his vnlucky stares, or the hard fortune which had euer followed so good a man, so pius, so mercifull a judge, and so wise and so excellent an king, did in this action make knowin how he was deserted, yes, and betrayed, euen of those in whom he had greatest confidence.
>
> (Gordon 1844, p. 33)

Gordon portrayed Charles I as a pious, devout man, who had the misfortune to be betrayed by those close to him, but also by the failures of his army and its leaders, due, perhaps, to the effectiveness of the Scottish attempts at emotional manipulation. This was a turn of events that Gordon clearly hoped would elicit some sympathy from his audience. He subsequently noted of the defeat of the English:

> This greiued the good king so extreamly, that vpon the instant intreattie of the nobilitie, and large promises to sie all things redressed to his full contentment, and the Couenanters exactlye punished, he grantes them a parlement; and because the sinceritie and candor of his innocent soule could not harbour a thought, nor giue him libertie to beleeue, that vnder there many oaths and promises of fidelitie there could lurke any falshood or deceat, he grantes power to sitt ay and whill all things ware fullie pacefied, and a perfyt establishment of gouernement in both kingdoms satled; which, it seems, they had secretly concluded sould neuer be in his tyme.
> (Gordon 1844, p. 33)

Again, in this passage Gordon portrayed Charles I as a pious, innocent man, who could not conceive of the concept of falsehood, an attestation that was probably just as hard to believe at the time of writing as it is today. Nevertheless, for Gordon Charles I was the one who was truly deserving of sympathy and pity, as he had been duped and abused by the rebellious Covenanters. However, Gordon did not write this account only from a sense of devotion to Charles I and the crown. Rather, this account stemmed from a desire to refute the accusations of the Covenanters, as well as the Scottish Anglican bishop George Wishart, that Patrick Gordon's chief, the Marquis of Huntly, was disloyal (Gordon 1844, pp. xi–xii; Wishart 1819). This in itself is fascinating, as it highlights the fact that there was not necessarily a clear delineation of sides in this conflict. Gordon wrote an emotional account of the events of 1640, portraying the Scots as the rebellious aggressors, and Charles I as a devout, innocent Christian, as a response to a work produced by another supporter of the King and episcopacy.[5]

Edward Hyde, the first Earl of Clarendon, probably began writing his account around 1646, apparently at the earlier behest of Charles I. It would not be finished for many years, however, and did not appear in print until 1702, almost three decades after his death. Concerning the defeat of the English he stated that the Scots 'put our whole Army to the most shameful and confounding Flight that was ever heard of' (Hyde 1717, pp. 144–145). It is interesting to note the allusion to shame over a defeat that had taken place possibly as much as 30 years earlier. Indeed, Hyde seems to have taken the defeat almost as a personal affront, and was keen to place the blame for this embarrassment squarely upon the English command. He stated:

> The Lord *Conway* never after turning his Face towards the Enemy, or doing any thing like a Commander, though his Troops were quickly brought

together again, without the loss of a dozen men, and were so asham'd of their Flight, that they were very willing as well as able to have taken what Revenge they would upon the Enemy, who were possess'd with all the fears imaginable, and would hardly believe their own success, till they were assur'd that the Lord *Conway* with all his Army rested quietly in *Durham*, and then they presum'd to enter into *New-Castle*.

(Hyde 1717, pp. 145)

It was clearly very important for Hyde to stress that the victory of the Scots shocked them as much as it did the English. The Scots were portrayed as still fearing the English even after they had fled, and refusing to enter Newcastle until they knew that the English would not retaliate. The English, on the other hand, were painted as quickly regaining their composure after a brief withdrawal, and as being eager to return and exact revenge upon the Scots. Of course, in reality, the English lost more than a dozen men, and the Scots can hardly be said to have been terrified. Had they so desired they could have chased the English down and destroyed them, but were constrained from doing so by Leslie, who held to the earlier promises of minimising violence, and preferring to capture rather than kill (Terry 1899, p. 120). For Hyde, however, it was important that the decision not to pursue the English came from fear. In Hyde's mind the Scots feared the English, and the English were defeated through the shameful actions of their commanders.

Possibly the most fascinating of the later accounts of the Battle of Newburn comes initially from a manuscript history completed in 1679 by James Somerville, by right the eleventh Lord Somerville. Somerville's father, also James Somerville, had been a part of the Covenanter army under Leslie, but following the execution of Charles I in 1649 he had begun to rethink his political beliefs, and it is highly likely that he passed these new beliefs onto his son. Indeed, in his *Memorie of The Somervilles* Charles I was described as 'soe religious and generous a prince, whose favours was as watter spilt upon the ground to that untoward and ungrate generatione' (Somerville 1815, p. 208). Clearly the younger of the Somervilles agreed with Patrick Gordon that Charles I was a pious and innocent man. What is of particular interest, however, is the way in which Somerville described the result of the battle. In his account the English engaged in 'A vile and shamefull retreat, altogither unworthy of men of honour, as most of them wer . . .' (Somerville 1815, p. 204). From the likes of Edward Hyde, or possibly even Patrick Gordon, this statement would have been completely understandable and expected, but Somerville's father had been part of Leslie's army. Although his politics changed later in life it still seems strange that his son would go so far as to describe the flight of the English as shameful. For Somerville, however, there were other considerations. As he had stated earlier in the text, the actions of the Covenanters were unforgivable, as 'ther being noe lawes sacred or human to warrand subjects to take up arms against their prince, upon any account, whether religious or civill' that could possibly excuse the events of 1640 (Somerville 1815, p. 201). For Somerville, even as a Scot, the actions of the Covenanters were wrong and rebellious. The English defeat was shameful in that they failed to prevent the Scottish occupation of Northern England, an act of aggression against the rightful king. Additionally, setting aside international politics, as a member of the aristocracy Somerville would have believed that the English commanders should not have retreated, even in the face of defeat, as that was not what was done by 'men of honour'. Their retreat was shameful, and their shame was clearly felt by other members of the aristocracy, such as Somerville, despite his father's role in the battle.

Conclusion

As has been argued throughout this chapter the Battle of Newburn was a significant event in many ways, and not least in the emotions it created, curated, inspired and manipulated on both sides of the conflict. In letters, literature, history and official proclamations, emotions were present but also presented to the audience, and this was done in order to foster certain responses to the battle, both before and after the fact.

Prior to the battle there were attempts made by the Scots to reduce fears the English people may have had, but also to engender in them a spirit of friendship and neighbourly love. This was done in order to reduce any resistance they may have met upon crossing the border, but also from a genuine desire for friendlier relations between the two nations, based upon a shared understanding of religion. The Scots not only desired tolerance of their own religious choices, they also wanted their closest neighbours to understand their earnest desires that this be the case. The Scots entered England not as invaders, but as supplicants to a king who would not hear them, and they tried desperately to convince the northern English of this. The English attempted to counter this with propaganda depicting the Scots as an invading horde hell-bent on destruction, thereby stirring up the fears of a people who had heard tales of old of the behaviour of their supposedly barbarous neighbours to the north. The Scots in turn endeavoured to spread fear through the English command with the size of their force and attempts to convince the English that many of their number had joined with the Scots, in order to weaken their resolve and instil a reluctance to meet the expeditionary force.

After the battle, the Scots continued in their strategies to quieten the fears of the English populace, particularly as they were now there as an occupying force, but they also attempted to convince the King they truly wanted nothing more than to profess their loyalty and to have their grievances heard. Again, on both sides of the conflict there were attempts to describe the opposing force in unflattering terms; in at least one instance the English were portrayed by an English supporter of the Scots as cowards who had abandoned those they were charged with defending, and the Scots were portrayed as ungracious conquerors. Within Scotland the Scots were reminded by Zachary Boyd of their debt to God for the victory of the Covenanters at Newburn Ford, as it was in defence of the Covenant that had caused them to cross the border in the first place.

What is particularly interesting in this case is for how long emotional accounts of the battle continued to be produced. That accounts were produced by many people for years and decades to come is not surprising at all; this was an international conflict at a time of unrest and political uncertainty. What is surprising is that in at least one instance an account was produced four decades after the battle that still described the defeat as shameful. Forty years after the battle the English were being told that they should still feel ashamed of their defeat. Even more fascinating is that this came from a Scottish account, but not one aimed at reminding the English of their defeat from a position of pride, but rather a position of solidarity. Somerville shared the English shame at their defeat. The emotions inspired by the Bishops' Wars, the Battle of Newburn, and the period of conflict that led to the Wars of the Three Kingdoms were clearly profound, and had an effect that could be seen in writings decades and centuries later.[6] Somerville may have been attempting to affect the emotions of those who had allowed, as he saw it, a rebel force to defeat those loyal to the king, but he himself was inspired by the lingering emotional responses to a decades-old battle.

Notes

1 I would like to thank the Australian Research Council for funding the Postdoctoral Fellowship (project number CE110001011) from which this chapter has been drawn.
2 For an in-depth account of the battle and surrounding events see Terry (1899, pp. 88–138).
3 For a much more detailed study of these events see, for example, Stevenson (1973), or Fissel (1994).
4 John Rushworth, writing in 1659, certainly believed that this was an attempt at emotional manipulation (Rushworth 1659, p. 1236).
5 The opposing sides in the Bishop's Wars, and, indeed the subsequent conflicts known as the Wars of the Three Kingdoms, were not simply a matter of Scotland and England, or Covenanter and Royalist. They went deeper than that, and allegiances could and did shift and change dependant on various factors, including politics, religion, and personal gain. Lewis Gordon, the fourth Marquis of Huntly, typified these shifting allegiances, fighting for the Royalists during the First Bishop's War, and for both the Royalists and Covenanters at different stages of the Scottish Civil War, which led to subsequent accusations of disloyalty to the King. That Patrick Gordon wrote his work as a response to the accusations of a fellow Royalist shows that even within the same camp there were different factions, and following the Restoration these conflicts surfaced once more. The emotional bond Patrick Gordon shared with his clan chief was clearly stronger than the religious bond shared with George Wishart, and his loyalty towards the Marquis of Huntly could be expressed following the Restoration.
6 In 1913 James King Hewison wrote of the shameful flight of the English and noted the honour of the Scots who buried their fallen foemen (Hewison 1913, p. 350).

Reference list

Balfour, J. 1824, *The Historical Works*, vol. 2, Edinburgh.
Boyd, Z. 1643, *The Battel of Nevvbvrne: Where the Scots Armie obtained a notable victorie against the English Papists, Prelats and Armininians, the 28 day of August, 1640*, Wing-B142, George Anderson, Glasgow.

Buchanan, D. 1645, *Truth its Manifest: or, A short and true Relation of divers main passages of things (in some whereof the Scots are particularly concerned) from the very first beginning of these unhappy Troubles to this day*, London.
Fenwicke, J. 1643, *Christ Ruling in midst of his Enemies; or, Some first Fruits of the Churches Deliverance*, Wing F719, Benjamin Allen, London.
Fissel, M. C. 1994, *The Bishops' Wars: Charles I's Campaigns Against Scotland, 1638–1640*, Cambridge University Press, Cambridge.
Gardiner, S. R. 1884, *History of England from the Accession of James I to the Outbreak of Civil War, 1603–1642*, vol. 9, Longmans, Green & Co., London.
Gordon, P. 1844, *A Short Abridgement of Britane's Distemper, from the yeare of God M.DC.XXXIX. to M.DC.XLIX*, Printed for the Spalding Club, Aberdeen.
Hamilton, W. D. (ed.) 1880, *Calendar of State Papers, Domestic Series, of the Reign of Charles I, 1640*, Longmans & Co., London.
Hamilton, W. D. (ed.) 1882, *Calendar of State Papers, Domestic Series, of the Reign of Charles I, 1640–41*, Longmans & Co., London.
Hewison, J. K. 1913, *The Covenanters, a History of the Church in Scotland from the Reformation to the Revolution*, vol. 1, 2nd edn, John Smith & Son, Glasgow.
Hyde, E. 1717, *The History of the Rebellion and Civil Wars in England, Begun in the Year 1641*, vol. 1, part 1, Printed at the Theatre, Oxford.
Information from the Estaits of the kingdome of Scotland, to the kingdome of England, 1640, STC-21916, J. Bryson, Edinburgh.
Information from the Scottish Nation, to all the true English, concerning the present Expedition, 1640, STC-21917, Edinburgh.
Rushworth, J. 1659, *Historical Collections of Private Passages of State*, vol. 3, London.
Somerville, J. 1815, *Memorie of The Somervilles; being a History of the Baronial House of Somerville*, vol. 2, James Ballantyne & Co., Edinburgh.
Stevenson, D. 1973, *The Scottish Revolution 1637–1644: the Triumph of the Covenanters*, David & Charles, Newton Abbot.
Terry, C. S. 1899, *The Life and Campaigns of Alexander Leslie, First Earl of Leven*, Longmans, Green & Co., London.
The Intentions of the Army of the Kingdome of Scotland, Declared to their Brethren of England, By the Commissioners of the late Parliament, and by the Generall, Noblemen, Barons, and others, Officers of the Army, 1640, STC-21919, Robert Bryson, Edinburgh.
The Lawfulnesse of ovr Expedition into England Manifested, 1640, STC-219235, Robert Bryson, Edinburgh.
Wishart, G. 1819, *Memoirs of the Most Renowned James Graham, Marquis of Montrose*, Archibald Constable & Co., Edinburgh.

10

'THIS HUMBLE MONUMENT OF GUILTLESS BLOOD'

The emotional landscape of Covenanter monuments[1]

Dolly MacKinnon

A striking woodcut (Figure 10.1) from Alexander Shields's account of the sufferings of the Church of Scotland during the second half of the seventeenth century depicts the gruesome fate of Presbyterian martyrs between 1660 and 1685. Such 'cruelty' met out by a tyrannical King and parliament was detailed in his evocatively titled *A Hind let loose, or, An Historical Representation of the Testimonies, Of the Church of Scotland, for the Interest of Christ, with the true State thereof in all its Periods* (Preface, A3). Shields (1687, front matter) stated that, 'Some had y^r hands st^{r}uck off & hanged others beheaded. Some hanged & quartered Some Tortured by boots thumbkins firematches. Some taken & instantly shot in fields. Some banished, others perished in ship-wrack. women hanged, others drowned at stakes in the sea'. The men and women who died as martyrs demonstrated that 'the Courage and Zeal of the Lovers of Christ was blazing', for 'the more they were afflicted the more they grew . . . the more did the number of Witnesses multiply . . . so that the then shed blood of the Martyrs became the seed of the Church . . .' (Shields 1692, p. 31; 1687, pp. 196–197). For Shields, the fight for Reformation in seventeenth-century Scotland was ongoing and caused by the

> Miseries & Mischiefs, that the pride of Prelacy and Tyrannical Supremacy had multiplied beyond measure upon this Church & Nation, and at the hight of all their haughtiness, when they were setting up their *Dagon* [a Philistine national deity from the Bible depicted as a fish-tailed man], and erecting Altars for him, imposing the *Service Book,* [introduced in Scotland in 1637] and the book of *Canons* &c. the Lord in Mercy remembered His people, and surprised them with a sudden unexpected Deliverance, by very despicable means.
>
> (1687, p. 61)

164 Dolly Mackinnon

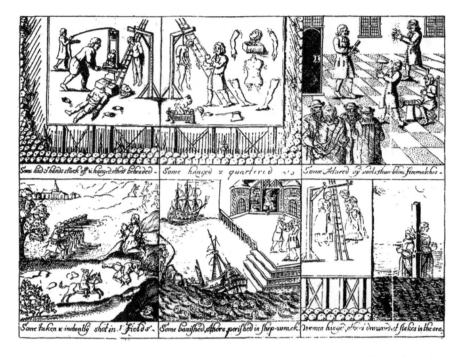

FIGURE 10.1 Frontispiece, [Alexander Shields] *A Hind let loose, or An Historical Representation of the Testimonies, of the Church of Scotland, for the Interest of Christ, with the true State thereof in all its Periods: Together With A Vindication of the present Testimonie, against the Popish, Prelatical, & Malignant Enemies of that Church . . . : Wherein Several Controversies of Greatest Consequence are enquired into, and in some measure cleared; concerning hearing of the Curats, owning of the present Tyrannie, taking of ensnaring Oaths & Bonds, frequenting of field meetings, Defensive Resistence of Tyrannical Violence . . . / By a Lover of true Liberty.* ([Edinburgh], 1687).
Source: Union Theological Seminary (New York, N. Y.) Library.

This chapter focuses upon those members of the more extreme Covenanters, known as Cameronians, an emotional and spiritual congregation specifically associated with field conventicles and martyrdom, and named after the field preacher Richard Cameron (c.1648–1680) who was killed at Ardsmoss. This Cameronian community existed within a more moderate community of Presbyterians. From the mighty to the humble, the Cameronians were united in their struggle to complete a thorough Reformation in Scotland, which also saw their opposition to the Union of 1707. For them, Scottish identity hinged on an allegiance to King Jesus, and not to a mortal monarch ruling over three kingdoms with an Episcopalian church government. The Cameronians saw 'even the opposition of a few weak women, at the begining of that Contest, which, ere it was quashed, made the Tyrant tumble headless off his throne' (Shields 1687, p. 61). According to this emotional community, martyrdom was God's gift to them. As such, their printed testimonies, and their physical monuments to their fallen martyrs, placed in the Scottish landscape over subsequent generations, marked their emotional practices within the Scottish landscape.

The inscription language of Covenanter monuments can be treated, in conjunction with the language of written and printed testimonies, as evidence of a continuing emotional community that reads Scottish national history in terms of the fate of the national Covenant, and those martyrs who died for it. This community is created and recreated through the acts and the effects of memorialisation, and the sharing of the language of the national covenant, reformation, blood and grace in the name of King Jesus. This chapter analyses the powerful emotions connected with silence, memory and remembrance by focusing on three case studies of memorialisation to individual Covenanter martyrs: William Gordon (1679), Airdsmoss (1680) and the Wigtown Martyrs (1685). The Cameronians relied upon word of mouth, print culture, the erection of memorial stones containing uniform inscriptions, as well as trans-generational memory (where memories, over time, were transformed through retelling into the remembering) of the performance of their emotions. Their forms of memorial (unmarked and marked stones, as well as print culture) constructed a virtual emotional religious community that, devoid of a Kirk to worship in, was an emotional expression of their conscience practised in the illegal conventicles held in the private houses, fields and rugged terrain of early modern lowland Scotland under constant threat of discovery. The key stages of this emotional community I discuss includes the following: the deaths of the martyrs; their recognition as martyrs and the emotional and physical marking (frequently through the use of traditional unmarked stones) of their place of murder; the marked and printed memorialisation practices of the following generations and the ongoing reverence and rehabilitation of the persecuted covenantors in the centuries afterwards in the formation of Scottish national identity.

From a methodological standpoint, this chapter takes the innovative work of Monique Scheer who articulated the potential of 'emotional practice' as a framework for analysing and understanding emotions in action (Scheer 2012, p. 193). Emotions are not simply internal entities, for, as the philosophical work of Robert C. Solomon has challenged us, emotions are 'not entities *in* consciousness' but rather 'acts of consciousness'; emotions are not something we 'just have', but rather they 'are indeed something we do' (Solomon 2007 cited in Scheer 2012, p. 194). As Scheer (2012, p. 211) notes 'emotional practices can be carried out alone, but they are frequently embedded in social settings'. In order for emotional practice to function within emotional communities, they must be actively 'mobilizing, naming, communicating and regulating emotions' (Scheer 2012, pp. 193, 209–220). Emotional practices 'are stored in the habitus, which provides socially anchored responses to others' and 'is dependent and intertwined' with speaking, gesturing, remembering, manipulating objects, and perceiving . . . spaces' (Scheer 2012, pp. 209, 211). All of these elements are dynamic in emotional ritual practices 'as a means of achieving, training, articulating, and modulating emotional for personal as well as social purposes' (Scheer 2012, p. 210). As this chapter demonstrates, those emotional practices are dynamic, and occur within short and long timeframes. Scheer concludes that 'centuries of reflection on the effects of observing others' bodies and voices on the stage, on the soapbox, or in the pulpit have elaborated, refined, and revised emotional practices' (2012, p. 211). My analysis of emotional practice centres of the Cammeronian community of Covenanters in order to reconstruct and identify 'the specific situatedness of . . . [their] doings', as well as 'look at bodies and artifacts on . . . [their] past' (Scheer 2012, p. 217).

The Restoration of Charles II in 1660 had reinstated Episcopacy, and dismantled the Solemn League and Covenant that were pivotal pieces in the Covenanter Revolution of 1650 (Stewart 2016). The fiscal punishments, executions, banishments they experienced under the law, as well as the summary executions, especially in the 1680s, created a culture of fear. For those Covenanters who refused to declare their allegiance to the King, death was the penalty. For those emotional communities affected, living memory kept the names of their dead, albeit spoken in hushed and revered tones, on the lips of the living, for survivors had a duty to remember. A stone was placed to mark the place of the site of the burial, until such time – years, decades, even centuries later – a monument with an inscription might be erected, or in some cases replaced. This traditional practice of marking death in the landscape was a shared common response to sudden death (Maddrell 2015). For example, the Reverend Mr Robert Laws (1818, p. 230) recounted the case of a 'dragoon [who accidentally shot himself] . . . through the heart' after he had stopped at the roadside 'to ease nature'. Laws (1818, p. 230) added that 'he is buried where he died, and a small heap of stones cast upon him, as a remembrance of that fact'. Here death is given a material marker through the placement of stones of remembrance, which were intended to commit the event to memory, and to mark this lesson in the emotional landscape of the community. No inscription was necessary, as word of mouth communicated the tragic event, while the stones marked the spot.

It was therefore a collective and calculated endeavour by the Cameronians to utilise the traditional practices of religious martyrdom for their memorialisation. First, they collected accounts of the martyrs that were printed as their last testamentary statements. The emotional material culture of the godly, comprising swords, bibles and the military banners of the Christian soldiers were kept secretly by families. The places of summary execution and martyrdom, were committed to memory and identified by unmarked stones. If funeral monuments were later erected to these martyrs, together with inscriptions, they often incorporated the emotional symbols of the sword and the bible onto the stone. These emotional practices were initiated at and ratified by the general meetings of the covenanting communities that remained alive.

The creation of both unmarked and marked graves, during a period of ongoing persecution was entirely contingent upon the religious and political climate of fear. In this context fear was related not only to calamity and danger, but also to the capacity to revere the dead (MacKinnon 2016, pp. 157–175; Bähr 2013, pp. 269–282; Eber 1997, pp. 62–77). Only when the political climate allowed could formal monuments to these Covenanter martyrs be erected, by those who held memories of these events, and gathered the funds and support necessary to place these memorial stones in the landscape. Communities at the time and over time actively collected personal accounts of the sufferings from the living in the affected communities across Western Scotland, and printed these texts of their sufferings for the spiritual benefit of the emotional communities that survived. The blood of martyrs had seeped into the cobblestones and soil of urban and rural sites marking the places where stones of remembrance would be placed. Over time, these stones were then replaced with inscriptions, from the beginning of the eighteenth century onwards.

Covenanter historiography

The radical Covenanters have been the subject of intense interest from scholars, and in intervening centuries they have also engendered emotional responses through the rhetoric used to describe their history in literary and historical terms. For example, the stereotypical Covenanter appeared, in a literary form, in Sir Walter Scott's 1816 depiction of a real individual that Scott called 'Old Mortality', who frequented the 'deserted mansion of the dead' (1816, p. 6). Scott's emotional encounter described

> an old man. . . seated upon the monument of the slaughtered Presbyterians, and, busily employed in deepening, with his chisel, the letters of the inscription, which, announcing, in scriptural language, the promised blessing of futurity to be the lot of the slain, anathematized the murderers with corresponding violence.
>
> (1816, p. 6)

The old man's violent words and speech act as a metaphor, not only for the restoration of the monuments, but also for the renewal and regeneration of the emotional practice of remembering these martyrs. Through the act of deepening the inscription, the emotional practice of the scriptural language is reanimated, and the 'promised blessing of futurity' of the slain remembered, while with each hit of the chisel the old man 'anathematized' their 'murderers with corresponding violence'. Scott also acknowledges the emotional zeal of 'Old Mortality's endevors': 'He considered himself as fulfilling a sacred duty, while renewing to the eyes of posterity the decaying emblems of the zeal and sufferings of their forefathers, and thereby trimming, as it were, the beacon-light which was to warn future generations to defend their religion even unto blood' (1816, p. 7). The beacon-light once trimmed, burns more brightly. Scott in his text used the terms found in the seventeenth and eighteenth-century Covenanter monument inscriptions, such as 'blood', 'sufferings and religion' and 'murdered'.

In 1844, the painter Thomas Duncan portrayed the shocking events of the summary execution of John Brown (in 1685) in an intensely-emotional depiction of Brown's dead body and that of his dead dog lying in front of his distraught wife and children.[2] The emotional layers of Brown's murder were added to and exemplified with each reiteration of the tale over the intervening centuries. In 1937, Agnes Mure Mackenzie recounted her emotions as a school child when she first encountered Brown's story from May 1685, at the height of the 'Killing Times'. MacKenzie (1937, p. 261) wrote of that 'famous case of John Brown, over whose death, as recorded in popular fiction, many readers of this book will have wept, as did its writer, in their schooldays . . .'. MacKenzie's account demonstrates how the retelling of the Covenanter's executions perpetuated this emotional practice over time. Each retelling provided an emotional touchstone in the creation of Scotland's national past in the nineteenth and early twentieth centuries. The emotional language of grace attending martyrdom for the true faith created and embraced this emotional community of readers in a debate about nineteenth and twentieth-century Scottish faith and nationalism.

Previous studies have either catalogued these Covenanter memorials, or referred to them, as part of the nineteenth-century rehabilitation of the Covenanters for the purposes of the creation of Scottish identity. For example, James J. Coleman in *Remembering the Past in Nineteenth-century Scotland: Commemoration, Nationality and Memory* (2014) has discussed how, from the nineteenth century onwards, 'different localities within Scotland invoked Covenanting memory as a means of celebrating their own contribution to Scotland's nationality' for the express purposes of defining Scottish identity and nationalism in the present (Coleman 2014, pp. 135–153; Pentland, Nixon & Robert 2012, pp. 28–49). Antiquarians too, have recorded these monuments and their inscriptions for posterity, most notably J. H. Thomson's *Martyr Graves of Scotland* (1881). Couched in the form of a handbook that sits comfortably in the palm of the hand, James Gibson's *Inscriptions on the Tombstone and Monuments Erected in Memory of the Covenanters, with Historical Introduction and Notes* (1881) enabled readers to conduct their own personal pilgrimages across the landscape (physical, spiritual and metaphorical) to these remote places of emotion, and gather with others in prayer to remember their martyrs. Most recently in the twentieth century, Thorbjörn Campbell's *Standing Witnesses: An Illustrated Guide to the Scottish Covenanters* (1996) provided a survey as part of, and in response to, 'repeated calls . . . for the cataloguing of war memorials throughout the United Kingdom because of their rapid deterioration' (1996, p. vii). Magnus Magnusson (2000, p. 486) observed that 'there are scores of sad, proud and often neglected monuments and headstones all over Scotland commemorating the martyrs to the Covenant during the 'Killing Time' (1685).

These are monuments to religious wars. As I have shown elsewhere, the emotional practice of constructing memorials, as well as the conflicts surrounding the form those memorials to past battles took, coincided with points of religious and political crisis in the present (MacKinnon 2016, p. 208). Covenanter memory in the immediate aftermath of the events of the 1680s, demonstrates these emotional communities continuing to struggle to achieve the supremacy of King Jesus, over what they understood to be the false claims of King, parliament, and the 1707 Union.

In analysing the evolution of the early practice of memorialisation that occurred in these emotional communities in the immediate aftermath of the Killing Times (1685), I can demonstrate the emotional practice of the Covenanters. Using the specific case studies of William Gordon (1679), Airdsmoss (1680) and the Wigtown Martyrs (1685), I trace these practices within the Covenanters from the late seventeenth into the early eighteenth centuries. I also analyse the inscription texts purposefully created for these monuments to male and female martyrs. The lens of emotional practice informs my methodology and is applied to both the archives and material cultural evidence within the Scottish landscape.

Emotions methodology

Barbara H. Rosenwein (2006, p. 15) has demonstrated how emotional communities in the Middle Ages valued the collective importance of emotional states in societies, showing that 'privilege or disregard' was afforded to each emotion, and that each community determined the 'feeling rules' they imparted to society. In dealing with Covenanter communities historians 'need to realize that certain communities must share emotional styles if they are to communicate and understand each other' (Rosenwein 2006, p. 15). What is also clear is that emotional communities are linked to their landscapes through their emotional practices. It is in the Covenanter emotional landscapes that the concept of their emotional practices – that is actions driven by states of emotion – occur. For the Covenanters, this allows us to analyse the emotional practices of a community that did not always leave direct written testimony. Memories relive, in Monique Scheer's sense, the 'emotional practices' of life that 'make use of the capacities of a body trained by specific social settings and power relations' (2012, pp. 193–194). Central to this concept of emotional practice are Scheer's four types of emotional practice: mobilising, naming, communicating and regulating emotion. Scheer's contention is that 'emotional arousals that seem to be purely physical are actually deeply socialised' (2012, p. 220). Scheer (2012, p. 220) demonstrates that emotions 'not only *follow* from things people do, but *are* themselves a form of practice, because they are an action of a mindful body', and 'that this feeling subject is not prior to but emerges in the doing of emotion'. Here the individual is part of an emotional community in Rosenwein's sense, but a community where emotion, the mind, and the body function as 'a locus for innate and learned capacities deeply shaped by habitual practices' (Scheer 2012, p. 220).

We must also consider how historians have, through their historical writing, championed the experience of the individual over emotional communities with respect to these violent episodes in Scottish history. For example, Michael Lynch, in *The Oxford Companion to Scottish History* (2001) summarised the succession of James VII and II, an ardent Catholic, and his government, as a period of vigorous, and violent enforcement of religious conformity. The consequence of these state-sanctioned actions was 'to culminate in the frenzy of concentrated violence known as the 'Killing Times' in which almost 100 individuals, nearly all belonging to the radical Cameronian party, were summarily executed over a short period of months in 1685' (Lynch 2001, p. 114). Lynch (2001, p. 114) concluded that 'the martyrology and mythology of the 'Killing Times' has often dominated the historiography of this entire period despite that fact that it was a short-lived aberration affecting only the adherents of one tiny Presbyterian faction'. Lynch takes no account that these 'almost 100 individuals' were connected to their wider families, as well as their religious communities, making the numbers of those affected by these violent events in the hundreds. These events tore local communities apart, through the process of summary executions, battles and government pogroms, as well as the billeting of troops. The publication of texts recounting these events from 1687 onwards offered an alternative view of the impact of these conflicts on emotional communities, and the women, men and children who were ultimately affected and traumatised by these religious wars. While Lynch claims that the martyrology and mythology of the Killing Times has dominated, national histories play down or forget these emotional events, while those directly affected collectively and actively commemorated and remembered them in order to keep the struggle for Reformed Scotland alive. What the political historians have categorised as isolated and individual acts of violence actually generated an emotional ripple and resonance that travelled well beyond those present at such killings, and has fuelled the centuries following. Each individual was a family member, a sibling, spouse, aunt, or uncle, grandparent, a cousin or a spiritual friend. Let us now turn to the ways in which these communities performed their emotions in the emotional landscape of their early modern present.

William Gordon of Earlston in Galloway 22 June 1679

The monument to William Gordon charts the process from silent stone to inscribed monument between 1679 and 1772. William Gordon (d. 1679) was the Laird of Earlston, Kirkcudbrightshire, and an ardent Covenanter. After the Restoration of Charles II, he had refused to appoint an Episcopalian Incumbent to the Kirk, and was known to have held conventicles and private meetings in his own house. Shortly after the Battle of Bothwell Bridge (1679), where the Covenanters were overwhelmingly defeated by government forces, Gordon was apprehended by government troops. After refusing to comply with their requests, Gordon was summarily shot, and as there was no family present, his body was interred in the local Kirkyard. Initially, a pillar was erected with no inscription. Gordon's monument is an example of that process of trans-generational commemoration recounted in the text of the monument's inscription erected by Gordon's great grandson, Sir John Gordon, Bart. The inscription reads, 'To the memory of the very *Worthy Pillar* of the *Church, M William Gordon of Earlston in Gallo-way*'. Gordon had been 'Shot by a partie of dragoons on his way to Bothwell bridge, 22 June. 1679. Aged 65', and the monument was 'inscribed by this great grandson, *Sir John Gordon, Bart*, [on] 11 June 1772' during the period of the American War of Independence. The Covenanters represented a character of defiance against the tyranny that influenced Europe and North America, and fuelled republican sentiment. The initial absence of an inscription on this monument was explained as 'Silent till now full ninety years hath stood, This humble Monument of Guiltless Blood'. The politically volatile times due to 'Tyranick Sway, forbad his Fate to name Least his known Worth should prove the Tyrant's shame'. Gordon's 'Godly' purpose for the completion of an ongoing reformation was made clear by the inscription, for

> On *Bothwell* road with love of *Freedon* fir'd, The Tyrant's minions boldly him require'd. To stop and yield, or it his life would cost. This he disdain'd not knowing all was lost [that the Covenanters had lost the battle at Bothwell Bridge]. On which they fir'd. Heaven so decreed His doom. Far from his own laid in this silent Tomb.

His death and silent tomb were marked by his emotional community who fought on. The remainder of the inscription continues, 'How leagu'd with Patriots to maintain the Cause[.] Of true RELIGIOUS LIBERTY and Laws'. Gordon's martyrdom was demonstrated by his characteristics as a martyr, and evident by 'How learn'd, how soft his manner, free from Pride, How clear his Judgement, and how he liv'd and dy'd'. The emotional practice of the Covenanter community, was demonstrated by those witnesses who knew 'They well cou'd tell who weeping round him stood[.] On *Strevan* plains that drank his Patriot Blood'.

This eighteenth-century inscription is a highly emotional call to the collective emotional practices of those Covenanters that live on. Here the blood of martyrs seeps into the landscape and signifies the emotional memory of death, and the utilisation of the emotional language, such as 'guiltless blood' and martyrdom for King Jesus Christ, that appeared on these monuments. The 1772 monument was then, some 70 years later, 'REPAIRED By Sir *John Gordon Bart. Of Earlston*. His Representative, 1842'. This demonstrates the second and third trans-generational reiterations of these emotional communities' performances during the period of the American War of Independence, and again at the period of the Disruption of the Church of Scotland. First-hand memory, as well as remembering when living memory has ceased, is dependent upon the emotional performances of multiple generations of family and friends visiting these sites, in the following centuries, re-articulating the emotional narratives of martyrdom and remembering past martyrs for the purposes of the present. For example the inscription on Gordon's monument, on the other side of the stone, instructs viewers that, 'IF A HARD FATE DEMANDS, OR CLAIMS A TEAR, STAY, GENTLE PASSENGER, AND SHED IT HERE' (Gibson 1881, pp. 84–85). This phrase on Gordon's monument addressing the 'passenger' echoes the earliest monument erected to the martyrs by James Currie and Helen Alexander in Greyfriars Churchyard in Edinburgh in 1706. It too addresses 'a passenger', sure in the knowledge that members of this emotional community make pilgrimages to see the place of their martyrs, and hear the stories of their martyrdom. Here we have the emotional practices of a demonstrable community making memory tangible, permanent and recoverable. Monuments, archives and printed culture intersect and provide vital evidence of the Covenanters' collective emotional actions in early modern Scotland in their ongoing purpose of attaining a reformed and Covenanted Scotland.

Airds Moss, 1680

As Sir Robert Hamilton, on 4 March 1702, put pen to paper under the sobriquet of 'Robert Smith', he addressed his missive to 'My dear Billie' (*The National Records of Scotland* 1702, Ch.3.269.26). Written under the guise of aliases, the letter's purpose was plain: what form should the memorial to the Covenanter martyrs, who had died in 1680 at Airdsmoss, take? The Covenanters were intent upon erecting a monument to the Minister Richard Cameron (c.1648–1680), among others, who was killed in a skirmish at Airdsmoss. The Cameronian community felt the loss keenly, marking the spot with an unmarked stone, and collectively committed these events and their martyrs to living memory. The creation of the united societies, comprised local groups who, from the late 1680s, onwards, kept session records of their activities demonstrating their collective purpose and progress. For example, the 'Conclusion of the Gen. Meeting of CrafordJohn [Crawfordjohn in Scotland]' taken down on 29 October 1701 'first concluded that all the correspondances provide and make Ready stones as signs of Honour to beset upon the graves of the late Martyrs as soon as possible'. What is more, communities were also tasked with writing down the names of 'martyers with yr speaches and Testimany and by whom they were martyed or killed in houses or fields contrey or cities as far as possible', and that this information was 'to be brought to the Nixt Ge. Meeting'.[3] The 'Epitephs, and Likewise' were to be ratified at these gatherings.[4] Among these activities, in which the men and women present ordered and maintained their godly society, was the gathering of evidence for each martyr's death, the place of their burial, and a desire to commemorate them through the creation of funeral monuments with approved inscriptions.

Hamilton's letter describes the layout of the common monument style used by those left alive to commemorate and venerate their martyrs. The Covenanter symbols representing their open-air meetings comprised the sword of a Christian soldier, a bible proclaiming the word of God, and a military banner of Covenanted Scotland from Bothwell Bridge (1679). These were the symbols known to the gatherings of women, men and children who worshipped, regardless of the risk to their personal safety, as a trans-generational group, a covenanted group and an emotional community. These funeral monuments are still to be found throughout Scotland: many have been replaced and renewed in the following centuries. Most of these monuments are in remote and inaccessible places.

In discussing the collective endeavour to erect stones in remembrance of their martyrs, Hamilton told Billie that 'the ston is curiously wrought on our Lords servants at Airds Mose'. The 'Epitaph' comprised 'a bible, upon one hand, arm and shabbell [a short, crooked sword]', adding 'and ane other ston ready for laying on there I hoop to ye satisfaction of friends. the gentillmen in st countries offering to leed lym and stone for ye bricking a tomb wall about them if we will be of the pains to build it'. Hamilton's community were at pains that the monument was built through this collective emotional community. The inscription proclaimed,

>Here lyes the Corps of that famous and faithful/
>preacher of the Gospell Mr Richard Cameron, who with severall others fell/
>in an encounter with the bloody enemies/
>of Truth and Godliness July 20 Anno 1680.

This Covenanter monument was typical in that it addressed those it assumed were assembled before it, asking

>Halt curious passanger, come heer
>and read;
>our souls Triumph with Christ our
>glorious head
>In self defence we murdered here
>do ly,
>To witness 'gainst this Nations perjury
>M
>R C
>Michael Cameron Robert Dick
>John Hamilton Cap. John Fuller
>John Gammell Robert Patteron
>James Gray Thomas Wattson

While the inscription claimed that 'Here lyes the Corps of that famous and faithful', James Gibson's (1881, p. 185) account stated that 'the head and hands of Richard Cameron were cut off by Robert Murray, who delivered them to the Council in Edinburgh'. The implementation of the treason laws saw the emotional impact of the dismembering of victims' bodies. The severed hands simultaneously represented those who had signed the National Covenant in allegiance to King Jesus for some, as well as those deemed traitors to King and country.

The New Statistical Accounts of Scotland, Volume 5, Ayr – Bute (1845, p. 323), makes reference to Cameron's monument as located in 'a cold and bleak district, . . . Airds Moss occupies the centre of it for about four miles on its eastern boundary, – which tends to give it an aspect of barrenness in that direction. . .'. The account noted that 'near the head of Airds Moss, is to be seem the monument erected to the memory of Richard Cameron, who was here overtaken and slain by the dragoons, on the 20th of July 1680' (The New Statistical Accounts of Scotland, Vol. 5: Ayr, Bute, 1845, p. 325). The sequence of monuments erected upon this site is also accounted for, as 'it consisted till lately of a flat stone with his own name [Cameron], and the names of the other individuals who were slain along with him, inscribed upon it' (The New Statistical Accounts of Scotland, Vol. 5: Ayr, Bute, 1845, pp. 325–326). This is the monument referred to by the Minutes of the United Societies' and Hamilton's letter. Gibson's volume claimed the 'original gravestone is placed upon four high pillars, with Cameron's name on the head of it, the form of an open Bible, with the other names round the side of the stone' (Gibson 1881, p. 186). The trans-generational processes of remembering saw a new monument erected, for 'a more conspicuous memorial of his life and death was reared some years ago from the proceeds of a collection made at a sermon delivered near the spot' (The New Statistical Accounts of Scotland, Vol. 5: Ayr, Bute, 1845, p. 326). It was 'in the year 1832, [that] the gravestone was set up on a platform, three feet high by ten feet square; in the centre an obelisk was erected, which may be seen from the railway . . . [and] the date of its erection, 1832, is cut on one of the sides' (Gibson 1881, pp. 186–187). The significance of this place in the Cameronian emotional landscape is demonstrated by these perpetual memorial practices.

Wigtown martyrs

The Wigtown martyrs comprised two women, drowned on 11 May, and three men hanged on 12 May 1685. The deaths of the two women martyrs have been commemorated, contested, and by some, categorically denied and recast as part of a fictitious Protestant martyrology (Napier 1863; Stewart 1869; Wodrow 1828–1830; Thomson 1871; Adams 2014). The seventeenth- and early eighteenth-century covenanter monuments commemorating these two women and three men in Wigtown represent the ongoing Covenanting communities' emotional practices, memory and acts of remembering. These events were not disputed in early modern Kirk session records for the surrounding area. The monuments erected from the early eighteenth century onwards are found in three separate locations: a series of funeral monuments to the three men and two women in the Kirk-yard c.1711–1730; a monument at Windyhill in Wigtown to the women and men erected in 1858; and a monument to the women only on the Bladnoch tidal river flats erected in c.1937. The names of those recorded on the gravestones are those of Margaret Wilson, Margaret Lachlane (also spelt McLaughlin, McLuachlison, Lauchlison et al.), William Johnston, John Milroy and George Walker. 'None of these were Wigtown Parish inhabitants, but were all commemorated for having been executed there on May 11 & 12 1685' (Wigtown's Heritage 2004). Shield had depicted the women first in his Frontispiece to *A Hind let Loose* in 1687, and then in a textual account of their deaths in 1690. The Wilson sisters are commemorated outside of Wigtown, in a nineteenth-century monument in Stirling, and there is also a monument to Margaret Wilson in a theological college in Canada.

Protestant martyrology was intended to make a record of these past events for the living, so the faithful could then garner strength from these examples to face their own struggles ahead. This was also history in an antiquarian sense, as documentary evidence was brought together with oral testimonies, and integrated in order to write and document that past. For example, Robert Wodrow (1679–1734) 'had many close relationships' with men and women 'who had suffered', and this included members of 'his own family' and 'in-laws' who had gone into hiding, been imprisoned and exiled during the Killing Times (Starkey 1974, pp. 488–489). Wodrow said of the Wigtown martyrs that he had this event 'fully vouched by witnesses whose attestations are now in my hands' (Starkey 1974, p. 496). In 1711, the General Meeting of 6 October [at Crawfordjohn], asked 'The several correspondences were appointed to take cop[i]es of the Epitaphs, Engraven upon the martyrs gravestones in yr several bounds to be Brought to the next meeting and that they be Inquisative qt Account can be had of any Remarkable Instance of Gods judgement upon persecuters in the for said Bounds . . .' (*The National Records of Scotland* 1711, Ch.3.269.1, p. 2).[5] *A Cloud of Witnesses* (1714, pp. 245–247) and Robert Wodrow's *The History of the Sufferings of the Church of Scotland* (1721–1722, 2 vols.) collected together for the first time the accounts of the sufferings of the Church of Scotland.[6] *A Cloud of Witnesses* (1714, pp. 245–247) takes its title from Hebrews 12:1: 'Wherefore, seeing we also are compassed about with so great a cloud of witnesses, let us lay aside every weight, and the sin which doth so easily beset *us*, and let us run with patience the race that is set before us' (King James Bible, 1661), and has been used by writers to discuss Protestant martyrs since the sixteenth-century Reformation in Europe. Wodrow's text, which included the two Margarets, was supported by an account of the events furnished to him by Thomas Rowan, minister of Penninghame, which was taken verbatim from the Penninghame Session Minute Book of 1711 (Starkey, p. 496). Alexander Shields's *A Hind Let Loose* (1687) would also have formed part of his evidence.

Only a minimal trail of evidence exists in official records about the Wigtown martyrs. What is known is kept in the memory of those who had witnessed these events and lived still. As Kuijpers and Pollmann (2013, p. 182) conclude, 'public silence was also a political imperative, with memories of revolt oftentimes an unwanted remembrance of disloyalty'. From both the Covenanters' and State's points of view, '[t]he policy of the actors was to suppress the story, and to ignore it in official records, and the wisdom of the friends of the sufferers was "to keep silence, because it was an evil time"' (Wylie 1875–1876, p. 870). Here, we have simultaneous acts of remembering and forgetting.

By February 1685, Thomas Wilson (aged 16), Margaret Wilson (aged 18), and Agnes Wilson (aged about 13) were being pursued by the authorities for not taking the Oath of Abjuration (Gibson 1881, pp. 282–283). Thomas is said to have kept to the hills around Wigtown, but Margaret and Agnes decided to head into town to see friends. It was while they were visiting a house in Wigtown that they were discovered, along with Margaret McLachland (aged 63) and Margaret Maxwell (in middle age) (Campbell 1996, p. 183). The women were imprisoned in the Wigtown Tollbooth, charged and found guilty of committing acts of rebellion, including being present when the Covenanters had fought the King's troops at Bothwell Bridge (Battle 1679) and Airds Moss (Battle 1680). They were also accused of attending 20 field conventicles and 20 house conventicles. Maxwell took the Oath of Abjuration, the others did not (Campbell 1996, p. 183). To have been present at the Battle of Bothwell Bridge, this would have made Margaret Wilson aged 10, Agnes aged seven, and Margaret McLachland aged 57, and for the Battle of Airdsmoss in 1680, Margaret Wilson was aged 11, Agnes aged eight, and Margaret McLachland aged 58. While McLachland was old enough to be part of the baggage train, and the young girls also, there is no archival evidence indicating they had been present at either battle site.

The women were found guilty and condemned to death by drowning. A petition for Margaret McLauchlison survives for 29 April 1685 requesting she be allowed to take the Oath of Abjuration. An incomplete stay of execution and pardon of 1685 also survives for Wilson and McLauchlison (Paton 1929, p. 33). Historians in support of the martyrs have claimed the links to the battles are unfounded, but certainly Margaret McLachlan, a widow, was old enough to have been part of a baggage train for this army. Margaret Wilson's younger sister Agnes was also accused but her father pleaded a bond of £100 Scots for Agnes and she was freed. Both Margarets were granted an undated pardon in Edinburgh, though it is unknown if, and unlikely that, the incomplete pardon ever reached Wigtown before 11 May.

In the case of the Wigtown martyrs, it was not until 1704 and then 1708 that public expressions of this event could be made. These took two forms: a Kirk pardon to one of the participants (1704) and the declaring of a Public fast in 1708. Wigtown Kirk was now led by the Reverand Thomas Kerr, who was appointed in 1701. Thus when in the Minutes of the Presbytery of Wigtown, Scotland on 8 July 1704, Bailie M'Keand, [the] elder, addressed Mr. Thomas Kerr (minister from 1701–1729) and the Kirk 'session for the privilege of the sacrament [which has been denied him for 19 years]", he did so out of his sense of grief. Before the assembled Session he was 'declaring his grief of his heart that he should have sitten in the seize of these women who were sentenced to die in this place in 1685' (Presbytery of Wigtown 1711, cited in Stewart 1869, p. 95). He not only sought redress from within his community, but also 'it had also been frequently his petition to God for true repentance and forgiveness for that sin' (Stewart 1869, p. 95). M'Keand then 'being removed, the session' discussed the matter further and, without M'Keand present, set to 'enquiring into this affair and the carriage of the said bailie since that time, and being satisfied with his conversation since, and the present evidence of repentance now, they granted him privilege' (Stewart 1869, p. 95). What can also be inferred from this account is that the evidence regarding the events in 1685 was also discussed, and the facts of the five deaths were not disputed, implying that the events must have taken place. Those that sat at the Kirk Sessions were well acquainted with the events nearly two decades earlier, for the Session included those who had lived through them. Present were members of families who had been fined for nonconformity. For example, Patrick M'Kie, who was a member of the Kirk Session, was the son of Katherine Lauder, the wife of Patrick M'Kie of Auchlean. Katherine herself had confessed to withdrawing from the church for the two years between 1682–1684, and was fined £250 [Scots] (Stewart 1869, p. 96). The quartering of troops with nonconformist families, was a physical hardship and fiscal mechanism used by the authorities to try to stem the tide of religious rebellion. When this failed, summary execution proved to be the only option. In these emotional communities, these events echoed across the following generations.

For example, in 1708 the Wigtown Kirk Sessions on 28 January declared a Public Fast because 'the sins of the late unhappy times have not been th[o]roughly search[ed] out, laid to heart, and mourned over' (Wigtown Kirk Session 1708, cited in 'The Wigtown Martyrs' 1864, p. 142). By 1711, the Kirk Session minutes for Penninghame dated 19 February recorded

> A brief information of the sufferings of people which are most remarkable in the paroch of Penninghame within the shire of Wigtoun upon the account of their adherence to the Reformation of the Church of Scotland and their refusing to conform with prelacie, with the occasions of their trowbles especiallie from the year 1679 to the year 1689.
> (The National Record of Scotland 1696–1729, Ch.2.1387.1
> Minutes, Records of the Penninghame Kirk Sessions)

Yet the physical evidence of the funeral monuments to the two women and three men in the Kirk-yard was interpreted by the nineteenth-century writer Napier as an example of fraudulent action set up in order to vouch for the earlier printed texts by Alexander Shields. Detractors saw these women in the historical record as fictional martyrs; a trope first deployed against Shields (1687). Napier even stated that their early eighteenth-century funeral monuments erected in the Kirk-yard at Wigtown were fabricated. Yet, '[a]ccording to "The Cloud of Witnesses", Margaret Wilson's memorial-stone was to be found in the churchyard prior to 1714' and 'that [monument] of Margaret McLachlan before 1730, when the third edition of this work was published' (Rogers 1871, p. 355). Wilson's family had continued to live on the family farm and her brother Thomas, who escaped arrest in 1685, returned to Wigtown and erected a monument to his sister in the early eighteenth century. That monument was 'originally placed against the north wall of the church', before it was then later grouped with the other martyr memorials after 1730 (Rogers 1871, p. 355). The monuments are plain in their support for the ongoing Reformation and a Covenanted Scotland, and apart from the individual names they contain, and the stark words of 'drowned' and 'murdered', intent upon an 'Adherence to Scotland reformation covenants national and solemn league' and that they were 'condemned' and 'suffered for Christ Jesus sake', as stated in the monument's inscription.

Covenanter memories were also passed down to others who remembered them and recounted them to younger generations. For example, in 1685 Margaret Maxwell, who had been imprisoned with Wilson and Macklachan was, according to her sentence, 'paraded through the town . . . [to be scourged on three successive days]' (Walker 1827, cited in Wylie 1875–1876, p. 870). The recollections of one man who had been a boy at the time were remembered and recounted by his granddaughter Miss Heron: 'the people retired into their houses, kept away from their windows, and hardly a child was seen in the streets' (Walker 1827, cited in Wylie 1875–1876, p. 870). The reason being that 'such was the Cruelty of these Days, that all who retained any Thing of Humanity towards their Fellow-creatures, abhorred such Barbarity; so that all the three Days the foresaid *Margaret* was punished and exposed, there was scare one open Door or Window to be seen in the Town of *Wigtown,* and no Boys or Girls looking on' (Walker 1827, cited in Wylie 1875–1876, p. 870). The veracity of the accounts was equated to Miss Heron being 'a lady of birth, who lived in Wigton [*sic*] when she herself was a girl, used constantly to visit her father's house' (Walker 1827, cited in Wylie 1875–1876, p. 870). That this was the testimony of a first-hand witness is demonstrated by the claim 'that her grandfather was an eye-witness of the execution of the two women, and had himself spoken of it to her, mentioning that the people were awestruck, and could not interfere' (Walker, 1827, cited in Wylie 1875–1876, p. 870). Those assembled then turned to King Jesus, and 'formed themselves into groups, uniting in prayer for the sufferers (Wylie 1875–1876, p. 870).

These emotional histories of the Covenanters would be reworked and recast over the following centuries. As James Gibson's evocative nineteenth-century account of the emotional landscape of Covenanter memorials proclaimed, 'the moors and kirkyards were visited only for the purposes of planting stones of remembrance' (Gibson 1881, p. 24). They also utilised emotive language, such as 'blood', 'martyrs', 'suffering', 'murder', 'drowned', to create an emotional covenanter community set on attaining a 'Reformation' of a 'Covenanted Scotland' for 'Christ' that spoke to those who visited these memorials. The collective emotional practices of the Covenanters, over time, purposefully transformed the lives of martyrs from the living testimonies of witness survivors into the tangible permanent and then inscribed markers in the Scottish landscape, in an ongoing, reciprocal cycle.

Notes

1 This research was funded by the Australian Research Council Centre for Excellence in the History of Emotions, Europe 1100–1800 (CE110001011) through my Associate Investigator Grant (2011–2014), 'Emotional Landscapes: English and Scottish Battlefield memorials 1638–1936' and my collaborative Australian Research Council Discovery Grant DP:140101177: Battlefields of memory: places of war and remembrance in medieval; and early modern England and Scotland. (2014–2016) The research was written up as part of my Visiting Fellowship at the Institute of Advanced Studies in the Humanities at The University of Edinburgh in early 2016.
2 T. Duncan, *The Death of John Brown of Priesthill* (1844), Glasgow Museums, Scotland.
3 Ewart Library, Dumfries, Scotland: GGD255 Minutes of the Proceedings and Conclusions of the General Meeting of the Witnessing Remnant of Presbyterians in Scotland.
4 Ewart Library: GGD255.
5 Conclusion of the General Meetings held at Crafordjohn 6th October 1711.
6 Shields (*A Hind Let Loose* 1687, p. 200) states 'In the beginning of this killing-time, as the Country calls it, the first author and authorizer of all these mischiefs, Charles II, was removed by death'.

Reference list

A Cloud of Witnesses, for the royal prerogatives of Jesus Christ; or, the last speeches and testimonies of those who have suffered for the truth, in Scotland, since the year 1680 (1714) Edinburgh.

Adams, S. 2004, 'Wilson, Margaret (1666/7–1685)', *Oxford Dictionary of National Biography*, ed. L. Goldman, viewed accessed 7 May 2014, www.oxforddnb.com.ezproxy.library.uq.edu.au/view/article/29677

Arnade, P. 2010, 'The City Defeated and Defended: Civism as Political Identity in the Habsburg-Burgundian Netherlands', in R. Stein & J. Pollmann (eds), *Networks Regions and Nations: Shaping Identities in the Low Countries 1300–1650*, Brill, Leiden.

Bähr, A. 2013, 'Remembering Fear: The Fear of Violence and the Violence of Fear in Seventeenth-Century War Memories', in E. Kuijpers, J. Pollmann, J. Muller & J. van der Steen (eds), *Memory before Modernity: Practices of Memory in Early Modern Europe*, Brill, Leiden & Boston.

Barnes, T. D. 2010, *Early Christian Hagiography and Roman History*, Mohr Siebeck, Tubingen.

Campbell, T. 1996, *Standing Witnesses: An Illustrated Guide to the Scottish Covenanters*, Saltire Society, Edinburgh.

Coleman, J. C. 2014, *Remembering the Past in Nineteenth-Century Scotland: Commemoration, Nationality, and Memory*, Edinburgh University Press, Edinburgh.

Eber, R. 1997, 'Fear of Water and Floods in the Low Countries', in P. Roberts & W. G. Naphy (eds), *Fear in Early Modern Society*, Manchester University Press, Manchester.

Gibson, J. 1881, *Inscriptions on the Tombstones and Monuments Erected in Memory of the Covenanters with Historical Introduction and Notes*, Dunn & Wright, Glasgow.

Jardine, M. 2014, 'The History of John Brown of Priesthill', Jardine's Book of Martyrs, 20 April, viewed 10 November 2016, https://drmarkjardine.wordpress.com/2014/04/20/the-history-of-john-brown-of-priesthill/

Kuijpers, E. & Pollmann, J. 2013, 'Why Remember Terror? Memories of Violence in the Dutch Revolt', in M. Ó Siochreú & J. Ohlmeyer (eds), *Ireland 1641: Contexts and Reactions*, Manchester University Press, Manchester.

Law, Rev. Mr. R. 1818, *Memorials . . . 1638 to 1684*, Archibald & Co, Edinburgh.

Lynch, M. (ed.) 2001, *The Oxford Companion to Scottish History*, Oxford University Press, Oxford.

Mackenzie, A. M. 1937, *Passing of the Stewarts*, Alexander Maclehose & Co, London.

MacKinnon, D. 2015, '"Correcting an Error in History": Battlefield Memorials at Marston Moor and Naseby', *Parergon*, vol. 32, no. 3, pp. 205–236.

Maddrell, A. 2015, 'Mapping Grief: A Conceptual Framework for Understanding the Spatial Dimensions of Bereavement, Mourning and Remembrance', *Social & Cultural Geography*, vol, 17, no. 2, pp. 4–23.

MacKinnon, D. 2016, 'Jangled the Belles, and with Fearefull Outcry, Raysed the Secure Inhabitants': Emotion, Memory and Storm Surges in the Early Modern East Anglian Landscape', in J. Spinks & C. Zika (eds), *Disaster, Death and the Emotions in the Shadow of the Apocalypse, 1400–1700*, Palgrave Macmillan, London.

Magnusson, M. 2001, *Scotland: The Story of a Nation*, HarperCollins, Hammersmith & London.

Napier, M. 1863, *The Case for the Crown in re the Wigtown Martyrs proved to be Myths versus Wodrow and Lord Macaulay*, Patrick the Pedlar and Principal Tulloch, Edinburgh.

Parker, G. 2002, 'The Etiquette of Atrocity: The Laws of War in Early Modern Europe', in G. Parker (ed.), *Empire War and Faith in Early Modern Europe*, Allen Lane, London.

Paton, H. (ed.) 1929, *The Register of the Privy Council of Scotland, A.D. 1684–1685*, 3rd ser., vol. 10, HM General Register House, Edinburgh.

Paton, H. (ed.) 1929, *The Register of the Privy Council of Scotland, A.D. 1685–1686*, 3rd ser., vol. 11, HM General Register House, Edinburgh.

Pentland, G., Nixon, M. & Robert, M. 2012, 'The Material Culture of Scottish Reform Politics c.1820-c1884', *Journal of Scottish History*, vol. 32, no. 1, pp. 28–49.

Raingard Eber, R. 1997, 'Fear of Water and Floods in the Low Countries', in P. Roberts & W. G. Naphy (eds), *Fear in Early Modern Society*, Manchester University Press, Manchester.

Rosenwein, B. H. 2006, *Emotional Communities in the Early Middle Ages*, Cornell University Press, Ithaca & London.

Rogers, C. 1871, *Monuments and Monumental Inscriptions in Scotland*, vol. 1, Charles Griffin & Co, London.

Scheer, M. 2012, 'Are Emotions a Kind of Practice (And Is That What Makes Them Have a History)? A Bourdieuian Approach to Understanding Emotion', *History and Theory*, vol. 51, no. 3, pp. 193–220.

Scott, Sir Walter 1816, *Old Mortality*, W. P. Nimmo, Hay & Mitchell, Edinburgh.

Shields, A. 1687, *A Hind let loose, or An Historical Representation of the Testimonies, of the Church of Scotland, for the Interest of Christ, with the true State thereof in all its Periods: Together With A Vindication of the present Testimonie, against the Popish, Prelatical, & Malignant Enemies of that Church . . . : Wherein Several Controversies of Greatest Consequence are enquired into, and in some measure cleared; concerning hearing of the Curats, owning of the present Tyrannie, taking of ensnaring Oaths & Bonds, frequenting of field meetings, Defensive Resistance of Tyrannical Violence . . . / By a Lover of true Liberty*, <sic>, Edinburgh.

Shields, A. 1690, *A short memorial of the sufferings and grievances past and present of the Presbyterians in Scotland: Particularly of those of them called by Nick-name Cameronians*, no details.

Shields, A. 1692, *The History of Scotch-Presbytery: Being an Epitome of The Hind Let Loose*, By Mr. Shields, J Hindmarsh, London.

Solomon, R. C. 2007, *True to Our Feelings: What Our Emotions Are Really Telling Us*, Oxford University Press, Oxford.

Starkey, A. M. 1974, 'Robert Wodrow and the History of the Sufferings of the Church of Scotland', *Church History*, vol. 43, no. 4, pp. 488–498.
Stewart, A. 1869, *History Vindicated in the Case of the Wigtown Martyrs*, Edmonston & Douglas, Edinburgh.
Stewart, L. 2016, *Rethinking the Scottish Revolution: Covenated Scotland, 1637–1651*, Oxford University Press, Oxford.
The New Statistical Accounts of Scotland (1845), vol. 5, Ayr – Bute, William Blackwood & Sons, Edinburgh & London.
'The Wigtown Martyrs' (1864) *Reformed Presbyterian Magazine*, pp. 140–142.
Thomson, J. (ed.) 1871, *A Cloud of Witnesses*, Johnstone, Hunter & Co, Edinburgh.
Thomson, J. 1881, *Martyr Graves of Scotland*, Oliphant, Anderson & Perrier, Edinburgh & London.
Walker, P. 1827, *Biographia Presbyteriana*, DS Peare, Edinburgh.
Wigtown's Heritage 2004, viewed 2 May 2013, http://freespace.virgin.net/harold.hall/angchurch.htm [link no longer active].
Wodrow, R. 1828–30, *The History of the Sufferings of the Church of Scotland from the Restoration to the Revolution*, ed. R. Burns, 4 vols, Blackie, Fullarton & Co, Edinburgh.
Wylie, J. A. 1875–1876, *The Scots Worthies: Their Lives and Testimonies*. William Mackenzie, London.

11
PARADOXES OF FORM AND CHAOS IN THE POETRY OF WATERLOO

Robert White

Before battle, form rules the ranks. Armies are in straight lines, men move symmetrically and in 'formation', clothed in 'uniforms', which, as such words suggest, are all the same and seek to erase personal differences, each side differentiated, like sporting teams, only by colours. There seems something harmlessly aesthetic about such sights, whether satirised through the 'hobby-horse' of Uncle Toby Shandy, the military veteran of the Seven Years' War who continually replays this world war (1756–1763) in his garden fortifications, or simulated by modern soldiers trained in computerised war-games or sending armed mechanical drones hundreds of miles away. By contrast, when violent combat is engaged, form and order are rapidly lost and the orderly scene degenerates into chaos. The pattern played itself out at Waterloo. There is nothing so levelling and reduced to formlessness as the results of bayonets to stomachs, bullets to heads, horses staggering and dying, or body parts blown to the winds by cannon shot, while even visibility is lost in engulfing smoke. After battle, violated and fragmented bodies are the remaining marks of individuation that military forms had sought to occlude. In representing war, then, writers face an extreme quandary in tensions between the subject matter and the act of writing; as Kate McLoughlin puts it in *Authoring War: The Literary Representation of War from the Iliad to Iraq* (2011, pp. 6–7), 'War . . . resists depiction . . . . Yet even as it resists representation, conflict demands it'. This chapter will explore some aspects of the quandary in terms of how English writers responded in print to the Battle of Waterloo.

The story of Waterloo was told many times soon after the event, from many points of view. Seamus Perry writes of 'the conjuring of Waterloo into a metaphor', wondering at how 'the mere facts were conjured so swiftly into myth' (Perry 2016, p. 58), but that myth was capable of bearing many interpretations. The Battle of Waterloo in 1815, like that of Agincourt exactly 400 years earlier, was an occasion conveniently transformed into legendary status through poetry, a medium that sometimes glorifies heroism while at other times lamenting suffering, and occasionally both. Philip Shaw in *Waterloo and the Romantic Imagination* (2002) argues that the event decisively redefined the whole period of English Romantic literature, as well as underpinning new conceptions of English nationalism. Some poets, including Scott, Byron and Southey, visited the site of the field of Waterloo in the months and years following the Battle. The background to the later narrative shape given to the battle, is that Belgium, a hapless state which has often been sandwiched between warring opponents, to the extent that it has gained the name of 'Battlefield of Europe', had been virtually chosen as the theatre of war, mainly because Napoleon for political reasons could not risk defeat on French soil, while Britain and Prussia regarded the Belgian community as a relatively reliable, and perhaps dispensable ally (Muir 2015, p. 37). 'Theatre of war' is a term advisedly chosen here. Historical circumstances provided a ready-made dramatic form to the sequence of events at Waterloo, structured as a stage play, drawing on the dimension of 'theatre' as a terminology of war: 'Act One' takes place on the evening before the day of the battle, as a glittering ball at Brussels. 'Act Two' includes the scene before battle and the conflict itself, with its vignettes of violence and heroism. 'Act Three' is the aftermath of appalling sights and sounds of suffering and agonising deaths of men and horses, on a battlefield where medical attention was not comprehensive, professional or systematic – to those who saw it, a scene from hell. This chapter explores how the tripartite sequence was shaped into poetic form, depending on each poet's relative perspective and attitude to war. Each example raises in different ways a paradox or contradiction faced by its writer, how to present war in the shapely formality of poetry, while also charting the steady descent of military conflict itself, from orderly formations and established etiquette, into the inchoate chaos of human destruction and desecration of nature. Whether the individual poet's ordering principle is patriotic celebration, religious affirmation of God's design, or anti-war sentiment, all the poets face the paradox of conveying the formlessness of violence through the structured form of poetry, and their main vehicle lies in controlling emotional expressiveness through the deployment of words in rhythm.

In one early prose account, the 'mere facts' of a basic narrative of the battle, as seen by the English, are summarised in 'Circumstantial Detail' by a 'near observer', 'An Englishwoman' identified as Jane Waldie Watts.[1] Her visit was something of a family affair:

> On Saturday, the 10th of June, 1815, my brother, my sister, and myself sailed from the pier of Ramsgate at three in the afternoon, in company with Sir—, Major—, extra Aide-de-camp to the Duke of Wellington, a Mr.—, an English merchant; together with an incongruous assemblage of horses, dogs, and barouches; Irish servants, French valets, and steerage passengers, too multifarious to mention, all crowded into a wretched little packet.
>
> (Watts 1817, pp. 1–2)

Troops were ordered for readiness on the 15th, with reports coming in that the allied Belgians under their commander Blücher had briefly joined combat, but, reinforcing the tone of a social occasion, the English entourage prepared themselves for a ball in the evening:

> Yes, a ball! For the Duke of Wellington, and his aides-de-camp, and half of the British officers, though they expected to go to a battle to-morrow, were going to a ball to-night, at the Duchess of Richmond's; and to the ball they did accordingly go.
>
> (Watts 1817, p. 32)

To capture the tone, Watts quotes the poetry of 'the Scottish Chief' in John Home's *Douglas: a Tragedy* (1756), in which the call to 'Prepare the feast!' holds a terrible contradiction between the night's revelry and the morrow's slaughter:

> This night once more
> Within these walls we rest: our tents we pitch
> To-morrow in the field. Prepare the feast! –
> Free is his heart who for his country fights:
> He on the eve of battle may resign
> Himself to social pleasure: sweetest then,
> When danger to a Soldier's soul endears
> The human joy that never may return.
>
> (Watts 1817, p. 32)

The Duke of Wellington received news at the ball that Napoleon was advancing. Distant explosions were heard from the village of Quatre Bras, at first dismissed as thunder but gradually recognised as cannon fire. Realising that the English should march immediately to support the Belgians, Wellington acted with *sang-froid* so as not to break the decorum of the occasion, and was apparently aware of his coming status as man of historical destiny:

> We were afterwards told, that upon perusing them he seemed for a few minutes to be absolutely absorbed in a profound reverie, and completely abstracted from every surrounding object; and that he was even heard to utter indistinctly a few words to himself. After a pause he folded up the dispatches, called one of his staff officers to him, gave the necessary orders with the utmost coolness and promptitude; and, having directed the army to be put in motion immediately, he himself staid at the ball till past two in the morning.
>
> (Watts 1817, p. 41)

Next morning the Highland regiments marched off,

> with their bagpipes playing before them, while the bright beams of the rising sun shone full on their polished muskets, and on the dark waving plumes of their tartan bonnets. We admired their fine athletic forms, their firm erect military demeanour and undaunted mien.
> (Watts 1817, p. 41)

Others followed in the same orderly fashion:

> Regiment after regiment formed and marched out of Brussels; we heard the last word of command – March! the heavy measured uniform tread of the soldiers' feet upon the pavement, and the last expiring note of the bugles, as they sounded from afar.
> (Watts 1817, p. 46)

The phrase 'the heavy measured uniform tread' works overtime in mirroring both the rhythm of marching and the rhythm of the prose itself reaching towards poetic intensity.

As the day wore on, information and misinformation, rumours and reports ebbing between alarming and triumphant, flowed back to the civilians: 'This dreadful uncertainty and ignorance made us truly wretched' (Watts 1817, p. 59). Even in the town the scenes became ones of 'tumult and confusion' (Watts 1817, p. 101), expressed through a suggestive image of 'the turbulence of the unruly cattle', which stampeded. The writer spares an empathetic thought for foes as well as friends, as the suffering on the battlefield gradually becomes known in Act Two of the unfolding drama:

> Not even imagination could form an idea of the dreadful sufferings that the unfortunate soldiers of the French and Prussian armies, who were wounded in the battles of the 15th and 16th June, were condemned to endure. It was not until nearly a week afterwards that surgical aid, or assistance of any kind, was given to them. During all this time they remained exposed to the burning heat of the noon-day sun, the heavy rains, and the chilling dews of midnight, without any sustenance except what their importunity extorted from the country people, and without any protection even from the flies that tormented them. Numbers had expired; the most trifling wounds had festered, and amputation in almost every instance had become necessary. This, and every other necessary operation, was most unskilfully and negligently performed by the Prussian surgeons. The description I heard of this scene of horror, from some respectable Belgic gentlemen who were spectators of it on the Wednesday following, is too dreadful to repeat.
> (Watts 1817, pp. 103–104, fn)

It was a hot day for all,

> but if we felt the rays of the sun beneath which we journeyed to be so oppressive, what must be the situation of the poor unsheltered wounded, exposed to its fervid blaze in the open field, without even a drop of water to cool their thirst? What must be the sufferings of our own unfortunate men, above all, of those who were not only wounded but prisoners, and at the mercy of the merciless French?
>
> (Watts 1817, p. 104)

Feelings of grief and horror sink in as the writer thinks of the 'gallant soldiers, whom in the morning we had seen march out so proudly to battle, and who were now lying insensible in death on the plains of Quatre Bras' (Watts 1817, p. 65). Watts identifies the imagination as the worst form of knowledge, at first insufficient in the face of suffering but then the only tool left for understanding. This provides the basis for Act Three:

> Never – never till this moment had I any conception of the horrors of war! and they have left an impression on my mind which no time can efface. Dreadful indeed is the sight of pain and misery we have no power to relieve, but far more dreadful are the horrors imagination pictures of the scene of carnage; the agonies of the wounded and the dying on the field of battle, where even the dead who had fallen by the sword, in the prime of youth and health, are to be envied! – the thought was agony, and yet I could not banish it from my mind.
>
> (Watts 1817, p. 105)

The English allies won victory on 18 June. It has been estimated that among all combatants 71,000 were killed or wounded in the battle itself, to which consequential casualties should be added making a total of 120,300 (Roberts 2005, p. 120). Every one of them, whether English, French or Belgian, was an individual imbued with the sanctity of human life, and each left grieving and bereft families and communities. For days afterwards the cries and groans of the wounded continued to pierce the air, and pillaging was rife. It was a triumphant win for the victors, but for those who witnessed or suffered the consequences, it was also the traumatic loss of innocence expressed by Jane Watts, shattering any prior illusions about the glory of war.

The historical importance of the event and its outcome included, it has been variously argued, the final death knell not only of French military might and Napoleon's imperialistic aspirations, but of the French Revolution itself, since the Bourbons of the *ancien régime* were soon to be reinstated. The Battle of Waterloo produced a consolidation of the British Empire, and the inception of the American Empire as French control of its own colonies weakened. Jeffrey N. Cox (2014) has argued that the younger Romantics responded to the Napoleonic Wars and their aftermath as to a time of 'global war', and the long-term consequences seem to justify such a description. Even the hope that the economic hardship of the war years in Britain might be lifted in peacetime came to naught, since depression and mass unemployment immediately followed. A third conclusion, then, might be that Waterloo achieved nothing but further destruction, into the distant and apparently unending future. Wars are not only visible signs of destruction in the past but also portend ruins to come. One transient benefit could not be justified by the mass suffering and negative outcomes, but undoubtedly, as Bennett writes, the conflict had a galvanising effect on its British critics:

> The end of the war signified the beginning of an unflagging struggle by the working and middle classes for liberty and justice, a struggle which was to continue throughout the nineteenth century.
> (Bennett 1976, p. 91)

A range of poetic responses among British writers followed Waterloo. Many undistinguished poems were written on the occasion of the Battle, and some can be found by scouring through the indispensable anthology of *British War Poetry in the Age of Romanticism* edited by Betty Bennett (1976), now selectively online. Both Simon Bainbridge (1995) and Jeffrey N. Cox (2014, p. 166) 'place the number of poems – which presumably would include newspaper verse – in the hundreds'. There were, of course, many who celebrated the victory at Waterloo in patriotic ways that helped consolidate its mythic, nationalistic status. Representative of these were poems by the writer signing himself Wm Thos Fitzgerald whose poetic voice was unleashed on any public occasion, to the irritation of Byron (1810, ll. 1–2): 'Shall hoarse Fitzgerald bawl / His creaking couplets in a tavern hall . . .?', the latter protested. After Waterloo, Fitzgerald claimed the mantle of a bard, crowing loudly on behalf of the victors over the defeated Napoleon as 'vile oppressor of mankind':

> Such Bard, in strength and loftiness of lays,
> May soar beyond hyperbole of praise,
> And yet not give the tribute that is due
> To BRITONS, WELLINGTON, led on by you!!
> For to the plains of WATERLOO belong
> The magic numbers of immortal song!
> (Bennett 1976, p. 7)

Fitzgerald was one among many stirred by victory into writing celebratory poetry, and even though other like-minded poets offered generous acknowledgement to the allied nations who helped, they regarded it as first and foremost a military triumph of British heroism. They held on to this ideological position as guiding the form of their writing.

Other poets assuming a bardic posture offered more subtle and mixed celebration of the victory at Waterloo. Wordsworth and Southey had joined public celebrations for the defeat of Napoleon on top of Mount Skiddaw in the Lake District (Bainbridge 1995, p. 153). Wordsworth's poem, known as 'Thanksgiving Ode', while mourning the dead, included the lines ridiculed by Byron and Shelley and damned by a horrified Hazlitt, lines seeing man as God's instrument: 'Man – arrayed for mutual slaughter, – Yea, carnage is thy [God's] daughter!' (Wordsworth 1989, p. 188), confirming that the slaughter was part of God's plan. This sentiment is expressed in the context of a poem which is, throughout, primarily religious in intention, rather than expressing simply a conventional, secular patriotism. For Wordsworth, there is a pattern and a form even in the chaos, though it is visible only to an omniscient God, and perhaps an equally omniscient poet. When he twice republished the poem almost 30 years later, Wordsworth dropped the lines, perhaps made aware by reviewers of their potential offence.

Wordsworth also wrote two sonnets in February 1816. 'Occasioned by the Battle of Waterloo' is centrally focused not on what has happened, but on the power of 'The Bard, whose soul is meek as dawning day' to see through 'the array / Of past events' with an 'experienced eye' and 'vision clear'.

> He only, if such breathe, in strains devout
> Shall comprehend this victory sublime;
> Shall worthily rehearse the hideous rout,
> The triumph hail, which from their peaceful clime
> Angels might welcome with a choral shout!

In some way it is a strange way to view 'the hideous rout' as somehow self-aggrandising the poet's visionary and prophetic powers, but Wordsworth asserts it, again as an example of willed form subjugating emotional complexities of substance. The other sonnet, 'Occasioned by the Battle of Waterloo', is more straightforwardly patriotic, praising the 'Intrepid sons of Albion!' as 'Heroes!' for their courage in quelling 'that impious crew : 'But death, becoming death, is dearer far, / When duty bids you bleed in open war'. Horace's epigram (*Odes* 2.3.13) comes to mind: '*Dulce et decorum est pro patria mori*'. *Decorum* ('becoming') is rich with implicature, suggesting both literary and ethical appropriateness of form; it raises profound questions about the extent to which human suffering is justified to achieve this decorum. The implicit paradox renders vulnerable Horace's *sententia* to the kind of dark parody and sarcasm in Wilfred Owen's famous poem of the same name, when transplanted to the actual scene of battle. In the case of Wordsworth's sonnet the somehow complacent rhyme between 'hideous rout' and 'choral shout' provides its own unintended irony.

But the sight of the place itself may have taken its subtle revenge on Wordsworth. He and his sister Dorothy made a visit some years afterwards in 1820, and the result was another sonnet, 'After Visiting the Field of Waterloo', which conveys a wider spectrum of feelings about the experience. It is more disconcerting, as though the sense of place is too sobering to sustain the sense of triumph. Initially 'A winged Goddess, clothed in vesture wrought / Of rainbow colours' hovers over the 'far-famed Spot' as though investing it with a benign, holy aura. This, however, vanishes:

> . . . leaving prospect blank and cold
> Of wind-swept corn that wide around us rolled
> In dreary billows, wood, and meagre cot . . .

At this moment, 'glory seemed betrayal' and 'patriot zeal / Sank in our hearts', to be replaced by a haunting sense of treading upon the dead:

> . . . we felt as Men should feel
> With such vast hoards of hidden carnage near,
> And horror breathing from the silent ground.

Given his generally celebratory tone, it may not be likely that Wordsworth quite knew or intended that he had written in an anti-war vein, but the shift in tone is so marked that it seems the progression and immediacy of thought has broken out of the sonnet form designed to immortalise Waterloo, as though a bubble of thought has been punctured and momentarily allowed entrance to something darker and chaotic.

Inevitably there were poems written from a range of different viewpoints about Waterloo. Some poets such as Shelley and Byron saw Wellington's victory not as Britain's but more narrowly as that of the English Tory party, intent primarily on 'regime change' in France after the Revolution. Occasionally a poet willing to risk the charge of Jacobinism, such as one writing under the name of 'P. Cornwall' in the Whig-leaning *The Morning Chronicle* (21 October 1815), offered condolences to the fallen hero Napoleon, now bereft of fair-weather friends and supporters (Bennett 1976, p. 10). Hazlitt, biographer of Napoleon, openly grieved, and Byron confessed himself 'd—d sorry' (Cathcart 2015). Some were intentionally anti-war. 'W. A.' expressed at least ambivalence over Waterloo, and although showing relief at the allied victory, also lamented that once again the 'embattled plain / . . . Lies heaped with myriads of its victims slain'. In this poem 'the fiend' is not a military enemy but war itself in its indiscriminate destruction of the innocent:

> But pause! and contemplate this scene of blood,
> This endless widowhood,
> To many a thousand sorrows, joys, and fears:
> The mother's sighs,
> The Orphan's cries,
> The parent's grief,
> In agonising strains assail our ears –
>
> (Bennett 1976, p. 11)

Among anti-war literary responses, Leigh Hunt appended to his allegorical ballad *Captain Sword and Captain Pen* a summary of Robert Southey's searing eyewitness prose account of an earlier battlefield at Blenheim, 'The Horrors of War', with its descriptions of the wounded and dying presented with polemical impact. Hunt's poem plays out its metaphorical theme that the pen is mightier than the sword, and, as I have argued elsewhere, in his Appendix Hunt was envisioning and contributing to the function of the Red Cross, though its inception lay over 50 years into the future (White 2015).

By contrast with subsequent wars fought either in trenches away from communities or later by strategies of purposeful and genocidal mass aerial bombing of civilian areas, the Battle of Waterloo was waged right in the middle of a farming community. The action was closely observed at the time by nearby cottage dwellers, and bullet holes in their homes bore witness to the proximity. Their farms were destroyed and their animals were among the victims. The conflict was heard by nearby citizens, including anxious families of officers staying in towns nearby.

The battlefield of Waterloo, later regarded as a kind of shrine, was visited after the event by writers. Sir Walter Scott was there by August, as one of the first civilians to arrive, and he was followed soon by Southey and a year later Byron and Wordsworth.[2] The artist J. M. W. Turner went in 1817, and his darkly brooding painting 'The Field of Waterloo', exhibited in 1818, has the profound atmosphere of a mourning vigil by mankind and nature, as grieving relatives from both sides search by night the mountain of corpses for loved ones. This raises, in the context of pictorial art, the kind of paradox of form and formlessness we are observing in poetry, as control of aesthetic form is deployed to depict chaos, and emotions drive the process. In art, we are encouraged to conceive of form as organic and natural even though it can be imposed and even unnaturally regular. The aim of the artist in representing war is to create a form and principle of order, which can unobtrusively guide the eye and the feelings to see as the artist does, even when what we see is a version of chaos. Turner's painting, in Romantic-era terms is not picturesque but sublime, and as powerful a statement on the inchoate horrors of war as Picasso's *Guernica* and Goya's series on *The Disasters of War*. Such works are paralleled at Waterloo more conventionally by the works of famous war artists of the time, Matthew Dubourg and Heaviside ('Waterloo') Clark.

In form, interestingly, two modes of poetry commonly adopted in the poems of Waterloo are among the most rhythmically regular, the ballad and Spenserian stanzas. These are genres designed to create a feeling of 'long ago' times that belong as much to legend and allegory as historical fact. Both forms were revived during the later eighteenth century into the Romantic period, after publication of Percy's *Reliques of Ancient English Poetry* in 1765. Wordsworth in the year of Waterloo, 1815, proclaimed Percy's work as central to his own age's poetic enterprise: 'I do not think there is an able Writer of verse of the present day who would not be proud to acknowledge his obligations to the Reliques; I know that it is so with my friends; and for myself, I am happy in this occasion to make a public avowal of my own' (Wordsworth 1815). (His own works on Waterloo, however, comprised an ode and sonnets.) Ballads and Spenserian stanzas are used in poems about Waterloo for stylistic reasons: the pace and straightforward rhythms and rhymes of the ballad emphasise narrative, and lend an anonymous poetic stance; while the Spenserian form was linked with nationalistic pride, and – through its conscious archaisms – evoked an 'olde worlde'. Associations with the allegorical apparatus of *The Faerie Queene* also added a heightened sense of historical significance to the perspective.

In 'The Poet's Pilgrimage to Waterloo', written on visiting the battlefield in October, Southey in some ways fuses the two forms to suit his purposes. This poem uses a story mode of the pilgrimage as journey followed by battle, and then the allegory of the second Part, titled 'The Vision', to celebrate British bravery in fulsome terms while demonising Napoleonic tyranny. The long work also ambitiously aspires to epic proportions, structured in two main sections each divided into four Parts of about 50 stanzas each. As poet laureate from 1813 to 1843 (which he declares in his subtitle) he could hardly have done otherwise. Southey reminds us of this public responsibility, consciously and fairly consistently adopting the self-aggrandising stance suitable to the writer of a bardic lay, beginning with a strong assertion of ego:

> Me most of all men it behoved to raise
> The strain of triumph for this foe subdued,
> To give a voice to joy, and in my lays
> Exalt a nation's hymn of gratitude,
> And blazon forth in song that day's renown,
> For I was graced with England's laurel crown.
>
> (Southey 1838, p. 14)

He speaks of emulating accounts of 'tilts in days of old, And tourneys' graced by chieftains of renown, / Fair dames, grave citizens, and warriors bold . . .', again distancing his own story from the present in a framework including balladry and Spenserian historical perspective. The primary aim is to celebrate the allied victory, but in Southey's poem there are more disquieting notes that break through in spite of the poet's political beliefs. Briefly, Southey had once been a radical, but to the exasperation of younger Romantics such as Hazlitt, he became more and more conservative – hence his laureateship. But pockets of radicalism remained latent in his mind, especially in his condemnation of war. We know from his journal mentioned above, published as *The Horrors of War*, that his 'pilgrimage' had traumatised him with the manifest evidence of suffering. This strain, however powerful, enters his poem in an almost smuggled way to qualify the more ostentatious nationalism and distancing devices. He speaks from observation of the hospital where, even after three months, men were dying in 'wretchedness and pain':

> Her inmost chambers trembled with dismay;
> And now within her walls, insatiate Death,
> Devourer whom no harvest e'er can fill,
> The gleanings of that field was gathering still.
>
> (Southey 1838, p. 26)

The imagery ironically reprises the likening of war to a grotesque feast, in this case harvest. Memories must have been triggered of images he had seen before, of casualties of war as limbless invalids being carried exhausted and helpless on wagons, only just able to draw the breath which was the only outward sign of the fact they were alive, prelude to 'pain through hopeless years of lingering death'. There 'comes with horror to the shuddering mind' the groans and cries breathed in mortal pain by ally and enemy alike on the battlefield, and fleetingly and unexpectedly, as though from his unconscious, Southey touches the nerve and brings a moment of undeniable outrage to his mind by envisaging the distortions of form caused by violent conflict:

> Here might the hideous face of war be seen,
> Stript of all pomp, adornment, and disguise;
> It was a dismal spectacle I ween,
> Such as might well to the beholders' eyes
> Bring sudden tears, and make the pious mind
> Grieve for the crimes and follies of mankind.
>
> (Southey 1838, p. 27)

If the poem had proceeded along this sombre line, it would hardly have endeared itself as much as it did to the Tory press such as the *Anti-Jacobin*. Instead, however, the intrusively indecorous note passes immediately from outrage to regret, and then into a diatribe of blame against France as 'the guilty nation', which had fallen under 'a Tyrant's yoke' and had brought on the conflict. Southey later returns to the note of inner resistance in a gentler key when he imagines the local villagers who lived nearby, their fields of green corn trampled and blood-soaked 'like water shed', 'ancient groves and fruitful orchards wide' destroyed, small holdings littered with dead and dying men and horses, cottage walls peppered with musket holes and flecked with streaks of blood, wives and children fled 'to some near retreat' to tremble in fear for their husbands left behind as helpless and hapless observers. There is even a hint of less than patriotic regret from Southey, 'Alas to think such irreligious deed / Of wrong from British soldiers should proceed!'. Throughout 'The Poet's Pilgrimage to Waterloo' we observe at work the paradox in a new key. An uncomfortable part of Southey's affective memory keeps obtruding to disturb and disrupt the overlaid order and form which his ideology of patriotism seeks to impose. The result is both psychologically and artistically a more complex and emotionally honest poem than Southey may have been fully aware of.

Sir Walter Scott's 'The Field of Waterloo' was widely panned by conservative critics at the time because of its perceived lukewarm partisanship for the English cause. John Gibson Lockhart, an editor reviled by literary historians as one who destroyed Keats's budding reputation, was scathing. Lockhart used criticism of style as a stalking horse to mask his political antipathy, based on his perception that Scott had been far more impressive when writing about his own nation's Battle of Bannockburn, the first war of Scottish independence in 1314, than he was of a victory claimed generally as led by the English because of Wellington's generalship (Lockhart 1914, p. 120). Although the poem is neither ballad nor, until its end, Spenserian in form, but mainly in the metre of Scott's *Marmion*, the perspective is comparable to these genres. Generally speaking, Scott is, like other patriotic poets, seeking to mythologise Waterloo in Spenserian terms as a late 'flower of Chivalry' opposed to 'a dragon foe', and his comparisons are with Agincourt and Cressy, though such heroics, despite ending the poem, are not consistent with the overall impression it makes. However, his effort was considered lukewarm and hackneyed by the critics, and it was even parodied by rival poets. The overt thrust is to describe the conflict, to praise Wellington and denigrate Napoleon, and also to evoke a sense of place. However, amidst generalities Scott allows a more critical pattern of thought to assert itself. The poet gives visualised glimpses of the post-battle scene where a stronger, more melancholy and dismayed tone emerges:

> And ere the darkening of the day,
> Piled high as autumn shocks, there lay
> The ghastly harvest of the fray,
> The corpses of the slain.
>
> (Scott 1910, pp. 609–628, stanzas 5, 6)

Even two months after the fray, bodies are vestigially visible from evidence of a 'trenched mound' while 'pestilential fumes' still hang in the air, either metaphorically or literally. The reader is then led into the specific landscape of the poem gradually, allowing us slowly to realise how the initial impression of the battle scene differs from the human triumphalism of the victory. The emphasis develops into stanza 20 where 'Triumph and Sorrow border near', bringing us closer to the living victims, and in stanza 23 environmental destruction is emphasised as the price paid for human glory. In a more subtle way perhaps than other poets, Scott develops the full significance of visiting the battlefield *after* the event, when the place is visibly different and reveals as much human degradation of nature as of humankind. Scott's intention was to send profits from the poem's publication to a fund for soldiers' widows and orphans, the Waterloo Subscription. Despite critical denigration, it was in fact successful with the public, 6,000 copies selling out initially, sending it into a second and third edition, so it succeeded in its aim of aiding victims.

Lord Byron's attitude to war was somewhat equivocal depending on the political motives behind a particular conflict (White 2008, pp. 188–190). He was opposed to war as such, especially when it was for imperialistic reasons or to acquire territory, but he supported wars of independence waged by oppressed populations, such as the one in Greece which he funded himself and during which he died. Needless to say, he was scathing about Waterloo, which he saw as an unnecessary war fought for purely nationalistic and aggressive reasons on both sides – by the imperialist Napoleon and by the conservative British government opposed to the French Revolution. Canto III, stanza XVIII of *Childe Harold's Pilgrimage* stands alone as one of the great anti-war poems, and it is built upon the self-sufficient episode which, when anthologised, goes under the name 'The Eve of Waterloo'. Byron makes specific reference to the ball at Brussels on the evening before battle, like Scott who was himself reproved by the critics for its inclusion. This event was regarded ambivalently in Britain, as either a gesture of heroic audacity or of extravagance, complacency and arrogance. Byron, clearly in the latter camp, uses the 'night before' to contrast with and intensify the unnecessary suffering during the two days to come, as Leigh Hunt was to do later in his overtly pacifist ballad *Captain Sword and Captain Pen*. Byron wrote 'The Eve of Waterloo' in exact Spenserian stanzas, consistent with the whole of *Childe Harold*. Characteristically, he varies and adapts the form opportunistically to suit his intentions, sometimes parodying or even burlesquing it, sometimes to attack anti-quarian attitudes to nationalism and religion, and sometimes to accentuate an allegorical tendency. Here he uses it as a framework to universalise the event, which happened in 'this place of skulls', not in Southey's and Scott's spirit of moral and military triumph, but rather to exemplify the futility of war itself. Spenser, no pacifist himself in his public role as apologist for English genocide in Ireland in his *View of the Present State of Ireland*, may not have approved of Byron's message, but the poetic deployment of his stanzaic form is true to his own mission of making myths out of poetry.

Brussels rings to the 'sound of revelry by night' and the ball is described with the vocabulary of 'Chivalry' laced with Byron's seductive trademark of a language of love soon to be brutally halted in its lulling romanticism:

> A thousand hearts beat happily; and when
> Music arose with its voluptuous swell,
> Soft eyes look'd love to eyes which spake again . . .
> (Byron 1980, pp. 832–837)

As the poem's perspective widens, nature itself becomes a horrified, lamenting spectator:

> And Ardennes waves above them her green leaves,
> Dewy with nature's tear-drops, as they pass,
> Grieving, if aught inanimate e'er grieves,
> Over the unreturning brave, – alas!

> Ere evening to be trodden like the grass
> Which now beneath them, but above shall grow
> In its next verdure, when this fiery mass
> Of living valour, rolling on the foe
> And burning with high hope, shall moulder cold and low.
>
> (Byron 1980, pp. 832–837)

Like Turner, Byron sees nature as implicated in the condemnation of man, 'if aught inanimate e'er grieves', and the grass trodden down by men will grow over them when they are dead. At the end of the fragment, the poem returns to its opening, with a poignant reminder of the 'lusty life' of youthfulness 'in Beauty's circle proudly gay', in order to throw into relief the hideous and formless chaos after the battle, lamented even by nature and the reproving weather:

> The thunder-clouds close o'er it, which when rent
> The earth is covered thick with other clay
> Which her own clay shall cover, heaped and pent,
> Rider and horse, – friend, foe, – in one red burial blent!
>
> (Byron 1980, pp. 832–837)

What had been a scene of human 'revelry' has, through war, been turned into a site of indiscriminate slaughter of animals, allies and enemies alike, an exercise of 'mutual slaughter' deliberately undermining attitudes such as those in Wordsworth's pious complacent theocracy. 'Thick with other clay' is a disturbing image. The sheer pointlessness of war in general as chaos overthrows form, love and human aspirations, is Byron's target in this brief but powerful poetic episode.

One more work, this time in prose and written long after the event, provides our *coda*. Thackeray's historical novel *Vanity Fair* may draw on Byron's poem, and if so it carries an extra, allusive richness. Published in 1848 but set during the Napoleonic Wars, a decisive turning point in the narrative is the Battle of Waterloo (Thackeray 1968).[3] The male characters are regimental officers who, with their wives and children on the night before battle, attend the ball organised in Brussels for 'such a brilliant train of camp-followers as hung around the Duke of Wellington's army'. In the hint behind the words 'hung around', we already see something of the writer's distancing and derogatory attitude, not to speak of the buried metaphor of camp followers as a string of 'brilliant' baubles strung around their leader. The narrator comments acidly, 'I have heard from ladies who were in that town at the period, that the talk and interest of persons of their own sex regarding the ball was much greater than in respect of the enemy in their front' (Thackeray *Vanity Fair*, ch. xxix). New dresses and ornaments are flaunted, fine wines drunk, and but for sardonic asides of poetic irony, such as the parenthetic reference to the Captain's 'wife (or it might be his widow's) guardianship', and the solitary anxieties of the stolid and faithful Dobbin for his beloved Amelia in the event of defeat, nobody gives a realistic thought to the impending dangers.

Realistic in her own mercenary way is Becky Sharp who coldly calculates how much she will inherit should her husband Rawdon Crawley be killed. As news arrives that battle will be engaged, reactions oscillate between George Osborne's mounting excitement and his wife Amelia's fear. As dawn bugles awaken the soldiers to combat, the novel's gaze remains behind with the women, children and Jos Sedley who all stay at the hotel, along with the narrator: 'We do not claim to rank among the military novelists. Our place is with the non-combatants' (Thackeray *Vanity Fair*, ch. l.c.). An unobtrusively ominous note is sounded when, having flirted with Rebecca at the ball, George says goodbye to his apprehensive wife and child but callously reflects on the social and emotional awkwardness, 'Thank heaven that is over', not realising that human contact is over forever. The chapter ends, 'The sun was just rising as the march began – it was a gallant sight – band led the column, playing the regimental march ... then George came marching, and passed on; and even the sound of the music died away' (Thackeray *Vanity Fair*, ch. xxx). News from the battle is carried back to the town during the fateful day, while the private imbroglios and fine dining proceed. In the fluctuating fortunes, it looks like the British forces will be defeated, and reports come back of feats of heroism by Osborne and Dobbin, murmurs of generalised suffering, and acts of unobtrusive heroism which provide a gloss on the novel's subtitle, *A Novel Without a Hero*. Jos, afraid for the women and for himself since he realises he will be mistaken for a soldier, tries to organise them all to flee, knowing they will be 'butchered' by the French forces, a very real prospect because of the proximity of the town to the battle. At the distant rumble of cannons, rumours are rife, and all Jos can do is simply drink champagne with feelings of shame and fear. When news of victory comes, Thackeray's narrator slips in his crucial and chilling climax almost inadvertently with controlled, throwaway casualness at the end of a chapter, as post-battle silence begins to fall:

> No more firing was heard at Brussels – the pursuit rolled miles away. Darkness came down on the field and city: and Amelia was praying for George, who was lying on his face, dead, with a bullet through his heart.
> (Thackeray *Vanity Fair*, ch. xxxii)

The narrator's apparently wry self-exemption ('We do not claim to rank among the military novelists. Our place is with the non-combatants') is multiply meaningful, acting as an implied rebuke to others who focus on the heroism exhibited in battle to glorify the dead and the cause, and also identifying Thackeray's own commitment to the lowlier but equally powerful emotions of the non-combatants who must live with their own loss as best they can.

Military organisation in war has always been based on conspicuously over-determined strategies and patterned ordering of formations: from the lines and rectangular ranks of soldiers advancing in compact squadrons, to their crisp and identical uniforms. The soldiers even have their 'orders' to follow in a different sense, and obedience draws them into mirroring each other's exact behaviour.

A strictly imposed hierarchical line of officers descending to privates contains, and further coerces, the massed blocks into imposed relationships. The blare of bugles and beat of drums add a layer of compelling musical drama designed to sublimate emotions of fear into courage, and puffs of distant powder seem more an aesthetic adornment than emanations from deadly cannon designed with no purpose in mind except murder. It is astonishing that the assertion of extreme control in all this preparation is calculated to persuade combatants to think that an adverse result must be by chance, while success is part of a divine order. In reality, the result in every case is the same and entirely inevitable, 'mutual slaughter'. As each of the writers – with their very different motivations in writing of the Battle of Waterloo – make affectively and starkly clear, the 'Morning After' exposes war itself as the exact reverse of order and form. It is revealed rather, as a formless and terrible destruction of human order, forms and potential, with no purpose or pattern, and leaving each family of a slaughtered human without livelihood, deracinated and grieving. At the same time, however, in some instances such as Scott's poem and Turner's painting, the order and form conferred by conventions of art and driven by emotional conviction can create a higher order, a dark sublimity perhaps, giving dignity, sympathy and humanity to the individual protagonists caught up in the chaos.

Paradoxically, it is the formal arrangement of poetry into rhythms, rhymes and genres such as ballad or Spenserian stanzas, and the rhetorical patterning of heightened prose, which can most movingly direct, and heighten the reader's emotional engagement and apprehension of significance in the disruption of forms. In yet another sense, however, as we have seen in the poems of Southey and Wordsworth in particular, the poet's attempt to impose a consistent point of view based on an ideology can also be undermined and disordered from within, by the imagination stretched in moments of dismay to break its own willed boundaries and borders. A century after Waterloo, and in a very different war, Wilfred Owen (1931, p. 31) was to write memorably, 'Above all I am not concerned with Poetry. / My subject is War, and the pity of War. / The Poetry is in the pity'. Among its many available resonances, the statement shifts the emphasis away from form for its own sake or the sake of decorum, to the unruliness of emotional content, and the feelings aroused by war.

Notes

1 I am grateful to Katrina O'Loughlin for providing me with a copy of this text.
2 Byron's visit in August 1816 was (somewhat surprisingly) reported in a letter from 'A Sexagenarian' in *The Sydney Gazette and New South Wales Advertiser*, on Saturday 6 March 1830, p. 4. The letter-writer asked Byron his opinion of Scott's 'Field of Waterloo', to which the reply was 'I am sure there is no poet living who could have written so many good lines on so meagre a subject, in so short a time'.
3 The ambiguity of Thackeray's time scheme, hovering as it does between 1815 and the 1840s, is analysed by Hammond in 'Thackeray's Waterloo: History and War in *Vanity Fair*', *Literature and History*, third series 11 (2002), pp. 19–38.

Reference list

Astbury, K. 2015, 'Witnesses, Wives, Politicians, and Soldiers: The Women of Waterloo', *The Conversation*, June 12: http://theconversation.com/witnesses-wives-politicians-soldiers-the-women-of-waterloo-42648, accessed 5 September 2016.

Bainbridge, S. 1995, *Napoleon and English Romanticism*, Cambridge University Press, Cambridge.

Bennett, B. (ed.) 1976, *British War Poetry in the Age of Romanticism 1793–1815*, Garland Publishing, New York. Online at www.rc.umd.edu/editions/warpoetry/1815/1815_7.html, accessed 12 June 2016.

Byron, Lord 1810, *English Bards and Scotch Reviewers; A Satire*, James Cawthorn, London.

Byron, Lord 1980, *Lord Byron: The Complete Poetical Works*, ed. J. J. McGann, Clarendon Press, Oxford.

Cathcart, B. 2015, *The News from Waterloo: The Race to Tell Britain of Wellington's Victory*, Faber & Faber, London.

Cox, J. N. 2014, *Romanticism in the Shadow of War: Culture in the Napoleonic War Years*, Cambridge University Press, Cambridge.

Favret, M. 2009, *War at Distance: Romanticism and the Making of Modern Wartime*, Princeton University Press, Princeton, New Jersey.

Gottlieb, E. 2009, 'Fighting Words: Representing the Napoleonic Wars in the Poetry of Hemans and Barbauld', *European Romantic Review*, vol. 20, pp. 327–343.

Hammond, M. 2002, 'Thackeray's Waterloo: History and War in *Vanity Fair*', in *Literature and History*, vol. 11, no. 2, pp. 19–38.

Hunt, L. 1990, *Leigh Hunt: Selected Writings*, ed. D. J. Dibley, Carcanet Press, Manchester.

Lockhart, J. G. 1914, *Lockhart's Life of Scott*, ed. O. L. Reid, The Macmillan Company, New York.

McLoughlin, K. 2011, *Authoring War: The Literary Representation of War from the Iliad to Iraq*, Cambridge University Press, Cambridge.

Muir, R. 2015, *Wellington: Waterloo and the Fortunes of Peace 1814–1852*, Yale University Press, New Haven.

Owen, W. 1931, *The Collected Poems of Wilfred Owens*, ed. E. Blunden, Chatto & Windus, London.

Perry, S. 2016, 'Waterloo and the Poets', *Keats-Shelley Review*, vol. 30, pp. 57–62.

Roberts, A. 2005, *Waterloo: The Battle for Modern Europe*, Harper Collins, London.

Scott, Sir Walter 1910, *The Poetical Works of Sir Walter Scott*, ed. J. L. Robertson, Oxford University Press, Oxford, pp. 609–628.

Shaw, P. 2002, *Waterloo and the Romantic Imagination*, Palgrave Macmillan, London.

Southey, R. 1838. *The Poetical Works of Robert Southey Collected by Himself*, vol. 10, Longman, Hurst, Rees, Orme, & Brown, London.

Thackeray, W. 1968, *Vanity Fair*, The Penguin English Library, Harmondsworth.

Watts, J. W. 1817, *Narrative of a Residence in Belgium During the Campaign of 1815; and of a Visit to the Field of Waterloo*, 10th edn, John Murray, London.

White, R. S. 2008, *Pacifism and English Literature: Minstrels of Peace*, Palgrave Macmillan, London.

White, R. S. 2015, 'Victims of War: Battlefield Casualties and Literary Sensibility', in N. Ramsay & G. Russell (eds), *Tracing War in British Enlightenment and Romantic Culture*, Palgrave Macmillan, London.

Wordsworth, W. 1815, 'Essay Supplementary to the Preface', *Lyrical Ballads*, 2 vols, Longman, Hurst, Rees, Orme & Brown, London.

Wordsworth, W. 1989, *Shorter Poems, 1807–1820 by William Wordsworth*, ed. C. H. Ketcham, Cornell University Press, Ithaca.

12
WAR AND EMOTION IN THE AGE OF BIEDERMEIER

The *United Service Journal* and the military tale

Neil Ramsey

Following the close of the French Revolutionary and Napoleonic Wars (1792–1815), European culture settled into what Virgil Nemoianu terms the Age of Biedermeier (Nemoianu 1984). It was, Nemoianu argues, a decidedly prosaic age. Coming at the tail end of the great outpouring of art and literature associated with High Romanticism, the Biedermeier was an era when the poetry of Romance was tamed, domesticated or disciplined by the spread of a commercial spirit and a nascent middle class. Literature thus underwent a 'reduction to scale, a lowering of sights' as it moved away from its aspirations to epic poetry and turned, instead, towards the modern realist novel and a proliferation of literary magazines (Nemoianu 1984, p. 195). In his more recent study of the British Biedermeier, however, Richard Cronin has insisted that the literature of this period is also therefore fundamentally shaped by a sense of historical memory (Cronin 2002). If the period was being formed by the emergence of unheroic modern commerce, it nonetheless also saw itself as coming belatedly after the great and tumultuous events of the recent wars. Franco Moretti (2013, p. 177) has also complicated arguments about the coterminous rise of the novel and the Victorian middle-classes by insisting that what characterises the nineteenth-century novel is its failure to align completely with bourgeois values. Basing his views on a quantitative analysis, or what he has termed 'distant reading', of the vast corpus of adventure novels of the nineteenth century, Moretti (2013, p. 178) suggests that the period's literature was equally driven by the continuity of 'pre-modern traits' that he identifies, primarily, with war.

As much as Britain saw itself during the Biedermeier era as a modern nation progressing towards a future of commercial peace and prosperity, it was also a memorialising culture that lay in the shadow of war.[1] One of the starkest examples of this was the emergence in the 1820s of a sizeable body of military literature dedicated to commemorating the wars, and which included not only military histories, journals and biographies, but also a range of newly significant forms of soldiers' personal accounts such as military memoirs, novels and short tales (Ramsey 2011). Alongside a taming or dissolution of Romance by the modern world, it is possible to see in this military writing one way that Romance, defined by Ian Duncan (1992) as the 'narrative form of historical otherness, a representation discontinuous with modern cultural formations', might be seen to have persisted within the modern nation. This chapter considers the publication and reception of military tales in the leading military and naval journal of the period, the *United Service Journal*, which played a central role not only in disseminating such stories, but also in offering extended discussions about how they might be understood as a species of literature. By situating military stories in relation to work on the entanglements of generic forms in this period, the interconnections of emotion, fact, poetry and prose, this chapter considers how such stories commemorated individual soldiers' suffering as a form of sublime feeling.[2] On the one hand, the military journal's publication of ordinary soldiers' personal tales, as opposed to tales of the nation's great heroes such as Lord Nelson, can be situated in relation to late Romantic literature more generally, with its reduced aspirations in the Biedermeier period and its focus on everyday life. But on the other hand, tales of war, along with the commentary that the *United Service Journal* developed around them, helped to establish a militarised aesthetic of historical memory that could redirect and develop ideas of intense, sublime feelings for an emergent Victorian era, even developing a basic equation between war and intense emotionality that could be seen to underpin modern ideas of war literature.

The *United Service Journal* and personal histories of war

The *United Service Journal* was established when the publisher Henry Colburn took over the proprietorship of *The Naval and Military Magazine* in 1829, which had itself been established only two years earlier. Military and naval journals had first appeared in Britain during the French Revolutionary and Napoleonic Wars. They were modelled on German military periodicals that had themselves been first published in the 1770s and 1780s, such as Andreas Böhnn's *Magazin für Ingenieurs und Artilleristen* (1777–1789) and Gerhard Scharnhorst's *Neues Militarisches Journal* (1788–1793 and 1797–1805) (Gat 2001). British military periodicals included a number of short lived periodicals such as *The Soldier's Pocket Magazine* (1798), *The British Military Library* (1799) and *The Monthly Military Companion* (1801–1802), but also several longer running serials, from the *Military Panorama, or Officers Companion* (1812–1814) to the *Royal Military Chronicle* (1810–1817) and the even more enduring *The Naval Chronicle* (1799–1818). The journals featured articles on various aspects of military and naval service, from reports of parliamentary debates on military matters to discussions of nautical or military technologies, accounts of recent military campaigns and information about military promotions, regulations and courts martial (Ramsey 2014). They were also published as wartime journals and thus saw themselves as not simply addressing readers in the military and navy, but equally the reading nation more generally. As such they also featured a range of patriotic literature, from biographical tales of British generals and admirals, through to war themed poetry and dictionaries of military terms.

Being wartime publications, however, the military and naval journals were largely discontinued at the close of the wars. The longest lasting, *The Naval Chronicle*, ceased publication in 1818 soon after the Napoleonic wars because, its editors claimed, there were no longer any notable naval events worth reporting. The re-emergence of military journals after the wars thus represents something of a shift away from this wartime role as such journals began to devote attention to developing the professional and scientific identity of the military and navy. They can in large part be linked to a broader proliferation of journals at the end of the Romantic era that was central to the emerging hegemony of the middle classes and its growing emphasis on the importance of reading and intellectual culture (Klancher 1987). These developments are reflected, for example, in the *Naval and Military Journal*, which announced in the preface to its first volume that it was 'a publication which should exclusively devote itself to the interests of the military and navy' (*The Naval and Military Journal* 1827, p. iii). Similar comments appear in the first volume of the *British Indian Military Repository*, in which the editor states that it was set up in order to provide a repository for 'the honourable achievements of the British Indian Army' (*The British Indian Military Repository* 1822, p. iv). The *United Service Journal* likewise proclaimed that it had nothing to do with politics and party factions but was solely concerned with supplying information relevant to the military and navy as professional institutions (*The United Service Journal* 1829a, p. 1). Indeed, the success of the *United Service Journal* was central to the subsequent formation of the United Service Institute in London in 1831, which was established in an effort to further advance military science as a legitimate and recognisable field of study. Scientific institutions flourished in the late 1820s and start of the 1830s. Although they had their origins in earlier arts and science institutes they nonetheless operated with rigid disciplinary boundaries and clear separations between science and the arts, divisions that were reflected in the proliferation of professional journals that, as Jon Klancher (2013, pp. 224–225) observes, 'registered the increasingly heterogenous play of sociolects – the discourses of emerging professions, conflicting social spheres, men and women'. Intimately linked with such developments, the *United Service Journal* was central to the consolidation of the professional and disciplinary identity of the military services.

In noting how audiences were fragmented across late Romantic periodicals, Clifford Siskin (1998, pp. 186–187) argues that a countervailing development nonetheless also emerged in the journals as they began to take a keen interest in the review and discussion of novels. Composed around the ordinary details of national life, novels were stories with which any and all members of the nation could potentially identify. By the end of the Romantic era novels had also come to be seen as central to the very idea of writing, a development Siskin (1998, p. 22) terms 'novelism' or the 'subordination of writing to the novel', and thus novels were seen to possess an intrinsic affinity with the expansion of the reading public. Novels were able to define a national reading public by enabling the diverse parts of the nation to come together imaginatively as a unified whole (in some sense even filling the role that war had formerly played in unifying the nation against its hostile French 'Other') (Siskin 1998, p. 186). Although the *United Service Journal* was aware that as a military publication it could hardly concentrate as extensively as other journals on 'poetry and literature', it was also highly conscious of its relationship to the general reading public and their interest in such material (*The United Service Journal* 1829a, p. iii). To some extent, this literary dimension can be seen in earlier, wartime military journals (which included poetry and military biography), while both the *Naval and Military Journal* and the *British Indian Military Repository* continued some of this interest by including biographical accounts of illustrious officers. The *United Service Journal* also included biographies of notable generals and admirals, but a literary dimension to the journal was principally formed by its inclusion of officers' 'personal histories' of war (along with extensive reviewing of such publications), which, the journal claimed, would be of 'the greatest value' to military officers, while to the public at large they would constitute 'subjects of the most exciting interest' (Blakiston 1829, p. 382). These stories, the journal suggested in the preface to its first volume, would appeal to 'the boundless and exuberant domains of fancy and feeling' and would be enjoyed equally by officers and the public more generally, even to 'our accomplished countrywomen' (*United Service Journal* 1829a, p. 2). Personal tales of war could be seen to have worked for the *United Service Journal* in a manner analogous to the discourse of novelism in journals more generally. If novels helped anchor the diverse audiences of the journals within a unified idea of the nation, so military tales and their concern with the ordinary details of the nation's soldiers helped the *United Service Journal* speak to a national audience despite its institutional status.

Although the *United Service Journal* was the first military journal to include soldiers' personal tales of war, personal accounts of war were not themselves new in Britain, having been published throughout the eighteenth century. However, by the end of the eighteenth century accounts of military life were beginning to draw on elements of sentimental literature, meaning that they were both increasingly personal in their focus and also far more concerned with themes of suffering (Harari 2008). Because sentimental literature foregrounded suffering, it had an ambiguous relationship with the nationalist ideals of war. As Marilyn Butler (1981, p. 31) has argued, sentimental reflections on war were typically perceived as having an anti-authority bias, their focus on the suffering of ordinary individuals at odds with the grandeur and political power associated with the nation's wars. That a military journal should have taken an interest in personal tales of war's hardships was, therefore, something unusual. It is a development that can be traced to the unprecedented commercial success of two military memoirs published by British officers in the mid-1820s about their experiences during the Peninsular War (1808–1814), Moyle Sherer's *Recollections of the Peninsula* (1823) and George Gleig's *The Subaltern* (1825). Despite drawing on sentimental traditions of war writing as an account of an individual's suffering, Gleig and Sherer nonetheless wrote in such a way as to redefine the hardships and the horrors of war as a version of an ennobling pastoral experience in nature. Campaigning with the army not only allowed Sherer to enjoy the picturesque beauties of the Iberian Peninsula, but to be uplifted by his experience of war's privations. War's 'carnage', he felt, must be talked of with pleasure because 'in the very peril of sudden and violent death, or cureless wounds, and ghastly laceration, excitement, strong, high, and pleasurable, fills and animates the bosom: hope, pride, patriotism, and awe, make up this mighty feeling, and lift a man, for such moments, almost above the dignity of his nature' (Sherer 1824, p. 40). Sherer (1824, p. 40) concludes of his military experiences that '[s]uch moments are more than equal to years of common life'. Reflecting on his experiences with the army, Gleig (1845, p. viii) similarly saw the hardships of campaigning as having been an experience of 'piety and true devotion' absent from the idle comfort of civilian society. 'They who write and speak of war as of a succession of horror, and nothing else', he reflected, 'know not what they are describing' (1845, p. ix).

Both memoirs were not only greeted enthusiastically by major review magazines, they also inspired numerous imitations by other military and naval officers. By the 1830s it was common for reviewers to remark upon the growth of a popular 'school of writing' that could be traced to these early 'experiments' by Sherer and Gleig (*The Gentleman's Magazine* 1831, p. 68). The *Quarterly Review* even suggested in 1832 that the *United Service Journal* was itself an outgrowth of this expansion in writing and had become, if somewhat implausibly, the most widely read journal in Britain (*The Quarterly Review* 1831, pp. 166–167). Colburn's involvement may well have been because of the commercial opportunities afforded by publication of military tales in the journal. A considerable portion of its pages were, therefore, devoted not to scientific accounts of war, but were taken up with reviews and excerpts from military tales that echoed this celebration of war's hardships, carnage and horror found in Sherer and Gleig's earlier work. The first volume of the journal, for example, featured the anonymously written 'A Hussars Life on Service', a series of private letters in which the narrator delights in the youthful energies of his life on active military service during the Peninsular War. The first letter opens with the narrator's surprise that his correspondent should be less interested in accounts of military victories than 'our general mode of life while "campaigning"', but acknowledges that such minor details will be useful for the sake of posterity (*The United Service Journal* 1829a, p. 427). He goes on to explain that hussars had a particularly arduous existence on campaign because they were always riding in advance of the army, being required to form picket lines, arrange forage and scout enemy positions. Despite therefore being constantly employed in the face of the enemy, the author is as resolute as Gleig and Sherer that he took instruction and pleasure from his experiences, observing 'that in danger and risk there is pleasure, if not happiness' (p. 428). So too, he notes that a friendly discourse eventually emerged between the French and British officers, the whole contributing to the emergence of 'right feeling' in relation to the war (p. 431). The author even goes so far as to offer his wartime letters as 'the best philosophy of life' for the English gentleman at ease at home (*The United Service Journal* 1.1 1829, p. 428).

Other military stories featured in the journal similarly reveal war's unequalled suffering, even as they find some form of solace and consolation within that very privation. The anonymous 'Recollections in Quarters' was composed as a disconnected series of anecdotes about the narrator's active service during several campaigns with the army. One anecdote relates the narrator's recollections of the night before the Battle of Salamanca, in which he describes the hushed, tense and apprehensive mood that came over him and his fellow soldiers as they contemplated the prospect of the next day's combat. Taking a walk about the camp, the narrator comes to a quiet spot, 'as tranquil as a churchyard', where he notices two soldiers kneeling together in prayer and realises they are father and son (*The United Service Journal* 1829b, p. 94). During the next day's battle the son is killed, leaving behind his father who dutifully locates his son's body and performs the burial. The author himself confronts his own emotions at the prospect of death during the siege of St Sebastian. While he sees one artilleryman killed by a cannon 'running him against a wall and squeezing his bowels out' he nonetheless insists that he was not afraid but had, rather, a feeling of 'extreme suspense and surprise' (p. 96). War is, throughout these anecdotes, brutal, heart rending and frightening, yet the narrator, like that of 'A Hussar's Life', persistently draws his reader back to consolatory feelings of equanimity, duty, suspense and elation. One correspondent to the journal complained that revelations of soldiers' feelings in battle were deleterious to the army because they contained implications of cowardice. The editors dismissed the correspondent's fears, suggesting that what mattered was simply the 'truth and power' that such stories presented to their readers (p. 108).

In a pair of sketches of the 'Storming of Ciudad Rodrigo' and 'Storming of Badajoz', the anonymous narrator emphasises a broader commemorative element as he writes of the appalling loss of life when the British stormed the breaches of these two fortifications. At one point the officer describes meeting his comrade during the assault of Ciudad Rodrigo in as much graphic detail as the author of 'Recollections' witnessed the death of a disembowelled artilleryman:

> I went towards the large breach, and met Uniacke of the 95th; he was walking between two men. One of his eyes was blown out, and the flesh was torn off his arms and legs. I asked who it was; he replied Uniacke, and walked on. He had taken chocolate with our mess an hour before.
> (The United Service Journal 1829a, pp. 63–64)

The narrator proceeds to describe the desultory aftermath of the combat – the ground is covered in dead British soldiers, including General McKinnon who has been stripped near naked following his death. The narrator ponders the cause of his fate, concluding that it must not have been from an explosion or his face should have been 'scorched' (p. 65). He also describes meeting two mortally wounded friends, Madden and Merry, after the storming of Badajoz: the first lies dying covered in his own blood while the second insists he will die from a knee shattered by grape shot. The story not only foregrounds the officers' familiarity with the shocking experience of suffering and misery, highlighted by the radical disjunction between Uniacke taking chocolate and the brutal violence of military combat that tears, scorches and shatters flesh and bone. It equally signals the office's unparalleled fortitude and courage in meeting such horrors, a courage that effaces all marks of rank and distinction. The sketches conclude with reflection on the noble qualities that thus found their expression in the sacrifices of the soldiers at Badajoz, demanding of the reader 'Look on those blood stained uniforms; gaze on these noble forms stretched on the earth, and think on their agonies!' (p. 169).

Narrating the romance of war

The *United Service Journal* not only featured military tales, however, it also engaged in an extended discourse on the nature of such stories, emphasising in particular what it saw as their unparalleled emotional intensity. In doing so, the journal drew on a discourse of emotionality that had already been developing in response to Sherer and Gleig and the 'school' of military writing they had helped launch, albeit a discourse that had placed the intense feelings of their stories in relation to the very fact that they wrote prosaic and factual accounts of their personal experiences. In its review of the two authors, the *Quarterly Review* (1826, p. 407) insisted that their tales of war were compelling in so far as they employed 'plain intelligible language' that 'shunned affectation' and recorded only the straightforward observations of the writers. The *Monthly Review* similarly remarked that *The Subaltern* provided a 'natural' picture of war that allowed the reader to stand 'side by side' with the subaltern himself. It similarly observed that Sherer had written with a simple clarity, in which he presented scenes of the Peninsular War as though it were in a 'in a camera obscura' that allowed the reader to be transported to the scene of conflict (*The Monthly Review* 1826, p. 54; 1823, p. 132). This plain and unaffected language was seen to be of vital importance as it meant that Sherer and Gleig's writing could clearly express an emotional intensity inherent to the soldiers' life itself, characterised as it was by 'wild adventures' and the extremes of 'human nature ... the horrible and the ludicrous, the savage and the pathetic' (*The Quarterly Review* 1826, p. 408). War was, according to the reviews, fundamentally equated with the most intense and extreme realms of felt experience, meaning that the power of Sherer and Gleig's writing came from its simple record of this emotional intensity.

Their accounts of military service thus even seemed to reviewers to partake of the poetic. The *Monthly Review* (1823, p. 132) noted of Sherer that '[f]ew writers, indeed, who are not poets by profession, have the art of painting in words, with so much vividness and distinctness, the various objects which surround their view'. The same journal imagined Gleig as composing poetry like William Wordsworth, reflecting in tranquillity on the turbulent emotions he had formerly experienced:

the *quondam* subaltern, it may be easily imagined, looks back in a calm and contemplative mood to the scenes of violent excitement in which a part of his life was passed; his mind retraces them as it might the visions of some strange dream; it seems as if he even wrote minutely, in order to convince himself that he was not writing a fiction.

(The Quarterly Review 1826, p. 408)

In its review of Sherer, the *United Service Journal* insisted that his '"recollections" . . . are truth, and his language is poetry' (*The United Service Journal* 1829b, p. 220). That the plain and factual language of a military author could be described as a version of poetry is a development that needs to be set in relation to early nineteenth-century views about the capacious nature of narrative form. While traditionally understood in terms of the rise of the proto-Victorian novel, as exemplified by the novels of Sir Walter Scott and Jane Austen, the period is equally characterised by formal experimentation that worked to redefine borders between fact and fiction, realism and romance, even poetry and prose (Behrendt 2009, pp. 189–205). What characterises much of the proliferation of narrative in the era is what Amanda Gilroy and Wil Verhoven (2001, p. 150) term its 'generic hybridity'. Poetry itself had come to be understood in the Romantic period less as a species of formal composition than as an expression of imagination and emotional intensity. Given its most famous expression in Wordsworth's insistence that 'there neither is nor can be any essential difference' between the language of poetry and prose, this was an idea that had become a commonplace, as can be seen for example in Hugh Blair's work on rhetoric, where he defined poetry as 'the language of passion, or of enlivened imagination' (quoted in Rowland 2008, p. 150). The novel, in turn, could be seen as even more emotionally compelling than poetry or romance in so far as it dealt with factual truth. Commenting on Sir Walter Scott's novels, William Hazlitt echoed reviewers' descriptions of Gleig and Sherer's writing by proposing that 'facts are better than fiction, that there is no romance like the romance of real life' (quoted in Gilory & Verhoeven 2001, p. 149). This elision of generic distinctions around narrative forms has even been linked to the emergence of a modern idea of literature itself in the Romantic period and the association of literature with imaginative writing in general (Rowland 2008, p. 123). As Jacques Rancière (2011, p. 184) argues, a modern 'literary revolution' in the Romantic period was primarily about 'undermining the distinction between discourses and destroying the opposition between a world of poetry and a world of prose'. Literature thus consolidated itself around the passionate intensity that circulated through the 'bare life' of ordinary individuals' experiences (Rancière 2016).

One such version of generic hybridity, as Gilory and Verhoven (2001, p. 150) point out, are the military tales that achieved popularity in the 1820s, and which had come to occupy the pages of the *United Service Journal* because of their evocation of 'fancy and feeling'. Soldiers' tales can be seen to have developed, while clearly redirecting, a traditional association between war and poetry.

The idea that poetry could be seen simply as emotional intensity or passionate language was itself, in large part, derived from a primitivist strain of Enlightenment thought that identified poetry with more savage states of society, and hence with societies that were not only more emotional but also more warlike (Rowland 2008, p. 122). It was a viewpoint expressed, for example, in Thomas Love Peacock's *The Four Ages of Poetry* (1820). Peacock frames poetry within a stadial history of modern progress by reversing Ovid's four-stage progress of society from peace to war in order to suggest that societies not only progress from war to peace, but that they thereby become ever less poetic as they progress. For Peacock (1961, p. 569), poetry originally stemmed from the desire to celebrate warlike deeds, 'in which rude bards celebrate in rough numbers the exploits of ruder chiefs, in days when every man is a warrior'. In turn, it is specifically because societies progress beyond their warlike origins and towards a modern state of peaceful commerce that poetry fades from the world, replaced, as Nemoianu suggests of the 'Biedermeier period', by a prose of rationalism, science and commerce. However, a contrary view had also emerged over the course of the eighteenth century that insisted modern developments in warfare, the use of gunpowder, science and massed armies, were inherently unpoetic (Bainbridge 2003, pp. 123–124). Although warfare had thus acquired a degree of sublime grandeur because of the vast spectacle of modern battle, for many its very scale and destructiveness precluded the possibilities for meaningful individual action that might be celebrated in poetry (St Clair 2004, p. 287).

With the growth of soldiers' tales in the late 1820s, however, war's emotional force comes to be seen in relation to the ordinary, the personal and the bodily: the passionate intensity of 'bare life', rather than in the sublimity of war's magnificence and scale. War, however, is not rendered poetic because it preserves a pre-modern heroism, but rather because of the way it presents an emotional and physical intensity otherwise absent from the prosaic modern world. In their emphasis on the emotional intensity of the soldier's unparalleled bodily suffering, soldiers' stories even share affinities with a Kantian version of the sublime, in which war becomes sublime through the operation of standing ground courageously in the face of danger (Harari 2008, p. 155). Yuval Noah Harari (2008) suggests that this is how we can conceptualise the modern soldier's story emerging at this time: that, at heart, these narratives elaborate an account of the soldier's confrontation with bodily suffering that is absent from ordinary, domestic life. On the one hand, such stories can therefore be related to a democratisation of feeling that Rancière associates with the emergence of modern literature. Rather than offer celebrations of war's heroes that Peacock saw at the origins of poetry, soldiers' tales record a reduction of war into the most basic elements of bodily life and suffering that could thereby speak to the nation as a whole (Rancière 2011, pp. 9–11). But viewed as sublime or poetic stories of courage, soldiers' tales also arrested what might be seen as the troubling implications of war's suffering and fear, even the potential unruliness of feeling in general that had begun to preoccupy the proto-Victorian era (Faflak & Sha 2014, pp. 8–10). Tales of war could not only elicit the strongest emotions, they could do so without fear that such emotion might disrupt the demands of national discipline and order. If there is an imaginative element of 'fancy' in the soldier's story, it is not to be found in a departure from fact, but rather in the evocation of the extraordinary conditions that the soldier himself undergoes, in which his real life inherently appears as a 'fiction' or 'strange dream'.

The personal tale of war, with its plain language and truthful accounts of ordinary military life, was thus coming to be widely celebrated by the end of the Romantic era as possessing the same sublime feelings found in the best romance or poetry. The *Monthly Review* (1826, p. 278), for instance, observed that: 'Such works, if composed only with simplicity, truth, and common intelligence, have an irresistible charm, for they blend all the excitement of romance with the important realities of history'. The *London Magazine* (1826, p. 267; 1827, p. 108) applauded these stories as 'one of the most amusing parts of literature', while insisting that, '[f]ew people have more to tell than they who have seen seventeen years of service abroad and at home: and few, that which is better worth hearing. Military authors, we are glad to observe, are accumulating'. If it found the *Naval Sketch Book* (1826) mostly dull, *The London Magazine* (1826, p. 173; 1827, p. 108) nonetheless claimed that several tales in the volume showed a 'romance . . . [that] . . . discovers genius', and in the *Military Sketch Book* (1827) a display of literary talents evinced through 'the force and reality of . . . his sketches' (1827). *Blackwood's*, which had originally published Gleig's *The Subaltern* in serial form, similarly reflected that a true narration of life at war was more engaging than the 'fine poetry' of Romance: 'Dang your Spenserian stanza – your octosyllabics – your long and shorts; your heroics and blank-verse, feckless as blank-cartridge – but give us Jack himself . . . spinning a long yarn' (*Blackwood's Edinburgh Magazine* 1826, p. 361). The magazine observed that if a military tale is written with a simplicity that could produce a 'vivid and affecting picture . . . [w]e read it with all the avidity with which we peruse a romance, and with a deeper interest, arising from a knowledge of its truth, than ever a romance excited' (*Blackwood's Edinburgh Magazine* 1821, p. 181). By 1835 the magazine was even insisting that sailors and soldiers' tales – tales of the 'moving accidents of flood and field' – have an attraction for every one because '[w]ar is heroic poetry put into action' (*Blackwood's Edinburgh Magazine* 1835, p. 957). In his faithful description of the British courage at the Battle of Albuerra, where the British soldiers continued to fight despite three in every four becoming casualties, William Napier had produced 'the most spirit stirring specimen, in any tongue, of the Moral and Physical Sublime' (*Blackwood's Edinburgh Magazine* 1831, pp. 248–249).

The *United Service Journal* echoed this broader discourse of sublime and poetic emotion in its own commentary on soldiers' tales. Reviewing *Sailors and Saint* (1829) a fictionalised story of a British naval vessel's actions during the Napoleonic Wars, the journal argued that naval stories were 'connected with nature in its grandest and most terrible aspects, with art in its subtlest ingenuity, and with human enterprize and courage in their noblest achievement' (*The United Service*

Journal 1829a, p. 67). The journal thus ranked the novel alongside Coleridge's *Rime of the Ancient Mariner* as an immortal story of the sea, arguing that nothing can excite our sympathies more than 'the details of a life exposed to such vicissitudes and perils' (*The United Service Journal* 1829a, p. 68). While the journal still distinguished poetry and prose, it valued poetry not as a generic or metrical form but simply as writing associated with 'the feelings and the fancy', terms that the journal equally used to describe personal histories of soldiers (*The United Service Journal* 1829a, p. 45). Extending such claims, the journal insisted that the military life is itself an inherently 'eventful and romantic calling', while it suggested tales of war:

> Amidst agents and elements so pregnant with excitement and contrast, the force of circumstancs and the operations of human impulses and passions have naturally created scenes and situation in which every ingredient of dramatic effect is powerfully comprised; while the disruption of ties, widespread desolation, and bitter sacrifices and suffering, inseparable from the conflict of nations, combine to invest reality with so much of the sentiment of romance, that a double attraction and a deeper sympathy are attached to a tale of war.
> (*The United Service Journal* 1829b, pp. 502, 216)

It elsewhere concluded that a military funeral, the epitome of the soldier's courageous heroism, is far greater than the 'most elaborate efforts of poetry and painting' (*The United Service Journal* 1829a, p. 503).

If the journal celebrated military tales as though a species of poetry, it also reframed poetry itself around what it saw as the greater emotional intensity and power of the military author. The journal articulates such an argument in a review of Byron's *Don Juan*, which the editors included in their hopes of contributing 'a few facts to the history of contemporary literature' by discussing Byron's 'wonderful poem' (*The United Service Journal* 1829a, p. 221). But even as the journal applauded what it termed the 'splendid genius' of Byron, it chastised his poetry by taking issue with his descriptions and use of an unacknowledged source in the shipwreck scene at the start of Canto 2 (*The United Service Journal* 1829a, p. 221). It threw cold water on Byron's intimation that the source for the scene was his own grandfather's narrative, while simultaneously discrediting the *Literary Gazette*'s earlier efforts to track down the source of the scene in the published account of the shipwreck of the *Medusa*. Instead, it offered evidence that the unacknowledged source of the scene was the 1812 collection *Shipwrecks and Disasters at Sea*, which contained many descriptions directly paralleled in *Don Juan*. For example, Canto 2, Stanza 45, of *Don Juan* describes sailors preparing for their fate as the ship sinks: 'Some lashed them in their hammocks, some put on | Their best clothes as if going to a fair' (quoted in *The United Service Journal* 1829a, p. 225). These comments, the journal shows, were taken almost verbatim from Captain Ingleford's account of the sinking of the Centaur. The journal also drew attention to Byron's erroneous deviation from this original source. At one point in his poem, Byron states that the ship's crew cut down both the foremast and bowspit in an effort to correct the position of the ship in the water, after the storm had turned it side on to the waves. The journal points out that the foremast and bowsprit are in actual fact crucial for righting a ship in such a situation and so would not have been cut down.

The journal's strongest criticism is directed at Byron's description of cannibalism. Here, however, it does not fault Byron's use of the source, but rather the source itself:

> We believe that the accounts which are given of men in this extremity, adopting the horrible expedient of eating the bodies of their fellow-creatures, are, for the most part, fictions. It is not solid food for which the sufferers in such calamities yearn; but water to allay a burning and maddening thirst, which renders the mastication and swallowing of any substance nearly impossible, and therefore not wished for. This, upon a little reflection, would appear to be truth; and for the sake of humanity, we are glad to find this opinion confirmed by the testimony of a distinguished living officer, who, having been with others in an open boat many days, under the most distressing circumstances, states that not only were the bodies of their shipmates thrown overboard immediately after death, without any contemplation on the part of the survivors of making the revolting use of them which Lord Byron and others have alleged; but that even some biscuit which had been served out to the companions of our informant, lay unregarded at the bottom of the boat, the sole agony of the men being occasioned by intense thirst.
>
> (*The United Service Journal* 1829a, p. 226)

A vision of the prosaic humanity and factual, collective wisdom of the navy is presented by the journal in an effort to correct Byron's treatment of the shipwreck. On the one hand, the journal's engagement with Byron's poem resonates with Nemoianu's suggestions of a taming of Romance, in which, as Tilotoma Rajan (2006, p. 490) argues, the period can be seen witnessing the dissolution of poetic Romance by 'the prose of actuality', which is 'represented by the novel as civil society's disciplining of romance that brings it into conformity with the practices of everyday life'. But while at one level the journal disciplines Byron's romance with just such a 'prose of actuality' drawn from military's officers' accounts of shipwreck, we are nonetheless removed from any effort to bring the poem into conformity with the novel, civil society or the practices of everyday life. Rather, the journal insists that experiences such as a shipwreck are the most extreme events, that 'the incidents which arise in such calamities as those in question, are unlike what any other kind of human misery produces' (*The United Service Journal* 1829a, p. 221). The journal thus applauds Byron for borrowing from the sources of naval officers, arguing that he 'did well to consult the very words of such mariners as have given to the world narratives of their sufferings at sea; for of such occurrences he could himself know little or nothing' (*The United Service Journal* 1829a, p. 221). The sheer scale of these events is 'not to be supplied by imagination' (*The United Service Journal* 1829a, p. 221).

Arguing, in turn, that Byron's account of the shipwreck is the most popular scene in his most popular poem, the journal concludes in praise of 'power of truth, however homely in its expressions, over fiction, however ingenious and brilliant! In being content to transcribe rather than invent, Lord Byron has framed a story which will go down to remotest posterity' (*The United Service Journal* 1829a, p. 222). It is the officers in the navy and the military who not only understand and record the extremes of human emotion and experience but whose command of these extremes can keep their writing within the realm of the civilised, redirecting the sad or the revolting into the emotionally uplifting. The review disciplines the romance of Byron's poem by displacing the imagination of the poet with the sublime true tale of the military or naval officer. It appears hardly a coincidence that so many of the military stories featured in the journal were anonymous and anecdotal; they stood for a collective military experience, a heterogeneous multiplicity of voices that nonetheless came to one essential conclusion about the soldier's stoical endurance of suffering. The journal even concludes that the most interesting aspects of literature are constituted by the writing of military officers:

> When faithfully and forcibly depicted, the events and vicissitudes of war must either exalt or instruct, by acting as incentives to its higher aims and aspirations, or as antidotes to its inherent evils and incidental abuses. And who is more qualified than the soldier, by opportunity and experience, to paint man in his various shades of life and clime, and embody each variety of moral portrait amidst its own peculiar landscape?
>
> We will push our question even farther, and inquire what class of our intellectual community has executed this instructive task with greater truth and felicity?
>
> (*The United Service Journal* 1829a, p. 44)

The officer's experiential truth might transcend even the 'events and vicissitudes of war', the journal argues, to emerge with the noble and instructive powers of the finest imaginative poetry (*The United Service Journal* 1829a, p. 44). In writing of his experiences, the military author even appeared to assume a role resembling that of a national poet, producing work of a comparable vision, passion and romance.

War, emotion and the modern spirit of commerce

When, at the end of the 1820s, Thomas Carlyle famously proclaimed that Britain was now possessed of a mechanical spirit, he nonetheless also argued that Romance could still be found, merely that genuine Romance must be looked for in real lives. Life itself 'not only is Poetry, but is the sole Poetry possible' (Carlyle 1847, p. 2). In his essay on biography he thus turned his attention away from fictional forms altogether, because he believed that biographical glimpses of human life were capable of being, as Mark Saunders (2010, p. 79) elaborates, 'revelatory in ways that fiction cannot match'. Carlyle (1847, pp. 350–351) recognised that the recent wars presented one such way of seeing this romance in the present age, although he tempers his remarks by adding that they are only superficially Romantic. He personally saw the expansion of military writing, 'Tales by Flood and Field', as simply part of the innumerable and fleeting mass of publications that beset modern Britain, a literary 'foam' with no enduring or higher reality behind them (Carlyle 1847, p. 15). Carlyle's remarks are a useful reminder that the *United Service Journal* was, admittedly, making claims about military writing that seem more than a little overblown. Yet Carlyle's comments are also suggestive of the ways in which military tales were thought of in the era, that soldiers' personal narratives of their real lives could be seen to capture an unparalleled poetic intensity.

What was most important about the military tales, nevertheless, was their preservation of forms of feeling, of a Romance of the real that now seemed to lie outside of the prosaic world and its mechanical or commercial spirit. Moretti suggests that we might see the early nineteenth century's interest in war as the continuing circulation of pre-modern ideals in literature of the period, despite the rise of the middle classes. He proposes that even in its rise, the middle class continued to need a master, and in this sense were easily led by the appeal of war (Moretti 2013, p. 178). The military tale could in certain respects be aligned with the rise of modernity and a disciplining of emotion around military action and the military institution itself, but such tales could also be associated with a militarised romance that might keep alive a military spirit among the British reading public. Kant (cited in Harari 2008, p. 155) had noted this in his discussion of war's sublimity, that war lends a degree of sublimity to a nation, while peace leads to the formation of a 'commercial spirit' that simply 'degrades the character of the nation'. It was a viewpoint with which the *United Service Journal* would have concurred. The journal explained that it was not only designed to preserve military science, but to ensure that the 'martial spirit' of the population did not disappear (*The United Service Journal* 1832, p. 3). The *United Service Journal* was, in effect, developing an idea of Romance, a 'narrative form of historical otherness', that could continue to be operative for an emergent Victorian modernity, soldiers' tales serving as a vital corrective for the moral degradations of a modern, commercial age.

In her work on the First World War, Ute Frevert (2014) notes that literature was equally a major site for the production of nationalistic emotion during that, latter, war, a point that suggests some continuity between the ideas of the *United Service Journal* and subsequent conflicts. But the way military stories figured in the pages of the *United Service Journal* could be seen to point to an equally enduring connection in the modern era between war literature and emotion in general.

As the *United Service Journal* disseminated military tales to the public and helped to define how such stories should be read, so it also defined how the public could relate to war itself. What can be seen taking shape in the pages of the *United Service Journal* was an association between war and the modern 'literary revolution' that collapsed generic borders and installed imagination, feeling and passion as fundamental to literary production. Emotional intensity was, therefore, established as the very defining principle of stories of war written for the general public. The founding of the *United Service Journal* signalled, on the one hand, that the military was increasingly taking a scientific approach to war and that the military were as much a part of modern intellectual culture as other professions. On the other hand, the journal marked a moment at which the public, conversely, were seen to have a connection with war that was now to be almost wholly constituted by feeling and emotion. Even as the journal brought together a mixed readership of the military and the general public, so it overturned generic distinctions to recode war writing around a fundamental division between emotional and scientific forms.

Notes

1 Looking at the wider European context, Pfau (2005) describes the era as a melancholy culture following the trauma of the Napoleonic Wars. On the impact of war on post-war British culture, see also Shaw (2002), Walker (2009), and Cox (2014).
2 On the significant relationship in this period between war and feeling, see also Favret (2010) and Downes, Lynch and O'Loughlin (2015).

Reference list

Bainbridge, S. 2003, *British Poetry and the Revolutionary and Napoleonic Wars*, Oxford University Press, Oxford.
Behrendt, S. C. 2009, 'Response Essay: Cultural Transitions, Literary Judgements and the Romantic-Era British Novel', in M. L. Wallace (ed.), *Enlightening Romanticism: Romancing the Enlightenment British Novels From 1750 to 1832*, Ashgate, Aldershot, pp. 189–205.
Blackwood's Edinburgh Magazine 1821, vol. 9, no. 50, William Blackwood, Edinburgh.
Blackwood's Edinburgh Magazine 1826, vol. 19, no. 111, William Blackwood, Edinburgh.
Blackwood's Edinburgh Magazine 1831, vol. 30, no. 152, William Blackwood, Edinburgh.
Blackwood's Edinburgh Magazine 1835, vol. 37, no. 236, William Blackwood, Edinburgh.
Carlyle, T. 1847, 'Biography', in *Critical and Miscellaneous Essays: Collected and Republished*, 3rd edn, vol. 3, Chapman & Hall, London.
Carlyle, T. 1847, 'Diamond Necklace', in *Critical and Miscellaneous Essays: Collected and Republished*, 3rd edn, vol. 3, Chapman & Hall, London.
Christensen, J. 2004, *Romanticism at the End of History*, Johns Hopkins University Press, Baltimore.
Colley, L. 1992, *Britons: Forging the Nation*, Yale University Press, New Haven & London.
Cox, J. N. 2014, *Romanticism in the Shadow of War: Literary Culture in the Napoleonic War Years*, Cambridge University Press, Cambridge.
Cronin, R. 2002, *Romantic Victorians: English literature, 1824–1840*, Palgrave, Houndmills, Basingstoke, Hampshire; New York.

Downes, S., Lynch, A. & O'Loughlin, K. (eds) 2015, *Emotions and War: Medieval to Romantic Literature*, Palgrave Studies in the History of Emotions, Palgrave Macmillan, Basingstoke.

Duncan, I. 2005, *Modern Romance and Transformations of the Novel: The Gothic, Scott, Dickens*, Cambridge University Press, Cambridge.

Faflak, J. & Sha, R. C. 2014, 'Introduction: Feeling Romanticism', in J. Faflak & R. C. Sha (eds), *Romanticism and the Emotions*, Cambridge University Press, Cambridge, pp. 1–18.

Favret, M. 2010, *War at a Distance: Romanticism and the Making of Modern Wartime*, Princeton University Press, Princeton.

Frevert, U. 2014, 'Wartime Emotions: Honour, Shame, and the Ecstasy of Sacrifice', in U. Daniel, P. Gatrell, O. Janz, H. Jones, J. Keene, A. Kramer & B. Nasson (eds), 1914–1918 online: International Encyclopedia of the First World War, viewed 30 October 2016, http://encyclopedia.1914–1918-online.net/article/wartime_emotions_honour_shame_and_the_ecstasy_of_sacrifice.

Gat, A. 2001, *A History of Military Thought: From the Enlightenment to the Cold War*, Oxford University Press, Oxford.

Gilroy, A. & Verhoeven, W. 2001, 'The Romantic-Era Novel: A Special Issue: Introduction', *Novel: A Forum on Fiction*, vol. 34, no. 2, pp. 147–162.

Gleig, G. 1845, *The Subaltern*, Blackwood & Son, Edinburgh & London.

Harari, Y. N. 2008, *The Ultimate Experience: Battlefield Revelations and the Making of Modern War Culture, 1450–2000*, Palgrave Macmillan, Basingstoke.

Klancher, J. 1987, *The Making of English Reading Audiences, 1790–1832*, University of Wisconsin Press, Wisconsin.

Klancher, J. 2013, *Transfiguring the Arts and Sciences: Knowledge and Cultural Institutions in the Romantic Age*, Cambridge University Press, Cambridge.

Moretti, F. 2013, *Distant Reading*, Verso, London.

Nemoianu, V. 1984, *The Taming of Romanticism: European Literature and the Age of Biedermeier*, Harvard University Press, Cambridge, MA.

Peacock, T. L. 1961, 'The Four Ages of Poetry', in C. Wordring (ed.), *Prose of the Romantic Period*, Houghton Mifflin Company, Boston, pp. 569–580.

Pfau, T. 2005, *Romantic Moods: Paranoia, Trauma, and Melancholy, 1790–1840*, Johns Hopkins University Press, Baltimore.

Rajan, T. 2006, '"The Prose of the World": Romanticism, the Nineteenth Century, and the Reorganization of Knowledge', *Modern Language Quarterly*, vol. 67, no. 44, pp. 479–504.

Rajan, T. 2010, *Romantic Narrative: Shelley, Hays, Godwin, Wollstonecraft*, Johns Hopkins University Press, Baltimore.

Ramsey, N. 2011, *The Military Memoir and Romantic Literary Culture, 1780–1835*, Burlington, VT and Aldershot: Ashgate.

Ramsey, N. 2014, 'Wartime Reading: Romantic Era Military Periodicals and the Edinburgh Review', *Australian Literary Studies*, vol. 29, no. 3, pp. 28–40.

Rancière, J. 2011, *The Politics of Literature*, trans. J. Rose, Polity Press, Cambridge.

Rancière, J. 2009, 'The Reality Effect and the Politics of Fiction', public lecture at ICI Berlin, viewed 30 October 2016, www.ici-berlin.org/videos/jacques-ranciere/part/2/

Rowland, A. W. 2008, 'Romantic Poetry and the Romantic Novel', in J. Chandler & M. N. Mclane (eds), *The Cambridge Companion to British Romantic Poetry*, Cambridge University Press, Cambridge, pp. 117–135.

Saunders, M. 2010, *Self Impression: Life-Writing, Autobiografiction, and the Forms of Modern Literature*, Oxford University Press, Oxford.

Shaw, P. 2002, *Waterloo and the Romantic Imagination*, Palgrave Macmillan, Basingstoke.

Sherer, M. 1824, *Recollections of the Peninsula*, 2nd edn, Longman & Co, London.

Siskin, C. 1998, *The Work of Writing: Literature and Social Change in Britain, 1700–1830*, The John Hopkins University Press, Baltimore & London.
St. Clair, W. 2004, *The Reading Nation in the Romantic Period*, Cambridge University Press, Cambridge.
The British Indian Military Repository 1822, vol. 1. in B Marilyn (ed.) 1981, *Romantics, Rebels and Reactionaries: English Literature and its Background, 1760–1830*, Oxford University Press, Oxford.
The Gentleman's Magazine 1831, vol. 101.
The London Magazine, 1826, N.S. vol. 4, Hunt & Clarke, London.
The London Magazine, 1827, N.S. vol. 8, Hunt & Clarke, London.
The Naval and Military Journal, 1827, vol. 1, T Clerc Smith, London.
The Monthly Review, 1823, vol. 102, A & R Spottiswoode, London.
The Monthly Review, 1826, N.S. vol. 1, A & R Spottiswoode, London.
The Quarterly Review, 1826, vol. 34, John Murray, London.
The Quarterly Review, 1831, vol. 45, John Murray, London.
The United Service Journal 1829a, vol. 1, no. 1, H Colburn, London.
The United Service Journal 1829b, vol. 1, no. 2, H Colburn, London.
The United Service Journal 1832, vol. 4, no. 1, H Colburn, London.
Walker, C. 2009, *Marriage, Writing, and Romanticism: Wordsworth and Austen after War*, Stanford University Press, Stanford.

13

'A POSSESSION FOR ETERNITY'

Thomas De Quincey's feeling for war

Michael Champion and Miranda Stanyon

> In this Work he is of no Sect or Party [. . .] He draws no Consequences in his Notes; makes no oblique Glances upon any disputed Points, old or new. He consecrates this Work, as a κειμήλιον, a κτῆμα ἐς ἀεὶ [a treasure, a possession for eternity], a *Charter*, a *Magna Charta*, to the whole Christian Church; to last when all the Antient MSS [. . .] may be lost and extinguish'd.
> (Bentley 1721)

In several contributions to the conservative *Blackwood's Magazine*, De Quincey uses the phrase 'a possession for eternity'.[1] It may have been suggested to him by his reading of Richard Bentley, the eighteenth-century biblical scholar and champion of Anglican orthodoxy, who modestly referred to his own edition of the New Testament in this way. The passage in question, quoted by De Quincey in an 1830 review (DQ 7.129), unites several themes prized by the late Romantic writer: law (the charter), Englishness (the cherished magna carta), the Church militant, classical scholarship (for De Quincey styled himself a scholar and wrote extensively about Greek literature)[2] and a vision of eternity framed in terms of textual survival. Silently, it also links these fields to war and war writing: as De Quincey knew, the phrase *ktēma es aei*, 'a possession for eternity', was borrowed from Thucydides' *History of the Peloponnesian War*. Here it described the fifth-century historian's estimation of his own text, a history of the war between Athens and Sparta. The presence of Thucydides in the passage complicates Bentley's claims, since Thucydides, like Bentley after him, in fact failed to complete his work or to leave an intact text to posterity. De Quincey does not admit this irony in his 1830 review. For him, Bentley was 'the very Prince of scholars' (DQ 8.5), and his claim to noble impartiality was a heartfelt 'grand burst of enthusiasm' (DQ 7.129). Yet Bentley's self-presentation could also be satirised as atrocious hubris (one enemy indeed dubbed his grand scheme 'Bentley's Bubble', DQ 7.129).[3]

The link between the *ktēma es aei* and the moral-affective failing of hubris is significant: it hints at Thucydides' potential association with the failure of the endeavour to write histories, especially histories of war, unchanged by the passage of time. And beyond war writing, the ironies of the *ktēma es aei* might extend to the failure of wars themselves to deliver the successes and advances, or the worlds of stable and ordered forms, which they promise.

Our chapter explores this web of associations, examining De Quincey's feelings for war writing through his engagement with Thucydides.[4] At the outset, it is worth registering the peculiar emotional character De Quincey ascribes to Bentley – his bursting 'enthusiasm' for scholarship. If it seems paradoxical to associate uncontrolled enthusiasm with the controlled impartiality which Bentley claims as his method, then for De Quincey this paradox characterises the emotional style of the scholarly writer *per se*, and perhaps particularly the writer on war in the wake of Thucydides.

Thucydides is central to the Western tradition of war writing, and one aim of this chapter is to suggest the deep classical history of Romantic (and, by extension, current) feelings about war. But more is at stake than reception history. By probing questions of form and feeling through the lens of De Quincey's engagement with Thucydides, this chapter finds figures of a broader argument about war and form – taking the latter in the broad sense of a repeated and recognisable '*arrangement of elements – an ordering, patterning, or shaping*'.[5] Much modern writing on war, we might say, aligns form with goodness. Conservative advocates for war not infrequently view war as a good since it supposedly promotes order, cultural cohesion and advances in technological progress; left-wing responses often condemn war as disordered and chaotic, leaving the equation of form, order and culture intact.[6] Our reading of De Quincey points beyond both 'left-wing' and 'conservative' claims about the allegedly true formlessness of war – chaotic, disruptive and terrifying – or war as the stern, consoling teacher who gives rise to ordered cultural and emotional forms. It suggests that we should rethink both the dichotomy of form versus formlessness and the equation of form with goodness. We begin with Thucydides' reception, before turning to De Quincey's writings on war more generally to explore the entanglement of emotional styles in writing war with views about the form-creating or form-destroying power of war itself.

Thucydides' reception: patterns and possibilities

De Quincey drew on contemporary reception of Thucydides to set up and undermine contrasts between empirical, scientific, ordered, universal and detached history, and its converse: war writing which is subjective, rhetorical, disruptive, particular and overtly emotional. More and less ordered and controlled forms of writing are thus aligned with different aesthetic and moral judgements about war and its relationship to order. In the main, De Quincey associates Thucydides with a scientific form of historiography, contrasted with rhetorical anecdotage and cases. Yet instabilities in Thucydides' reception helped De Quincey to play with this contrast, questioning the identification of form, civilisation and goodness in the process. Ultimately, his ironic texts put pressure on the idea, common in the reception of Thucydides, that unemotional scientific historiography can truly be opposed to emotional literary genres, alongside the idea that emotive literary forms are the site of genuinely formless or form-testing outpourings of feeling.[7] In this way, De Quincey encourages his readers to undermine, on one hand, the pretentions to objectivity of supposedly unemotional war history – often the province of pro-war writers – and, on the other hand, the implicitly anti-war claim that subjective sincerity and the 'true' horror of war are revealed in those genres cast as emotional interruptions of or refuges from severe formal discourse.[8]

The complexity of the early modern reception of Thucydides is clear in method. From the enlightenment onward, Thucydides is taken as a model for empiricists, offering a 'true account' of the historical facts of 'what is real', as against historians like Herodotus who present mere fable (Voltaire 1765, cited in Morley 2014, p. 45). Similarly, his history is ordered by the application of strict rules: Rapin argues that 'whatever Rules may be given to history, none can be prescrib'd so severe than those Thucydides [has] observed' (Rapin 1694, preface).[9] Such a view enabled the co-option of Thucydides by champions of history as a science.[10] On this view, the Thucydidean historian, like the doctor, follows empirical prescriptions with the emotional 'detachment' and self-effacing 'reticence' necessary for 'objectivity' (Cochrane 1929, p. 31; Morley 2014, p. 68). Such a method was held to rely on moral-affective qualities including suppression of feeling and personality: 'a disinterested Meaning shine[s] in every thing he writes' because he is 'disengaged of Prejudice, Interest and Passion' (Rapin 1694, p. 8; Morley 2014, pp. 72, 82–83).

This view was encouraged by Thucydides' own comments on method.[11] In the words of a popular Victorian translation:

> far from permitting myself to derive [my narrative] from the first source that came to hand, I did not even trust my own impressions, but it rests partly on what I saw myself, partly on what others saw for me, the accuracy of the report being always tried by the most severe and detailed tests (*para akribeiai*) possible. My conclusions have cost me some labour from the want of coincidence between accounts of the same occurrences by different eye-witnesses, arising sometimes from imperfect memory, sometimes from undue partiality [. . .]. The absence of romance (*to mē mythōdes*) in my history will, I fear, detract somewhat from its interest; but if it be judged useful by those inquirers who desire an exact knowledge of the past as an aid to the interpretation of the future, which in the course of human things must resemble if it does not reflect it, I shall be content. In fine, I have written my work, not as an essay which is to win the applause of the moment, but as a possession for all time (*ktēma es aei*).
>
> (Thuc. 1.22.2–4, trans. Crawley 1866)

The rendering of *akribeiai* as 'severe and detailed tests' speaks to the power of the image of Thucydides as the detached empiricist. If somewhat overtranslated, it is not indefensible, given that *akribeia* was a prized possession of the doctors of his day, and Platonic *akribeia* distinguished skills based on knowledge from the orators' mere opinion (Plato *Philebus*, 55e–59d).[12] 'Absence of romance' neatly captures Thucydides' own attempt to distinguish himself from other purveyors of wisdom – poets, rhetoricians, and logographers – for whom myth had a role to play in historical explanation and political discourse. In this context, Thucydides' claim that history follows rules according to which the future simply '*must* resemble' the past is read as modern empiricism. De Quincey will thus sound a Thucydidean note when he writes in his essay 'War' (1848): 'The causes that *have* existed for war are the causes that *will* exist; or, at least, they are the same under modifications that will simply vary the rule' (DQ 16.286). For many admirers, Thucydides' principled method and his apparent view of war as itself governed by unchanging principles made his *History* an 'everlasting possession'.[13] It offered an objective analysis of society, politics and international relations which amounted to a cross-temporal political theory in an empirical and detached mode.

Yet this portrait of Thucydides as the detached scientist was contested. Modern writers also inherited a view of Thucydides as consummate rhetorician. Dionysius of Halicarnassus (b. 60 BCE) had praised the speed of Thucydides' narrative, which allowed 'full poetic licence' and displayed 'compactness and solidity, pungency and severity, vehemence, the ability to disturb and terrify and above all emotional power' (*On Thucydides* 24, LCL pp. 465, 526–531; *Second Letter to Ammaeus* 2, LCL pp. 466, 406–411). While the main line of the reception of Thucydides departed from the view that history should be rhetorical, prioritising instead emotional detachment and impartiality (Morley 2014, pp. 79–91), for Hobbes, Thucydides is useful because he is an artist who 'maketh his auditor a spectator' of human truths through his narrative (*Peloponnesian Warre*, p. viii). Pierre Le Moyne thought Thucydides wrote in the 'sublime character' most suited to histories that treat grand events and must therefore employ an elevated style approaching that of poetry (Le Moyne 1695, pp. 205–209).

This reception tradition could be understood as setting Thucydides the detached scientist against Thucydides the sublime, emotional artist. But for De Quincey, one resonance of this tradition is the tendency to equate, rather than oppose, artistry and emotional detachment and control. This resonates too with post-Kantian aesthetics, with its insistence on disinterested pleasure, and especially the sublime, where experience is compartmentalised so that cognitive and moral pain need not translate to aesthetic pain. Indeed, in the Kantian sublime, the violence to which the faculty of imagination is subjected enables the elevation of the faculty of reason, and the pleasure felt in judging sublime experiences (Kant 1973, pp. 25–27). The scientific historian can here converge with the artistic connoisseur. The idea of separate psychological faculties helps explain the personal feeling of the nonetheless detached historian. Compartmentalisation allows the historian both to feel with intensity and to write with detachment and control. The quality of this feeling is, for eighteenth- and nineteenth-century readers, that of the sublime: vehement, intense, enthusiastic, yet not aligned with everyday passions or emotions.[14] Thucydides might thus also be aligned with post-Kantian aesthetics and distinctions between passion and sublimity, in order to advance a style of scholarship allegedly isolated from the unruly passions, beliefs, and values of the everyday. This is a textbook case of what Benno Gammerl calls a 'detached' emotional style of history (Gammerl 2012, pp. 169–170); we could also call it a 'Thucydidean' style.

Beyond his importance for historical method and style, Thucydides was also drawn into contemporary politics by successive generations of readers. As the historian of the war that led to the demise of democratic Athens, he could be read as pro- or anti-democracy (Grote v. Hobbes), or as exploring how war puts democracy under pressures it is not equipped to withstand.[15] Thucydides also provided stimulus for political theorists probing connections between violence and progress.[16] Since the early modern period, Thucydides' analysis of the war's outbreak had offered rich material for proponents of pre-emptive strikes and of war as an instrument of progress. His opening chapters detail the advances in technology and social organisation associated with the wars (Thucydides, 1.1–19). Thucydides' treatment of the respective interests of Athens and Sparta became associated with Hobbesian theories of self-interest and the rights of power, and with social progress from a state of nature where individuals live in a war of all against all, into a nation state where individuals submit to an artificial sovereign, and conflict reigns between nations. In the words of a speech beloved of modern neo-liberals and war-hawks: 'Of the gods we believe, and of men we know, that by a necessary law of nature, they rule wherever they can'.[17]

De Quincey and Thucydidean history

By the nineteenth century, then, Thucydides was a name to conjure with in debates about historiographical form and style, the value of democracy and history, the connections between war and civilisation, and relationships between nations. On questions of form and style, De Quincey typically follows his contemporaries and portrays Thucydides as a forerunner to detached, impartial, orderly scientists. Yet, as we have begun to suggest, this portrait is often undercut. In 'On Style' (1840), Thucydides is represented as the first writer of 'stern philosophic prose', while Herodotus was 'an artist' who stood on an island 'between the regions of [epic] poetry and blank unimpassioned' prose (DQ 12.32).[18] Herodotus represents a 'splendid semi-barbarous generation' while Thucydides is 'experimental' (DQ 12.33). Herodotus is a 'son of nature, fascinated by the mighty powers of chance or of tragic destiny'; Thucydides 'was the son of political speculation, delighting to trace the darker agencies which brood in the mind of man – the subtle motives, the combinations, the plots which gather in the brain of "dark viziers," when entrusted with the fate of millions, and the nation-wielding tempests which move at the bidding of the orator' (DQ 12.33). Likewise, De Quincey's 'Appraisal of the Greek Literature' (1838) recognises Thucydides as 'affect[ing] to treat [...] [history] philosophically' (DQ 11.23), in common with the main line of the tradition. But he goes on to suggest mischievously that philosophical historians are in fact 'the corruptors of genuine history' (DQ 11.23). Against the tide of reception history, De Quincey laments Thucydides' self-proclaimed lack of romance, doubts his much-touted veracity, and questions the social standing and expertise in politics of the Athenian general turned historian:

> Thucydides, though writing about his own time, and doubtless embellishing by fictions not less than his more amusing brethren, is as dull as if he prided himself on veracity. Nay, he tells us no secret anecdotes of the times – surely there must have been many; and this proves to us, that he was a low fellow without political connexions, and that he never had been behind the curtain.
> (DQ 11.23)

Drawing a parallel between the demise of the refined and 'arrogant' Athenian empire on one hand, and the defeat of Revolutionary and Napoleonic France on the other, De Quincey observes that '[t]here was something to "point a moral" in the Peloponnesian war' (DQ 11.23). Yet Thucydides failed to moralise. He showed nothing of Athens's 'bloody abuse of power, or the bloody retribution' of Sparta; 'he is as cool as a cucumber upon every act of atrocity': 'all alike he enters in his daybook and ledger, posts them up to the [...] brutal Spartan or polished Athenian, with no more expression of his feelings (if he had any) than a merchant making out an invoice' (DQ 11.23–24).

Thucydides' historiographical failure to moralise is also a mercantile, ungentlemanly failure to feel. In the 'Appraisal', the only elements of Thucydides' narrative worthy of inclusion in world history are the Plague at Athens and the Sicilian Expedition (DQ 11.23). These show Thucydides at his most emotive, conjuring up heart-rending images of suffering and disaster. They are also comparatively rare moments in which he includes explicit authorial moral judgements – on Athens's quest for power, the moral degeneracy of Athenian politics, the instability of democratic decision-making, the virtue of the Athenian general Nicias and the value of traditional Athenian political virtues. Given the existence of these passages, De Quincey's attack on Thucydides can be read as tongue-in-cheek or at least hyperbolic. Yet it also intervenes in debates about method and politics. While the liberal progressivist reader might wish Thucydides had been more scientific and philosophical, and less absorbed by novelistic particularity, the conservative essayist and autobiographer De Quincey purports to wish Thucydides had been more anecdotal and passionate.[19]

The necessity of feeling in accurate historical accounts returns in De Quincey's 'Postscript' to the essays *On Murder, Considered as One of the Fine Arts*, probably drafted between 1827 and 1839. De Quincey plausibly began the series as a satire of gentlemen lovers of boxing after one prominent figure was found guilty of murder, and its first 'paper' ventriloquises for a speaker at a fictional society for the appreciation of murders. Nonetheless, the elaborate essays also suggest the real attractions of violence and the plausibility of an aesthetics of sublimity or tragedy.

As a straightforward satire, the piece suggests the problems with Thucydidean histories insofar as they are histories of social progress in and through violence, and insofar as they are connected with Hobbesian ideas about human progress from the state of nature into a less violent civil state, marked by form-ful wars rather than shapeless violence. In *On Murder*, as we plunge into detailed and concrete anecdotes of bloodshed, we see that violence holds an appeal *an sich*, and that more structure, more theory and more civilised sophistication do not necessarily mean less blood. In this vein, the preface to *On Murder* quotes approvingly the third-century church father Lactantius, in a diatribe against the amphitheatre:

> 'What is so dreadful,' says Lactantius, 'what so dismal and revolting, as the murder of a human creature? Therefore it is, that life [. . .] is protected by laws the most rigorous: therefore it is, that wars are objects of execration. And yet [. . .] Rome has devised a mode of authorising murder [. . .] and the demands of taste (*voluptas*) are now become the same as those of abandoned guilt.
>
> (DQ 6.112)[20]

De Quincey here cites a view of war and murder as cognate evils, which supposedly-advanced societies perversely manage to formalise and enjoy. The quotation from Lactantius links this anti-war and anti-progress argument to an implicit critique of the aesthetics of tragedy and the disinterested enjoyment of sublime spectacles:

> Now if merely to be present at a murder fastens on a man the character of an accomplice, – if barely to be a spectator involves us in one common guilt with the perpetrator; it follows [. . .] that, in these murders of the amphitheatre, the hand which inflicts the fatal blow is not more deeply imbrued with blood than his who sits and looks on [. . .] [or] gives his applause to the murderer.
>
> (DQ 6.112)

By applauding, Lactantius insists, we make aesthetic and ethical judgements. Vicarious enjoyment of violence – whether in the amphitheatre, war, or murder – is also vicarious guilt. Feelings are crucial here: pleasure and exaltation, not merely the act of watching, constitute an identification between gladiator and spectator. Affect allows agency to leach from person to person, individual to community.

In the 'Postscript', however, De Quincey suggests aesthetic enjoyment of violence is inevitable and, moreover, separable from ethical judgement:

> the tendency to a critical or aesthetic valuation of fires and murders is universal. If you are summoned to the spectacle of a great fire, undoubtedly the first impulse is—to assist in putting it out. But that field of exertion is very limited [. . .] after we have paid our tribute of regret to the affair, considered as a calamity, inevitably, and without restraint, we go on to consider it as a stage spectacle.
>
> (DQ 20.38)

De Quincey's speaker hereby claims the right to appreciate the *artistry* of murders, and particularly the spectacular Ratcliffe Highway murders of 1811, allegedly committed by John Williams. De Quincey quotes Thucydides in imagining Williams's sentiments and artistic production. Williams only struck in London, that 'great metropolitan *castra stativa* [permanent encampment] of gigantic crime' (DQ 20.40). 'In fact', De Quincey continues,

> the great artist disdained a provincial reputation; and he must have felt [. . .] the contrast between a country town or village, on one hand, and, on the other, a work more lasting than brass—a κτῆμα ἐς ἀεί—a murder such in quality as any murder that *he* would condescend to own for a work turned out from his own *studio*.
>
> (DQ 20.40)

This passage is counterintuitive in giving Thucydides' *ktēma es aei* as an apparent back-translation for the Horatian monument more lasting than bronze; but the Greek catchphrase is appropriate for its links to the history of violence (for the essays provide a mock history of murder), and to the archetype of the killer/writer who remains emotionally detached from his materials. This is hardly a straightforward appeal to the model of Thucydidean history and the passage holds further ironies. First, having ventriloquised for the 'artist', describing his works as possessions for eternity, the speaker claims a need to retell all the details of the murders, since they 'belong[] to an era that is now [. . .] forty-two years behind us', and which 'not one person in four [. . .] can be expected to know correctly' (DQ 20.41). Immediately afterwards, we hear the murders took place in 1812, rather than 1811: the chronicler has confused his chronology, and the everlasting possession has faded like other sensations.[21] De Quincey certainly does not play the role of the impartial Thucydidean historian here, carefully checking and cross-referencing existing reports. Rather, he admits that he was unable or unwilling to make revisions to his first draft due to the 'afflicting agitations, and the unconquerable impatience of [his] nervous malady' (DQ 20.37). In other words, he lets his emotions get the better of him. His nervous affliction is warlike (unconquerable), and disrupts the normal course of time: it is 'impatient' – unwilling to wait and unwilling to suffer or feel *patientia*, a word from the same root as passion, *passio*.

On Murder thus cites and samples contradictory images of the writer, spectator, and perpetrator of ordered violence; for war and murder, as the latter is understood in *On Murder*, are paradigmatic examples of order and civilisation through violence. We see in the writer, spectator and perpetrator emotional detachment or entanglement; his ability to give form to his materials; and their attainment of the kind of formal perfection or 'quality' that would make them eternal or classic. If Thucydides serves here as a placeholder for ideas of eternal laws, progress and emotional detachment – ideas ironised if not dismissed – then he also serves in De Quincey's exploration of war histories as timebound, non-progressive and emotional. This countermodel to 'Thucydidean' history is aligned with formlessness, but has its own particular rhetorical form: that of the anecdote or case.

Thucydides contra Thucydides? Anecdote and case

De Quincey's approach to anecdotes and cases responds to a complex Romantic-era body of writing. Romantic interest in these forms has been linked to the emergence of historicism, in the sense of a disposition to interpret history through specific cultures and circumstances rather than eternal principles (Chandler 1998; Fineman 1989). For Fineman, indeed, anecdotage 'uniquely *lets history happen* by [. . .] introduc[ing] an opening into the teleological, and therefore timeless, narration of beginning, middle and end' (Fineman 1989, p. 61). As De Quincey makes clear in essays such as 'Casuistry' (1839–1840) and 'War' (1848), both anecdotage and cases challenge the status of 'general law[s]', of conceptual and emotional abstraction (DQ 11.349). Both are empirical, concrete, small, often apparently trivial and scandalous, 'rare and anomalous' (DQ 11.348). Procopius' *Anekdota* (or *Secret History*) dealt in palace intrigues, the titillating goings-on 'behind the curtain' that Thucydides eschewed. By the nineteenth century, anecdotes are seen as lending novelistic 'charm' and 'colour' to history proper.[22] Casuistry is 'the science of cases' (DQ 11.350), developed to guide confessors encountering specific sins, but later exploited when cases were published and consumed as entertainment, exciting sensation and sentiment by 'exploring guilty recesses of human life' (DQ 11.348). There are *prima facie* reasons to censure these forms, then, as well as to celebrate the deviation they offer from detached history.

A telling example of anecdotage governs De Quincey's autobiographical *The English Mail-Coach, or The Glory of Motion* (1849), set during the Napoleonic wars. Like *On Murder*, the piece examines violence felt at a spectatorial distance, with its moral and affective implications. De Quincey recalls how the mail-coach system spread the news and the intoxicating feelings of battles on the Continent through the land – and through the body politic. One night, the mail-coach in which De Quincey is travelling grazes a fragile domestic vehicle and almost kills its occupants, two young lovers. De Quincey is transfixed by the sight of the young woman rising up and falling back on her seat in agitation, her feelings struck as the coach has been. He experiences a guilt that parallels his mixed feelings about spreading war news. For alongside official news of uplifting military victories comes news that is intimate and particular to soldiers' families: news of casualties and losses.

The incident of the woman and her lover struck by the mail-coach is certainly an anecdote – historical, momentary, particular. It is faintly scandalous in its spying into the 'recesses' of a private vehicle to reveal a midnight tryst between an unmarried couple. It also suggests a deeper scandal: De Quincey's supposed complicity in the grand violence of the state mail-coach service. The incident, like those in other anecdotes, is moreover trivial: the woman has nothing particular to do with wars or the state of nations, and neither does De Quincey. But for him it acts like a causative historical agent of huge proportions. This is in fact precisely the problem with anecdote as De Quincey will identify it in 'War'. Anecdotal history mistakes an 'occasion' or chance occurrence for a 'cause' of larger events (DQ 16.277). Anecdotage thus distorts cause and effect. In the *Mail-Coach*, this distortion symbolically disrupts progressive history and chronology: the incident transforms De Quincey's later dream life into endless play-backs of versions of the woman's imminent death, or her salvation in apocalyptic dream scenes. The anecdotal form helps to explain this incident's traumatic force in the imagination of the narrator, its compulsive return as a symbol or exemplum, since it cannot properly be assigned to a place in a fixed causal chain.

By making war a problem in this way, anecdotage represents an attractive alternative to impartial history. It may be over-engaged, emotionally lurid, even pathological. But it seems to show our conservative, often pro-war writer breaking out – perhaps against his will – into more human, compassionate, 'real' encounters with war and the pity of war.[23] To emphasise such anecdotes is an understandable response to Romantic war writing and De Quincey in particular. It affirms the liberal notion that war is genuinely horrible, and genuinely resistant to the stylistic and emotional formality and the form-orientedness associated with 'objective' Thucydidean history.[24] Nonetheless, it does not quite get at the fact that anecdote, too, has its conventions and formal features, and that it, too, is generic and not an overflowing of spontaneous feeling. Nor does it get at the dialectic De Quincey constructs between anecdote or case, and impartial history.[25]

The dialectic between emotionally detached and engaged literary forms can be approached through the surprising role Thucydides plays in De Quincey's defence of casuistry.[26] Within a series of examples, 'Casuistry' takes Thucydides' discussion of piracy and develops a general account of war's relation to civilisation. Thucydides reports that piracy was once 'held in the greatest honour', but developed into a crime (DQ 11.356; Thucydides 1.4–8). Piracy, De Quincey observes, is natural and just in 'rude nations' where the '*Bellum inter omnes* is the natural state of things'. Whereas in the state of nature the norm was war and arbitrary violence, as societies progress, violence is increasingly regulated by specific rules and exceptions, which together legitimise the nation state. Only 'amongst us civilized men' is peace the 'rule', insists De Quincey (DQ 11.357). And only among very civilised men (like the author) are extra-state privateering and other acts of war on principles of 'commerce' regarded as piratical and condemned. When humans enter Hobbesian society, war becomes national and public, and is thereby banned from the private realm of individuals – and by extension their commercial ventures.

Thucydides here appears as what we could call a historicist. He charts the development of violence from norm to anomaly (or crime) as civilisation progresses, and thereby charts the origins of war between civilised Athens and ruder Sparta. De Quincey himself builds from Thucydides' case (via Hobbes, who had translated the *Peloponnesian War*) to more abstract principles. But the appeal to Thucydides in this context also implies that his method was not simply opposed to the particular, engaged and time-bound. If Thucydides is associated with the view that the future 'must resemble' the past, and that men crave power 'by a necessary law of nature', then, nonetheless, his generalities might be seen to develop from specific cases, just as scientific laws emerge from empirical experiments, or common law from precedents.

This is precisely the relationship between case and rule articulated in 'Casuistry': that *'all law, as it exists in every civilised land, is nothing but casuistry'*, nothing but the use of potentially anomalous cases to test, modify and generate general laws (DQ 11.348). Such a method implies its own kind of eternity and form-orientedness. For cases are, according to the essay, 'special varieties which are for ever changing the face of [. . .] general rules. The tendency of such variations is, in all states of complex civilisation, to absolute infinity' (DQ 11.350). Evident in this text is a tendency towards the organicist understanding of form so important to Romanticism, which associates form with increasing complexity or structuring, rather than neoclassical simplicity and stability.[27] Form on this construction is progressive and infinite, an eternal process or principle rather than a possession.

Casuistry furthermore entails a particular emotional style that De Quincey's essay aligns with British civilisation, morality, empiricism, artistic interest and ornament. Far from casuistry being the province of absolutist Catholic barbarism, De Quincey argues, only a cruel, arbitrary judge would ignore specific cases and their 'palliations' (DQ 11.349). Implicitly, a stance of mercy and compassion belong to casuistry, and so to a general form of justice. This line of thinking is indebted to Aristotle, who argued that the most general form of justice takes all the particulars into account, and results in more lenient judgements than those demanded by harsh, retributive justice, which, in turn, often leads to war and violence (Aristotle 1890, 1130b–1138a). In Thucydides' famous Melian Dialogue (5.84–116), similar arguments are offered by the conquered Melians and rejected by the Athenians in favour of *realpolitik*. The connection between eternal principles and cases is thus also connected, in a long classical tradition, to emotional regimes of pity, sympathy and compassion in attempts to moderate anger, bellicosity and brutal detachment.

The centrality of war to this historiographical model, implicit in 'Casuistry', is developed in the later essay 'War'. War, for De Quincey, develops through cases of violence, and such cases build civilisation. The essay argues, against societies for perpetual peace, that war is both necessary given the human condition, and beneficial. In its course, it lays out a 'Thucydidean' argument that man's self-interest prompts social progress and formation.[28] War, so the underlying argument might go, prompts new technologies and stratagems, invents new laws, instills new discipline in armies, acquires new land to cultivate, and gives conquered lands new and better forms of government and commerce, drawing savages out of an inchoate state of nature. In De Quincey's elaborate version of this argument, war itself limits war in the sense of simple conflict, by giving violence form and boundaries, and it limits cases of war by generating international laws and treaties which increasingly regulate when wars may be waged.

'Banish war as now administered,' De Quincey insists, 'and it will revolve upon us in a worse shape, that is, in a shape of predatory and ruffian war, more and more licentious [. . .]. Will the causes of war die away because war is forbidden? Certainly not; and the only result of the prohibition would be to throw back the exercise of war from national into private and mercenary hands; and *that* is precisely the retrograde or inverse course of civilisation' (DQ 16.279). The alternatives are 'interminable warfare of a mixed character [. . .] infesting the frontiers of all states like a fever', or 'intermitting wars of high national police, administered with the dignified responsibility that belongs to supreme rank, with the humanity that belongs to conscious power, and with the diminishing havock that belongs to increasing skill in the arts of destruction' (DQ 16.279). Without well-administered warfare, then, violence lacks social, temporal, and spatial order and distinctions. Suppressing war thus increases chaotic violence, while cultivating war limits and transforms it:

> war has no tendency to propagate war, but tends to the very opposite result. To thump is as costly, and in other ways as painful, as to *be* thumped. The evil to both sides arises in an undeveloped state of law. If rights were defined by a well considered [international] code growing from long experience, each party sees that this scourge of war would continually tend to limit itself. Consequently the very necessity of war becomes the strongest invitation to that system of judicial logic which forms its sole limitation
>
> (DQ 16.283).

The final result is a less war-ridden world order, but also an improved world culture, enriched by militarism. As the essay concludes: 'Gradually the mere practice of war, and the culture of war though merely viewed as a rude trade of bloodshed, ripened into an intellectual art [. . .] were it only through impulses of self-conservation, and when searching with a view to more effectual destructiveness, war did and must refine itself from a horrid trade of butchery into a magnificent and enlightened science' (DQ 16.288).

The dialectical arguments in 'War' chime strongly with 'Casuistry', where colonisation through conquest was linked with uplifting and formative feelings:

> To imagine the extinction of war itself, in the present stage of human advance, is [. . .] idle. Higher modes of civilisation – an earth more universally colonized [. . .] must pave the way for *that* [. . .]. War on a national scale is

often ennobling, and one great instrument of pioneering for civilisation: but war of private citizen upon his fellow [. . .] is always demoralizing.

(DQ 11.357)

This contrast between ennobling and demoralising warfare blends moral and affective terms. To be de-moralised is to be made objectively less moral (and so less socially advanced). But demoralisation is clearly also a subjective feeling, connected with dejection, humiliation and the nebulous *loss of morale* to which failure in war is not infrequently attributed.[29] Note that the 'ennobling' feelings of war are public and national, isolated from the private sphere, just as the exhilarating feelings of the detached historian of war are isolated from his private emotions and interests.

Cultural-emotional formation through war comes to the fore in the later essay. War here improves our 'sensibilities', 'train[s]' our 'feelings' and 'the higher capacities of [the] heart', through 'what originally had been a mere movement of self-interest' and self-protection (DQ 16.287). Not only does man become more developed and well-formed through practices such as war; he also comes to appreciate and desire form: 'having thoroughy reconciled himself to a better order of things, [. . .] at length he begins [. . .] to perceive a moral beauty and a fitness in arrangments [. . .] so that finally he generates a sublime pleasure of conscientiousness out of that which' began 'in the meanest forms of mercenary convenience' (DQ 16.287). War thus has a providential teleological function. Unbeknownst to its practitioners, it works like 'the benignity of nature still watching for ennobling opportunities'. It eventually falls under the influence of 'the arts of ornament and pomp', becoming beautiful in itself (DQ 16.287). On this account, war is instrumental to what Norbert Elias would later call a 'civilising process' of increasing emotional and martial restraint, and linked for Elias with increasingly elaborate social forms at court and with state formation (Elias 1939).

We stress the role of art and ornament here not only because of art's links with sensibilities and with supposed civilisational progress, but also because of its link with anecdotage, a genre associated with literature rather than political science, with entertainment, trivial pleasures, and chance. In stern philosophical Thucydidean mode, 'War' explicitly condemns anecdotage and literary romance. Yet, like 'Casuistry', the essay ultimately suggests the mutual implication of eternal law and contingent case. Anecdotes, De Quincey begins, represent wars as unleashed by 'a point of ceremony' at court, 'a personal pique', 'a hasty word', the 'momentary caprice' of a minister or king's mistress; they are not the stuff of history writing proper but of 'French memoirs' and the discourse of the 'lady's tea-table or toilette' (DQ 16.273). In short, anecdotes are the product of a degenerate, foreign, effeminate sensibility. They suggest wars are caused not by the 'eternal *matrix* of disputes' between nations, but by 'trivial impulses', which 'a trivial resistance' might have diverted (DQ 16.273, 16.277). Even if factual, anecdotes therefore confuse contingencies with causes. '*All* anecdotes [. . .] are false' and 'all dealers in anecdotes are tainted with mendacity' (DQ 16.273).

Yet, De Quincey goes on, '[a]ll history' is in fact 'built partly, and some of it altogether upon anecdotage', and so all history 'must be a tissue of lies' (DQ 16.273). History cannot escape from the realms of literature and personal memoir into science or philosophy, from emotional engagement and accident into detachment. Ironically, not to say facetiously, this gives history its saving grace:

> Are these works then to be held cheap, because their truths to their falsehoods are in the ratio of one to five hundred? On the contrary, they are better and more to be esteemed on that account; because *now* they are admirable reading on a winter's night; whereas written on the principle of sticking to the truth, they would have been as dull as ditch water. [...] dealers in anecdotage are to be viewed with admiration as patriotic citizens, willing to sacrifice their own characters, lest their countrymen should find themselves short of amusement.
>
> (DQ 16.273–4)

Following the general two-pronged argument of 'War', we could say that the human condition makes anecdote *necessary* for history writing, just as war is necessary for mankind. Moreover, like war, anecdote is *beneficial*, 'often ennobling': an ornament and comfort of society, and a marker of civilisation. This logic integrates anecdotes with the larger pro-war logic of the essay. There is a symmetry here between the work of cases and anecdotes, around the axis of law and war. On one side, cases generate and advance general laws; on the other, general advances in society, driven by the 'eternal *matrix*' of international wars, promote the flourishing of anecdote. Far from representing an unruly alternative to detached 'Thucydidean' history, case and anecdote complete a larger – and in an important sense likewise Thucydidean – form of history.

Conclusions

Thucydides and his rich reception helped De Quincey set up contrasting accounts of war and writing war – as detached, progressive, form-giving and scientific, or as emotional, informal, anecdotal and literary. In 'War', the latter model is associated with a liberal and sentimental idea that war destroys order rather than propelling it, and should be abolished rather than perfected.[30] Anecdote can be seen as a wayward genre, and it is often self-consciously digressive in De Quincey's writings (indeed, the diatribe against anecdote in 'War' is explicitly labelled a 'digression', DQ 16.275). As such, it could be imagined as bursting out 'hydraulically' to show the true, personal and tragic nature of war.[31] Against De Quincey's conservative attempts to glorify war, anecdotes would reveal the 'non-compliant' emotions and scandals under the official logic of histories understood as sternly Thucydidean.[32] This opposition makes some intuitive sense, and resonates with some current strategies in arguing and emoting about war.

Yet for the purposes of analysing De Quincey, at least, we should move beyond this reading of a 'true' formless horror of war and a repressive or at best consoling response, which gives war and its feelings form. Just as the history of emotions insists on the non-opposition of feeling and reason, we need to unpick our subtle and deep-seated assumptions about the contrast of feeling and form. In our account, De Quincey not only sketches out but also undermines the strict opposition of form and formlessness in warfare, and between emotional, rhetorical anecdote, and stern, scientific history. In their shifting, sometimes deeply ironic appropriations of Thucydides, De Quincey's writings undermine a polar opposition between form and formlessness in war, and between anecdote as 'rhetorical', emotional and formless, and Thucydidean history as scientific, unemotional and ordered.

This study raises more general questions about writing on war. We might see three strands emerging from these texts. One is pro-war because war is formful, associated with order and a civilising impetus. This strand predominates in modern conservative or neo-liberal thinking. One strand, commonly associated with liberal and academic war writing, is anti-war, since warfare is chaotic and destroys order and sense. A third strand is more (ideologically) paradoxical, and more postmodern. Here, form itself looks suspiciously like a kind of violence stamping itself on things: as a response, we sing the praises of resistance to form, completion and articulation; we want to end with the open, liminal, unfixed, undone, incomplete.[33] In our reading of historical sources, this can result in a tendency, first, to credit past feelings about war, and forms of war writing, only when they 'reveal' the *Formwidrigkeit* of war. In the process, we can succumb to a hydraulic model of emotions, where pity, compassion or horror, simply well up and get the better of past writers; where 'emotions' undermine attempts to portray war as formful or to give form to wartime experience. Second, reflection on war might be prodded towards a double bind, where we both condemn war through arguments about its destructiveness and non-formativeness, and yet promote special varieties of formlessness in response. De Quincey might help think about this because of the tendency in some of his writings to suggest that form itself can be horrifying and violent; because of his engagement with classical and early-modern traditions on which we still draw; because of his play with literary or generic forms; and because of the way he undermines apparent distinctions between the formful and formless, praise and satire, the emotionless and emotional.

Notes

1 De Quincey 2000–2003, 7.129 (= vol. 7, p. 129), 8.41, 20.40. This edition is cited herafter by volume and page number as DQ.
2 His best known work, *Confessions of an English Opium-Eater* (1821), is subtitled *Being an Extract from the Life of a Scholar*.
3 De Quincey himself used the idea of a *ktēma es aei* to satirical effect in savaging the Whig writer Samuel Parr, for him a pseudo-scholar and the antithesis of Bentley (DQ 8.41).

4 We know no detailed study of De Quincey and Thucydides' reception, though see Morley 2016, p. 143; Agnew 2012, p. 93; Gummere 1909, pp. 34–38. Lee and Morley 2014 does not mention De Quincey.
5 Levine 2015, p. 3. The concept of form thus includes political and socio-cultural orderings as well as literary and discursive patterns, and suggests how the discursive can be imagined to reflect, shape, and disrupt the social.
6 See for example the arguments set out in Gat 2008 and Morris 2014.
7 The alignment of literary genres with emotion is commonplace. As Eagleton (2003, p. 22) put it, partly ventriloquising for Victorian writers: 'literature, as we know, deals in universal human values rather than in such historical trivia as civil wars [. . .] literature works primarily by emotion and experience, and so was admirably well-fitted to carry through the ideological task which religion left off. Indeed by our own time literature has become effectively identical with the opposite of analytical thought and conceptual enquiry: whereas scientists, philosophers and political theorists are saddled with these drably discursive pursuits, students of literature occupy the more prized territory of feeling and experience'.
8 In other words, if 'literature retains a particular power to take emotional understanding of war beyond the limits and disguises of "official" languages' (Downes, Lynch & O'Loughlin 2015, p. 11), then this power relies on 'disguises' and formal conventions of its own – in genres like lyric, for example, which can pose as outlets for the free expression of thought and feeling, or like the digressive anecdote, which can pose as a personal interruption of abstract rule-bound argumentation.
9 See Morley 2014 for a detailed analysis of characterisations and evaluations of Thucydides from antiquity onwards, to which this section is indebted.
10 See discussion in Morley 2014, 42–44.
11 For discussion and literature on this highly-contested passage, see Hornblower 1991, 59–62.
12 In his *Ethica Nicomachea*, Aristotle (1890, 2.6, 1106b 14–15) uses the term to unite intellectual and practical reasoning, which allows Thucydides to re-enter the fray as a moralist based on the scientific accuracy of his account.
13 This is Hobbes's translation of Thucydides I.22.4. See further Harloe and Morley 2012, pp. 7–8.
14 John Dennis's writings are a *locus classicus* for the distinction between the sublime's enthusiastic passions and ordinary or vulgar passions (Dennis 1701; Dennis 1704).
15 Hobbes claims he translated Thucydides to make people flee democracy (*rhetoras ut fugerent*) (Hobbes 1679, p. 4), aligning democrats with Sophists; Grote's Thucydides champions democracy. See Pope 1988, p. 276. For the modern view: e.g. Macleod 1977, Ober 1998, chapter 2, cf. Ober 2010.
16 Hoekstra 2012, p. 27.
17 Thucydides 5.105.2. For discussion, see Sahlins (2004, p. 3); Harloe and Morley (2012, pp. 13–18).
18 The contrast between Herodotus and Thucydides particularly echoes and modifies Macaulay's 1828 essay 'History' (1910/1968, pp. 2–12).
19 Note that the liberal Macaulay's essay chid Thucydides for being insufficiently scientific (Macualay 1910/1968, pp. 10–11) and regretted the defects of the French Revolution (18); for De Quincey, the failure of democratic Athens is like the failure of republican France: not a tragedy, but a commeuppance.
20 Compare Lactantius, *Epitome Divinarum Institutionum* 6, 20, 9–15. We quote the translation in *Selections Grave and Gay* (1854), which includes Lactantius' mention of war. See DQ 6.122 notes, *loc. cit.*
21 De Quincey's editors note that he commits 'a number of [other] factual errors' and embroiderings of truth about the murders (DQ 20.37).
22 Macaulay 1910/1968, pp. 36–37. On anecdotes more broadly, see recently Loselle (2009).

23 For Fineman (1989, p. 61), the anecdote 'uniquely refers to the real'.
24 Cf. Shaw 2013, p. 29.
25 On this point, De Quincey would bear comparison with both Macaulay's dialectic between the literary/anecdotal and abstract principle within the ideal history, and the dialectic Jolles (1930/1968, pp. 171–199) described between abstract norm/law and concrete instance/exception within the case form.
26 The surprise is not absolute: Macaulay's 'heterodox' opinion was that Thucydides specialised in 'deciding' on 'particular case[s]' but could not generalise (Macaulay 1910/1968, pp. 11–12); Fineman (1989) provocatively calls Thucydides the founding father of anecdotal history and hence historicism; Koselleck indicates his appeal for exemplary history (Koselleck 2004). Compare Chandler (1998, pp. 163, 173).
27 Cf., for example, Beiser (2002, pp. 361–368).
28 See e.g. Kaplan (2002, pp. 45–46), quoted in Sahlins (2004, p. 3).
29 On humiliation and Romantic war, see Favret 2014. According to the OED, 'morale' in the sense of a 'mental or emotional state (with regard to confidence, hope, enthusiasm, etc.)' was first used during the Napoleonic wars: 'the morale of the old soldiers is shaken very much' (F. S. Larpent, *Journal*, 1813). In the following six examples, three concern warfare, including one about the problems for '*morale*' if a 'soldier' has to attack 'citizens', that is, if warfare improperly mixes the public and private. The remaining examples concern other agonistic activities.
30 See especially the draft fragment towards 'War', DQ 16.514: 'Most of what has been written on [. . .] the cruelty of war [. . .], in connection with [. . .] the Old Testament, is (with submission to sentimentalists) false and profoundly unphilosophic. It is of the same feeble character as the flashy modern moralizations upon War.'
31 On the 'hydraulic' model of emotions, see Rosenwein (2006, pp. 13–15).
32 Cf. Downes, Lynch & O'Loughlin 2015.
33 Cf. Favret 2009.

Reference list

Agnew, L. P. 2012, *Thomas De Quincey: British Rhetoric's Romantic Turn*, Southern Illinois University Press, Carbondale & Edwardsville.
Aristotle 1890, *Ethica Nicomachea*, ed. I. Bywater, Clarendon Press, Oxford.
Beiser, F. 2008, *German Idealism: The Struggle against Subjectivism, 1781–1801*, Harvard University Press, Cambridge MA.
Bentley, R. 1721, *Dr. Bentley's proposals for printing a new edition of the Greek Testament, and St. Hierom's Latin version. With a full answer to all the remarks of a late pamphleteer*, printed for J Knapton, London.
Chandler, J. 1998, *England in 1819. The Politics of Literary Culture and the Case of Romantic Historicism*, Chicago University Press, Chicago.
Cochrane, C. 1929, *Thucydides and the Science of History*, Oxford University Press, Oxford.
Dennis, J. 1701, *The Advancement and Reformation of Modern Poetry*, Richard Parker, London.
Dennis, J. 1704, *The Grounds of Criticism in Poetry*, George Strahan and Bernard Lintott, London.
De Quincey, T. 2000–2003, *The Works of Thomas De Quincey*, ed. F. Burnwick, Pickering & Chatto, London.
Dionysius of Halicarnassus 2014, *On Thucydides*, trans. S. Usher, Loeb Classical Library [LCL] 465, Harvard University Press, Cambridge MA.
Dionysius of Halicarnassus 2014, *Second Letter to Ammaeus*, trans. S. Usher, Loeb Classical Library 466, Harvard University Press, Cambridge MA.

Downes, S., Lynch, A. & O'Loughlin, K. 2015, 'Introduction – War as Emotion: Cultural Fields of Conflict and Feeling', in S. Downes, A. Lynch & K. O'Loughlin (eds), *Emotions and War: Medieval to Romantic Literature*, Palgrave Macmillan, Houndsmill & New York, pp. 1–23.

Eagleton, T. 1996, *Literary Theory: An Introduction*, 2nd edn, Blackwell, Oxford.

Elias, N. 1939, *The Civilizing Process*, Blackwell, Oxford.

Favret, M. 2009, *War at a Distance*, Princeton University Press, Princeton.

Favret, M. 2014, 'The General Fast and Humiliation', in J. Faflak & R. Sha (eds), *Romanticism and the Emotions*, Cambridge University Press, Cambridge, pp. 124–146.

Fineman, J. 1989, 'The History of the Anecdote: Fiction and Fiction', in H. A. Veeser (ed.), *The New Historicism*, Routledge, New York, pp. 49–76.

Gammerl, B. 2012, 'Emotional Styles – Concepts and Challenges', *Rethinking History: The Journal of Theory and Practice*, vol. 16, no. 2, pp. 161–175.

Gummere, R. M. 1909, 'De Quincey and Macaulay in Relation to Classical Tradition', *The Classical Weekly*, vol. 3, no. 5, pp. 34–38.

Harloe, K. & Morley, N. (eds) 2012, *Thucydides and the Modern World: Reception, Reinterpretation and Influence from the Renaissance to the Present*, Cambridge University Press, Cambridge.

Hobbes, T. 1629, *Eight bookes of the Peloponnesian Warre written by Thucydiddes the sonne of Olorus. Interpreted with faith and diligence immediately out of the Greeke by Thomas Hobbes secretary to ye late Earle of Deuonshire*, Imprinted [at Eliot's Court Press] for Hen: Seile, and are to be sold at the Tigres Head in Paules Churchyard, London.

Hobbes, T. 1679 *Vitae Carmine Expressa*, [n. p.], London.

Hoesktra, K. 2012, 'Thucydides and the Bellicose Beginnings of Modern Political Theory', in Harloe, K. and Morley, N. (eds), *Thucydides and the Modern World: Reception, Reinterpretation, and Influence from the Renaissance to the Present*, Cambridge University Press, Cambridge.

Hornblower, S. 1991, *A Commentary on Thucydides*, Clarendon Press, Oxford.

Jolles, A. 1930/1968, *Einfache Formen: Legende, Sage, Mythe, Rätsel, Spruch, Kasus, Memorabile, Märchen, Witz*, 4th unrevised edn, Max Niemeyer, Tübingen.

Kant, I. 1973, *Kritik der Urteilskraft: Kant's Gesammelte Schriften*, vol. 5, ed. Königlich Preußische Akademie der Wissenschaften, Reimer, Berlin.

Kaplan, R. 2002, *Warrior Politics: Why Leadership Demands a Pagan Ethos*, Vintage, New York.

Koselleck, R. 2004, *Futures Past: On the Semantics of Historical Time*, Columbia University Press, New York.

Lactantius 1890, *Divinarum Institutionum*, ed. S. Brandt, Corpus scriptorium ecclesiasticorum latinorum 19, Tempsky, Vindobonae.

Le Moyne, P. 1695, *Of the art both of writing & judging of history with reflections upon ancient as well as modern historians, shewing through what defects there are so few good, and that it is impossible there should be many so much as tolerable / by the Jesuit Father Le-Moyne*, Printed for R. Sare & J. Hindmarsh, London.

Lee, C. & Morley, N. (eds) 2014, *A Handbook to the Reception of Thucydides*, Blackwell, Chichester.

Levine, C. 2015, *Forms: Whole, Rhythm, Hierarchy, Network*, Princeton University Press, Princeton & Oxford.

Loselle, A. (ed.) 2009, 'The Anecdote', *SubStance*, special issue, vol. 38, no. 1.

Macaulay, T. 1910/1968, *Lays of Ancient Rome; Essays and Poems*, Dent, London.

Macleod, C. W. 1977, 'Thucydides' Plataean Debate', *Greek, Roman, and Byzantine Studies*, vol. 18, no. 3, pp. 227–246.

Morley, N. 2014, *Thucydides and the Idea of History*, IB Tauris, London & New York.

Morley, N. 2016, 'The Anti-Thucydides: Herodotus and the Development of Modern Historiography', in J. Priestly & V. Zali (eds), *Brill's Companion to the Reception of Herodotus in Antiquity and Beyond*, Brill, Leiden, pp. 200–232.

Ober, J. 1998, *Political Dissent in Democratic Athens: Intellectual Critics of Popular Rule*, Princeton University Press, Princeton.

Ober, J. 2010, 'Thucydides on Athens' Democratic Advantage in the Archidamian War', in D. M. Pritchard (ed.), *War, Democracy and Culture in Classical Athens*, Cambridge University Press, Cambridge, pp. 65–87.

Plato 1903, *Platonis opera*, ed. J. Burnet, Oxford University Press, Oxford.

Pope, M. 1988, 'Thucydides and Democracy', *Historia*, vol. 37, no. 3, pp. 276–296.

Rapin, R. 1694, *Monsieur Rapin's Comparison of Thucydides and Livy Translated into English*, printed by L. Lichfield, for A. Peisley, Oxford.

Rosenwein, B. 2006, *Emotional Communities in the Early Middle Ages*, Cornell University Press, Ithaca and London.

Sahlins, M. 2004, *Apologies to Thucydides: Understanding History as Culture and Vice Versa*, University of Chicago Press, Chicago.

Scarry, E. 1985, *The Body in Pain: The Making and Unmaking of the World*, Oxford University Press, Oxford.

Shaw, P. 2013, '"On War": De Quincey's Martial Sublime', *Romanticism*, vol. 19, no. 1, pp. 19–30.

Thucydides 1866, *The History of Thucydides done into English by Richard Crawley*, [James Parker and Co.], Oxford and London.

Voltaire 1765, 'Histoire', in *L'Encyclopédie ou dictionnaire raisonné des sciences, des arts et des métiers*, vol. 8, Paris, pp. 220–230.

INDEX

Adams, T. 16–17
affect(s) 3, 4, 9, 19, 47, 74, 90, 132, 134–137, 140, 225
Åhäll, L. 4
Airds Moss 172–174
allies 63, 120
Alliterative *Morte Arthure* 77, 79–80, 86–87; and Malory's *Morte Darthur* 78
Amadís de Gaula 113–114
American Civil War 12–13
Amiens 57, 60, 63
amphitheatre 225
anecdotage 227–228, 231–232
anger 9, 16–17, 73; aristocratic 58–59, 65; languages of 57–68
anti-war 190–191
Aristotle 229, 234–235
Armagnac–Burgundian feud 57–68
arms 58, 60, 65–68, 114
army 66, 96, 98, 112, 118, 139–140, 176, 205–206; Armagnac 67; Covenanter 145–150, 152–158; Royalist Northern 138
array 1, 14, 16
Arthur 77–81; and kingship 80; and pity 79–80; and wars 42, 48
Athens 223–224

Bailey, M. L. 17
battle of: Agincourt 65; Airds Moss 176 (*see also* Airds Moss); Albuerra 210; Bannockburn 194; Bothwell Bridge 171, 176; Lepanto 6; Marston Moor 130; Modone 27, 28, 32; Newburn 1, 17, 145–159 (*see also* Newburn, battle of); Nicopolis 30, 31; Roosebeke 28; Saint-Quentin 107; Salamanca 206; Waterloo 16, 183–198 (*see also* Waterloo)
battlefield 23, 29–30, 33, 184, 186, 191; of Europe 184
Bayman, A. 92–93, 98
Bennett, B. 188, 190
Beowulf 6, 40
Bible 163, 167, 173
biography 1, 16, 24–33, 91, 133, 138, 204, 214
body/bodily practice 2, 40, 46, 53, 77, 79, 94, 137, 168, 169, 183, 206
border 146–148, 152
Bothwell Bridge 171, 173
Boucicaut: emotions of 28; and love 27; *see also* Jean II Le Meingre
Bourdieu, P. 2
bourgeois culture 2
Bourke, J. 9, 19
Britain 201–202, 204–205
British Indian Military Repository 203–204
Burgundy, Duke of 57–60, 62–66, 68; arms of 60
burial 11, 40, 75, 85, 166, 172, 196, 206

Index

Cameron, R. 173–174
Cameronians 164–166, 174
casuistry 227–231
Cavendish, M. 127; *Natures Pictures* 129–130; *Playes* 127, 129, 131
Cervantes, M. 5–6; *see also* Don Quixote
Charles I 145, 147
Charles V 59
Charles VI 59
Chaucer, G. 5, 7, 15, 19, 75–77, 80, 85, 87; *see also* Troilus and Criseyde
chivalry 5, 7, 11, 13, 115
chronicle 13, 15–16
Church of Scotland *see* Scotland
civilisation 221, 223, 227–232
civil war 3, 12–13, 129; *see also* American Civil War
Cole, S. 8–9, 19
combatants 11–12, 15, 18
commemoration 168
community 165–167, 169–170, 172; confessional 11; religious 165, 170
compassion 16, 74–75, 77, 81–83
conflict 3–6, 16, 93–94, 96, 98, 145, 147–148
correspondence 18, 23, 107, 108, 110, 112, 114, 116, 118, 130, 145, 152, 175
Cour amoureuse 57–61, 65
Covenanter monuments 163–174, 165, 167, 169, 171, 173; historiography of 167–169; *see also* monuments; memorials
Covenanters 165–167, 168–169, 171–172
Cox, Jeffrey N. 187–188
Crawford, Neta C. 4
Crocker, H. 9, 19
Crusades 5, 12

dauphin 57–59, 62, 64–65, 67–68
Davenant, W. 131, 140
The dead tearme 96; *see also* Dekker
Dekker, T. 89, 91–93, 95, 97, 98; choice of topics 92; and contemporary conflicts 92; war writing 90, 92–93, 96
De Quincey, T. 18, 219–233
diaries 2, 8, 23
disloyalty 64–65, 157
Don Quixote 5–6; *see also* Cervantes
Dreux 66–67
Duffy, C. A. 6–7
Dutch 96–101

emotion 1–5, 2, 4, 7–9, 14–16, 18–19, 38–41, 43, 45, 47, 49, 51, 53, 66, 68–69, 74–77, 79–80, 84–85, 127–131, 134, 136, 165, 168–170, 171, 213–215
emotional: attachment 43–44, 47; communities 165–173; cost (of war) 97; detachment 222, 227; education 131; engagement 7, 18; events 170; experience 1–2, 4, 6, 15–16; expression 18; forms 3, 14; intensity 207–209; life 2, 14; memories, collective 165; practices, collective 171; processes 76, 79–80, 84; regimes 41, 51; register 2, 15; responses 11, 14; states 79–80; styles 220; socialization 3; subjectivity 9, 14–15
Emotion, Politics and War 4
England 89, 91–97, 96–101, 98, 134, 136
English: authorities 146, 149–150; forces 149–151

famine 95–96, 98
The Faerie Queene 5, 192; *see also* Spenser
fear 9, 15, 19, 29–33, 63, 95, 98–99, 130, 134–135, 150–151, 159, 166–167, 198
feud leaders 58–59
fiction/fictionalisation 5, 16, 96, 102, 208, 210, 214,
Fineman, J. 227, 235
First World War/Great War 3, 4, 6, 214
Flecknoe, R. 132–133
Fontenay 66
Fortune 44–47
France 45, 77, 81–82, 107, 111–112, 114–115

Genoa 28, 32–33
Gerhard Scharnhorst's *Neues Militarisches Journal* 202
Gleig, G. 205, 207–208
Gohory, J. 114–115
Gondibert 131; *see also* Davenant
Gordon, W. of Earlston 165, 169–171
Gregory, T. 4
grief 6, 14, 27, 42, 47, 70n4, 129–130, 137–139

habitus 2, 165
Heaney, S. 6
Henri II 107–110; autograph letter from 111, 117; campaigns of 115; and chivalric romance 110–117; letters of 107, 110, 114; war correspondence of 112
Henry V 5, 7, 10, 13; *see also* Shakespeare
'Histories of Violence' 4
history of emotions 9, 53, 128, 233; methodology 169–170
Hobbes, T. 131, 135, 136
Homer 7, 8
Hundred Years War 5, 16, 23
Hungarians 30–31

inscriptions 1, 11, 15, 165–169, 171–178
Ireland 5, 89, 97, 195

Jean II Le Meingre 24, 26, 29, 32
Jean Le Bel 23–24
Jerusalem 48–49, 51–53
Jewish peoples, late medieval 52–53
journalism 6, 69, 89–90, 201–217, 227–228

'Killing Times' 168–170
Knights Templar 78–79, 86

landscape 166–169, 171
language: allegory 68; chivalric 39, 119, 195; effectiveness of describing war 7–8; emotional 18, 91, 94, 120, 128, 148, 165, 168, 171, 178; and love 120, 195; of soldiering 207–210; and violence 39
League of Gien 57–58, 63, 66
Lehoux, Françoise 108, 113–116
Libre qui es de l'ordre de cavalleria 5
literature/literary genres: epic 5, 15, 113, 192, 301; English Romantic literature 184; medieval 5, 9, 38, 54 79; novel 2, 18, 201–204, 208; poetry 3, 4, 6–9, 15–17, 27, 38, 41, 53, 57, 59, 60, 128, 155, 183–198, 201–202, 204, 207–211, 213, 214, 222, 223; romance 5, 8, 11, 13, 15, 16, 18, 24, 26, 27, 33, 43, 46, 74, 107–121, 201, 202, 207–214, 222, 224, 231
loyalty 11, 60–61, 64, 130, 153

Lydgate, J. 73–74, 80, 86
Lynch, A. 170

McLoughlin, K. 3, 183
Malory, T. 79–80, 86; *Morte Darthur* 78
martyrdom 164–165, 167–168, 171–172
martyrs 163, 165–169, 172–173
Massumi, B. 4
de' Medici, Catherine 107–113, 115–116, 118, 120–121
medieval period 4–5, 7; *see also* Middle Ages
medieval piety 46, 53
The Meeting of Gallants 96; *see also* Dekker
memoir 4, 17, 18, 202, 204–205, 231–232
memorials: Menin Gate 11; Covenanter 165–178; *see also* monuments
mercantilism 93–96
mercy 50, 51, 52, 74–76, 85, 187, 229
de Mézières, Philippe 82–83
Middle Ages 4, 15, 41, 169; *see also* Medieval period
Middleton, T. 90, 96, 98
Military Journal 202–204
military: life 204; memoirs 202, 204; science 203; stories 206; subplots 96–101; tales 202, 204–205, 208; veterans 23–24, 26, 33
militias 67
'misericorde'/'misericordia' 74, 75
modernity 14–15, 214
de Monstrelet, Enguerrand 62–65
Monthly Review 207
monuments, of war 11, 12, 17, 137, 140, 226; Airds Moss 172–174; Covenanter 163–174, 165, 167, 169, 171, 173; Gordon's 170–172; Horatian 226; Wigtown Martyrs 174–178
de Montmorency, Anne 107, 108, 113, 118
Morte Darthur 79–80, 84, 86
myths 131, 132, 170, 183, 188, 194, 195, 221–222

Nall, C. 3, 16, 47, 73
Napoleon Bonaparte 184–185, 189–190
Napoleonic Wars 188, 196, 201, 202, 203, 210, 227

nation 15, 140, 147–148, 163, 165, 192, 201–204, 214, 223
naval journals 202–203
Nemoianu, V. 201, 209
Netherlands 89, 94–95
Newburn, battle of 145–56; later representations of 156–159
New Statistical Accounts 174
Nicopolis 28, 30–31; expedition 24, 32

Orleanist-Burgundian conflict 59–65
Orleanists 57–58, 65
Orleans, Duke of 59–60, 62, 64–65; sons of 62–64
Ottoman Empire 30–31

pamphlets 89, 91, 93, 98
Paris 57, 63–64, 67–68
passions 7, 9, 12, 18–19, 49, 58, 90, 112, 120–121, 130–141, 208–209, 215, 223, 227; theatrical 128–128
peace 43, 52, 58, 62–65, 68, 81–82, 92, 94, 99, 101, 116, 119, 120, 133, 134–136, 153, 201, 209, 228, 229; negotiations 94–95; Peace of Auxerre 67; Peace of Bicêtre 64; Peace of Cateau-Cambrésis 107, 120; Peace of Chartres 62; Peace of God movement 40–41
Percy's Reliques of Ancient English Poetry 191
pestilence 95–96
Philip of Burgundy 59–62, 64–65
Pintoin, M. 61–62, 66–68
pity 16, 27, 31, 39, 40, 47, 49–53, 73–80, 156, 198, 228, 233; politics of 81–85
plague 91, 93, 95
Plamper, J. 3
Playes 127–141, 133–134; see also Cavendish
poetry 3, 4, 6–9, 15–17, 27, 38, 41, 53, 57, 59, 60, 128, 155, 183–198, 201–202, 204, 207–211, 213, 214, 222, 223; British War Poetry 188; celebratory poetry 188; see also Waterloo, poetry of
de Poitiers, Diane 107, 108, 110–121
prose 110, 113, 114, 120, 134, 184, 186, 191, 196, 198, 202, 208–210, 212, 223
Protesilaus 73–74

Quadrilogue Invectif 83
Quarterly Review 205, 207–208

Rapin, R. 221
Reformation (Scottish) 163–165, 171, 177, 178
De Regimine Principum 74, 85, 87
'rewþe' 74, 85
Romantic era 203, 208
Romanticism 14, 195, 201–202, 207–208, 229
Rome 25–26, 42, 44–45, 51

Scheer, M. 2, 165–166, 169–170
Schiff, R. P. 49
Scotland 145–152, 163–164, 168–169, 172–174; Church of 163–164, 172; Covenanter 172–173; Kingdom of 146–149
Scottish: army 145–146, 148, 152; commissioners 152–153; landscape 165, 169
Scott, W. 13, 17, 167–168
sentiment 41, 101, 107–108, 110, 114, 120–121, 171, 204, 227
The Seven Deadly Sinnes of London 90, 94
Shakespeare 5, 10, 13, 14, 128
Sherer, M. 205, 207–208
Sherman, S. 2
Shields, A. 163–164
Shoemaker's Holiday 90, 93, 96–97; see also Dekker
The Siege of Jerusalem 48–54, 53
soldiers 6, 8, 9, 11–12, 13, 40, 67–68, 93, 97, 99–100, 102, 150–151, 202, 204, 206–211, 213–214, 228; Christian 167, 173; returning 99, 102
soul 9, 10, 135–136, 157, 173, 189
Spain 89, 94–96
Spenser, E. 5; see also *The Faerie Queene*
Stendhal 15
Sterne, L. 8; see also *Tristram Shandy*

theatres 127–128, 131–134, 136; theatrical practices 131–132
Thebes 75
Theseus 75–77, 79–81, 85–87
Thomson's Martyr Graves of Scotland 168
Thucydides 220–224, 226–229, 232–235; historiographical failure 224; reception

220, 234; Thucydidean history 221, 223, 225–227, 232–233
trade 92–94; and war 93–96
Tristram Shandy 8; *see also* Sterne
Troilus and Criseyde 5; *see also* Chaucer

United Service Journal 201–208; and personal histories of war 202

Venetians 26–28, 32
vengeance 16, 26, 39, 47, 52, 66, 68, 74, 79, 81; divine 48–50
violence 6, 15–16, 19, 38, 40, 44–45, 47–48, 52, 74–75, 79–84, 184, 222–223, 225–230; and actions 39, 53; and compassion 73, 75, 77, 79, 81, 83, 85, 87; interpretation of medieval 40; subjective 58–59, 62; work 48

Wace 78
warfare 3–5, 11, 16, 38–39, 43–45, 92–93, 97, 233, 235
Wars of the Roses 5
Waterloo 183–185, 187–191; poetry of 183–198
Watts, J. W. 184–187
weeping 8, 73–74, 75, 77, 79, 85–86, 97, 98, 100, 127–128, 134, 137–139, 171
Wellington 184–185, 188
Wigtown Martyrs 165, 169, 174–178
women 75–77, 79, 82, 163, 170, 172–174, 228; as martyrs 174
Wordsworth, W. 189–191
A Worke for Armourers 90, 93–96, 98; *see also* Dekker

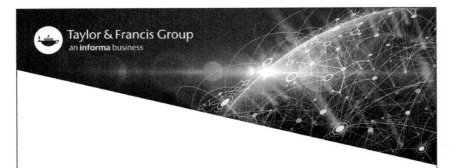

Taylor & Francis eBooks

www.taylorfrancis.com

A single destination for eBooks from Taylor & Francis with increased functionality and an improved user experience to meet the needs of our customers.

90,000+ eBooks of award-winning academic content in Humanities, Social Science, Science, Technology, Engineering, and Medical written by a global network of editors and authors.

TAYLOR & FRANCIS EBOOKS OFFERS:

- A streamlined experience for our library customers
- A single point of discovery for all of our eBook content
- Improved search and discovery of content at both book and chapter level

REQUEST A FREE TRIAL
support@taylorfrancis.com